CULTURAL ANTHROPOLOGY

A Problem-Based Approach

SECOND CANADIAN EDITION

Richard H. Robbins
State University of New York at Plattsburgh

Maggie Cummings
University of Toronto

Karen McGarry
York University

Sherrie N. Larkin
Western University

NELSON / EDUCATION

NELSON EDUCATION

Cultural Anthropology: A Problem-Based Approach, Second Canadian Edition
by Richard Robbins, Maggie Cummings, Karen McGarry and Sherrie Larkin

Vice President, Editorial Higher Education:
Anne Williams

Acquisitions Editor:
Maya Castle

Senior Marketing Manager:
Amanda Henry

Developmental Editor:
Jacquelyn Busby

Photo Researcher:
Carrie McGregor

Permissions Coordinator:
Carrie McGregor

Content Production Manager:
Claire Horsnell

Production Service:
Cenveo Publisher Services

Copy Editor:
Matthew Kudelka

Proofreader:
Jitendra Kumar Das

Indexer:
BIM Indexing Services

Senior Manufacturing Coordinator:
Ferial Suleman

Design Director:
Ken Phipps

Managing Designer:
Franca Amore

Interior Design:
Cathy Mayer

Cover Design:
Cathy Mayer

Cover Image:
© Morning Star by Alex Janvier Canadian Museum of Civilization, VI-D-276, photo Marie-Louise Deruaz, IMG2009-0085-0001-Dm

Compositor:
Cenveo Publisher Services

Library and Archives Canada Cataloguing in Publication Data

Cultural anthropology : a problem-based approach / Richard H. Robbins . . . [et al.]. — 2nd Canadian ed.

Rev. ed. of: Cultural anthropology / Richard H. Robbins, Sherrie N. [Larkin. 1st Canadian ed. © 2007.

Includes bibliographical references and index.ISBN 978-0-17-650272-0

1. Ethnology—Textbooks. I. Robbins, Richard H. (Richard Howard), 1940-

GN316.R62 2013   306
C2012-905024-5

ISBN-13: 978-0-17-650272-0
ISBN-10: 0-17-650272-6

A Note About the Book's Cover:

The image on this book's cover reflects Alex Janvier's *Morning Star*, which resides in the dome of the Grand Hall in the Canadian Museum of Civilization. According to Janvier, *Morning Star* refers to the morning star as a guiding light. The publisher of *Cultural Anthropology: A Problem-Based Approach*, second Canadian edition, hopes that the inquiry-based approach of this book guides students as they develop an inquisitiveness and openness to cultural diversity, especially to the culture and history of Aboriginal Peoples.

CULTURAL ANTHROPOLOGY

A Problem-Based Approach

SECOND CANADIAN EDITION

PUTTING THE WORLD IN PERSPECTIVE

Although all humans that we know about are capable of producing accurate sketches of localities and regions with which they are familiar, **cartography** (the craft of mapmaking as we know it today) had its beginnings in 16th-century Europe, and its subsequent development is related to the expansion of Europeans to all parts of the globe. From the beginning, there have been two problems with maps: the technical one of how to depict on a two-dimensional, flat surface a three-dimensional spherical object, and the cultural one of whose world view maps reflect. In fact, the two issues are inseparable, for the particular projection one uses inevitably makes a statement about how one views one's own people and their place in the world. Indeed, maps often shape our perceptions of reality as much as they reflect them.

In cartography, a **projection** refers to the system of intersecting lines (of longitude and latitude) by which part or all of the globe is represented on a flat surface. There are more than a hundred different projections in use today, ranging from polar perspectives to interrupted "butterflies" to rectangles to heart shapes. Each projection causes distortion in size, shape, or distance in some way or another. A map that correctly shows the shape of a landmass will of necessity misrepresent the size. A map that is accurate along the equator will be deceptive at the poles.

Perhaps no projection has had more influence on the way we see the world than that of Gerhardus Mercator, who devised his map in 1569 as a navigational aid for mariners. So well suited was Mercator's map for this purpose that it continues to be used for navigational charts today. At the same time, the Mercator projection became a standard for depicting landmasses, something for which it

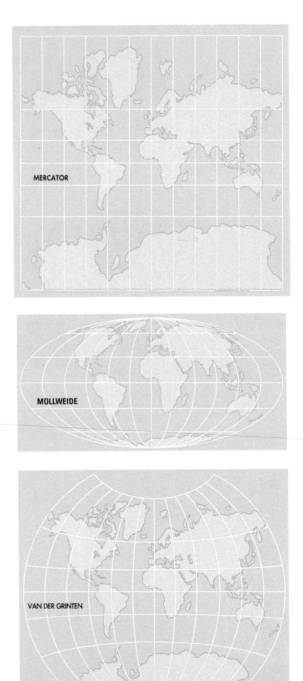

MERCATOR

MOLLWEIDE

VAN DER GRINTEN

ROBINSON

was never intended. Although an accurate navigational tool, the Mercator projection greatly exaggerates the size of landmasses in higher latitudes, giving about two-thirds of the map's surface to the northern hemisphere. Thus the lands occupied by Europeans and European descendants appear far larger than those of other people. For example, North America (19 million square kilometres) appears almost twice the size of Africa (30 million square kilometres), while Europe is shown as equal in size to South America, which actually has nearly twice the landmass of Europe.

A map developed in 1805 by Karl B. Mollweide was one of the earlier *equal-area projections* of the world. Equal-area projections portray landmasses in correct relative size, but as a result, they distort the shapes of continents more than other projections. They most often compress and warp lands in the higher latitudes and vertically stretch landmasses close to the equator. Other equal-area projections include the Lambert Cylindrical Equal-Area Projection (1772), the Hammer Equal Area Projection (1892), and the Eckert Equal-Area Projection (1906).

The Van der Grinten Projection (1904) was a compromise aimed at minimizing both the distortions of size in the Mercator and the distortions of shape in equal-area maps such as the Mollweide. Although an improvement, the Van der Grinten still emphasizes the lands of the northern hemisphere at the expense of the southern. For example, it shows Canada and the former Soviet Union at more than twice their actual size.

The Robinson Projection, which was adopted by the National Geographic Society in 1988 to replace the Van der Grinten, is one of the best compromises to date between the distortions of size and those of shape. Although an improvement over the Van der Grinten, the Robinson Projection still depicts lands in the northern latitudes as proportionally larger than those of the southern (i.e., the Third World). And like European maps before it, the Robinson Projection places Europe at the centre with the Atlantic Ocean and the Americas to the left, thus emphasizing the cultural connection between Europe and North America, while neglecting the geographic closeness of northwestern North America to northeastern Asia.

Each of the four maps on the following pages conveys quite a different cultural message. Included among them are the Peters Projection, an equal-area map that has been adopted as the official map of UNESCO (the United Nations Educational, Scientific, and Cultural Organization), and a Japanese map that shows us how the world looks from the other side.

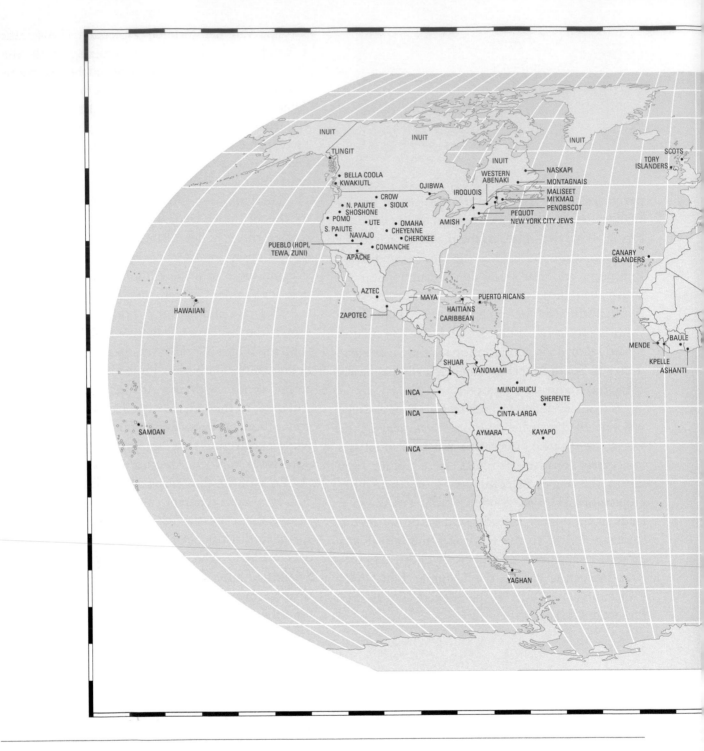

THE ROBINSON PROJECTION

This projection is used today by the National Geographic Society and Rand McNally. Although it distorts the relative size of landmasses, it does so much less than most other projections. Still, it places Europe at the centre of the map. This textbook uses the Robinson.

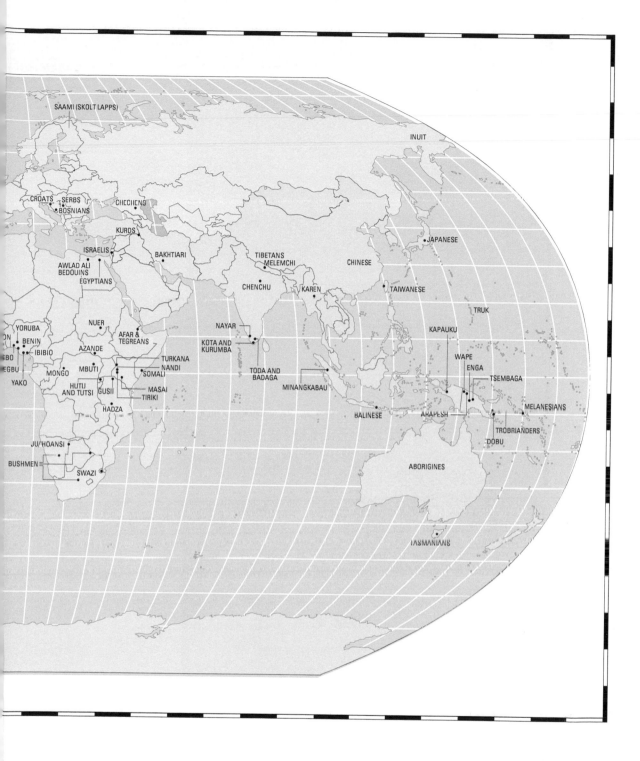

SAAMI (SKOLT LAPPS)

INUIT

CROATS SERBS
BOSNIANS
CHECHENS

KURDS

ISRAELIS
BAKHTIARI

JAPANESE

AWLAD ALI
BEDOUINS
EGYPTIANS

TIBETANS
MELEMCHI

CHINESE

CHENCHU

KAREN

TAIWANESE

TRUK

YORUBA
NUER

KAPAUKU

BENIN
AFAR &
TEGREANS
NAYAR

WAPE

IBIBIO
AZANDE
KOTA AND
KURUMBA
ENGA

GBU
TURKANA
TSEMBAGA

MONGO
MBUTI
NANDI
SOMALI
TODA AND
BADAGA

YAKO
HUTU
AND TUTSI
GUSII
MASAI
TIRIKI
MINANGKABAU

ARAPESH
MELANESIANS

HADZA
BALINESE
TROBRIANDERS

DOBU

JU/'HOANSI

ABORIGINES

BUSHMEN

SWAZI

TASMANIANS

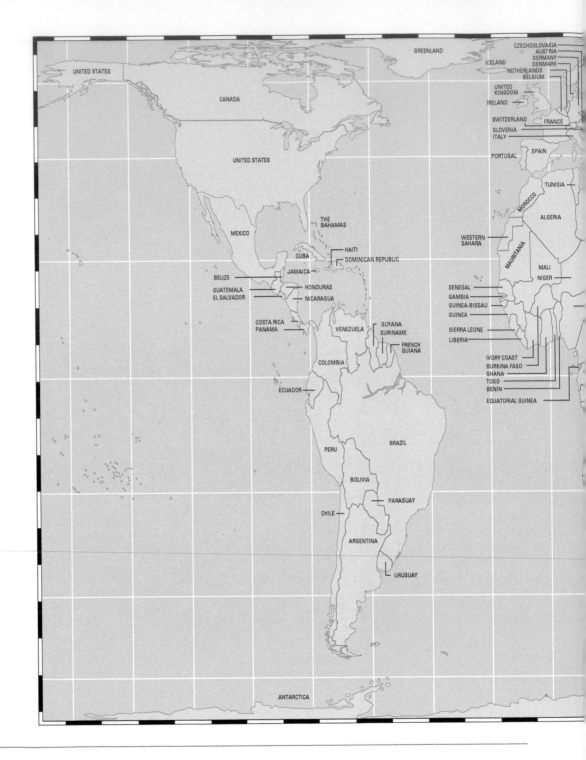

THE PETERS PROJECTION

This projection is based on the Peters. It distorts the continents (countries near the equator are vertically elongated by a ratio of 2 to 1), but it does show all the continents according to their correct relative sizes. Europe is still at the centre but is not shown as larger than the Third World.

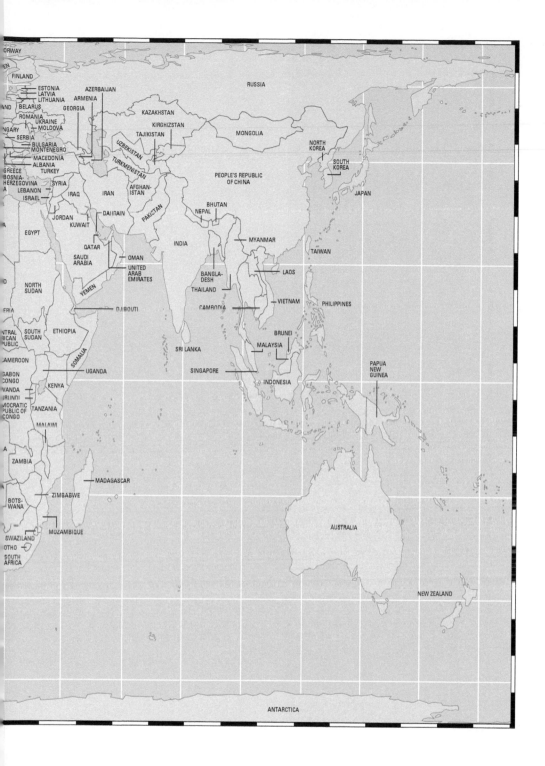

JAPANESE MAP

Not all maps place Europe at the centre of the world, This map, besides reflecting the importance the Japanese attach to themselves in the world, has the virtue of showing the geographic proximity of North America to Asia—a fact easily overlooked when maps place Europe at their centre.

GREENLAND

RUSSIA

UNITED
STATES

CANADA

UNITED STATES

MEXICO

THE
BAHAMAS

CUBA

HAITI
DOMINICAN REPUBLIC

BELIZE
GUATEMALA
EL SALVADOR
HONDURAS

JAMAICA
NICARAGUA

FRENCH GUIANA

VENEZUELA

COSTA RICA
PANAMA

COLOMBIA

GUYANA
SURINAM

ECUADOR

PERU

BRAZIL

BOLIVIA

PARAGUAY

CHILE

NEW
ZEALAND

ARGENTINA

URUGUAY

ANTARCTICA

BRIEF CONTENTS

CONTENTS

CHAPTER 3

THE SOCIAL AND CULTURAL CONSTRUCTION OF REALITY 76

PROBLEM 3: Why do people believe different
things, and why are they so certain that their

CHAPTER 6

THE CULTURAL CONSTRUCTION OF SOCIAL HIERARCHY 164

PROBLEM 6: Why are modern societies characterized by social, political, and economic inequalities? How are certain gender, class, racial, and other identities privileged or marginalized in various social contexts? 165

CHAPTER 7

GLOBALIZATION, NEOLIBERALISM, AND THE NATION-STATE 198

PROBLEM 7: What are the economic and cultural effects of globalization? What is the relationship between globalization, the nation-state, and national identity? 199

CHAPTER 8

THE CULTURAL CONSTRUCTION OF CONFLICT AND VIOLENCE   228

PREFACE

A NOTE TO STUDENTS: HOW TO READ THIS TEXTBOOK

"How can you begin to think like an anthropologist?"

Each of the chapters in this book addresses a series of questions and problems that are of concern to contemporary anthropologists. This text provides you with the necessary anthropological concepts and tools to begin to think "anthropologically" about these problems. For most of you, thinking anthropologically will involve re-evaluating and critiquing many core ideas and values you have probably been taught as being "true," "right," or "natural." Through cross-cultural examples and case studies, you will learn to appreciate the diversity of beliefs, traditions, and experiences of different cultures. This in turn will challenge you to think differently about aspects of your own culture, upbringing, and beliefs.

Each of the eight chapters in this text includes a problem, chapter questions, exercises, and critical thinking questions. Think of these as a "toolkit" to guide you through the text. Each chapter begins with a specific "problem." While reading a chapter, you should keep the relevant problem in mind so that, once you are finished reading, you will understand how the various cultural examples in the text can help you critically address the central problem/issue of the chapter.

In addition, in each chapter you will find questions that will help you think anthropologically and more specifically about the problem. To make the broad issues in the chapter manageable, we break down the problem into a series of related questions. Exercises interspersed throughout each chapter are derived from the chapter content; they aim to focus your attention on a meaningful critique of contemporary social practices and/or to apply the new knowledge and skills you are learning to particular social concerns. You should therefore attempt the exercises after you have read the chapter's corresponding section. Finally, the critical thinking questions, located at the conclusion of each chapter, ask you to reflect on broad issues discussed in the chapter. These questions should only be attempted once you have read the entire chapter thoroughly. These questions also make excellent study questions.

You will find key terms in **bold** font throughout this text. These are foundational concepts and ideas in anthropology, and it is important to understand how these key ideas are defined within the discipline. For instance, most people use the term "gender" in everyday language. However, "gender" has a unique meaning in anthropology. To help you remember these bolded key terms, we have provided a running glossary throughout the chapter, a list of the key terms and the page numbers where they can be found at the end of each chapter, and a full glossary at the end of the book.

FOR INSTRUCTORS

This text introduces students to the key concepts and methods utilized by sociocultural anthropology. One of our goals in writing this text is to encourage students to read, think, and write critically. Indeed, we believe that one of the main objectives of first-year sociocultural anthropology courses is to teach students to think differently about the world around them. The text facilitates this by encouraging students to analyze and critique many basic assumptions that they have brought with them to the course. For example, many of us are taught to think about our sense of identity (for example, gender, class, race, ethnicity, nationalism, family) as natural, biological, or fixed—as something we are born with. In this text, however, we place particular emphasis on the culturally constructed nature of our world—on the idea that many identities, as well as beliefs and practices, that we view as natural are both learned and the consequences of cultural differences.

We thus adopt a "problem-based approach" to the study of anthropology. Richard Robbins wrote the original edition of *Cultural Anthropology: A Problem-Based Approach* in the hope that such an approach would foster a classroom culture that, regardless of class size and instructional technique, would actively involve students in the learning process, promote critical thinking, and impress on students that they, along with the other people and cultures of the world, are cultural animals worthy of study. Each chapter is organized around an intellectual "problem" and then subdivided into a series of questions that address the problem from an anthropological perspective. Most sections of each chapter contain short exercises that encourage students to apply the knowledge and skills they have learned to foster a sense of reflexivity about their own behaviours and beliefs. Each chapter ends with a discussion of the ways in which a problem-based approach and anthropological perspective can be put to use outside academia. Ultimately, we hope that after reading this text, students will appreciate that culture, as the way that human beings make their lives meaningful, is fluid, dynamic, contradictory, and subject to critique. Moreover, we hope that students who read this book will understand why and how anthropology *matters* for anyone who wants to understand, and perhaps make a difference in, the contemporary world.

The material in this text is organized by problems and questions rather than by topics. Each of the eight chapters focuses on a specific problem of anthropological as well as general concern:

- How can people begin to understand beliefs and behaviours that are different from their own?
- How do we explain the transformation of human societies over the past ten thousand or so years from small-scale, nomadic bands

of hunters and gatherers to large-scale, urban-industrial states?
- Why do people believe different things, and why are they so certain that their view of the world is correct, and that others are wrong?
- What does a person have to know to understand the dynamics of family life in other societies?
- How do people determine who they are, and how do they communicate who they *think* they are to others?
- Why are modern societies characterized by social, political, and economic inequalities?
- What are the economic and cultural effects of globalization, and what is the relationship between globalization, the nation-state, and national identity?
- How do societies give meaning to and justify collective violence?

These problems have no definitive solutions, yet they drive much intellectual inquiry. Each problem/chapter is broken down into a series of specific questions, each of which can be "answered" by focusing on the ethnographic and theoretical contributions of anthropologists. Such questions include:

- Is it possible to see the world through the eyes of others?
- How do people come to accept social hierarchies as natural?
- What are the characteristics of peaceful societies?

Of course, the list of problems and questions included in the text is not exhaustive. However, the problems and questions that we have selected are those that are central to the concerns of the discipline, and include the topics and issues typically covered in an introductory anthropology class. We have chosen problems and questions that we hope will capture students' imaginations and whet their appetite for further study in the discipline. The Topics–Questions Correspondence Chart, which links topics to questions considered in the text, can be used in guiding discussion and in course planning.

TOPIC AND QUESTION CORRESPONDENCE

Topic	Corresponding Chapter or Question
Aboriginal Peoples	Question 2.2; Question 2.3; Question 2.5; Question 3.1; Question 3.4; Question 3.5; Question 5.6; Question 6.4; Question 7.3; Question 8.1
Applied Anthropology	Question 1.6; Question 2.5; Chapter 3 (Conclusions); Question 4.6; Question 6.6
Caste	Question 6.1
Colonialism	Question 2.2; Question 2.3; Question 3.4; Question 7.3
Conflict	Chapter 8
Corporations	Question 7.2
Cultural Relativism	Question 1.3
Culture Change	Chapter 2
Culture Concept	Chapter 1
Ecology	Question 1.5; Question 2.3; Question 2.5; Question 7.2
Economic Anthropology	Chapter 2; Chapter 6; Chapter 7
Education	Question 7.3; Question 5.1
Ethnocentrism	Question 1.3
Family Organization	Chapter 4
Feminist Anthropology	Question 4.5; Question 5.1; Question 6.4; Question 8.3
Fieldwork	Question 1.2; Question 1.3 ; Question 8.6
Food Production	Question 2.1; Question 2.3; Question 7.2
Foragers	Question 2.1; Question 8.2
Gender	Chapter 4; Question 5.1 ; Question 6.3; Question 8.3
Gift Giving	Question 4.3; Question 5.5
Globalization	Question 2.2; Question 2.3; Chapter 7
Human Rights	Question 1.3; Question 6.6
Identity	Chapter 5
Industrialization	Question 2.2; Question 2.3
Inequality	Chapter 6
International Development	Question 2.3; Question 2.5; Question 5.6
Kinship	Chapter 4; Question 5.2; Question 5.3; Question 6.4
Language and Culture	Question 1.4; Question 3.1; Question 5.3; Question 6.3; Question 8.5
Law and Anthropology	Question 1.6
Marriage	Chapter 4

(Continued)

TOPIC AND QUESTION CORRESPONDENCE *(Continued)*

Topic	Corresponding Chapter or Question
Medical Anthropology	Question 1.6; Question 2.4; Question 4.6; Question 6.6
Nation-State	Chapter 7; Question 8.4
Neoliberalism	Chapter 7
Peasants	Question 2.1; Question 2.3; Question 2.5; Chapter 4
Political Ecology	Question 1.6
Political Organization and Control	Chapter 6; Question 6.5; Question 8.2; Question 8.3; Question 8.4
Race and Racism	Question 6.2; Question 6.3
Religion/World View	Question 1.1; Question 1.3; Chapter 3; Question 5.5; Question 8.1
Ritual	Question 1.4; Question 1.5; Question 2.4; Question 3.2; Question 3.3; Question 5.4 ; Question 5.5; Question 5.6
Sexual Stratification	Question 4.1; Question 4.2; Question 4.3
Sexuality	Question 4.3; Question 4.5; Question 4.6; Question 6.3
Social Stratification	Chapter 6
Status and Rank	Question 2.1; Question 2.2; Question 2.3; Chapter 6; Question 8.1
Subsistence Techniques	Question 2.1; Question 2.2
Symbolism	Question 1.1; Question 1.4; Question 1.5; Question 3.1; Question 3.2; Question 3.3; Question 5.4; Question 5.5
Systems of Exchange	Question 5.5
Tourism	Question 7.4

A key pedagogical feature of this text is the inclusion of exercises that give students the opportunity to apply what they have read, to think about the implications of the material for their own lives, and to attempt to think about various problems "like an anthropologist." These exercises are interspersed throughout the text and can be used in various ways by students and instructors. They might serve as discussion questions in lectures, tutorials, or online discussion posts, or they could be used as the basis for group work. They could also be treated as informal writing assignments, with students preparing brief reading responses based on the exercises, which would then be used as a starting point for classroom discussion. However they are used, the exercises are designed to give first-year students a chance to engage in intellectual debate and to highlight the real-world implications of what they have learned.

In addition to the exercises, each chapter concludes with several critical thinking questions, a new feature in this edition. The questions, together with the new, end-of-chapter glossaries of key terms, encourage students to review what they have learned in two different ways. The lists (whose terms appear in bold throughout the chapter) allow students to review each chapter's material quickly: names, terms, and theories. The critical thinking questions give students the opportunity to rethink the material in a way that underscores what they have learned through the problem-based approach.

One new feature of this edition of *Cultural Anthropology: A Problem-Based Approach* is the inclusion of maps, which appear throughout the chapters. The inclusion of the different projections that open this book exemplifies one of the key pedagogical goals of an introductory anthropology class: to show how one's entire world is shaped by one's cultural perspective. In addition to these maps, each of the chapters includes two or three smaller maps, each of which corresponds with one of the ethnographic examples in the text. These are intended to help orient students toward the material, especially for places that, in our teaching experience, students tend to be less familiar with (such as the Trobriand Islands).

Another key feature that contributes to learning stems from Richard Robbins's conviction—evident in the earlier editions and maintained here, and which we share—that students learning about the cultures of others cannot fully appreciate them without first understanding something of their own cultural perspective. In order to appreciate that other people construct their worlds, they must appreciate that they themselves do so as well. Accordingly, we have included numerous comparisons of world cultures with North American cultures, both in the text and through the exercises.

NEW IN THIS EDITION

In this Second Canadian Edition of *Cultural Anthropology: A Problem-Based Approach*, we retain the spirit of Richard Robbins's account of what anthropology is all about. We also build on Larkin's efforts in the first Canadian edition to provide interesting and important examples of the research that Canadian anthropologists are doing, both in Canada and beyond. Larkin's strong focus on Canadian anthropological work with First Nations, Inuit, and Métis peoples remains important as well. In order to give students a sense of both the history of the discipline and its ongoing dynamism and potential, we have

added new ethnographic examples from around the world, both classic and contemporary. In response to instructor feedback, and based on our own experiences in the classroom, we have made several additions and enhancements throughout the text. These include the following:

Chapter 1

- A new question (1.2), "How Do Anthropologists Learn About Culture?" This section includes an expanded discussion of fieldwork and the culture concept in the context of late-19th- and early-20th-century anthropology and the pioneering work of anthropologists like Bronislaw Malinowski. We go on to outline how fieldwork has changed over the past century (this includes, for example, discussions of the multi-sited ethnography and virtual communities).
- A new discussion under Question 1.6 of the subfield of medical anthropology.
- Explicit discussion of what makes anthropology unique among the social sciences and why an anthropological perspective might be important inside and outside of academia.

Chapter 2

- This chapter is reframed as an explicitly critical discussion of narratives of progress and development.
- An expanded discussion of the relations among globalization, economic development, and cultural diversity.
- A new Canadian case study on the Lubicon Cree.

Chapter 3

- A stronger focus on the role of metaphor in creating and maintaining one's world view.

- Updated examples and discussion of mythology in contemporary popular culture (zombies and vampires).

Chapter 4

- An updated introduction that notes some of the significant features of kinship using contemporary examples that will be well known to Canadian students.
- A new discussion in Section 4.6 of the ways that medical anthropologists can apply their kinship expertise to create better HIV prevention campaigns. The ethnographic example here is about the Ju/'hoansi, one of the cultural groups discussed in detail throughout the chapter.
- Additional attention throughout the chapter to North American kinship and patterns of family relations. Students are encouraged throughout the chapter to critically question their own understandings of what makes a family.

Chapter 5

- A new emphasis on the significance of thinking about identity as learned rather than natural (5.1).
- Discussion of Canadian identity as a learned identity (5.1) and as an example of an imagined community.
- Discussion of anthropological debates about nature, nurture, and identity (5.1).
- Addition of a discussion of Helen Gremillion's work on gender, identity, and body image in North America.
- Discussion in section 5.4 of rites of passage in contemporary Canadian society.

Chapter 6

- A revised introduction that emphasizes the significance of taking a critical approach to social hierarchies that are often taken for granted as natural.

- A revised discussion of caste and class (6.1).
- New sections on race (6.2) and gender (6.3) as forms of social hierarchy.
- A new case study on race, gender, class, and plastic surgery in Brazil.
- A new discussion of gender stratification and hegemonic masculinities.

Chapter 7

- Chapter 7 was formerly Chapter 3. This chapter now addresses globalization and neoliberalism as well as the nation-state.
- A detailed explanation of the development and history of neoliberalism and its role in economic globalization (7.1).
- Definitions and explanations of the interrelated issues of globalization, the nation-state, and neoliberalism (7.2).
- A discussion of the cultural impact of globalization on identity (especially national identities), with examples on tourism, art, and sport (7.4).
- An explanation of the ambiguous cultural effects of globalization, including new case studies from Canada and abroad (Vanuatu) (7.4).

Chapter 8

- A new section, 8.6, about doing fieldwork amidst violent conflict.
- New material that addresses contemporary conflicts in Iraq and Afghanistan (the Human Terrain System and Canadian soldiers in Kandahar).
- Discussion (moved here from the former Chapter 3) of the relationship between the nation-state and violence, touching on ethnocide, genocide, and refugees.
- A new case study of East Timorese refugees in Australia.

Finally, in addition to the new pedagogical features (updated exercises, critical thinking questions, and maps) and the new material discussed above, we are excited about the addition of colour photographs and design elements to this edition. This adds to the visual excitement of the text; we also hope that the new, visually engaging style will enhance learning outcomes for those students who are visual learners. There are also more photographs in this edition than in the last, but they have been added in such a way that they complement rather than undermine a key strength of the earlier editions: the inclusion of many in-depth case studies that encourage close reading. This text should appeal to students with a number of learning preferences: visual learners, active learners, and those who learn through reading. These styles come together in the new opening pages for each chapter, each of which includes a visual element (such as a photo) that is explicitly connected, in its caption, to a text element (the epigraph), which in turn exemplifies the issues for active learning articulated in the chapter problem. Furthermore, on the online platform CourseMate, students can engage with Interactive Maps Exercises and an interactive book.

ACKNOWLEDGMENTS

We are indebted to Richard Robbins and Sherrie Larkin for their work on earlier editions of this text. In the first Canadian edition, published in 2007, Sherrie Larkin did an excellent job of adapting Robbins's text for a Canadian readership. Much of this second edition is an extension and elaboration of their earlier efforts.

We also thank Maya Castle and Jacquelyn Busby at Nelson Education Canada for their encouragement, patience, and support throughout the writing of this second edition. Thanks also go to Matthew Kudelka, the copy editor. Maggie would like to thank Karen for being an imaginative, thoughtful, and patient co-editor and a wonderful colleague. And Karen thanks Maggie for her patience, organization, and creativity during the planning, writing, and editing of this text.

We would also like to thank the reviewers, past and present, for their valuable feedback:

Anna K. Boshnakova, Sheridan College
Blair Rutherford, Carleton University
Branka Maleševi, University of Windsor
Bruce Miller, University of British Columbia
Barbara Wilkes, University of Calgary
Charisma Thomson, University of Regina
Chris Holdsworth, University of Calgary
Edward J. Hedican, University of Guelph
Ellen Facey, University of Northern British
    Columbia
Mark Tate, Memorial University
Sam Migliore, Kwantlen Polytechnic University
Sean Connaughton, Kwantlen Polytechnic
    University
Teresa Holmes, York University

We would be very grateful to receive questions, comments, and suggestions for improvement from instructors and students. Our email addresses are mcummings@utsc.utoronto.ca and mcgarry@yorku.ca.

Maggie Cummings and Karen McGarry

ANCILLARIES

Instructor Ancillaries

neta The **Nelson Education Teaching Advantage** **(NETA)** program delivers research-based instructor resources that promote student engagement and higher-order thinking to enable the success of Canadian students and educators.

Instructors today face many challenges. Resources are limited, time is scarce, and a new kind of student has emerged: one who is juggling school with work, who has gaps in his or her basic knowledge, and who is immersed in technology in a way that has led to a completely new style of learning.

In response, Nelson Education has gathered a group of dedicated instructors to advise us on the creation of richer and more flexible ancillaries that respond to the needs of today's teaching environments.

The members of our editorial advisory board have experience across a variety of disciplines and are recognized for their commitment to teaching. They include:

Norman Althouse, Haskayne School of Business, University of Calgary

Brenda Chant-Smith, Department of Psychology, Trent University

Scott Follows, Manning School of Business Administration, Acadia University

Jon Houseman, Department of Biology, University of Ottawa

Glen Loppnow, Department of Chemistry, University of Alberta

Tanya Noel, Department of Biology, York University

Gary Poole, Senior Scholar, Centre for Health Education Scholarship, and Associate Director, School of Population and Public Health, University of British Columbia

Dan Pratt, Department of Educational Studies, University of British Columbia

Mercedes Rowinsky-Geurts, Department of Languages and Literatures, Wilfrid Laurier University

David DiBattista, Department of Psychology, Brock University

Roger Fisher, Ph.D.

In consultation with the editorial advisory board, Nelson Education has completely rethought the structure, approaches, and formats of our key textbook ancillaries. We've also increased our investment in editorial support for our ancillary authors. The result is the Nelson Education Teaching Advantage and its key components: *NETA Engagement, NETA Assessment,* and *NETA Presentation.* Each component includes one or more ancillaries prepared according to our best practices, as well as a document explaining the theory behind the practices.

NETA Engagement presents materials that help instructors deliver engaging content and activities to their classes. Instead of Instructor's Manuals that regurgitate chapter outlines and key terms from the text, NETA Enriched Instructor's Manuals (EIMs) provide genuine assistance to teachers. The EIMs answer questions like *What should students learn?, Why should students care?,* and *What are some common student misconceptions and stumbling blocks?* EIMs not only identify the topics that cause students the most difficulty, but also describe techniques and resources to help students master these concepts. Dr. Roger Fisher's *Instructor's Guide to Classroom Engagement (IGCE)* accompanies every Enriched Instructor's Manual. (Information about the NETA Enriched Instructor's Manual prepared for *Cultural Anthropology: A Problem-Based Approach,* Second Canadian Edition, is included in the description of the IRCD below.)

NETA Assessment relates to testing materials. Under *NETA Assessment,* Nelson's authors create multiple-choice questions that reflect research-based best practices for constructing effective questions and testing not just recall but also higher-order thinking. Our guidelines were developed by David DiBattista, a 3M National Teaching Fellow whose recent research as a professor of psychology at Brock University has focused on multiple-choice testing. All Test Bank authors receive training at workshops conducted by Professor DiBattista, as do the copy editors assigned to each Test Bank. A copy of *Multiple Choice Tests: Getting Beyond Remembering,* Professor DiBattista's guide to writing effective tests, is included with every Nelson Test Bank / Computerized Test Bank package. (Information about the NETA Test Bank prepared for *Cultural Anthropology: A Problem-Based Approach,* Second Canadian Edition, is included in the description of the IRCD below.)

NETA Presentation has been developed to help instructors make the best use of PowerPoint® in their classrooms. With a clean and uncluttered design developed by Maureen Stone of StoneSoup Consulting, *NETA Presentation* features slides with improved readability, more multi-media and graphic materials, activities to use in class, and tips for instructors on the Notes page. A copy of *NETA Guidelines for Classroom Presentations* by Maureen Stone is included with each set of PowerPoint slides. (Information about the NETA PowerPoint® prepared for *Cultural Anthropology: A Problem-Based Approach,* Second Canadian Edition, is included in the description of the IRCD below.)

IRCD

Key instructor ancillaries are provided on the *Instructor's Resource CD* (ISBN 0176662413), giving instructors the ultimate tool for customizing lectures and presentations. (Downloadable Web versions are also available at www.robbins2ce.nelson.com. The IRCD includes:

- **NETA Engagement:** The Enriched Instructor's Manual was written by Blair Rutherford, Carlton University. It is organized according to the textbook chapters and addresses seven key educational concerns, such as typical stumbling blocks students face and how to address them. Other features include a guide to using group inquiry in the classroom.
- **NETA Assessment:** The Test Bank was written by Charisma Thomson, University of Regina. It includes more than 200 multiple-choice questions written according to NETA guidelines for effective construction and development of higher order questions. Also included are true/false, short answer, and essay questions. Test Bank files are provided in Word format for easy editing and in PDF format for convenient printing, whatever your system.
- **NETA Presentation:** Microsoft® PowerPoint® lecture slides for every chapter have been created by Terry Webb, Western University. There is an average of 30 slides per chapter, many featuring key figures, tables, and photographs from *Cultural Anthropology: A Problem-Based Approach.* NETA principles of clear design and engaging content have been incorporated throughout.

- **Image Library:** This resource consists of digital copies of figures, short tables, and photographs used in the book. Instructors may use these jpegs to create their own PowerPoint presentations.
- **DayOne:** Day One—Prof InClass is a PowerPoint presentation that you can customize to orient your students to the class and their text at the beginning of the course.

CourseMate  CourseMate

Engaging. Trackable. Affordable.

Nelson Education's *Cultural Anthropology* CourseMate brings course concepts to life with interactive learning and exam preparation tools that integrate with the printed textbook. Students activate their knowledge through quizzes, games, and flashcards, among many other tools.

CourseMate provides immediate feedback that enables students to connect results to the work they have just produced, increasing their learning efficiency. It encourages contact between students and faculty: You can select to monitor your students' level of engagement with CourseMate, correlating their efforts to their outcomes. You can even use CourseMate's quizzes to practise "Just in Time" teaching by tracking results in the Engagement Tracker and customizing your lesson plans to address their learning needs.

Engagement Tracker. How do instructors assess their students' engagement in the course? How do instructors know their students have read the material or viewed the resources assigned?

Good practice encourages frequent contacts between students and faculty: with CourseMate, instructors can use the included Engagement Tracker to assess student preparation and engagement. Instructors can use the tracking tools to see progress for the class as a whole or for individual students. This helps instructors identify students at risk early in the course, uncover which concepts are most difficult for the class, monitor time on task, and keep students engaged.

Interactive Teaching and Learning Tools. CourseMate includes interactive teaching and learning tools:

- Quizzes
- Flashcards
- Map exercises
- Crossword puzzles
- and more.

The variety of tools in CourseMate respect diverse ways of learning and give students ample opportunity to actively engage with the course concepts. Students receive prompt feedback, which helps them focus their learning efforts on the concepts they have yet to master. Time plus energy equals learning, and CourseMate offers an engaging way for students to increase their time on task.

Interactive eBook. In addition to interactive teaching and learning tools, CourseMate includes an interactive eBook. Instructors can use it as a supplement to the printed text, or as a substitute. Students can take notes, highlight, search, and interact with embedded media specific to their book. To access CourseMate, please ask your Nelson Sales Representative for an SSO account. To provide your students with access to CourseMate, please direct them to www.nelsonbrain.com.

The National Geographic Learning Reader Series

This groundbreaking series is brought to you through an exclusive partnership with the National Geographic Society, an organization with a unique tradition of exploration, scientific research, discovery, conservation, and nonpareil publishing. Readers of interest to students of anthropology include: Archeology, Biological Anthropology, and Cultural Anthropology. The readers bring learning to life by featuring compelling images, media, and text from National Geographic. Each article has an introduction to provide context as well as focus questions that suggest ideas to think about while reading the selection. Rich photography and compelling images are used throughout to further enhance understanding of the selections. The chapter culminating section includes discussion questions to stimulate both in-class discussion and out-of-class work. Additional resources are available via a media-rich eBook that contains videos as well as the capability to highlight, take notes, search and bookmark. For more information, visit www.cengage.com/community/natgeo, or contact your Nelson Education sales representative.

CourseReader

CourseReader is an easy-to-use and affordable option to create your own online collection of readings for your course. Simply go online to search or browse Cengage Learning's collection of thousands of text documents and media clips. In just a matter of minutes you can preview, select, and create your customized collection from across many disciplines. To view a demo of CourseReader visit www.cengage.com/coursereader. To learn more about money-saving bundles, please contact your local Nelson sales representative.

LETTER FROM THE PUBLISHER

Dear Instructor,

CourseMate CourseMate, Nelson Education's online engagement and assessment platform, is built with you and your students in mind.

CourseMate is designed to support your wonderful efforts to create an interactive, engaging online course, whether it accounts for 5 percent or 100 percent of your students' course experience. The digital assets found in this platform were selected for their pedagogical utility. Each digital asset contributes to the creation of an enriching online learning experience that respects diverse learning preferences and supports better student outcomes.

Our development of this learning tool has been guided by Arthur Chickering and Zelda Gamson's seminal work, "Seven Principles of Good Practice In Undergraduate Education" (*AAHE Bulletin,* 1987), and the follow-up work by Chickering and Stephen C. Ehrmann, "Implementing the Seven Principles: Technology as Lever" (*AAHE Bulletin,* 1996). Our attention to these principles ensures CourseMate appropriately reflects the core goals of contact, collaboration, multimodal learning, time on task, prompt feedback, active learning, and high expectations.

You can use CourseMate in several ways, including the following:

- **To help students prepare for class:** Instructors can assign the interactive quiz questions before class. Students receive immediate feedback to the pre-test, including ebook excerpts covering the concepts they have yet to master. To confirm whether students have completed their pre-class assignment, instructors consult the Engagement Tracker for immediate insight into each student's time on task and achievement. Engagement Tracker helps instructors identify at-risk students early so they can intervene as needed.

- **To engage students:** Students can read about fieldwork in the *Meet the Scientist* boxes and answer critical thinking questions. They practise comprehension by adding notes to the embedded eBook and highlighting important passages, as well as by using interactive flashcards and answering quiz questions.

- **To help students develop their critical thinking skills:** Students can challenge their higher-order thinking skills with the critical thinking questions that conclude almost all of the digital assets, including the Interactive Map Exercises.

- **To assess students:** Instructors can attach grades to student responses to the quizzes and critical thinking questions. Instructors might also choose to load the text's Test Bank to their learning management system (LMS).

- **To create an online learning community:** Instructors can ask students to read one of the passages or read one of the boxed assets (such as the *Meet the Scientist* box). Rather than have each student respond to the culminating critical thinking question, some instructors post the critical thinking question to the discussion board on their LMS. Yet others assign the question for in-class discussion or a small group response via email.

However you choose to incorporate CourseMate into your course, we sincerely hope it supports the construction of an online community of engaged learners. To access CourseMate, please ask your Nelson Sales Representative for an SSO account.

Should you wish to contact me, please feel free to do so by emailing Maya.Castle@nelson.com.

Warmest wishes,

Maya Castle

Maya Castle
Acquisitions Editor
Nelson Education
Canada's Learning Advantage

ABOUT THE AUTHORS

RICHARD H. ROBBINS Richard H. Robbins is a distinguished teaching professor of anthropology at the State University of New York at Plattsburgh. His teaching interests include courses on global problems, utopian societies, comparative religion, and activist anthropology. He has conducted research among indigenous peoples of Canada and fishing communities in northeastern New Brunswick. His recent books include *Global Problems and the Culture of Capitalism,* Fourth Edition; *Darwin and the Bible: The Cultural Confrontation* (with Mark Cohen); and *Globalization and the Environment* (with Gary Kroll). Professor Robbins is the recipient of the 2005 American Anthropological Association Award for Excellence in Undergraduate Teaching.

MAGGIE CUMMINGS Maggie Cummings (Ph.D. 2009, York University) is an assistant professor of anthropology at the University of Toronto, Scarborough. For the past decade, she has done fieldwork on gender, modernity, and social change in Vanuatu. She is currently working on two research projects: the first explores the transformation of cultural understandings of masculinity in Vanuatu among men who work in the burgeoning tourist industry and/or as temporary agricultural workers in New Zealand. The second project take place closer to home, and focuses on long-distance running, embodied ethics, and corporate charities such as Run for the Cure. Since beginning her teaching career in 2006, she has designed and taught over a dozen undergraduate anthropology courses, including Introduction to Anthropology, Fieldwork in Sociocultural Anthropology, Genders and Sexualities, and Culture through Film and Media. She has also been involved in several fieldwork-based student learning initiatives at UTSC, including an interdisciplinary project on citizenship, belonging, and urban life in East Scarborough.

KAREN MCGARRY Karen McGarry is a cultural anthropologist at York University in Toronto, Ontario. Much of her fieldwork and research involves ethnographic studies of elite, high-performance sport, with an emphasis upon the production, distribution and reception of particular representations of athlete's bodies in the mass media. Broadly speaking, she is interested in the intersections among gender, race, class, ethnicity, and Canadian nationalism. She has conducted fieldwork among Olympic figure skaters, divers, and swimmers.

SHERRIE N. LARKIN Dr. Sherrie Larkin is the undergraduate chair of the Anthropology Department at Western University (formerly the University of Western Ontario). The focus of her research has been temporary international labour migration from the Caribbean to Canada, specifically agricultural workers who travel from the Eastern Caribbean Island of Saint Lucia to live and work on farms in Ontario. This focus includes questions about the role of the Canadian state and its immigration requirements, the ways in which Ontario growers organize their labour needs, the experiences of Caribbean employees working in Ontario, and the effects of labour migration on both the Caribbean and rural Ontario.

PROBLEM-BASED PEDAGOGICAL FRAMEWORK

One doesn't need to change one's instructional approach to adopt a problem-based book. If you'd like your students to question, inquire, think critically, and analyze material, the problem-based pedagogical framework of this text can support that intention.

A thorough, robust map program

Expanding students' geographical awareness can be achieved through a comprehensive map program. Global ethnographic examples within the chapters are grounded by maps in the prefatory and in-text material. The maps give students a visual sense of both the global diversity of human culture, and of the geographical breadth of anthropology as a discipline. Each chapter includes two or three smaller maps which correspond with one of ethnographic examples in the text. These are intended to help to orient students towards the material, especially for places with which, in the authors' teaching experience, students tend to be less familiar.

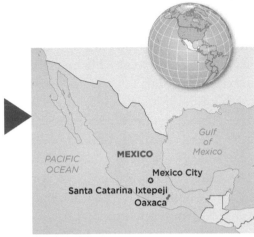

Problems

At the centre of the problem-based approach is the problem that frames each chapter. The material in this text is organized by problems rather than topics, to encourage students to make connections between pressing issues, anthropological lenses, and anthropologists' work. Each of the eight chapters of the book focuses on a specific problem of anthropological, as well as general, concern. Although these problems may have no definitive solutions, they drive much intellectual inquiry.

PROBLEM 3

Why do people believe different things, and why are they so certain that their view of the world is correct and other views are wrong?

Questions

Each problem/chapter is broken down into a series of specific questions, each of which can be "answered" by focusing on the ethnographic and theoretical contributions of anthropologists.

QUESTIONS

In examining this problem, we will consider the following questions:

3.1 How does the use of metaphor affect the meanings people assign to experience?

3.2 How does symbolic action reinforce a particular view of the world?

3.3 How does the way we live affect our beliefs and rituals?

3.4 What happened to local worldviews when they were confronted by the religions of the European colonizers?

3.5 How can people reorder their view of the world if it becomes unsatisfactory?

Exercises

A key pedagogical feature of this text is the inclusion of exercises that give students the opportunity to apply what they have read, to think about the implications of the material for their own lives, and to attempt to think about various problems "like an anthropologist." These can be assigned for homework, worked through in class, or posted to your learning management system. Students can complete them in groups or individually.

EXERCISE 3.3

1. Take a few minutes to think about your own beliefs about the relationship between the cultural life of humans and the natural world. Are they connected to a particular religious or secular world view (or both)? How do these beliefs reinforce the life you live (and vice versa)?

2. If you believed that all the entities of the world are somehow connected and have the same rights as humans, how would this belief change the way you think about resources such as the foods you eat, the gas you put in your car, the disposal of your garbage, and the electricity and water you use in your house?

CRITICAL THINKING QUESTIONS

1. If reality is culturally and socially constructed, can there be such a thing as objective truth? What are the implications of taking a social constructionist approach to reality for the pursuit of knowledge? Is objectivity possible? What obstacles might this present for the anthropological study of culture?

2. Do we need to believe in rituals in order for them to be effective?

3. How have the forces and circumstances of globalization shaped belief systems around the world?

Critical Thinking Questions

To extend the inquiry-based philosophy of the text, the authors have introduced critical thinking questions to the end of each chapter, a new feature in this edition. The questions encourage students to review what they have learned by giving students the opportunity to rethink the material in a way that underscores what they have learned through the problem-based approach. These can be assigned for homework or used for in-class discussion.

Running Glossary

Also new to this edition is a running glossary where key terms are highlighted and defined on the page in which they first appear. The glossary (whose terms appear in bold throughout the chapter) allows to students to review quickly the chapter's material: names, terms, and theories.

totemism
Fake copy the belief that people are related to particular animals, plants, or natural objects by virtue of descent from common ancestral spirits.

ritual
a dramatic rendering or social portrayal of meanings shared by a specific body of people in a way that makes them seem correct and proper (see also symbolic actions)

CULTURE AND MEANING

© iStockphoto/Thinkstock

As noted in the epigraph from Rupert Ross, it is nearly impossible to accurately interpret people's acts when we do not understand the meanings they attribute to those acts. Egyptian hieroglyphics provide an apt metaphor for potential pitfalls of misinterpretation. What do you see when you look at this hieroglyph? How do you make sense of it? Unless you are well versed in Egyptian myth and history, it is likely that your interpretation says more about your own cultural context than that of the ancient Egyptians. Understanding human beliefs and behaviours requires a similar attention to meaning in context.

Acts are never merely acts. They are also signals of attitude. Those signals, however, are often culture specific. When acts are seen, but their signal-content misinterpreted, it is impossible to avoid forming inaccurate interpretations of others. Until we understand what particular acts mean to the other, we will continually ascribe motivations and states of mind that are well off the mark.

Rupert Ross, Dancing with a Ghost

PROBLEM 1

How can people begin to understand beliefs and behaviours that are different from their own?

INTRODUCTION

The World Behind Everyday Appearances

In **sociocultural anthropology** we strive to look beyond the world of everyday experiences to discover the patterns and meanings that lie behind that world. Take, for example, the typical classroom chair with attached desk.

In our taken-for-granted, everyday world, this piece of furniture is a utilitarian object: something to sit on, or to write on, or even to put our feet on. But for the sociocultural anthropologist, the classroom chair tells some interesting tales and poses some interesting questions. For example, why do we have chairs at all? Many societies don't; instead, people sit or squat on the ground or the floor or sit on stools or benches. Historically, the chair likely first appeared in Europe or the Near East, but it wasn't common even in Europe until the 18th century. Another question: Why does the classroom chair take the form it does? Why don't we sit on stools? One feature of the chair that anthropologists might explore as they try to decipher the meaning of the classroom chair and desk is the erect position into which it forces the body, compelling it, in effect, to "pay attention." We might take a clue from the French philosopher Michel Foucault, who refers to the shaping of the human body as a "political anatomy." By this, he means that people's bodies are controlled by others to operate with the necessary speed and efficiency. Political anatomy produces, he says, "docile bodies."

> **sociocultural anthropology**
> An anthropological approach that retains the British focus on social anthropology at the same time as it adds the American focus on culture to produce something slightly different from either one.

Sociocultural anthropologists find patterns of meaning even in objects as simple as a classroom chair.

© Ursula Alter/iStockphoto

An anthropologist might suggest that the classroom chair and desk are part of the political anatomy of educational settings—part of the system of relations that gives meaning to the classroom. In other words, this piece of furniture forms the body into a shape that prepares it (or forces it) to attend to a teacher and not to others in the same room. Moreover, it is appropriate to its unique setting in the classroom, as are other objects of furniture. Imagine, for example, replacing classroom chairs with bar stools, whose main purpose is to promote bodily mobility and conversation with others.

Once alert to the idea that the classroom chair might serve as an instrument of control, we might notice other ways in which classroom design serves as a mode of discipline. The distribution of people in space, with each person in a particular "spot" in neat, ordered rows, serves to discipline people to "pay attention" to the classroom centre and not to others around them. We might also notice the distinctive ordering of time and the use of clocks, bells, and whistles to control the movement and activities of people in school settings. We can even take our analysis a step further and examine the discipline of the school setting sequentially, from kindergarten through high school. Contrast, for example, the wide-open space of the kindergarten classroom,

with its open, movable chairs and tables and teacher's desk set off to the side, with the enclosed, partitioned space of a second- or third-grade classroom, with its neatly arranged desks facing the centred desk of the teacher. This is the evolution of classroom discipline.

Students, of course, do not always obey the subtle commands that direct their bodies to do certain things at certain times. One only has to examine the strange bodily contortions of students as they resist the form into which the classroom chair tries to force them. We also try, occasionally, to resist the isolation imposed by the arrangement of classroom furniture or the timetables set by clocks, bells, and whistles.

The ways in which specific societies order behaviour through the arrangement of space and time is but one small area examined by sociocultural anthropology, but it serves as an example of how, from an anthropological perspective, we cannot take anything about even our own beliefs and behaviour for granted, let alone the behaviour and beliefs of those whose backgrounds and histories differ from our own.

This book is about how sociocultural anthropology can help us see beyond our taken-for-granted world. We will be examining how sociocultural anthropology helps us understand others and, in the process, better understand ourselves. We will also be examining how knowledge of others and ourselves is relevant to careers in social and economic development, public policy and planning, education, medicine, and conflict resolution.

What Makes Sociocultural Anthropology Unique?

The term "anthropology" comes from two Greek words: *anthropos*, meaning "human beings," and *logia*, meaning "the study of" or "the knowledge of." This study of, or knowledge of, human beings includes everything that humans do currently or have done in the past. It also includes collecting evidence of how and when we became human and comparing humans to other organisms in the world. If asked to describe a typical anthropologist, you might envision an intrepid explorer, like Indiana Jones, searching for priceless artifacts or painstakingly excavating ancient fossils. But it would be more realistic to imagine a sociocultural anthropologist equipped with a notebook and a voice recorder rather than a shovel or a trowel. The kind of knowledge about human beings that sociocultural anthropologists are interested in is acquired by spending time with people, talking to them, observing what they do, and trying to understand their lives—as anthropologist Bronislaw Malinowski aptly put it—"from the native's point of view" (see section 1.2).

In North America, anthropology is divided into four different approaches to the study of humans. Although these four subdisciplines address some of the same questions about what it means to be human, they focus on different aspects of the anthropological question (hence the differences among the tools—notebooks versus shovels—used by different kinds of anthropologists). The subdisciplines are biological anthropology, archaeology, linguistic anthropology, and sociocultural anthropology (known as cultural anthropology in the United States and social anthropology in Britain). To understand what makes sociocultural anthropology unique among the subdisciplines (and among the social sciences in general), it is important first to understand the points of convergence and divergence among these subdisciplines.

Biological anthropology, the oldest of the four subdisciplines, focuses on human beings as one of a great multitude of organisms that inhabit the earth. Some biological anthropologists specialize in paleoanthropology, which is the study of fossil remains of the earliest humans, and attempt to understand the history of human biological evolution. Other biological anthropologists specialize in primatology, or the study of our closest nonhuman relatives. The newest branch of biological anthropology is forensic anthropology, which is the study of human remains for identification and cause of death.

Archaeology is the branch of anthropology that studies human history and its artifacts. Archaeologists typically look at the material remains of human groups in order to learn how people lived. Tools, pottery shards, and other artifacts offer clues about the social and cultural lives of societies that existed thousands of years ago.

Linguistic anthropologists examine the relationship between language and culture. They are interested in how people use language, both in a physical sense with regard to how communication is structured, and in a historical sense with regard to how different languages have developed and spread throughout history.

Finally—and most importantly for our purposes in this text—*sociocultural anthropologists* look at how societies are structured and how cultural meanings are created. Although these anthropologists are interested in differences among peoples throughout the world, they also look for similarities in how people construct their own versions of what it means to be human. Sociocultural anthropologists, then, explore both the universal and the particular, moving back and forth between these two levels of inquiry and analysis in their work. They do fieldwork (see section 1.2) among the societies and cultures they study, gathering data by talking to people and by participating in and observing their day-to-day lives.

This focus on social structures and cultural meanings, in all their forms, is what makes sociocultural anthropology unique among the subdisciplines. Many people—including some anthropologists themselves—wonder whether sociocultural anthropology should be characterized as a science or as one of the humanities. At its best, sociocultural anthropology incorporates aspects of both: the methodological and analytical rigour of the sciences, and the interpretive insights and nuances of the humanities. Eminent anthropologist Eric Wolf (1964, 88) perhaps put it best when he described anthropology as "the most scientific of the humanities, [and] the most humanistic of the sciences." This combination of versatility and breadth is precisely what makes anthropology such an interesting and dynamic discipline.

Moreover, the unique perspective on humanity provided by sociocultural anthropology is well suited to thinking about the complexity of the contemporary world and the human condition. This book is organized around eight general problems that arise from the human condition—problems such as how to understand people with different beliefs and behaviours; why ways of life change; how people justify violence; and whether it is possible to solve problems of social inequality. These problems concern everyone, not just sociocultural anthropologists, but definitive solutions are not possible. So the goal, instead, is to achieve a greater understanding of why those problems exist and what might be done to address them. Sociocultural anthropologists can ask specific questions concerning them, applying their unique disciplinary perspective and methodologies. We will be focusing on these eight general problems in this text. At various points you will be asked to supply your own answers to questions and, perhaps, to discuss your answers with others.

Understanding others requires you to recognize that your behaviours and beliefs, as well as those of people in other societies, are socially patterned and constructed. For that reason, you will find in this text many comparisons between North American life and life in other societies. Whether or not you pursue a career in anthropology, or a career that explicitly requires anthropological expertise, learning to approach and understand human beliefs and behaviour from an anthropological perspective is a valuable skill in the contemporary world.

QUESTIONS

1.1 Why do human beings differ in their beliefs and behaviours?

1.2 How do anthropologists learn about culture?

1.3 Is it possible to see the world through the eyes of others?

1.4 How can the meanings that others find in experience be interpreted and described?

1.5 What can learning about other peoples tell anthropologists about their own societies?

1.6 How can an anthropological perspective be used outside of academia?

QUESTION 1.1: WHY DO HUMAN BEINGS DIFFER IN THEIR BELIEFS AND BEHAVIOURS?

From an anthropological perspective, members of a society view the world in a similar way because they share the same **culture**; people differ in how they view the world because their cultures differ. What do anthropologists mean by culture? A good place to start to understand the concept of culture is with the fact that members of all human societies experience specific life events such as birth, death, and the quest for food, water, and shelter. All societies have what are for them appropriate rules for courtship, ideas about child rearing, procedures for exchanging goods, methods of food production, techniques for building shelters, and so on. But from one society to the next, the meanings people assign these events differ. We learn these meanings from, and teach these meanings to, other members of our culture. Our working definition of culture, therefore, is as follows: "culture is the system of meanings about the nature of experience that is shared by a people and passed from one generation to another." This definition encompasses the meanings that people give to things, events, activities, and people. As we will see in section 1.2, throughout the history of the discipline, anthropologists have debated—and often disagreed about—the substance of culture and the best ways to study it. Our working definition of culture highlights those aspects of this complicated and contentious term upon which most anthropologists *can* agree: culture is about meaning; cultural meanings must be learned; and, once learned, meanings are shared by members of a particular

---

culture
The system of meanings about the nature of experience that are shared by a people and passed on from one generation to another, including the meanings that people give to things, events, activities, and people.

culture. Culture enables human beings to make sense of their life experiences and to understand those experiences as meaningful in particular ways. All human beings share certain basic experiences: hunger, sex, and death, for example. Why, though, do people from different backgrounds understand these experiences in different ways? Thinking about culture begins to suggest an answer to this question.

Attitudes toward death provide one example. For some people, death marks the passage of a person from one world to another. For others, death is an ending, the final event in a life span; and still others view death as part of a never-ending cycle of birth, death, and rebirth. The Kwakwaka'wakw of British Columbia, for example, believe that when a person dies, the soul leaves the body and enters the body of a salmon. When a salmon is caught and eaten, a soul is released and is free to enter the body of another person.

Some societies fear the dead; others revere them. In rural China until recently, each household contained a shrine to the family ancestors. Before any major family decision, the head of the household addressed the shrine to ask the ancestors' advice, thus making the dead part of the world of the living. In southern Italy, by contrast, funeral customs were designed to *discourage* the dead from returning. Relatives placed useful objects such as matches and small change near the body to placate the soul of the deceased and to ensure that it did not return to disturb the living.

A Chinese bride makes an offering to an ancestral shrine.

In some societies, death is accepted as natural and inevitable; in others, death is always attributed to the malevolent act of some person, often involving sorcery. In these societies, every death elicits suspicion and a demand for vengeance. Still other societies require great demonstrations of grief and mourning for the deceased. Thus, the Dani of New Guinea require a close female relative of a recently deceased person to sacrifice part of a finger. When the Wari' in of western Brazil still lived independent of Western civilization, they disposed of the bodies of their dead by eating the roasted flesh, certain internal organs, and sometimes the ground bones. They ate the dead not because they needed the meat or because they liked the taste of human flesh, but rather out of a respect and compassion for the dead person and the dead person's family (we will explore this example in section 1.3). In southern Europe, widows were required to shave their heads; at one time in India, widows were cremated alive at their husbands' funerals, a practice known as *sati*. In most North American societies, survivors of the deceased are expected to restrain their grief almost as if it were a contagious disease. To many North Americans, the sight of southern Italian women pulling their hair and being restrained from flinging themselves into an open grave is as bewildering as their own restraint of grief would be to southern Italians.

Food provides another telling example of how a culture takes the "raw materials" of human life and makes them meaningful. All humans need to eat; however, no society accepts all items in their edible universe as "good to eat." Only a relatively few items are so designated. Insects such as grubs, beetles, and ants are acceptable fare in some societies, while people in others are horrified by the thought of eating insects. North Americans generally do not define insects as food (although U.S. federal regulations do allow a certain percentage of insect matter to be included in processed food). Most North Americans like and are encouraged to drink milk, yet some people in China consider milk undrinkable. Conversely, the Chinese raise dogs for meat—something that would horrify most

North Americans. North American children who have raised pet guinea pigs would have a hard time accepting the Peruvian practice of raising guinea pigs for food. Of all the two million or so species of living organisms that inhabit the earth, only humans dwell largely in worlds that they themselves have created by giving meanings to things. This creation is what anthropologists mean by the term "culture." Human beings are cultural animals; they ascribe meanings of their own creation to objects, persons, behaviours, emotions, and events and then proceed to act as if those meanings are real. All facets of their lives—death, birth, courtship, mating, food acquisition and consumption—are suffused with meaning.

Clifford Geertz suggests that human beings are compelled to impose meaning on their experiences because without those meanings to help them comprehend experience and impose an order on the universe, the world would seem a jumble, "a chaos of pointless acts and exploding emotions" (1973, 46). Geertz writes that human beings are "incomplete or unfinished animals who complete themselves through culture—not culture in general, but specific forms of it": Balinese, Italian, Ilongot, Chinese, Kwakiutl, Canadian, and so on (1976, 49). When people share the meanings they give to experiences, they share and participate in the same culture.

Differences in culture arise in part from the fact that different groups of human beings, for various reasons, create, share, and participate in different realities; as a consequence, they assign different meanings to death, birth, marriage, and food. Objects, persons, behaviours, emotions, and events in a human world have meanings ascribed to them by those who share, use, or experience them. The clothes people wear, the foods they eat (or refuse to eat), even their gender, are defined through the meanings that people give them. Understanding culture, and the culturally situated meanings that flourish in various cultural contexts, is therefore the main object of anthropological study. In the next section, we will explore how anthropologists have approached the study of culture and how unique research methods have emerged as the discipline of anthropology has developed.

QUESTION 1.2: HOW DO ANTHROPOLOGISTS LEARN ABOUT CULTURE?

The Formative Years of Anthropology

Anthropology began at a particular time in history: "the Age of Exploration," which was launched by Christopher Columbus when he arrived in the Americas in 1492 and which lasted until the early 17th century. It was during these centuries that Europeans first encountered people who looked and behaved very differently (Barrett 1996, 3). Travellers and explorers returned home with stories about the seemingly "strange" people they had met in faraway places, sometimes bringing back live native "specimens" as well. Those at home debated at length whether these beings were actually human. European countries established colonies throughout the world, often sending missionaries along to "civilize" the strange people; those missionaries then documented their encounters. One of the most famous of these accounts is the *Jesuit Relations*, first published in 1632, which describes the interactions between the Jesuit missionaries and the indigenous peoples in southern Ontario. These missionaries' writings were a type of proto-anthropology, though it must be added that missionaries and anthropologists today have very different motivations for the work they do.

Notwithstanding these early cross-cultural interactions, anthropology did not emerge as a formal discipline until 1883, when Edward Tylor was appointed to the first position of anthropology in Britain. Decades later, in 1925, Thomas F. McIlwraith became the first anthropology appointment at the University of Toronto. Canada's first Department of Anthropology was founded at the same university in 1936.

In the late 1800s, as anthropology grew in popularity throughout Europe and North America, many early anthropologists like Tylor were **armchair anthropologists**. That is, instead of visiting various peoples and conducting their own first-hand research, they stayed at home and amassed diaries, reports, and various documents written by others who had come in contact with various non-Western peoples. Sitting in their "armchairs," or perhaps at their university office desks, these anthropologists applied a comparative method to explore differences and similarities in social institutions and belief systems in a variety of societies. Based on their comparisons, armchair anthropologists would attempt to make cross-cultural generalizations about such things as warfare, family structures and marriage, religion, and other phenomena.

Tylor relied on the accounts provided by travellers and missionaries as sources of information for his book, *Primitive Culture*. But he did so uncritically—that is, he did not acknowledge the inherent biases in their writings, instead taking their work at face value (as did many other armchair anthropologists of his day). It is worth noting the ways in which Tylor's own 1871 definition of culture reflected the methodological approach that he shared with his fellow armchair anthropologists. According to Tylor, "culture or civilization, taken in its wide [comparative] ethnographic sense, is that complex whole which includes knowledge, belief, art, morals, law, custom, and any other capabilities and habits acquired by man as a member of his society" (1871, 1). As in our working definition of culture outlined in section 1.1, Tylor's definition emphasized the shared and learned aspects of culture. However, he and other Victorian anthropologists wrote about culture in the singular, believing that some peoples or cultural groups might have more or less culture or civilization than others. In this sense, both their methodology and their understanding of culture were not merely comparative, but hierarchical as well. Contemporary anthropologists remain interested in the differences and similarities between cultures, but they no longer resort to hierarchies when comparing human beliefs and behaviours.

> **armchair anthropologist**
> Refers to an approach to the study of various societies that dominated anthropology in the late 1800s. It involved the collection, study, and analysis of the writings of missionaries, explorers, and colonists who had sustained contact with non-Western peoples. Armchair anthropologists used these documents to make comparisons and generalizations about the ways of life of various groups.

Ethnographic Fieldwork

Anthropologists such as Bronislaw Malinowski and Franz Boas (often regarded as the "fathers" of social and cultural anthropology, respectively) would soon move beyond the armchair anthropology of Tylor and his contemporaries. In the United States, Boas sought firsthand knowledge among the Inuit and the Kwakwaka'wakw. After Malinowski went to live in the Trobriand Islands during the First World War, extended periods of fieldwork became the required methodology of sociocultural anthropology.

Anthropologists, like other social scientists, use surveys, written documents, historical accounts, and questionnaires as part of their research toolbox. But the unique feature of sociocultural anthropology is the **ethnographic method**—investigators immerse themselves in the lives of the people they are trying to understand and thereby attain some level of understanding of the meanings those people ascribe to their existence. This immersion process entails **participant observation**, defined as the active participation of observers in the lives of their subjects.

The ethnographic method is only part of the anthropological enterprise. The anthropologist also seeks to explain why people view the world as they do and to contribute to the understanding of human behaviour in general. But this enterprise begins with fieldwork, which involves the meeting of at least two cultures: that of the researcher, and that of the people the researcher is trying to understand. Anthropological researchers must set aside their own views of things and attempt to see the world in a new way. In many respects, they must assume the demeanour and status of children who must be taught by their elders the proper view of the world.

Bronislaw Malinowski (1884–1942), Polish-born and British-trained, was one of the first anthropologists to abandon the armchair approach. He would revolutionize anthropology by stressing the primacy of **fieldwork**. In Malinowski's time, fieldwork usually involved conducting first-hand, long-term, qualitative research with a group of people. This meant that anthropologists had to get out of their armchairs and travel to live among non-Western (usually indigenous) peoples. Having arrived at their research site, they would spend at least a year carrying out fieldwork—conducting interviews and surveys, taking photographs, and recording songs and oral narratives, among other things. In 1915, Malinowski arrived in the Trobriand Islands as the guest of British colonial officials. Soon after his arrival, he concluded that it would be necessary to spend each day with the Trobrianders if he hoped to obtain a comprehensive understanding of their daily lives. So he left the comfort of his colonial household, acquired a

Bronislaw Malinowski in the Trobriand Islands. Malinowski was one of the first anthropologists to conduct long-term fieldwork.

© London School of Economics, Malinowski/3/18/2

ethnographic method
The immersion of researchers in the lives and cultures of the peoples they are trying to understand in order to comprehend the meanings these people ascribe to their existence.

participant observation
An element of fieldwork that can involve participating in daily tasks, and observing daily interactions among a particular group.

fieldwork
Anthropologists engage in long-term interactions (usually a year or more) with various groups of people. This often involves living with people, observing and contributing to daily chores and tasks (participant observation), and conducting interviews. Most fieldwork in anthropology has historically been qualitative in nature.

tent, and set up camp in a nearby Trobriand village. By living with Trobrianders, observing and participating in their daily tasks, and learning their language, he established the importance of participant observation as a fieldwork strategy.

Participant observation requires long-term engagement with a group of people and their daily lives. This may involve living with them as well as observing and participating in daily tasks, no matter how mundane. This fieldwork technique would become a defining feature of contemporary anthropological fieldwork. Even today, anthropologists regularly observe and participate in such things as gardening, harvesting, cooking, recreation, and various rituals and ceremonies.

Malinowski took detailed field notes by hand during his interactions with Trobriand Islanders. In the evenings, he typed up his notes. Later, he would transform these into an **ethnography**, defined as a written description and analysis of an anthropologist's experiences and interactions with a group of people. In essence, the ethnography is the end product of a fieldwork experience.

Malinowski felt that by carefully documenting their experiences and observations with field notes, and combining this with participant observation and other qualitative fieldwork techniques, anthropologists would be able to obtain "the native's point of view" (Malinowski 1961, 25). This approach, also referred to as the "emic" or "insider" perspective, implies that the goal of anthropology is to understand people's beliefs and culture *from their own perspective*. Until Malinowski's time, armchair anthropologists had tended to privilege "etic" or "outsider" explanations for human behaviour. The categories of "insider versus outsider" have been challenged in recent years as a result of globalization's destabilizing impact on unitary identities such as "insider" and "outsider" (see, for example, Narayan 1993). This does not at all detract from Malinowski's contribution, for he was instrumental in establishing the importance of long-term fieldwork for understanding various cultures, and in challenging the cultural generalizations that the

comparative, armchair approach tended to produce. The differences between Edward Tylor's definition of culture and Malinowski's reflect the differences between armchair anthropology and ethnographic fieldwork. Malinowski was less interested in hierarchical comparisons than in understanding each culture on its own terms. His view was that cultures arise in order to meet the particular needs of specific peoples. Culture, in this sense, can be understood as plural. For Malinowski, culture was

> the integral whole consisting of implements and consumers' goods, of constitutional charters for the various social groupings, of human ideas and crafts, beliefs, and customs. Whether we consider a very simple or primitive culture or an extremely complex and developed one, we are confronted by a vast apparatus, partly material, partly human, and partly spiritual, by which man is able to cope with the concrete, specific problems that face him. (1944, 36)

Changing Notions of Fieldwork

Malinowski's insistence on long-term fieldwork and participant observation would have lasting effects on the discipline. These days, PhD students in anthropology are still required to spend at least a year in the field, and they often incorporate participant observation as a fieldwork technique. However, fieldwork has also changed over the last century, and many of Malinowski's original ideas about fieldwork have been challenged.

In the late 19th century, anthropology was about the study of non-Western peoples and places. Most anthropologists were upper-class, educated, white men from Europe, Australia, Canada, and the United States. From their perspective, indigenous peoples were the most

---

ethnography
A written description and analysis of a particular group of people, usually based upon anthropological fieldwork.

appropriate subjects of study. In a somewhat pater-nalistic way, these early anthropologists viewed indigenous peoples as groups in need of "rescue." Thus, a great deal of early-20th-century anthropology in North America was an outgrowth of **salvage anthropology**—an idea espoused by Franz Boas, among others, who felt that indigenous peoples throughout the world were undergoing rapid assimilation and would eventually disappear. He thus felt that anthropologists had an obligation to document and collect the various traditions and cultures of these groups. Boas and his students began documenting Inuit and Northwest Coast indigenous cultures so to "preserve" them before they disappeared (which they never did). Museums at the time took on the same task. Indeed, museums became integral to this culture of collecting and would play a prominent role in the development of Canadian anthropology. In 1911, the Anthropology Division of the Geological Survey of Canada was established, with Edward Sapir, Marius Barbeau, and Diamond Jenness on its staff. In the 1920s, this unit became part of the National Museum of Canada, since renamed the Museum of Civilization (Ervin 2001, 15).

Regna Darnell, an anthropologist at the University of Western Ontario who has conducted extensive research on the history of Canadian anthropology, contends that although there are no features of Canadian anthropology that set it apart as utterly unique, "the national discipline combines features of disciplinary organization and historical context in patterns that *are* unique" (1998, 155). It is difficult to define exactly what is "Canadian" about Canadian anthropology,

but Darnell has an interesting suggestion: "In Canada, a critical mass of First Nations languages and cultures maintains them with a saliency in the national forum unparalleled in the United States" (2000, 170). Many Canadian anthropologists focus on First Nations peoples, but they also conduct research in Latin America, the Caribbean, Asia, Africa, Europe (Eastern and Western), New Zealand, Australia, Melanesia, Polynesia, and the Middle East. Throughout this book, we will be looking at the work of many Canadian anthropologists as well as that of anthropologists in other places in the world.

Many anthropologists continue to focus on indigenous groups. However, ideas about appropriate "field sites" and subjects of study have changed since the days of Malinowski and Boas. Anthropologists no longer restrict themselves to the study of non-Western peoples and places. These days we are just as likely to see anthropologists studying aspects of their own culture. This shift in thinking has had consequences for how anthropologists conduct their fieldwork. The field "site" is not necessarily a faraway place. Today, anthropologists might study office culture in Vancouver, homelessness in Toronto, or separatist ideologies in Quebec. As such, they do not necessarily travel long distances for fieldwork, and many no longer live among their informants for extended lengths of time.

Globalization (which we discuss in more detail in Chapter 7) also has transformed how anthropologists perceive and study societies. Television, the Internet, and other media technologies have transformed the ways we form and maintain social relationships. Today we are creating a sense of community not only through face-to-face interactions but also through Internet sites, chat rooms, online games, Skype, and Facebook, among others. Given that our contemporary interactions are mediated by technology, we increasingly see anthropologists conducting fieldwork online as well as face to face. For example, Tom Boellstorff's ethnography, *Coming of Age in Second Life* (2008), documents his research on the three-dimensional, online gaming

---

salvage anthropology
An approach to anthropology that arose in the late 1800s when anthropologists witnessed the extinction and/or assimilation of indigenous groups throughout the world. In response, some anthropologists, such as Franz Boas, suggested that anthropologists rapidly document the oral stories, songs, histories, and other traditions of indigenous groups before they disappeared.

world of "Second Life." Boellstorff conducted all of his fieldwork online. He justified this by stating that this virtual space is a productive one for studying the unique "cultural logic" of gaming and gamers. In other words, the online communities created by gamers are just as valid an object of study as traditional face-to-face communities have been. Interestingly, Boellstorff cites Tylor's understanding of culture as a "complex whole," asking, "What is a virtual world if not a complex whole, however networked?" (2008, 66). He goes on to explain that he is not studying "virtual culture," but rather "culture in virtual worlds" (ibid.).

Given that globalization has resulted in increasingly fragmented communities and highly mobile groups, it is often no longer tenable for anthropologists to stay in one location for a long period. Malinowski advocated in-depth research in one specific location, but anthropologists today often conduct multi-locale fieldwork, or fieldwork in multiple locations. Other anthropologists advocate the use of multi-sited fieldwork, a term coined by George Marcus in 1995. **Multi-sited fieldwork** involves connecting the localized events and experiences of a community with broader regional, national, or global processes. This approach often goes hand in hand with multi-locale approaches. For instance, Canadian anthropologist Andrew

© Tom Boellstorff

Tom Boellstorff conducted his fieldwork for *Coming of Age in Second Life* entirely online.

Walsh (2010) has studied the commodification of sapphires and the growing preference for "natural" gems (sapphires that have not been subject to heat treatment to enhance their colour) from multiple perspectives. He has interviewed Malagasy miners and local sapphire traders in Madagascar as well as gemologists and jewellers in North America. His work has taken him not only to Madagascar but also to international gemological trade shows. In essence, Walsh is attempting to track the multiple meanings and relationships that form around the international sapphire trade, and he explores how international demand for "natural" sapphires is affecting the lives of miners in local communities in Madagascar.

Fieldwork has undergone changes since Malinowski's time; but the *content* of fieldwork, or data collection, has undergone relatively few changes. Another key aspect of doing anthropology that remains relatively unchanged is that, as anthropologists, through our ethnographies we create bodies of knowledge about the people we are studying. Issues of how to accurately and ethically represent human beliefs and behaviours therefore remain central to the discipline.

Representation and Culture

Because they create knowledge about culture and relay other people's stories about themselves, anthropologists are concerned about issues of **representation.** That is why they try to think

multi-sited fieldwork
This term, coined by George Marcus in 1995, refers to the process of connecting localized experiences of fieldwork with broader, global processes. It necessitates understanding various issues from multiple "sites" or perspectives.

representation
The way in which a group of people is depicted in writing or through images. Anthropologists are increasingly conscious of the fact that when they write about a group of people, they are constructing particular representations that may have positive or negative long-term effects for a group of people.

CULTURE AND MEANING

critically about how they depict the people they are studying, be it in writing, photographs, art, films, and other media or on the Internet. Representations can be created by anthropologists, by the media, or by the informants themselves. Increasingly, anthropologists are speaking out against racist, sexist, or homophobic representations produced by the mass media. In the wake of 9/11, for example, many mainstream American media outlets depicted Islamic people (especially men) as violent terrorists or as "uncivilized," "backward," "primitive." The mass media have tended to resort to **essentialism** when representing particular groups. In essentialist representations, groups of people are depicted in ways that tend to homogenize and stereotype them (Mattingly, Lawlor, and Jacobs-Huey 2002). When essentialist representations are consumed by a public that is too often uncritical, racism is perpetuated, and domestic and foreign policy are affected for the worse.

With respect to representation, anthropologists also turn a critical lens upon themselves. An anthropologist who takes a photograph or writes an ethnographic account is crafting a particular representation of a group of people. This raises an important issue: Who has the right to produce representations of another group of people, and is there such a thing as a misrepresentation?

The people whom anthropologists study are becoming increasingly critical of how they are depicted. American anthropologist Margaret Mead travelled to American Samoa in 1925 to study adolescent girls' sexual habits; this led to the publication of her now famous ethnography, *Coming of Age in Samoa* (1928). Throughout her book, Mead painted a picture of Samoan society as peaceful; she also noted that the girls were free to experiment with pre-marital sex. This contrasted sharply with American attitudes at the time regarding sexuality, where pre-marital sex was viewed as taboo. Her ethnography, which was widely read by anthropologists, students, and the mainstream public, cultivated (perhaps unintentionally) a romanticized and "exotic" representation of Samoans for a largely Western audience. Later generations of Samoans critiqued her work, often denying that teenagers engaged in gratuitous sex (Marshall 1993). Some anthropologists are quick to point out that the "missionization" of Samoans has contributed to the development of stricter moral ideals of sexuality—ideals that in turn have affected their perceptions of Mead's text. Even so, their objections raise some interesting questions for anthropology students. What if the anthropologist's interpretations of culture

© Gerard Sioen/Anzenberger/Redux

Images, like this one, that depict the Yanomamo as fierce and warlike have resulted in essentialist representations of the tribe.

---

essentialism
The act of creating generalizations or stereotypes about the behaviour or culture of a group of people.

differ from those of his or her informants? And what are the consequences of the representations cultivated by anthropologists?

There are no clear-cut answers for those questions, but it is worth noting that the representations crafted by anthropologists can have long-term ill consequences for the groups being depicted. For example, Napoleon Chagnon studied the Yanomami, an Amazonian indigenous group in Brazil and Venezuela. He often labelled them as "fierce" and warlike. In fact, the title of his ethnography about them is *The Yanomamo: The Fierce People* (1968). Other anthropologists who have studied the Yanomami (e.g., Ferguson 1995) have challenged his interpretation of the Yanomami as fierce. Terence Turner (2005) has argued that representations of the Yanomami as "fierce" have done them harm. For instance, in the early 1990s, the British government wanted to provide financial assistance for various Amazonian groups for education and medical clinics. But after reading Chagnon's work, they decided that the money would be better spent on reducing levels of "violence" in the community.

Clearly, representations put forward by anthropologists, the mass media, and others have social, economic, and political consequences for various groups. So it is important for anthropologists to consider the long-term impact of their work in various communities.

EXERCISE 1.2

Find a Canadian newspaper or magazine article that discusses a particular event involving a "minority" group. Outline how the author of the article represents this group. What words does the author use? What sorts of pictures (if any) are displayed? What is the tone of the article? Who was it written by, and for what audience?

QUESTION 1.3: IS IT POSSIBLE TO SEE THE WORLD THROUGH THE EYES OF OTHERS?

This question lies at the heart of the anthropological enterprise. The anthropologist must be able to look beyond everyday appearance to decipher the often hidden meanings of beliefs, objects, and behaviours, while at the same time setting aside her or his preconceptions about what is normal or proper. But in addition to that, the anthropologist must also learn one culture and then relate what he or she has learned to members of another culture in order to translate the meanings of one world into the meanings of another. Like children making their way in a world they do not fully comprehend, anthropologists often find themselves in awkward, embarrassing, or dangerous situations and must be prepared to learn from those moments.

The Embarrassed Anthropologist

Awkwardness and embarrassment are a part of fieldwork, as well as a part of the process through which the fieldworker learns about another culture. Richard Scaglion spent over a year with the Abelam of Papua New Guinea. Shortly after he arrived in the field, he observed and photographed an Abelam pig hunt in which the men set out nets and waited while the women and children made lots of noise to drive the pigs into the nets. Soon after, he was invited by the Abelam to participate in a pig hunt, and he took this as a sign of acceptance, that the people "liked him." He started to go with the men, but they told him they wanted him to go with the women and children to beat the bush, explaining, "We've never seen anyone who makes as much noise in the jungle as you." Later, wanting to redeem himself, Scaglion offered to help an Abelam who was planting crops with a digging stick. A crowd gathered to watch as he used a shovel to try to dig a demonstration hole. After he had struggled for several minutes to get the shovel into the hard-packed soil, someone handed him a digging stick, and he was amazed at how easy it was to use. Later, he found out that several Abelam had shovels but rarely used them because they didn't work.

After months of answering Scaglion's questions about their view of the natural world, such as the moon, sun, and stars, some Abelam asked him about *his* views of the universe. Feeling on safe ground, he gave the usual grade school lecture about the shape of the earth, its daily rotation, and its travels around the sun. Using a coconut, he showed them the relative positions on the earth of New Guinea, Australia, Europe, and the United States. Everyone listened intently, and Scaglion thought it had gone well—until a week later, when he overheard some elders wondering how it was that North Americans walked upside down!

Beginning again, Scaglion used the coconut to explain how, as the earth rotates, sometimes the United States is upright and New Guinea is on the bottom. The Abelam rejected this because they could see that they were *not* upside down, and no one, not even some of the old people in the community, remembered ever having walked upside down. Scaglion began to draw on the physics he had learned at university. As he tried to explain Newton's law of gravity (or "grabity," as his friends pronounced it), he suddenly realized that he didn't understand "grabity" either. It was something he had accepted since grade three, a concept that even physicists simply take for granted as a convenient concept.

EXERCISE 1.3A

Think of some awkward or embarrassing situation created by something you did or didn't do, said or didn't say. What was inappropriate about your behaviour, and why did it lead to misunderstanding or embarrassment? What did you learn from the experience about the meaning of your or others' behaviour?

Confronting Witchcraft in Mexico

Awkward or embarrassing moments in the field may help anthropologists understand a culture and even question their own view of the world. But the question of whether one can ever see the world through others' eyes remains a contentious one among anthropologists. Obviously, to communicate with anyone—even members of their own society—people must share some of the meanings they ascribe to objects, persons, behaviours, emotions, and events. What happens, then, when views of the world are completely different?

Michael Kearney travelled to the town of Santa Catarina Ixtepeji in the valley of Oaxaca, Mexico, with the intention of studying the relationship between the people's view of the world and their social arrangements and environment. He began his work secure in his knowledge of the scientific and materialist view of the world in which he was reared, but he was often fascinated by the differences between his view and that of the people of Santa Catarina Ixtepeji. Their world was controlled by mystic notions of "fate," the will of God, and

malevolent witches and other harmful and sometimes lethal spiritual forces. He became familiar with the Ixtepejanos' world view, never doubting that it was "unscientific"—albeit justified, perhaps, by a life in which suffering, disease, and death were common.

Kearney's faith in his own world view was momentarily shattered by an incident that began innocently enough. While walking to an appointment, he came upon an obviously distressed woman, Doña Delfina. She was known as a witch, and Kearney had been trying unsuccessfully to interview her. When they met she explained that her sister-in-law had a "very bad disease in her arms" and that she wanted him to help. Kearney accompanied Doña Delfina to her house, where he found that the sister-in-law's arms were ulcerated with deep, oozing lesions that looked to him like infected burns. They rejected his offer to take the sick woman to a doctor for medical treatment, so Kearney said he had some ointment that might help, and they eagerly agreed that he should use it. He got the ointment, which contained an anaesthetic, and daubed it on the woman's sores. Much to the amazement of Doña Delfina, her sister-in-law immediately felt better. By the afternoon, her arms had greatly improved; by the following morning, scabs had formed; the day after, she had completely recovered.

Kearney was credited with a "miraculous cure." But the same day, a Ixtepejano friend asked Kearney what he had done and he proudly explained. The friend replied, "Why did you do that? It was not a good thing to do." The sick woman, he said, had been the victim of black magic; another woman, Gregoria, was trying to take Delfina's brother away from his wife and was using black magic to make Delfina's sister-in-law sick. Delfina was using *her* magic to keep her brother in the household, but Gregoria was winning. Now, the friend explained to Kearney, he had intervened, tipping the balance of power back to Delfina but creating a powerful enemy in Gregoria. "Maybe you should leave town for a while until Gregoria calms down," Kearney's friend suggested. Kearney did not take the danger seriously, and he might never have done so were it not for two incidents that occurred soon afterward.

A young doctor in town asked Kearney, who had medical training, to assist in an autopsy of a man who had died in a fall off a truck. It was a particularly long and gory autopsy accomplished only with rusty carpenter's tools in a dimly lit room. Images of the scene and the cadaver disturbed Kearney's sleep over the next few days. One night, about a week later, as the wind beat cornstalks against his house, Kearney felt an itching on his arm. Rolling up his sleeve, he discovered several angry welts that seemed to be growing as he watched them. Immediately he thought of the chancrous arms of Delfina's sister-in-law, realizing at the same time that Gregoria's house was only 50 metres from his and that she could be trying to kill him. "She got me!" he thought. The image of the cadaver on the table jumped into his mind, followed by a wish that he had got out of town while there was still time. As Kearney put it, he was witnessing the disintegration of his scientific, materialist view of the world and grappling with forces with which he was unprepared to deal.

Kearney is not sure how long his initial terror lasted—seconds, perhaps minutes. As he struggled against it, he realized that he was suspended between two worlds, his own and that of the Ixtepejanos. He was questioning a world of meanings that he had until then taken for granted. Kearney is not sure how long he was able to truly believe that the world was as the Ixtepejanos saw it, but as he retrieved his own view of the world, the Ixtepejano's world view, filled with witchcraft and magic, ceased to be only intellectually interesting. It acquired a reality and a sense of legitimacy for him that it had not had before he experienced the real fear that he had been bewitched. He came to realize through his experience that systems of belief are eminently reasonable when viewed from within that system.

The experiences of these anthropologists, Kearney and Scaglion, highlight certain features of the ethnographic method. They especially illustrate anthropologists' attempts to appreciate the views of others while at the same time questioning their own views of the world. They also illustrate what makes the ethnographic method unique: by participating in the lives of others and in their cultural practices, anthropologists can take *themselves* as subjects of investigation. Those who succeed in seeing the world as others do, if even for a brief moment, find it far easier to understand and describe that world. It also helps the anthropologist understand how others can believe what they do. Claude Levi-Strauss, one of the greatest anthropologists of the 20th century, once said that fieldwork, and anthropologists' attempts to immerse themselves in the world of others, makes them "marginal" men or women. They are never completely native because they cannot totally shed their own cultural perceptions, but they are never the same again after having glimpsed alternative visions of the world. Anthropologists are, as Roger Keesing put it, outsiders who know something of what it is to be insiders.

Scaglion and Kearney both succeeded because they were able to see things, at least temporarily, from the native's point of view or an insider's perspective. This is by no means easy, especially when we are faced with practices and beliefs that we find incredible or troublesome. We may be able to overcome our initial shock or bewilderment on confronting different cultures if we understand something about why cultural differences exist. But how should we react if the meanings that others ascribe to experiences differ from our own? It is difficult enough to look beyond everyday appearances at our own beliefs and behaviours; it is far more difficult when we confront beliefs and behaviours of others that we initially consider wrong, horrible, or bizarre. As we shall see in the next section, being able to overcome, or at last set aside, our own cultural biases is one of the major challenges that anthropologists face when they attempt to study and understand cultural beliefs and practices.

How Do People Judge the Beliefs and Behaviours of Others?

Richard Scaglion is fond of telling the story of his friend, a member of the Abelam tribe of Papua New Guinea, who was looking through an issue of *Sports Illustrated*. The friend, dressed in full ceremonial regalia with a feather through his nose, was laughing uncontrollably at a woman shown in a liquor advertisement. When he managed to stop laughing long enough to explain what he thought was so funny, he said, "This white woman has made holes in her ears and stuck things in them." When Scaglion pointed out that his friend had an ornament in his nose, the reply was "That's different. That's for beauty and has ceremonial significance. But I didn't know that white people mutilated themselves."

Scaglion's friend was confronting a problem that many do when the behaviour or beliefs of others seem to differ from their own, and his response was not unusual. He was both shocked and mystified at the strange behaviour. And this suggests a dilemma: Since there are so many versions of what the world is like, how do we go about trying to understand each of them without making positive or negative judgments? Which version of the world is correct? Are there any such versions that we *can* reject or condemn? Can we say, as so many have, that one culture is superior to another?

In the catalogue of human behaviours and beliefs, it is not difficult to find practices or ideas that may seem bizarre or shocking even to trained anthropologists. Sociocultural anthropologists have described the beliefs of the Ilongots of the Philippines, who must kill an enemy to obtain a head that they can throw away in order to diminish the grief and rage they feel at the death of a kinsman or kinswoman. They have studied the historical records of the Aztecs in Mexico, who believed that the universe underwent periodic destruction and that the only way to ward off disaster was to pluck

Abelam villager in ceremonial costume.

the hearts from live sacrificial victims to offer to the gods. They have also studied modern states that routinely engage in or sanction torture, terror, and genocide. How, then, should we react to practices and beliefs such as these?

The Ethnocentric Fallacy and the Relativist Fallacy

If we do condemn or reject the beliefs or behaviours of others, we may be embracing the **ethnocentric fallacy**, which is the idea that our beliefs and behaviours are right and true, while those of other peoples are wrong or misguided. Sociocultural anthropologists have long fought against **ethnocentrism**, that is, the tendency to judge the beliefs and behaviours of other cultures

from the perspective of one's own. They try to show that what often appears on the surface to be an odd belief or a bizarre bit of behaviour is functional and logical in the context of a particular culture. They find the ethnocentric fallacy *intellectually* and *methodologically* intolerable; if everyone everywhere thinks that they are right and that others must be wrong, an intellectual and social dead end is inevitable. Furthermore, if we, as anthropologists, assume that we have all the right answers, our study of other cultures becomes simply the study of other people's mistakes.

Because of the intellectual and methodological implications of ethnocentrism, sociocultural anthropologists emphatically reject this position. But the opposite pole to ethnocentrism, **cultural relativism**, raises issues of its own. Cultural relativism, simply stated, holds that no behaviour or belief can be judged to be odd or wrong simply because it is different from our own. Instead, we must try to understand a culture on its own terms and to understand behaviours or beliefs for the purpose, function, or meaning they have to people in the societies in which we find them. In other words, cultural relativism holds that a specific belief or behaviour can only be understood in relation to the culture—the system of meanings—in which it is embedded.

For example, according to Renato Rosaldo (1989), the ceremonies and rituals accompanying a successful headhunting expedition help the Ilongot psychologically manage their grief over the death of a kinsperson. However, relativism poses a *moral* predicament. Once we concede, say, that it is

---

ethnocentric fallacy
The mistaken notion that the beliefs and behaviours of other cultures can be judged from the perspective of one's own culture.

ethnocentrism
The tendency to judge the beliefs and behaviours of other cultures from the perspective of one's own culture.

cultural relativism
The attempt to understand the beliefs and behaviours of other cultures in terms of the culture in which they are found.

permissible to rip the hearts out of living human beings, provided that you believe it necessary to save the world, or that it is permissible to subject young girls to genital modification to protect family reputations, we find ourselves falling quickly into the **relativistic fallacy**, which is the idea that it is impossible to make moral judgments about the beliefs and behaviours of others. This, of course, seems morally intolerable because it implies that no beliefs or behaviours can be condemned. So we are left with two untenable positions: the ethnocentric alternative, which is intellectually and methodologically unsatisfactory, and the relativist alternative, which is morally unsatisfactory. How do we solve this problem?

Virginity Testing in Turkey and Cannibalism Among the Wari'

To illustrate further the dilemma of relativism and the difficulty of appreciating the cultures of others without making moral judgments, some time ago a human rights group based in the United States issued a report condemning the practice of virginity testing in Turkey. Traditionally, young women in Turkey, as in some other cultures, are expected to avoid sexual relations prior to marriage, although the same rule does not apply to men. In this tradition, the bride's virginity is revealed by displaying, the morning after the wedding, the sheet that was spread on the couple's wedding bed with the tell-tale hymeneal blood stain. The human rights report condemns the traditional testing as well as the reported practice of forcing tests on hospital patients, students, and applicants for government jobs. As anthropologists, we must ask: Is the human rights group being ethnocentric in judging Turkish customs by North American cultural norms, or is it correctly

identifying abuses of women that must be corrected? Might it help if we better understood the logic behind the belief?

In her book on Turkish village society, *The Seed and the Soil,* anthropologist Carol Delaney describes how virginity testing relates to the way in which Turkish villagers conceptualize and explain the reproductive process. They see producing children as analogous to the planting and growing of crops; the man provides the "seed" with his semen, and the woman serves as the "soil" in which the seed germinates and grows. As a metaphor for reproduction, the idea of the seed and the soil provides villagers with a way of thinking about and understanding reproduction. However, the metaphor of seed and soil has at least one very important implication; since seeds do not have a limited life span, as we know semen to have, villagers believe that once planted, the seed (semen) may grow at any time. Consequently, if a woman has had sexual relations with a man other than her husband at any time prior to her marriage, the paternity of the child will be in doubt. Since descent in traditional Turkish villages is closely tied to many things, including property rights, uncertainty about the identity of the true father can have major implications. Thus in the context of Turkish beliefs about procreation, virginity testing may be said to make sense. Furthermore, Turkish beliefs about conception are not that far removed from our own, since our language draws from the same agricultural metaphors as those of Turkish villagers to explain reproduction. We talk about women being "fertile" or "barren" and semen "fertilizing" "eggs." "Sowing one's oats" as an expression of sexual activity is still heard in parts of the United States and Canada. Furthermore, these views are reinforced by religious proscription, legitimized in the Koran and the Old Testament. Thus, before we either condemn or accept the Turkish villagers for their treatment of women, we need to examine what their beliefs tell us about our own. Ours may be equally problematical.

---

relativistic fallacy
The idea that it is impossible to make moral judgments about the beliefs and behaviours of members of other cultures.

But what of cannibalism, such as the Wari' practice of roasting and eating the dead? Surely there is no way to justify that. Cannibalism, as Beth Conklin points out in her study of Wari' cannibalism, *Consuming Grief*, pushes the limits of cultural relativism, guaranteeing reactions of revulsion and fascination. But in addition to that, it has political implications: for centuries, cannibalism was the ultimate smear tactic. To accuse one's enemies or people one wished to degrade or dominate of cannibalism was the ultimate justification for conquest, domination, and exploitation. In 1503, Queen Isabella of Spain decreed that Spaniards could legally enslave specifically those American Indians who were cannibals. Pope Innocent IV, in 1510, ruled that Christians could punish, by force of arms, the sin of cannibalism. By claiming moral superiority in this way, Christians were claiming the right to decide ultimately what is right and what is wrong. Armed with that power, they felt justified in imposing their own views and way of life. What Queen Isabella and Pope Innocent IV conveniently overlooked, however, was that Europeans at the time themselves practised cannibalism. As Conklin notes, medicinal cannibalism—the consumption of human body parts for curing purposes—had a long tradition in Europe. Up until two centuries ago, European physicians prescribed the consumption of human flesh, heart, bones, and other body parts as cures for such afflictions as arthritis, reproductive disorders, sciatica, warts, and skin blemishes. Human blood was thought to be a cure for epilepsy, and physicians recommended that it be drunk immediately after the supplier died. Physicians also thought that the blood of someone who died violently was particularly effective. Thus, in Denmark, epileptics would stand around the scaffolds, cups in hand, waiting to catch the blood of executed criminals. And almost every apothecary kept dried and powdered human body parts on hand for anxious customers.

The people of medieval Europe accepted in their own lives the same types of practices they condemned in others. Furthermore, they failed to understand the practices from the point of view of the others. The Wari' ate their dead, for example, because they believed it was the compassionate thing to do. As Conklin puts it, "More painful than having the corpse eaten would have been to have it *not* eaten" (2001, 81). For the Wari', a corpse left intact was a painful reminder of the deceased. People unrelated to the deceased ate the corpse, even when the smell or taste repulsed them, in the belief that it would help family members come to terms with their loss. Furthermore, the Western practice of burying the dead (which missionaries and government officials forced the Wari' to do after contact) was almost as horrific to the Wari' as their cannibalism might have been for non-Wari'. "It's cold in the earth," a father who had recently lost a two-year-old son explained to Beth Conklin. "We keep remembering our child, lying there, cold. We remember and we are sad. It was better in the old days, when the others ate the body. Then we did not think about our child's body much. We did not remember our child as much, and we were not so sad" (xv).

Burying the body also violated many fundamental Wari' values. For them, the ground was "dirty" and "polluting." They never sat directly on the dirt, and discarding things on the ground was considered disrespectful. Special ritual objects were never supposed to touch the ground.

Without a deeper understanding of Wari' culture, we cannot know how consuming the dead aligns with the meaning they impose on their world, including how they deal with their emotions. By consuming the dead, Wari' are trying to obliterate the painful memories of their loss. The memory of the body is painful, but equally painful are the material objects associated with the deceased and the very mention of the deceased's name. Thus, the Wari' not only consume the body but also burn the house and personal possessions of the deceased. And for months, they walk into the forest to find places associated with the deceased—where a hunter made a kill or a woman felled a fruit tree, or where there was something such as a favourite log on which she or he liked to sit—cut the vegetation around it, and, after it has dried, burn the spot, changing the appearance of the last earthly places to which memories of the deceased might cling. As they "sweep" (the Wari' term for it), they cry over the memories; but once done, "it is different," "there is not much sadness there." For most North Americans, a dead body is only a shell, its soul or spiritual essence gone. Thus some societies can prepare the dead to look as they did in life and think of them buried in that way. The Wari', by contrast, want to separate the dead from the living; thus, obliterating their memories is perfectly logical. And they are not the only group to do so.

There are other aspects of Wari' beliefs about consuming the dead. For example, they believe that the spirits of the dead ultimately enter the bodies of animals they depend on for food, thus creating a cycle of eating and being eaten. The point being made here is that when we impose our own meanings on practices such as cannibalism

EXERCISE 1.3B

Wari' attempt in their funeral practices to obliterate the memory of the dead, as do many other societies. Other societies, however, memorialize the dead; forgetting them would be an act of disrespect. Think about your own cultural background and whether or not you are encouraged to memorialize the dead. List the ways that you try to keep the memory of deceased persons alive, and speculate as to why you do that instead of trying to forget them. If you are encouraged to forget the dead, how is that accomplished? Why? Compare your beliefs and practices with those of your classmates.

and fail to see those practices the way others do, we miss a great deal.

But does this mean that *any* practice or belief, once we understand it from "the native's point of view," is acceptable? Does understanding the cultures of others require that we accept and justify all beliefs and practices?

Objectivity and Morality

For anthropologists, the conflict between ethnocentrism and relativism is not just a theoretical one. When choosing their research subjects, anthropologists may face this dilemma: Should they maintain a "moral distance" from those they are studying and remain "objective," or should they engage in criticizing behaviour or beliefs they encounter (e.g., virginity testing).

The contradiction between "objective" anthropology and a politically committed anthropology became apparent to Nancy Scheper-Hughes when she returned as an anthropologist to a shantytown in Brazil where, previously, she had worked as a community organizer. The women with whom she had worked in the past became angry. Why, they asked, when as a community organizer she had helped

The Taj Mahal, a monument built to honour a 17th-century Mughal emperor's wife, who died in childbirth.

them organize to fight for clean water, decent wages, and protection from police brutality, was she now, as an anthropologist, so passive, so indifferent to the destruction around her? She tried to explain that as an anthropologist her work was different—she was there now to observe, document, and write about their lives as truthfully as she could. The women refused to accept this and insisted that if they were to work with her, she would have to work with them to fight for better lives. "What," they said, "is anthropology to us?"

On the basis of that experience, Scheper-Hughes (1995, 416) now argues for a politically committed, morally engaged, and ethically grounded anthropology. "Those of us who make our living observing and recording the misery of the world," she writes, "have a particular obligation to reflect critically on the impact of the harsh images of human suffering that we foist upon the public."

Scheper-Hughes proposes what she calls a more "womanly" anthropology, one that is concerned with how people treat one another. Moral relativism, she says, is no longer appropriate to the world in which we live, and anthropology, if it is to be worth anything at all, must be "critically grounded." Anthropologists cannot ignore the massacres and disappearances of vulnerable people that often occur in the communities in which anthropologists work. Anthropologists must, she insists, serve as witnesses and reporters of human rights abuses and of the suffering of the poor and the oppressed.

But serving as a witness for the poor and oppressed can itself lead to moral dilemmas for the anthropologist when the people with whom the anthropologist works engage in behaviour that may appear morally questionable. Scheper-Hughes confronted this question when she discovered and reported that impoverished women in the Brazilian shantytowns sometimes allowed their starving infants to die in the belief that they were doomed anyway. When Philippe Bourgois studied the world of crack dealers on the Upper East Side of New York City, he worried about the negative images he would be conveying if he reported the personal violence, sexual abuse, addiction, and alienation he witnessed. He recalled the advice of anthropologist Laura Nader, who advised others not to study the poor and powerless, because whatever you say will be used against them.

Human rights activists, in particular, are skeptical about cultural relativism. If, they say, we must tolerate the beliefs and practices of other cultures because to do otherwise would be ethnocentric, how can we ever criticize what seem to be violations of basic human rights, such as the right to bodily integrity, or the right to be free from torture, arbitrary imprisonment, slavery, and genocide? Cultural relativism, they say, makes arguments about human rights meaningless by legitimizing almost any behaviour.

Take the case of the practice in some areas of India of *sati*, the burning of a widow on her husband's funeral pyre. In 1987, Roon Kanwar, an 18-year-old girl, was burned alive on her husband's pyre. Women's rights groups protested, but relatives claimed that it is an ancient Indian custom and accused the protesters of being Western imperialists imposing their own cultural standards on them. Although India has outlawed the practice, prosecutors rarely enforce the law because of the difficulty of obtaining evidence. Would it matter if Roon Kanwar committed *sati* voluntarily? What would happen if she objected? Does it matter that it is only women who are burned? Is the purpose of *sati* to deny a widow the inheritance of her husband's family's land? Elizabeth Zechenter, who makes the argument for universal principles of human rights, says that cultural relativists are right to contend that the endorsement or rejection of some foreign customs risks imposing one's own cultural prejudices on others. But she adds that the idea that we can make no judgments without being ethnocentric is illusory: "One simply cannot avoid making judgments when faced with oppression and brutality masquerading under the guise of cultural tradition. Such a nonjudgmental tolerance of brutality is actually an ultimate form of ethnocentrism, if not an outright ethical surrender" (1997, 336).

There is obviously no easy answer to the question of when, if ever, it is proper to judge the beliefs and practices of others to be right or wrong, or when, if ever, it is proper to work to change behaviours or beliefs judged to be wrong. Ideally, our attempts to understand what at first seemed puzzling in some cultures, and our arrival at some solution to that puzzle, should lead us to ask ourselves what made the behaviour or belief seem puzzling in the first place. We also need to bear in mind that when cultures order the world in certain ways for their members, they are in effect masking other ways of viewing things. We need to appreciate that there are perspectives different from our own and that our ethnocentric biases may blind us to those alternatives. In other words, while culture provides us with certain meanings to give to objects, persons, behaviours, emotions, and events, it also shields us from alternative meanings. What our culture hides from us may be more important than what it reveals.

EXERCISE 1.3C

You have been doing anthropological research in Canada with a religious group that believes they must live the life described in the Christian Bible, particularly as described in the Book of Acts. They live communally, sharing all property; they believe that women should be subservient to their husbands, and they enforce rules against drinking alcoholic beverages, smoking, and so on. The group has lately come under attack by a group in the local community as being a "dangerous cult." You know that, although their beliefs and practices differ from those of the larger society around them, they are not dangerous and, in fact, lead lives of harmony. They have asked you to speak in their defence. Can you do this without sacrificing your objectivity?

QUESTION 1.4: HOW CAN THE MEANINGS THAT OTHERS FIND IN EXPERIENCE BE INTERPRETED AND DESCRIBED?

In one Sherlock Holmes detective story, Dr. Watson, Holmes's assistant, decides to teach the great detective a lesson in humility. He hands Holmes a pocket watch owned by Watson's late brother and challenges Holmes to infer from the watch the character of its owner. Holmes's interpretation: "[Your brother] was a man of untidy habits—very untidy and careless. He was left with good prospects, but he threw away his chances and finally, taking to drink, he died."

Watson, astounded at the accuracy of Holmes's description of his late brother, asks if it was guesswork. "I never guess," replies Holmes:

I began by stating that your brother was careless. When you observe the lower part of the watch case, you notice that it is not only dented in two places, but it is cut and marked all over from the habit of keeping other hard objects, such as coins or keys, in the same pocket. Surely it is no great feat to assume that a man who treats [an expensive] watch so cavalierly must be a careless man. Neither is it a very far-fetched inference that a man who inherits one article of such value is pretty well provided for in other respects.

"But what about his drinking habits?" asks Watson. Holmes responds:

Look at the innerplate which contains the keyhole [where the watch is wound]. Look at the thousands of scratches all around the hole-marks where the key has slipped. What sober man's key could have scored those grooves? But you will never see a drunkard's watch without them. He winds it at night, and he leaves these traces of his unsteady hand. Where is the mystery in all this?

Had Holmes been an anthropologist, he might have been tempted also to draw some inferences about the society in which the watch was manufactured, particularly about its conceptions of time. For example, in some societies time is task oriented, not clock oriented; time might be measured by how long it takes to cook rice, as in Madagascar. In other societies, time patterns depend on natural events such as the rising of the sun or the ebb and flow of tides. British anthropologist E.E. Evans-Pritchard, in his classic account of the Nuer of the Sudan, noted that

> *the Nuer have no expression equivalent to "time" in our language, and they cannot, therefore, as we can, speak of time as though it were something actual, which passes, can be wasted, can be saved, and so forth. I don't think they ever experience the same feeling of fighting against time because their points of reference are mainly the activities themselves, which are generally of a leisurely character. Events follow a logical order, but they are not controlled by an abstract system, there being no autonomous points of reference to which activities have to conform with precision. Nuer are fortunate.*

An anthropologist might also infer that clocks are instruments of discipline; they tell us when to get up, when to go to bed, when to eat, when to start work, when to stop work. Our work patterns themselves are defined by clocks, and our wages may depend on the constant repetition over time of a particular task. Historian E.P. Thompson notes that until the institution of modern notions of time and the need to measure it with clocks, work patterns were characterized by alternating bouts of intense labour and idleness, at least whenever people were in control of their own working lives. He even suggests that this pattern persists today, but only among a few self-employed professionals such as artists, writers, small farmers, and, he suggests, university students.

© SuperStock, Inc./Getty

Modern notions of clock-based time tell us a great deal about the culture we live in. What measures of time are most important in your life as a student?

Watson's brother's watch was a product of Western society, part of its culture. Holmes "read" the watch as if it were a collection of symbols or words, a **cultural text** that revealed the character of its owner. He could just as easily have viewed it as a text inscribed with the symbols that revealed the ideas about time and work that characterized the civilization that produced it.

One way to think about culture is as a text of significant symbols: words, gestures, drawings, natural objects—anything, in fact, that carries meaning. To understand another culture we must be able, as Holmes was with a pocket watch, to decipher the meanings of the symbols that comprise a cultural text. We must be able to interpret the meanings embedded in the language, objects, gestures, and activities that are shared by members of a society. Fortunately, the ability to decipher a cultural text is part of being human; in our everyday lives we both read and maintain the text that makes up our own culture. We have learned the meanings behind the

cultural text
A way of thinking about culture as a text of significant symbols—words, gestures, drawings, natural objects—that carries meaning.

CULTURE AND MEANING

symbols that frame our lives, and we share those meanings with others. Our task in understanding another culture is to take the abilities that have enabled us to dwell in our own culture and use them to understand the cultures of others.

Deciphering the Balinese Cockfight

To illustrate how an anthropologist might decipher a cultural text, imagine yourself coming upon a cockfight on the island of Bali. You see a ring in which two roosters with sharpened metal spurs attached to their legs are set at each other until one kills the other. Surrounding the fighting cocks are men shouting encouragement to their favourites, each having placed a wager that his favourite will kill its opponent.

What do you make of this? Your first reaction might be shock or disgust at the spectacle of the crowd urging the cocks to bloody combat. After a while you might begin to find similarities to events that are meaningful to you, such as some North American sports. But what if, like Sherlock Holmes (or like Clifford Geertz, from whom this example is taken), you want to understand the meaning of what is happening and what that meaning tells you about how Balinese view their world? If you assume that the cockfight is a feature of Balinese culture, a Balinese text filled with

symbols that carry meaning about what it is to be Balinese, how might you proceed to read this text?

You might begin by finding out the language the Balinese use to talk about the cockfight. You would no doubt discover that the double-entendre of cock both as a synonym for rooster and as a euphemism for penis is the same for the Balinese as it is for North Americans. The double-entendre even produces, says Geertz, the same jokes, puns, and obscenities in Bali as it does in North America. You would discover that *sabung*, the Balinese word for cock, has numerous other meanings and is used metaphorically to mean hero, warrior, champion, political candidate, bachelor, dandy, lady-killer, or tough guy. Court trials, wars, political contests,

In Balinese society, cockfighting is a major sporting event that is closely tied to cultural interpretations of manhood, competition, and status.

inheritance disputes, and street arguments are compared with cockfights. Even the island of Bali is thought of as being cock-shaped (in this case meaning the fowl). You would also find that men give their fowls inordinate attention, spending most of their time grooming them and even feeding them a special diet. As one of Geertz's Balinese informants put it, "We're all cock crazy."

Having discovered the importance of cockfights to the Balinese and the connections they make between cocks and men, you next examine the cockfight itself. You learn that cockfights are public events held in arenas of about 4.7 square metres from late afternoon until after sundown. Handlers, expert in the task, attach sharp spurs to the cock's legs; for a cock thought to be superior to an opponent, the spurs are adjusted in a slightly disadvantageous position. The cocks are released in the centre of the ring and fly at each other, fighting until one kills the other. The owner of the winning cock takes the carcass of the loser home to eat; the losing owner is sometimes driven in despair to wreck family shrines. You discover that the Balinese contrast heaven and hell by comparing them to the mood of a man whose cock has just won and the mood of a man whose cock has just lost.

You find out that while the Balinese place odds on cockfights, there are strict social conventions that dictate the wagering. For example, a man will never bet against a cock that is owned by someone of his family group or village or a friend's family group or village, but he will place large bets against a cock owned by an enemy or the friend of an enemy. Rarely is a cockfight without social significance (e.g., between two outsiders), and rarely do cocks owned by members of the same family or village fight each other. Moreover, the owners of the cocks, especially in important matches, are usually among the leaders of their communities. You might learn that cockfights come close to encouraging open expressions of aggression between village and kin-group rivals, but not quite, because the cockfight is, as the Balinese put it, "only a cockfight."

Given the social rules for betting and the ways in which odds are set, you might reason, as Geertz did, that the Balinese rarely make a profit betting on cockfights. Geertz says, in fact, that most bettors just want to break even. Consequently, the meaning of the cockfight for a Balinese has little to do with economics. The question is what meaning the cockfight *does* have for the Balinese. What is the cockfight really about, if it is not about money?

Geertz concludes that the Balinese cockfight is above all about status, about the ranking of people vis-à-vis one another. The Balinese cockfight is a text filled with meaning about status as the Balinese see it. Cocks represent men—more specifically, their owners; the fate of the cock in the ring is linked, if only temporarily, to the social fate of its owner. Each cock has a following consisting of the owner, the owner's family, and members of the owner's village, and these followers "risk" their status by betting on the cockfight. Furthermore, Geertz maintains that the more a match is between near equals, personal enemies, or high-status individuals, the more the match is about status. And the more the match is about status, the closer the identification of cock and man, the finer the cocks, and the more exactly they will be matched. The match will inspire greater emotion and absorption, and the gambling will be more about status and less about economic gain.

For Geertz, the cockfight is like any art form; it takes a highly abstract and difficult concept—status—and depicts it in a way that makes it comprehensible to the participants. The cockfight is meaningful to the Balinese because it tells them something real about their own lives, but in a way that does not directly affect their lives. They see the struggle for status that is part of everyday life vividly portrayed, even though, in the cockfight itself, no one really gains or loses status in any permanent sense.

A few words of caution are necessary concerning what we might learn about the Balinese from this particular cultural text. First, it would probably be a mistake to assume that the people gain status by being on the winning side or lose it by being on the side of the loser. The status outcomes of the cockfight do not translate into real life any more than the victory of your favourite sports team increases your status. Instead, says Geertz, the cockfight illustrates what status is about for the Balinese. The cockfight is a story the Balinese tell themselves about themselves. It would also be a mistake to assume that the character of the Balinese can be read directly from the cockfight; any conclusion that the cockfight is indicative of an aggressive, competitive, violent national character would quickly be dispelled. The Balinese are shy about competition and avoid open conflict. The slaughter in the cockfight is not how things are literally, but as they could be. Finally, the cockfight reveals only a segment of the Balinese character, as Watson's brother's watch revealed only a segment of its owner's character. The culture of a people, like the possessions of a person, is an ensemble of texts—collections of symbols and meanings—that must be viewed together to achieve a full understanding.

QUESTION 1.5: WHAT CAN LEARNING ABOUT OTHER PEOPLES TELL ANTHROPOLOGISTS ABOUT THEIR OWN SOCIETIES?

Anthropologists do not limit themselves to the study of cultures that are different from their own. They often apply concepts and techniques that are useful in understanding and interpreting other cultures as a means to understand and interpret their own. One objective of studying other cultures is to help us recognize the meanings we impose on our experiences. When Renato Rosaldo asked the Ilongots why they cut off human heads, they replied that rage, born of grief, drives them to kill others; by severing the heads of their victims, they are able to throw away the anger born of bereavement. Rosaldo found it difficult to accept the idea that the death of a kinsperson could cause anger or rage and that such rage in itself could drive a person to kill another. He questioned the Ilongots further but could obtain no other reason for their headhunting; he devised other theories to explain it, but none were satisfactory. Only his own experience of grief and anger at the accidental death of his wife, Michelle, while both were doing fieldwork among the Ilongots helped him realize how grief can generate rage and how grief drove the Ilongots to hunt the heads of their enemies. At the same time that he began to understand the Ilongots, he began to understand his own grief and reaction to death.

A Balinese Anthropologist Studies Canadian Hockey

Whether we approach other cultures as anthropologists, as travellers, or as professionals who need to communicate with people of other cultures, the confrontation with other ways of believing and behaving should cause us to reflect on our way of viewing the world. To illustrate, try to step outside yourself and objectify an experience whose meaning you take for granted. Pretend you are a Balinese anthropologist who suddenly comes upon a spectacle as important in its way to Canadians as the cockfight is to Balinese: a hockey game.

As a Balinese, your first reaction to this Canadian text might be one of horror and revulsion at seeing men and women speeding from one end of an ice pad to the other with long wooden sticks in their hands, rudely pushing one another out of the way while thousands cheer them on. As you settled in, however, you would soon find some obvious similarities between the hockey game and the cockfight you are familiar with at home. Both are spectator sports in which the spectators sort themselves into supporters of one side or the other. In fact, in hockey, the sorting is even more carefully arranged, since fans of one team are often seated on one side of the arena and fans of the other on the opposite side.

Your next step (as in interpreting the cockfight) would be to examine the language Canadians use to refer to the hockey game. You discover that they use similar expressions in talking about hockey and fighting, such as *roughing* and *slashing*. Coaches talk about getting "revenge" for defeats, as generals might talk about getting revenge on battlefields. You conclude that Canadians seem to feel the same way about hockey as they do about fighting. In fact, if you attend several hockey games, you will most likely witness a scene in which players of opposing teams take off their protective gloves and actually begin to punch each other.

You soon discover that winning and losing hockey games is as important to Canadians as winning and losing cockfights is to Balinese. Winners engage in frenzied celebrations called *victory parties*, and losers are often despondent in defeat. As anthropologists know, this is not always the case in other societies. When the Gahuku-Gama of the Highlands of New Guinea started playing soccer, they always played until a committee of elders decided that the score was tied, and then the match was considered completed. So you speculate that hockey is also about the meanings that Canadians give to the idea of success. You learn that success in Canada (like status in Bali) is a highly abstract idea; because it is abstract, its meaning is embedded in activities understood by members of the society. You need to find answers to certain questions about the meaning of success in Canadian society: How is success defined? How is it obtained? Why doesn't everyone who follows all the rules for gaining success attain it?

Through your fieldwork, you find that most North Americans believe that "all men are created equal" and that every person has (or at least should have) an equal opportunity to succeed. People compete for success, and they ought to compete on an equal footing, on a "level playing field," as some put it. Success, North Americans believe, comes from hard work, sacrifice, and self-denial. But you wonder why North Americans

An anthropologist might suggest that the meaning of hockey, for North Americans, is tied to our cultural understandings of success.

believe that hard work, sacrifice, and self-denial bring success. Aren't there instances where they do not? How do North Americans explain why women and minorities succeed less often than white males do? And why do some people achieve more success than others? You conclude that it is, in fact, impossible to prove directly in real life the correctness of this North American success model. Faith in the value of work and self-denial must be generated in other ways. As a Balinese anthropologist studying the Canadian custom of hockey, you conclude, then, that the meaning of Canadian hockey lies in its demonstration of the North American success model as it is supposed to work. But there is more to the Canadian game of hockey than simply a mirror of society: Canadian hockey is also a ritual that creates meaning.

Rituals do not just reflect society. As Yngve Lithman suggests, they also draw attention to something and provide an "explanation" for something. One of the reasons why Canadian hockey has become a national symbol is that it brings Canadians from different parts of the country together with a common focus. During the hockey season, a team from Calgary competes against a team from Montreal, a team from Vancouver plays in the same ice rink as a team from Toronto, and so on.

Anthropologist Noel Dyck points out that Canadian hockey "is not only one of Canada's proudest contributions to the world of sport but also a national passion" (2000, 10). Hockey becomes important to children very early in life, and it involves the whole family. Tiny players, called "Tim Bits," sponsored by the Tim Hortons coffee shops throughout Canada, begin their training so young that their mothers or fathers, or even their grandfathers or grandmothers, help them put on their protective clothing in the dressing rooms. Young teams of children are grouped according to age into categories such as "novice," "atom," "peewee," "bantam," and "midget," all progressing to secondary school and university teams. Those working toward professional play are called "Junior" and progress from "Junior D" to "Junior A." At the other end of the life cycle, older players have teams called "old timers," which are also grouped according to age.

Canadian hockey is also a ritual that anthropologists Peter Collings and Richard Condon suggest helps people adjust to sudden change by providing a way for players to gain status, achievement, and self-esteem. In the Kitikmeot region of the Northwest Territories, society is no longer based on hunting as a way of life, but communities are not yet fully integrated into the North American capitalist economy. In the Canadian Arctic, hockey has become a recreational activity that helps bridge this gap, and it consumes the passion of most communities.

At first, when radio and television were introduced to the Arctic, and to the community of Holman where Collings and Condon did their fieldwork in the 1980s, children played hockey on the snow-covered streets. Later, when a sporting organization in Yellowknife sent skates to Inuit communities, children started playing hockey on ice ponds. The initial hockey games were played Inuit style, with little emphasis on winning or losing, and were governed by flexible rules. Eventually, however, a league was established and competition began to take place between teams from different communities. With the formalization of hockey as a competition, violence became a standard feature of the game. Collings and Condon found that significantly more injuries were sustained playing hockey than during any other activity, including hunting, trapping, or fishing. Furthermore, being injured during a hockey game was a sure way to gain prestige, especially if an injured player returned to the ice before his injury was healed. Collings and Condon argue that the game of hockey, as it is played in Holman, models the values of achievement and self-reliance: "If achievement and self-reliance cannot be expressed in the conduct of everyday life, then it can be expressed on the ice while competing with one's peers. Status and control, so elusive to these young people in real life, become attainable goals when modeled in the context of play" (1996, 258).

Collings and Condon acknowledge the positive aspects of sports. Games such as hockey affirm the value of success, as well as a dramatic set of instructions on how it attain it. The games help build character and teach young people about cooperation. But Collings and Condon also suggest that there is a "darker side" to hockey. For some people, "games can teach violence, verbal aggression, subterfuge, cheating, poor sportsmanship, and other undesirable traits" (261). At the same time, hockey demonstrates the limits of acceptable violence. When players break the rules of how the game is supposed to be played they incur penalties, just as citizens are penalized for breaking the laws in Canada. When players score a high number of points, they are rewarded with both prestige and, in the case of professional hockey, wealth. Violence and competition are part of Canadian life, and the game of hockey shows how both are important to Canadians, but both must be controlled.

Anthropologists therefore can conclude (as did Collings and Condon) that hockey provides for Canadians, as the cockfight does for the Balinese, a small-scale rendering of a concept (status in the case of the Balinese, both status and success in the Canadian case) that is too complex to be directly comprehended.

Hockey is compelling because it is a vivid demonstration of the value of success, as well as a dramatic set of instructions on how to attain it. Consequently, the audience for a hockey game is led to believe that if the rules that govern the world of hockey are equated with the rules that govern success outside the rink, then the principles that govern success on the hockey rink must also apply in the outside world. That is, if hard work, dedication, submission to authority, and teamwork lead to success in a game, they will lead to success in real life. The rules by which success is achieved in hockey can also be applied to life to succeed in the real world.

Of course, hockey is also a game that people enjoy. Analyzing it should not reduce our enjoyment of it but rather should heighten our fascination with it. By looking at hockey from the same perspective as Geertz viewed the cockfight, we should gain an understanding of why the meaning carried by the game is important. While understanding the cockfight heightens our appreciation of the hockey game, it also helps us see similarities between Canadians and Balinese. If you were shocked by the cockfight, seeing the similarities to hockey should lessen that shock, at the same time making hockey seem just a bit more exotic.

An Anthropologist Looks at a "Happy Meal"

Nothing is too mundane to provide some insights into the culture of which it is a part. Take the "Happy Meal" advertised by one of the many fast food establishments in North America. It consists of a hamburger, French fries, a cola drink, and a plastic toy, generally a "Barbie" doll or a "Hot Wheels" car. What can we learn about the culture of North America by looking beyond the "taken for granted" quality of this meal? Among other things, we can get some idea of North American demographic and ecological patterns, agricultural and industrial history, and gender roles.

Why, for example, is meat the centre of the meal? Most cultures have diets centred on some complex carbohydrate—rice, wheat, manioc, yams, taro—or something made from these—bread, pasta, tortillas, and so on. It is the spice, vegetables, meat, or fish that when added to these foods give cuisine its distinctive taste. However, meat and fish are generally at the edge, not the centre, of the meal. Why is beef the main ingredient, rather than some other meat, such as pork?

Anthropologists Marvin Harris and Eric Ross note that one advantage of beef was its suitability for the outdoor grill, which became more popular as people moved from cities into suburbs. Suburban cooks soon discovered that pork patties crumbled and fell through the grill, whereas beef patties held together better. In addition, to reduce the risk of trichinosis, pork had to be cooked until it was grey, which makes it very tough.

In the United States, beef farmers, as well as the farmers who grew the corn fed to beef to achieve a desirable fat content, benefited from the definition of a hamburger set by the United States Department of Agriculture: "'Hamburger'" shall consist of chopped fresh and/or frozen beef with or without the addition of beef fat as such and/or seasonings, shall not contain more than 30 percent fat, and shall not contain added water, phosphates, binders, or extenders. Beef cheek (trimmed Beef cheeks) may be used in the preparation of hamburgers only in accordance with the conditions prescribed in paragraph (a) of this section" (quoted in Harris 1987, 125).

As Marvin Harris noted, we can eat ground pork and ground beef, but we can't combine them and still call it a hamburger. Even when lean, grass-fed beef is used for hamburger. Also, fat must be added as

CULTURE AND MEANING

a binder, and the fat must come from beef scraps, not from vegetables or a different animal. This definition of the hamburger protects both the beef industry and the corn farmer, whose income is linked to cattle production. Moreover, it helps the fast food industry, because the definition of hamburger permits the use of inexpensive scraps of fat from slaughtered beef to make up to 30% of its hamburger. Thus an international beef patty has been created that has overcome what Harris calls the "pig's natural superiority as a converter of grain to flesh."

The cola drink that accompanies our hamburger is the second part of the fat and sugar-centred diet that has come to characterize our culture. People in Canada consume, on average, about 38.6 kilograms of sugar a year. Why so much? Sugar, as anthropologist Sidney Mintz suggests, has no nutritional properties, but it provides a quick and inexpensive energy boost for hard-working labourers with little time for a more nutritious meal. Sugar also serves as an excellent complement to the fat in hamburgers, because it has what nutritionists call "go-away" qualities that remove the fat coating and the beef aftertaste from the mouth.

We can also learn from the "Happy Meal" that the fat-and-sugar diet is highly environmentally destructive. Beef raising is among the most environmentally inefficient and destructive forms of food raising. For example, the amount of water used to produce 10 pounds of steak equals the household consumption of a family for an entire year. Thirty-three times more water is needed to produce a kilogram of beef protein than an equivalent amount of plant protein.

Cattle raising is playing a major role in the destruction of tropical forests in Brazil, Guatemala, Costa Rica, and Honduras, where forests have been levelled to create pasture for cattle. Since most of the forest is cleared by burning, the creation of cattle pasture also creates carbon dioxide and, according to some environmentalists, contributes significantly to global warming.

Sugar is no less destructive a crop. Sugar production alters the environment in a number of ways.

Forests must be cleared to plant sugar; wood or fossil fuel must be burned in the evaporation process; waste water is produced when sucrose is extracted from the sugar cane; and more fuel is burned in the refining process. Contemporary sugar production in Hawai'i has destroyed forests, and waste products from processing have severely damaged marine environments. "Big Sugar," as the sugar industry is called in Florida, is largely responsible for the pollution, degradation, and virtual destruction of the Everglades.

Thus one of the "texts" that anthropologists can read from a Happy Meal relates to the extent to which consumption patterns associated with our culture create waste and environmental damage. Because of these consumption patterns, the average child born in the United States or Canada will, in the course of his or her lifetime, do twice the environmental damage of a Swedish child, 3 times that of an Italian child, 13 times that of a Brazilian child, 35 times that of an Indian child, and 280 times that of a Chadian or Haitian child.

And what of "Barbie dolls" and "Hot Wheels"? Clearly there is a message about the definition of gender roles, as dolls are expected to be chosen by girls, and cars by boys. But one can deduce, if you look closely enough, even more about our culture from this meal.

EXERCISE 1.4

We've examined some of the lessons we can learn about our culture from the "Happy Meal." There are obviously others. See what you can deduce about the following dimensions of life in North America from the "Happy Meal."

1. What can you say about gender roles in North America?
2. What can you deduce about race relations?
3. What can you say about the physical attributes of people favoured in North America?

QUESTION 1.6: HOW CAN AN ANTHROPOLOGICAL PERSPECTIVE BE USED OUTSIDE OF ACADEMIA?

What Can You Do with a BA in Anthropology?

Students taking anthropology classes often say, "I like anthropology, but what can I do with it?" A more or less typical response is "Anything that you can do with any liberal arts major." However, that doesn't get us very far. Being a professional anthropologist—teacher, researcher, consultant—generally requires an advanced degree. However, an anthropological perspective and methodology can be invaluable in all sorts of career areas, so much so that one national newspaper recently labelled anthropology a "hot major." This does not necessarily mean that you will see scores of job postings looking specifically for candidates with an anthropology degree. However, the demand for candidates with ethnographic skills is on the rise. A recent LinkedIn search using "ethnography" as a keyword yielded many hits that included jobs at Netflix, Skype, Microsoft, VISA, and Google. These examples are all from the corporate world, but many anthropologists are employed in the public sector or by nongovernmental organizations (NGOs) as well. Why are these companies looking for ethnographers? Anthropology, like any discipline, deals with problems and questions, which is what any career or profession does. In the contemporary lingo of Human Resources departments, ethnographers "add value" to the companies they work for by bringing their unique perspective to bear on the problems and questions that they address, and they often have distinctive insights and are able to suggest innovative solutions that accountants, marketers, doctors, or lawyers cannot.

What kinds of problems can ethnographers help solve? People in management must address the problem of how to structure relationships among staff; people in government must address problems involved in designing public policy initiatives, such as reducing juvenile crime. Someone in a medical field may face the problem of how to educate the young regarding sexually transmitted disease, while someone employed in the tourist industry must address the problem of how to minimize the negative consequences of tourism for local populations. The solutions to all of these and other problems can benefit from an anthropological perspective, because all involve ways that people give meaning to their experiences. Throughout the remaining chapters of this book, we will be examining various examples of how anthropological perspectives are applied to careers outside of academia. The best way to understand what anthropology is, and the problem-solving potential of ethnographic insights, is to look at what anthropologists and ethnographers do and at how they approach various kinds of social problems. The examples below, while they are drawn from the experiences of professional anthropologists, nonetheless demonstrate the very important ways in which anthropological knowledge and ethnographic expertise matter in the "real world," and begin to suggest some of the ways that anthropology can be put to use outside of academia.

Applied Anthropology

Applied anthropology is the branch of anthropology that specializes in putting anthropological knowledge into practice outside of academia. Sociocultural anthropology is about social and cultural differences, whether they occur from one country to another or within a single classroom. The fact that different peoples assign different meanings to events, objects, individuals, and emotions is a source of considerable conflict, miscommunication, and misunderstanding. Anthropologists seek to explain this diversity, to help people understand one another better, and, in the process, to apply their experience and knowledge to solving social, economic, educational, and political problems created by diversity.

In Canada, applied anthropologists have been involved in research that has helped document the validity of First Nations land claims. Edward Hedican writes that more and more Native band administrations are employing anthropologists to conduct research in areas that the band finds useful. This makes anthropological research easier because, as Hedican suggests, "people will certainly be more willing to cooperate with researchers if they are able to see that the work has some direct relevance to their lives" (1995, 226).

Law and Society

Another important branch of sociocultural anthropology involves the area of law and society, sometimes called political anthropology. Sally Falk Moore describes this approach as one that "inquires into the context of enforceable norms: social, political, economic, and intellectual. This includes, but goes farther than, what Western governments and courts define as law. In anthropology, while the 'socio-legal' includes formal juridical institutions and their social surroundings, it also encompasses law-like activities and processes of establishing order in many other social domains, formal and informal, official and unofficial, in our own society and in others" (2005, 1).

Anthropologists who study legal issues in a particular place ask questions about power, such as "who makes the rules, who can undo them, how are they normalized and enforced, and how are they morally justified" (2). These questions were first asked in egalitarian societies where legal institutions, such as courts and police, were absent; anthropologists tried to understand what prevented total chaos. Other questions are now being asked in relation to the possible lasting effects of colonialism on "native laws," as the colonial powers enforced their own sense of what was right and just.

In his book *Culture and Power*, Stanley Barrett argues that globalization has increased conflict throughout the world and that anthropology's interest in the political is likely to grow. He suggests that "power, authority, influence, manipulation, and coercion (or force) constitute the basic terms in this field of inquiry" (2002, 19). With these concepts in mind, anthropologists have extended their interest in legal issues to include, for example, indigenous claims on the state and global human rights. They also look at global issues that involve international labour, immigration patterns and obstacles, and development schemes, continually asking, "Who is in control? Whose interests are being served?" We will touch on many of these issues in the chapters that follow.

Political Ecology

A relatively new branch of sociocultural anthropology that is gaining popularity is political ecology, defined by Blaikie and Brookfield (1987, 17) as a field of study that "combines the concerns of ecology and a broadly defined political economy." One of the directions this approach has taken has involved challenging dominant explanations for environmental degradation and contesting some of the popular solutions to environmental problems (Paulson, Gezon, and Watts 2003, 205). Analyzing the politics of environment may uncover the interests of powerful elites who profit from directing public inquiry away from their activities and toward those of less powerful peoples, such as indigenous groups, who are forced into parts of the rain forest, where they clear plots of land to grow subsistence products.

Although political ecology usually focuses on land scarcity and access to material resources, two anthropologists at McMaster University have included community identity in their study of peri-urban political ecology. Tina Moffat and Beth Finnis combine a focus on access to land with access to education in a "squatter" community of 300 people called Nayabasti, in Kathmandu, Nepal.

As in many such communities, most of Nayabasti's people lack both sewers and indoor plumbing and build houses out of rudimentary materials. The people of Nayabasti were given the land informally by the municipal government 30 years ago, but they have no legal documentation and the only improvement that has been made is the partial installation of indoor toilets (unconnected to sewers) by a Danish NGO. When the community was first formed, there were few others close by. However, the area now includes monasteries that were built by Tibetan refugees, as well as the homes of wealthy urbanites who have moved from the core of Kathmandu to the outskirts because the land is cheaper and the air is cleaner. The arrival of these newcomers, who have clear title to their land, has placed the community of Nayabasti at even more risk.

Moffat and Finnis discuss the difficulties the community has faced in its efforts to provide education for local children. In 1998, the residents pooled their resources and set about searching for a place to build their own school. After a period of negotiation with the municipal government, a plot of land was found. The community provided almost all the labour to build the school, with Lumanti, a local NGO, providing financial support. Moffatt and Finnis caution that it is still uncertain whether the school will be sustainable in the long term, but the project did reinforce community identity, and the community's "ability to get this far is evidence of the incredible capacity of slum and squatter dwellers" (2005, 465).

Medical Anthropology

Medical anthropology is another branch of anthropology in which anthropologists are able to put their ethnographic skills and perspectives to good use. According to the Society for Medical Anthropology, it is "a subfield of anthropology that draws upon social, cultural, biological, and linguistic anthropology to better understand those factors which influence health and well being (broadly defined), the experience and distribution of illness, the prevention and treatment of sickness, healing processes, the social relations of therapy management, and the cultural importance and utilization of pluralistic medical systems."

This subfield of anthropology has moved in many directions. Medical anthropologists may analyze the politics of health care access, local interpretations and experience of health and illness, the cultural and historical context of contemporary medical practice and policies, or perceptions and experiences of risk and stigma related to various illnesses. Naomi Adelson is a medical anthropologist who has done fieldwork with the James Bay Cree of northern Quebec. In her ethnography, *Being Alive Well*, she notes that the Cree do not have a word that readily translates into what we call "health" in English. Rather, they talk about *miyupimaatisiiun*, or "being alive well." For the Cree, being alive well has less to do with individuals and physiology than with social and political relations. Adelson's informants asked, rhetorically, "If the land is not healthy, than how can we be?" (2000, 1). The Cree understanding and experience of health is grounded in what it means to "be Cree," which is itself grounded in connections to the land and to the past (25). Once, the James Bay Cree travelled and hunted across a vast swath of land in northwestern Quebec, but today many live in the village of Whapmagoostui at the mouth of the Great Whale River, hunting in the bush only on weekends. Since the 1970s, the Cree have been fighting with the provincial government of Quebec over the appropriate uses of the land and its resources, most famously in the building of the James Bay I hydroelectric dam and the failed James Bay II project. While the Quebec government saw the land as underused and underpopulated and as a untapped source of wealth and power, the Cree knew that the projects would drastically alter the ecosystem surrounding Whapmagoostui, changing the migration and survival patterns of land and sea mammals, fish, and birds. What would it mean to be

Cree in the face of such changes? How could they manage to "be alive well"? Adelson argues that "all definitions of health … are laden with ideological nuances and can never be separated from cultural norms and values" (1).

Since Adelson conducted her initial fieldwork, there has been a fusing, at the local level, of health and politics. Adelson distributed copies of her research to local political and health authorities, and her use of "being alive well" to explain Cree understandings of health has been incorporated, via *The James Bay Experience: A Guide for Health Professionals Working Among the Cree in Northern Quebec*, into the vocabulary of doctors, dentists, and other health care workers in the area (115).

CONCLUSIONS

This chapter has considered six questions, some having to do with the problem of how to understand ways of life that are different from our own and others with the problem of how to better understand our own lives. Why do human beings differ in what they believe and how they behave? One answer is that human beings, unlike other animals (or, at least, to a greater extent than other animals), create their own worlds and ascribe meanings to objects, persons, behaviours, emotions, and events, meanings that together constitute a culture. As Geertz suggests, human beings are compelled to create meanings if only to instill some sense of order in their lives. To understand such meanings from the native's point of view, we must go into the field (whether or not this is a singular, physical locale or site) to learn about them firsthand. Through long-term fieldwork, and the use of various qualitative methods such as participant observation and interviews, anthropologists develop a nuanced understanding of the different beliefs and cultural practices that they encounter in various societies. In addition, fieldwork helps us to comprehend how various societies are influenced by broader social processes, such as the effects of globalization, or colonialism.

The judgments we make about the beliefs and behaviours of other people create a dilemma. If, on the one hand, we assume that the meanings that others give to their experiences are wrong, silly, or absurd simply because they are different from ours, we are committing the ethnocentric fallacy. Ethnocentrism is intellectually awkward because it allows everyone to believe that their views are correct and that the views of others are wrong. This would make any kind of intercultural understanding virtually impossible. If, on the other hand, we conclude that the beliefs and behaviours of others can be judged only in the context of their cultures, we are confronted with the relativistic fallacy, which implies that any belief or behaviour is acceptable, provided it makes sense to the people of the society in which it occurs. This places us in a moral dilemma because we must then accept virtually any belief or behaviour.

One way we describe and interpret the meanings other people find in their experiences is to consider a culture as a text inscribed with symbols whose meaning can be deciphered. We can examine virtually any cultural activity in this way and find in it a portion of the overall view of the world of a people. If we approach our own culture in the same way we approach other cultures, we should gain a better understanding of the meanings we give objects, persons, and events. If we objectify our own beliefs and behaviour in the same way that we objectify the beliefs and behaviours of others, our own culture should become more exotic, while the cultures of others become less strange, shocking, or bizarre. It is this ability to make the familiar exotic and the exotic familiar that makes the anthropological perspective such an interesting one, and one that will serve you well whether you go into a career as a professional anthropologist, or simply apply your newfound insights to the world around you. Regardless of your career path, the anthropological approach developed within this text should provide you with critical thinking skills. You will perhaps question your own beliefs and understandings of the world as you study, and recognize that much of what we are taught to believe is "natural" is really the by-product of enculturation. In other words, our identities and worldviews are culturally constructed. This encourages us to recognize the dangers of thinking about our beliefs as "natural' or "biological." Ultimately, by recognizing how culture shapes our experiences, we are in a better position to understand both ourselves and others around us.

CULTURE AND MEANING

CRITICAL THINKING QUESTIONS

1. In the introduction, we discussed the way that an anthropologist might find cultural meaning in a classroom chair. Think about the kinds of classroom spaces you are taking classes in—lecture halls, labs, seminar rooms. What other aspects of the classroom set-up can you rethink from an anthropological perspective? How might an anthropologist explain your findings?

2. In section 1.2, we discuss participant observation, in which the anthropologist both observes and takes part in everyday life in order to understand the native's point of view. Is this objective knowledge or subjective knowledge or something in between? List the reasons for your answer.

3. Anthropologists explore the ways in which human beings make their experiences meaningful through culture. Is it possible to imagine life without systems of meaning to help us to make sense of it? What would a life without culture be like?

KEY TERMS:

armchair anthropologist (p. 9)
cultural relativism (p. 19)
cultural text (p. 25)
culture (p. 6)
essentialism (p. 14)
ethnocentric fallacy (p. 19)
ethnocentrism (p. 19)
ethnographic method (p. 10)
ethnography (p. 11)
fieldwork (p. 10)
multi-sited fieldwork (p. 13)
participant observation (p. 10)
relativistic fallacy (p. 20)
representation (p. 13)
salvage anthropology (p. 12)
sociocultural anthropology (p. 3)

CHAPTER 2

THE MEANING OF PROGRESS AND DEVELOPMENT

© Artwork by Ashley Cecil, http://www.ashleycecil.com

This painting by "painting activist" Ashley Cecil depicts Third World women's disappointment when their crops don't grow as well as they had hoped. As John Isbister points out in the epigraph to this chapter, modern technology has penetrated the Third World, particularly in farming, but the results have not always been positive.

One of the myths prevalent about third-world people is that they are unchanging, that their societies are static. One often hears the word traditional used to describe the network of relationships in which they seem trapped. The opposite is true, however. The third world is undergoing rapid and sometimes chaotic social change: populations are growing and becoming more urbanized. Public health measures are lowering death rates … Modern technology has penetrated the third world and transformed production. Education at all levels is spreading.

The lives of people in the third world are changing. They are not improving, however, at least for the majority. One can find privileged groups, or even entire countries and regions, in which economic conditions have progressed and human and political rights are respected … These are exceptions, though; most people in the third world are desperately poor.

John Isbister, Promises Not Kept *(2003)*

PROBLEM 2

How do we explain the transformation of human societies over the past 10,000 years from small-scale, nomadic bands of foragers to large-scale urban-industrial states?

INTRODUCTION

What Do We Talk About When We Talk About Progress?

Ten thousand years ago, all human beings lived in small, nomadic groups of 30 to 100 people, gathering wild vegetable foods and hunting large and small game as they had for thousands of years. Today, no human beings anywhere in the world live exclusively by foraging (hunting and gathering), although every society in existence is descended from such people.

Today's world is radically divided into wealthy nations and poor nations. Some enjoy a standard of living that gives them abundant food, comfortable shelter, and a plethora of consumer goods; but more than a billion people worldwide suffer from hunger and poverty, live in urban and rural slums, and lack even the basics of health care.

The gradual shift from a type of society that had flourished for at least 10,000 years, and the accompanying creation of a world divided into the wealthy and the poor, poses both a riddle and a moral predicament. The riddle is this: Why, after thousands of years of living as foragers, did some societies begin to change their way of life? Why did they begin to domesticate plants and animals and exchange their nomadic existence for a **sedentary** life in villages and towns? And how, over the next 10,000 years, did these villages and towns come to be divided into rich and poor states? The moral predicament involves our perceptions of the few remaining small-scale societies that still exist today and of the millions of people who go hungry each day. Should we assume—as many have and still do—that human beings *chose* to abandon a nomadic, foraging life because they discovered better ways of living? Should we assume that the few remaining small-scale tribal societies are remnants of an inferior way of life and that given the opportunity, their members would adopt modern farming, wage labour, or urban life? Should we assume that we can explain the world's division of wealth by saying that some nations have progressed while others have not? Or is the concept of **progress**—the human history has been a steady advance from a life dependent on nature's whims to a life of control and domination over natural forces—a fabrication of contemporary societies based on ethnocentric notions of technological superiority? Throughout this chapter, we will be trying to understand the monumental shift that has occurred in modes of livelihood and social organization over the past 10,000 years without relying on an uncritical use of the concept of progress. As we will see in section 2.5, many anthropological ideas about modes of livelihood can be put to good use outside of academia in the area of development; however, we will also see that "development" only works when we question the assumptions often inherent in the idea of progress. What, exactly, does progress mean, and for whom?

And who determines what counts as progress and what does not?

---

sedentary
A mode of livelihood characterized by permanent or semi-permanent settlements.

progress
The idea that human history is the story of a steady advance from a life dependent on the whims of nature to a life of control and domination over natural forces.

QUESTIONS

2.1 How and why did foraging societies switch to sedentary agriculture?

2.2 How can we explain the vast inequality between the rich and the poor?

2.3 How do globalization, economic development, and cultural diversity relate to one another?

2.4 Have progress and development improved human health?

2.5 How can we apply a critical anthropological understanding of progress and development outside of academia?

QUESTION 2.1: HOW AND WHY DID FORAGING SOCIETIES SWITCH TO SEDENTARY AGRICULTURE?

A thumbnail sketch of what we know about the course of cultural history, modes of livelihood, and social organization will provide a useful starting point for understanding the meaning of progress and development. Combining what we have learned about human history from the work of archaeologists and historians with information provided by cultural anthropologists who have worked among foraging and tribal societies creates a relatively clear picture of **culture change**. Until around 10,000 years ago, humans were scattered in small-scale, nomadic **bands** of 30 to 100 people, who lived by gathering wild plants and hunting small and large game. Because the search for food required mobility, it was probably not unusual for them to move every few days. With groups that were small and mobile, simple economic, social, and political arrangements sufficed; formal leaders were not needed, and there was little occupational specialization. If there was a specialist, it was likely to be a person who was believed to have special spiritual powers that could be used to cure illness or (if used malevolently) to cause illness or death. Kinship served as the main organizing principle of these societies, and social differences among people were based largely on age and gender. Because there was little occupational specialization and little difference in individual wealth or possessions, relations among people likely were of an egalitarian nature.

At some point in history, some foragers began to plant crops and domesticate wild animals. These groups became sedentary, living in permanent or semi-permanent settlements of 200 to 2,000 people. They practised **slash-and-burn** (or **swidden**) **agriculture**; they cleared forests by burning the trees and brush and then planted crops among the ashes. This land would be cultivated for one to three years; another plot of land would then be burned and planted. Because larger, more sedentary groups required more formal leadership, certain members assumed the roles of chief or elder, with the authority to make decisions and resolve disputes. Simple occupational roles developed. Villages consisted of extended family groups, and people organized themselves into **clans**—that is, groups of 200 to 500 people who claimed descent from a common ancestor. Now that leadership roles had developed, members of some groups were ranked in importance. Later in history, perhaps because of a need to defend themselves against other groups, settlements combined themselves under common leaders to form **states** consisting of many thousands of persons. The development of agriculture intensified, and slash-and-burn techniques were replaced by plough or **irrigation agriculture**. Leaders organized labour for the purpose of constructing public works such as roads (the Inca Highway), fortifications (the Great Wall of China), and religious structures (pyramids in Mexico, cathedrals in medieval Europe). Hereditary leaders emerged; settlements grew into cities; and competition between groups over available resources spurred the development of standing armies. As technological complexity increased, people began to develop specific skills and to specialize in occupational tasks (e.g., herder, baker, butcher, warrior, potter); that occupational specialization led to increased trade and to the evolution of a merchant class. Some 300 years ago, some of these hierarchical societies began to develop into large-scale, industrialized states, which are now found all over the world. Table 2.1 summarizes this sketch of human social and cultural history.

---

culture change
The changes in meanings that a people ascribe to experience and changes in their way of life.

bands
A term used by anthropologists to refer to egalitarian units of social organization, found mostly among foragers, that usually consist of fewer than 100 people.

slash-and-burn (or swidden) agriculture
A mode of livelihood in which forests are cleared by burning trees and brush, and crops are planted among the ashes of the cleared ground.

clans
A unilineal descent group whose members claim descent from a common ancestor.

state
A form of society characterized by a hierarchical ranking of people and centralized political control.

irrigation agriculture
A form of cultivation in which water is used to deliver nutrients to growing plants.

TABLE 2.1 SUMMARY OF THE DEVELOPMENT OF SOCIETIES FROM GATHERERS AND HUNTERS TO AGRICULTURAL STATES

	Hunters and Gatherers	Horticulturalists	State Societies
Population density	Approximately 1 person per 2.6 square kilometres	Approximately 10 to 15 people per 2.6 square kilometres	Approximately 300 people per 2.6 square kilometres
Subsistence	Hunting, gathering, and fishing	Slash-and-burn agriculture with mixed livestock herding	Plough or irrigation agriculture
Work, labour, and production	Very high yield relative to labour expended	High yield relative to labour expended	High labour needs relative to yield. High degree of occupational specialization.
Political organization	Informal political organization. Few, if any, formal leaders. Conflict controlled by limiting group size, mobility, and flexibility of group membership. Little intergroup conflict.	More formalized political organization, often with well-established leaders or chiefs. Increased population density and wealth result in increased potential for conflict. Intergroup warfare, motivated by desire for wealth, prestige, or women, is common.	Highly developed state organization with a clear hierarchy of authority. Often a two-class society with rulers (landowners) and peasants. Authority of the elite backed by organized use of force (police or army). Warfare for purpose of conquest is common. Well-established mechanisms for resolving conflict (e.g., courts) exist side by side with informal mechanisms.
Social organization	Small family groups, whose major purpose is economic cooperation. Few status distinctions other than those of sex and age. Marriage for economic partnership and interfamily alliance.	Emphasis on extended family groups. Descent important for the distribution of wealth and property. Status distinctions based on wealth are common, but status mobility is usually possible.	Emphasis on nuclear family. Family is strongly patriarchal, with women holding low status. Strong bonds of intergenerational dependence are built on inheritance needs. Social distinctions between people are emphasized, sometimes based on occupations. Little or no status mobility.

Does the Idea of Progress Help Us Understand the Shift from Foraging to Sedentary Agriculture?

As we have seen, the shifts in modes of livelihood from foraging to horticulture to agriculture were accompanied by major social and cultural shifts. From the earliest days of their discipline, anthropologists have sought to explain these shifts. One possible explanation for why societies transformed themselves in this way is that human inventions resulted in better ways of doing things; in other words, human culture progressed. In the past 30 years, however, anthropologists have begun to question the idea that the life of foragers was harsh and difficult. In this section, we discuss the work of two early and influential anthropologists, Lewis Henry Morgan and Leslie White, who developed explanations of culture change based on the idea of progress. We then explore case studies of foraging, slash-and-burn, and industrial agriculture; finally, we discuss the work of anthropologists who argue that agriculture is *not the* easiest mode of livelihood, nor is it the most efficient. If the notion of the steady march of progress through time does not adequately explain the shift in modes of livelihood, what does?

Evolutionary Explanations for Culture Change: Lewis Henry Morgan and Leslie White

One possible reason why foragers chose at some point to settle down and domesticate plants and animals is that sedentary agriculture was an easier, less dangerous, and more productive way to get food. People who discovered that they could plant and harvest crops and domesticate animals instead of searching for their food began to do so. According to this explanation, they had *progressed*.

The idea that change occurs because of a desire to progress is entrenched in Western societies; and beginning in the 19th century, anthropologists contributed significantly to this view. Lewis Henry Morgan, a lawyer in Rochester, New York, who took a great interest in the historical evolution of culture, offered his own idea of how humankind had progressed. Morgan became fascinated with the Iroquois of New York and later sent out questionnaires to travellers and missionaries all over the world asking them about the family organization and kinship terminology of the cultures they visited. In *Ancient Society* (1877), Morgan postulated a theory of human development in which human societies evolved through three stages that he labelled savagery, barbarism, and civilization. He further divided savagery and barbarism into early, middle, and late stages. Some societies—notably the United States, according to Morgan's theory—had evolved completely to civilization; others had yet to complete their transformation and remained in the stages of savagery or barbarism. The passage of societies from one stage to the next, Morgan reasoned, required some major technological invention. Thus, the advance from early to middle

savagery was marked by the control of fire; from middle to late savagery by the invention of the bow and arrow; from late savagery through late barbarism by the invention of pottery, agriculture, and animal domestication; and so on. Eventually, some societies had progressed to civilization. Other writers—including many anthropologists—elaborated on Morgan's scheme, assuming, as he did, that humankind was progressing and would continue to do so.

For example, in the mid-20th century, Leslie White formulated what would be one of the more influential evolutionary schemes to explain the historical development of culture. Like Morgan, White saw technology as the driving force of cultural evolution. From his perspective, human beings sought to harness energy through technology and to transform that energy into things they required for survival, such as food, clothing, and shelter. By means of technology, energy was put to work, and the amount of food, clothing, or other goods produced by the expenditure of energy was proportional to the efficiency of the technology available. Because foragers had only their own muscle power to work with, the amount of energy produced by their work was limited. Once technological advances—such as the plough, the water wheel, and the windmill—enabled people to grow more crops and to domesticate animals, they were able to harness more and more energy for their own use. Still later, new forms of energy in the form of coal, oil, and gas were harnessed by means of steam engines and internal combustion engines, and the amount of energy human beings could control again leaped forward.

From White's perspective, cultural development varied directly with the efficiency of the tools employed. Technology that was more efficient allowed human societies to transform more energy to fulfill their needs; these societies could then produce more food and support larger populations. At some point, increased efficiency in food production allowed a few people to produce enough food for everyone, freeing others to develop other skills and thereby promoting occupational specialization. Specialization led to widespread trade and the development of commerce. Population growth and increased contacts among groups led to the development of states capable of coordinating group activities and organizing armies to defend the group's wealth.

What Are the Shortcomings of These Theories of Progress?

White's view of technology as the driving force in cultural evolution was highly influential in 20th-century anthropological theory. But more relevant to us, his theories encapsulated a point of view that many people hold to this day: that technology is the true measure of progress, and that the more energy human societies can harness through the development of new power sources, the more social, economic, and political problems they will solve.

Technological progress remains a popular explanation for why societies transformed themselves, and many people continue to view technology as the solution to ongoing world problems. Yet even during the 20th century, anthropologists were questioning the progress theory. Spurring these new doubts were studies of foraging societies that suggested that the life of a nomadic forager was not nearly as harsh and dangerous as had been supposed. In fact, some anthropologists, such as Marshall Sahlins, were beginning to suggest that foraging represented "the original affluent society," with minimal work and plenty of leisure time.

One of the first suppositions about life in foraging societies to be challenged had to do with the roles of males and females. Studies found that contrary to common belief, the gathering activities of women produced by far the greater share of food in these societies; men hunted, but, except in areas such as the Arctic and Subarctic, meat and fish constituted only about one-quarter of the diet. A second supposition—that foragers often went hungry—proved to be unfounded. Apparently, they had plenty of food. Moreover, contrary to opinion,

they did not have to work very hard to get it. Which raises the question: Why did most foragers shift away from their mode of livelihood? And why do we often explain this shift in terms of progress?

Life Among Foragers: The Hadza and Ju/'hoansi

When James Woodburn studied the Hadza in the 1960s, they were a small group of nomadic foragers in Tanzania. Woodburn described their territory as dry, rocky savanna, characterized by one traveller as "barren land" and "desert." Foragers are often depicted as living on the verge of starvation, yet Woodburn found the Hadza area rich in food and resources. Wild game such as elephant, giraffe, zebra, and gazelle was plentiful. Plant foods—roots, berries, and fruits—were also abundant for those who knew where to look and constituted about 80 percent of the Hadza diet. The Hadza spent about two hours a day obtaining food.

Hadza women were responsible for almost all the plant food gathered; hunting was exclusively a male activity. The men hunted with bow and poisoned arrows; at the time Woodburn lived among them, they used no guns, spears, or traps. The Hadza considered only meat as proper food and would say they were hungry when there was none; but there was, in fact, plenty of food available. For a Hadza to go hungry, Woodburn noted, was almost inconceivable. Plant food was so plentiful that the Hadza made no attempt to preserve it. Physicians who examined Hadza children in the 1960s found them in good health by tropical standards. Woodburn found that from a nutritional point of view, the Hadza were better off than their agricultural neighbours.

The Ju/'hoansi★ peoples of Namibia's Kalahari Desert are another foraging society that has contributed extensively to what anthropologists

---

★ The terms that societies use to refer to themselves are often different from those assigned by others. Unfortunately the latter sometimes become more widely accepted than the former. The Ju/'hoansi, for example, were referred to as Bushmen by Europeans, and later as !Kung by anthropologists.

have learned about small-scale societies. Lorna Marshall, assisted by her children Elizabeth and John, began research among the Ju/'hoansi in the 1950s. Their work, along with intensive studies by Richard Lee and others, has provided us with a good description of Ju/'hoansi foraging activities. There is some controversy in anthropology over whether the Ju/'hoansi have always been foragers, but that was the way they lived when they were visited by the Marshalls and Lee through the 1960s.

Ju/'hoansi groups lived around water holes, from which they would wander as far as 10 kilometres in search of plant and animal foods. Their groups numbered from 30 to 40 people during the rainy season, when water holes were full and plentiful, but increased to 100 to 200 during the dry season, when only the larger holes retained water. Lee found that the food quest was constant among the Ju/'hoansi, as it was among the Hadza. They did little food processing, so they had to get food supplies every third or fourth day. Vegetable foods constituted 60 to 80 percent of the diet, and women gathered most of it, producing two to three times as much food as men.

Lee reports that the Ju/'hoansi never exhausted their food supplies. The major food source was the mongongo nut, which is far more nourishing than our own breakfast cereals and contains five times the calories and ten times the protein of cooked cereals. Mongongo nuts provided more than 50 percent of the Ju/'hoansi caloric intake; there are 1,260 calories and 56 grams of protein in 300 nuts (see Table 2.2). Ju/'hoansi territory contained more than 80 other species of edible plants, most of which they didn't even use, although they did eat about 20 species of roots, melons, gums, bulbs, and dried fruits. In addition, meat was provided by an occasional giraffe, antelope, or other large game animal, as well as by the more usual porcupine, hare, or other small animal. Their meat intake was between 80 and 90 kilograms per person per year—an amount comparable to the meat consumption in developed countries.

In other words, Lee found that the environment of the Ju/'hoansi provided ample

Readily available plant foods, such as the nutrient-rich mongongo nut, were the mainstay of the Ju/'hoansi diet. Here, Ju/'hoansi women return to camp after foraging for mongongo nuts to feed their families.

readily accessible food. Their diet consisted of some 2,300 calories a day, with a proper balance of protein, vitamins, and minerals. If the Ju/'hoansi diet was deficient, it was in carbohydrates, since there was no equivalent to our white bread, pasta, rice, or sugar.

The Ju/'hoansi did not spend much time getting food. Lee conducted a careful study of Ju/'hoansi work habits. During the first week in which he recorded the amount of time spent getting food, he found that individuals averaged 2.3 days at this work, with a typical working day of six hours. Overall, the average time spent getting food was 2.4 days, or less than 20 hours of work per week. The most active person Lee observed worked at getting food an average of 32 hours a week. Other time was spent doing housework or mending tools.

Lee concluded that, contrary to the stereotype that foragers must struggle with limited technology to obtain the food they need for survival, they do not have to work very hard to make a living. He added that the idea that foraging societies struggle for existence is an ethnocentric notion that assumes that our own technologically oriented society represents the pinnacle of development. If Lee, and others, are correct about foragers' ease of survival, and if their life is not harsh and dangerous, why

TABLE 2.2   THE MONGONGO NUT*—NUTRITION FACTS

Serving Size 100 g			
Total fat		57 g	
Saturated fat		10 g	
Polyunsaturated		14 g	
Monounsaturated		10 g	
Protein		24 g	
Calcium	193 mg	Magnesium	527 mg
Iron	3.7 mg	Copper	2.8 mg
Zinc	4 mg	Vitamin B1 (Thiamine)	0.3 mg
Vitamin B2 (Riboflavin)	0.2 mg	Vitamin B3 (Nicotinic Acid)	0.3 mg
Vitamin E	565 mg		

* Mongongo nuts, the main staple of the Ju/'hoansi diet, are rich in nutrients and provide the core of a balanced diet.

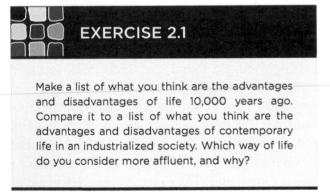

EXERCISE 2.1

Make a list of what you think are the advantages and disadvantages of life 10,000 years ago. Compare it to a list of what you think are the advantages and disadvantages of contemporary life in an industrialized society. Which way of life do you consider more affluent, and why?

did those foragers of 10,000 years ago abandon their old practices, begin to domesticate crops and animals, and settle in permanent villages and towns?

The Transition to Agriculture

There is a perspective on cultural change that views the gradual shift from foraging to modern, industrial society less as development or progress and more as a necessary evil. This perspective emphasizes the influences of population growth and **population density**—defined here as the number of people living in a given area. To understand this point of view, we need to examine the transition from foraging to agriculture while also exploring the reasons for the eventual change from relatively simple slash-and-burn agriculture to more complex, labour-intensive irrigation agriculture. Comparing modern agricultural techniques with less complex methods used in the production of potatoes will also illustrate the point.

Anthropologist Mark Cohen set out to explain why individuals or groups abandoned foraging for agriculture and why so many did so in a relatively

population density
The number of people in a given geographic area.

short period of time. First he examined the reported food-gathering strategies of foraging societies. Foragers settle in a given area to collect food; then, as food resources decline in one spot, they enlarge the area within which they travel in search of them. Imagine this area as a series of concentric circles; as the outer circles are approached from the centre, the group may decide to move to another area where food is more plentiful in order to reduce the distance that members must travel. Cohen suggests that when population density in a given geographical area reached a point where different groups began to bump into one another, or when groups found they had to travel farther and farther to get enough food to feed a growing population, they began to cultivate their own crops. He notes that anthropological and archaeological evidence suggests that they knew how to do this all along, but chose instead to gather crops until the labour involved in travelling to new food sources surpassed the labour involved in growing their own crops. In other words, the historical transition from foraging to simple agriculture was a necessary consequence of population growth rather than a consequence of a discovery or invention that was adopted because it made life better. In a limited way, of course, this transition from gathering to cultivating did make life easier; when people began to harvest crops in a limited area and remained in villages, groups no longer needed to travel as much. However, Cohen and others argue that agriculture didn't make life better at all; in fact, it made life worse (we'll explore that claim a little later in this chapter).

In most parts of the world, when societies abandoned foraging they likely began to utilize slash-and-burn agricultural techniques. Slash-and-burn or swidden agriculture can be practised by relatively small, kinship-based groups. As a form of growing crops, it is highly efficient and productive. The Kuikuru, who inhabit the central Brazilian rain forest, annually produce about 5 million calories per hectare of land farmed—enough to feed 5 people for a year. Moreover, the Kuikuru work only about two hours a day.

However, swidden agriculture requires large tracts of available land because after a plot is farmed for a couple of years, it must lie fallow for 20 to 30 years to allow the brush and trees to grow back so that it can be used again. If the population and thus the amount of land needed to feed it both increase, plots must be used more frequently, perhaps every five or ten years. But when land is cultivated more frequently, the yield per acre declines. Thus swidden agriculture is efficient only as long as the population and the amount of land available remain constant.

Farmland may become scarce not only because of increasing population but also because of environmental changes or the encroachment of other groups. Then new agricultural techniques must be developed to increase the yield on the available land. The digging stick may be replaced with the plough, or irrigation systems may be devised, and developments like these require a great deal of labour. In other words, the more food the group needs to produce, the more complex the technology needed to produce it; and the more complex the technology, the greater the amount of work involved. Note that this contradicts the idea that the shift from simple to complex technologies always makes life easier.

Tables 2.3 and 2.4 demonstrate the relationships among land, labour, population, and methods of agriculture. Table 2.3 indicates that the amount of labour required to produce a harvest increases with the complexity of agricultural techniques. For example, it requires up to 10 times more labour to produce a harvest with irrigation agriculture than it does to produce one with swidden agriculture.

Why, then, abandon swidden agriculture? The answer: because there is not enough land to support the population. Table 2.4 lists the amount of land needed to feed 100 families using various agricultural methods. For example, as little as 36.5 hectares of land are required to feed 100 families if irrigation agriculture is used, while around 1,200 hectares are needed if swidden agriculture is used. If a group has enough land, it might as well keep its farming

TABLE 2.3 DAYS OF LABOUR PER ACRE PER HARVEST BY TYPE OF AGRICULTURE

Type of agriculture	Days of labour per acre
Advanced swidden	18–25
Plough cultivation	20
Hoe cultivation	58
Irrigation agriculture	90–178

Source: Data from Eric R. Wolf, *Peasants* (Englewood Cliffs, N.J.: Prentice Hall, 1966).

TABLE 2.4 LAND NEEDED TO FEED 100 FAMILIES USING DIFFERENT AGRICULTURAL METHODS

Agricultural method	Number of hectares needed to feed 100 families
Swidden agriculture	1,200*
Swidden with garden plots	650*

*Includes unworked land that must be allowed to lie fallow to regain fertility.

Source: Data from Eric R. Wolf, *Peasants* (Englewood Cliffs, N.J.: Prentice Hall, 1966).

methods simple, changing them only if population increases or the supply of land decreases.

But the history of humankind has been marked by an increase in population and an increase in the ratio of people to land. Robert L. Carneiro outlines the consequences of population density for cultural change.

The increase in the number of people relative to the available land creates two problems. First, if there are more people than there is available land to feed them, conflict may arise between people vying for the available resources. Second, if a growing population decides to intensify methods of growing crops, there is a need for greater societal organization. Irrigation agriculture, for example, requires the digging of ditches, the building of pumps to bring water to the fields and to drain water from them, and the coordination of one and sometimes two harvests a year. Thus, whether a society deals with an increasing ratio between land and people by intensifying efforts to produce more food, or addresses the problem by denying some people access to the necessary resources, the groundwork is laid for a stratified society to emerge, with the concommitant need for a state organization.

Anthropologists like Cohen and Carneiro are suggesting, then, that the change from foraging to gradually more labour-intensive methods of agriculture was not a matter of choice. Slash-and-burn agriculture wasn't easier than foraging, and plough and irrigation agriculture wasn't more efficient than slash-and-burn agriculture. Rather, changes in food production techniques were necessary responses to increases in population or population density, and this in turn created the need for more formal, more elaborate political and social institutions, both to organize labour and to maintain order among more and more people.

We might conclude from this—which not all anthropologists do—that the transition from foraging to complex agriculture, and the associated social, political, and economic transformations, do not represent progress. But isn't it safe to say that at the very least, Western societies—particularly in North America—use agricultural techniques that are vastly superior to those of small, tribal societies? Those who claim that modern food production techniques are far more efficient than any others point out that in Canada and the United States only 1 calorie of human energy is needed to produce 210 calories for human consumption; by contrast, foragers produce fewer than 10 calories of food for every calorie they use collecting the food. Others, however, argue that these figures are deceptive. At the same time that we have vastly decreased the amount of human labour required to produce food, they say, we have vastly *increased* the amount of nonhuman energy required. From that perspective, we expend 1 calorie of nonhuman energy in the form of nonrenewable fossil fuels (e.g., oil and coal) for every 8 calories we produce.

Industrial Agriculture: Producing Potato Calories

To make this point about energy, John H. Bodley compared the production of sweet potatoes in New Guinea with potato production in the United States. In New Guinea, people cultivate sweet potatoes by slash-and-burn agriculture; plots of land are burned, cleared, and planted using digging sticks. When the crops are ready, sweet potatoes are cooked in pits and eaten. In one New Guinea community, sweet potatoes accounted for 21 percent of the diet of 204 people. Some of the sweet potatoes were fed to pigs, thus producing protein and accounting for an even larger proportion of the diet. The people used only 10 percent of the arable land, and there was no danger of resource depletion. With their agricultural techniques, the New Guinea farmers could produce about 12.4 million calories per hectare.

Potato farms in Canada and the United States produce more than twice as many calories per acre as New Guinea farmers—about 29.6 million calories per hectare. However, as Bodley points out, in addition to the human energy that goes into North American farming, vast amounts of nonhuman energy are expended. Chemicals must be applied to maintain soil conditions and to control insects and fungus. For example, in Washington State in the 1960s, 60 percent of the potato acreage was airplane-sprayed five to nine times per season to control insects; another 40 percent was treated for weeds. American potato farmers need specialized machines to cut, seed, harvest, dig, and plant. In 1969, 36,000 tons of fertilizer were applied to 25,300 hectares—more than 1,120 kilgrams per hectare. Thus, while the American system produced more potatoes, the actual energy costs per calorie were lower in New Guinea. Moreover, all kinds of hidden costs from consequences such as soil erosion and pollution were incurred in the United States.

North Americans must also deal with distribution costs, which are minimal in traditional cultures, where most households consume what they themselves produce. In modern industrial societies, where 95 percent of the population is urban, the energy expended in distributing the food now exceeds the energy expended in producing it. Taking the food-producing process as a whole—the manufacture and distribution of farm machinery, trucks, and fertilizer; irrigation projects; food processing; packaging; transportation; truck manufacturing; industrial and domestic food preparation; and refrigeration—the American food industry expends 8 to 12 calories of energy to produce a single calorie of food!

Thus, the human and nonhuman energy required to convert a potato into potato chips is far greater than the energy expended in New Guinea to produce a more nutritious sweet potato! Moreover, North Americans do not fully appreciate the health risks of adding some 2,500 substances to our foods to colour, flavour, or preserve them.

QUESTION 2.2: HOW CAN WE EXPLAIN THE VAST INEQUALITY BETWEEN THE RICH AND THE POOR?

Even if we agree that hunters and gatherers don't struggle for food and that simpler forms of agriculture are more efficient than modern techniques, we still have not explained the vast divisions in the modern world between rich and poor. The pyramid in Figure 2.1 illustrates the economic disparities in the world economy. The top level consists of the roughly 1 billion people who live in developed nations and who make more than $20,000 annually. The bottom tier consists of the roughly 4 billion people who make less than $2,000 per year.

If progress is not the reason, why do most people in the industrial world enjoy a standard of living superior to those who live in underdeveloped countries? That question requires a complex discussion of 300 years of world history. Rather than try to pack three centuries into the next few pages, let's see what we can learn from the story of the expansion of one industry, in one country, during one phase of its development—the textile

industry in England in the last half of the 18th century and the first half of the 19th. This period coincides with the **Industrial Revolution**, which was marked by urbanization, by the factory system, and by a shift in production from agriculture to industrial goods.

Before the Industrial Revolution in Europe, the world was significantly different in its distribution of wealth. China was arguably the richest country in the world during the 16th and 17th centuries as gold and silver taken from the mines of South America by the Spanish and Portuguese was funnelled into China to pay for Chinese silks, spices, teas, and luxury goods; India was developing a thriving cotton textile industry as Indian calicoes flooded into Europe. Wealthy states developed in western Africa, and

FIGURE 2.1   THE GLOBAL ECONOMIC PYRAMID

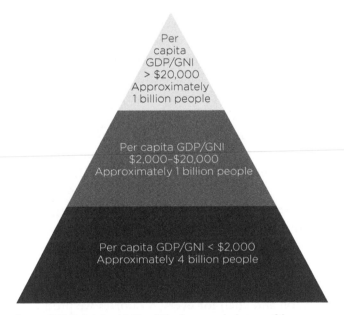

Per capita GDP/GNI > $20,000 Approximately 1 billion people

Per capita GDP/GNI $2,000–$20,000 Approximately 1 billion people

Per capita GDP/GNI < $2,000 Approximately 4 billion people

Source: C. K. Prahalad and S. Hart, "The fortune at the bottom of the pyramid," *Strategy + Business 26* (2002): 54–67; and S. Hart, *Capitalism at the Crossroads* (Philadelphia: Wharton School Publishing, 2005), 111.

Industrial Revolution

A period of European history, generally identified as occurring in the late 18th century, marked by a shift in production from agriculture to industrial goods, urbanization, and the factory system.

Islamic traders thrived from Africa to Southeast Asia. Seventeenth-century England was a largely rural and agricultural country; even by 1700, only 13 percent of the population lived in towns of 5,000 or more. England, however, had long enjoyed a thriving trade in raw wool and inexpensive wool textiles.

In its early days, textile production was largely a handicraft industry, and most steps in the production of wool cloth, from cutting and degreasing the wool, to dying and spinning the thread, to weaving the cloth, were in the hands of rural families or small cooperatives. The finished cloth or wool product might be sold at a local market or fair; more often, though, it was sold to urban-based merchants or traders for resale at fairs or for shipment overseas.

The trade in home-produced textiles was profitable for all. However, traders and merchants discovered that they needed to better control the type, quantity, and quality of cloth produced by spinners and weavers. The merchants' first solution to this problem was the **"putting out" system**, whereby merchants supplied weavers with materials and required them to produce cloth of the desired type. Some merchants supplied only the wool, cotton, or linen, while others supplied everything, including the looms. The merchants delivered the supplies and tools and picked up the finished products, generally paying the producers for each piece produced. Putting out had many advantages for textile merchants: it gave them more control over production; it ensured cheap labour, for it brought women and children into the production process; and if demand for textiles slackened, the merchant could easily control how much was produced by limiting the materials he put out.

Increasingly, however, beginning in the 18th century, English merchants found it expedient to transform the "putting out" system into a **factory system** by bringing the spinners, weavers, and others together in one location to produce the cloth. Factories were neither new nor unique to England—factories employing more than 15,000 workers existed in France as early as 1685. Furthermore, merchants were not particularly anxious to invest in factories. Profits from manufacture were not nearly as great as profits from trade, especially long-distance exchange. Moreover, removing people from home-based families to urban-based factories required new mechanisms of discipline and control—a fact that explains why early factories were modelled on penal workhouses and prisons. Finally, the entrepreneur, who in the past could have halted putting out when demand slackened, now had to keep his factories busy to pay for his investment in buildings and technology. Consequently, he had to create demands for his products.

The only things that made a manufacturing investment attractive were the various government subsidies or laws (e.g., vagrancy laws requiring people to have jobs) that ensured a flow of cheap labour. Textile manufacturers were able to draw on workers who had been forced from their land by the enclosure laws, which were pushing peasant farmers off their common lands at the behest of landowners, who wished to grow crops for sale to England's growing population. Since there were no minimum wage laws or laws restricting child labour, factory owners could exploit the cheap labour of women and children; thus, by 1834, children under 13 represented 13 percent of the British cotton industry, and by 1838, only 23 percent of textile factory workers in England were adult men. In addition, government played a major role in creating and defending overseas markets as well as sources of raw materials such as cotton.

The expansion of the textile industry had multiple effects. For one thing, it fuelled the growth of cities: by 1800, one-quarter of the English population

> **"putting out" system**
> A means of production, common in the 16th and 17th centuries and surviving today, in which a manufacturer or merchant supplies the materials and sometimes the tools to workers, who produce the goods in their own homes.
>
> **factory system**
> A system of production characterized by the concentration of labour and machines in specific places. It is associated with the Industrial Revolution.

Three inventions that revolutionized the textile industry (from left to right): the flying shuttle, the water frame, and the spinning mule.

lived in towns of 5,000 or more; and Manchester, a textile-manufacturing centre, grew from 24,000 inhabitants in 1773 to more than 250,000 by 1851. Moreover, factories spurred technological development. Mechanization of the textile industry began in earnest with Kay's flying shuttle in 1733, which doubled the weavers' output. However, since spinners could not keep up with the need for thread for the new looms, bottlenecks developed. To meet this need, James Hargreaves introduced in 1765 the spinning jenny. In 1769, Arkwright invented the water frame; then in 1779, Crompton developed a spinning mule that combined features of the water frame and the jenny. Finally, in 1790, steam

power was added to the production process. These inventions generated a staggering increase in textile production. A hand spinner in 18th-century India took more than 50,000 hours to process 100 pounds of cotton into thread; in England, Crompton's mule reduced that to 2,000 hours; the power-assisted mules of around 1795 reduced this time still further, to *300* hours. By 1825, it was taking only 135 hours to process 100 pounds of cotton.

The growth of the textile industry obviously produced great wealth and employed millions of workers. In economic terms, it transformed England into the wealthiest country in the world. And textiles were not, of course, the only industry that expanded—trade, the manufacture of iron, and food production further increased the wealth of the growing British Empire. The increase in technology and production created two problems, however: Where was the market for all these textile products to be found? And where were the raw materials—notably the cotton—to come from?

Some historians point to the large domestic market available to English textile producers in the wake of the growth of the English population from 6 million in 1700 to 9 million in 1800. Moreover, English textile manufacturers were able to sell much of their product to markets in Europe and the growing markets of the Americas. But there was still competition for these markets. England was not the only textile producer; Holland, France, and Spain were busy competing (and often fighting among one another) for overseas markets as well as for sources of raw materials. This competition, and the growing military superiority of Western Europe, often had dire consequences for once-prosperous industries in other parts of the world. The story of textiles in India is instructive.

The British in India

Mughal India of the 17th century was an empire created by Turks from Turkestan, who made their chief, Babur, the first Mughal emperor in 1527. India was a major trading country, and centuries-old trade networks linked India to Europe, the Islamic world, and China. In 1690 the British East India Company was granted a monopoly in East Asian trade by the British government. A relative latecomer to the Indian trade, it established a trading centre in Bengal, in the city of Calcutta. "John Company," as it came to be known, soon had some 150 posts in India, which traded for fine silks, cotton, sugar, rice, saltpetre, indigo, and opium.

In the 1750s the British provoked the rulers of Bengal into war, defeating them conclusively in 1757. In the aftermath of their victory in Bengal, they plundered the state treasury of some £5 million and gained control of 10,000 Bengali weavers. By 1765, John Company was the civil administration of Bengal. It promptly increased the tax burden on peasants and artisans, which led to serious famines in 1770 and 1783. From its base in Bengal, moreover, the company began to extend its control over much of the Indian Subcontinent.

Prior to the British military takeover, India had been producing cloth that was cheaper and better than English textiles; in fact, Indian cottons and calicoes—named after the city of Calicut—were the craze of Europe. To meet this challenge, the British government prohibited the British East India Company from importing calicoes into England. To take advantage of the import restriction, English factories began producing copies of popular Indian textiles for sale both in England and abroad. In addition, India was required to admit English manufacturers free of tariffs. These actions effectively destroyed what had been a thriving Indian textile industry. India was still a major producer of raw cotton. Indian cotton was not favoured by English or American manufacturers, although China was willing to import plenty of it.

The British, and Western European nations in general, had a problem with trade into China. Chinese products, notably tea, were in high demand, but the Europeans were producing little that the Chinese wanted or needed. There was a market in China for opium, however, and by 1773, the British East India Company had a monopoly over opium sales. Opium was illegal in China, but the Chinese state seemed incapable of cutting off supplies. Smuggling opium into China was hugely profitable for British merchants, as well as for the Americans and the French. When the Chinese government tried to halt the trade in 1839 by seizing opium held by British merchants in warehouses in Canton, the British government intervened militarily and forced the Chinese government to stop enforcing its own opium laws. An analogy today might be the government of Colombia sending troops to the United States or Canada to force acceptance of Colombian cocaine shipments. Moreover, the

THE MEANING OF PROGRESS AND DEVELOPMENT

British demanded and received additional trading rights into China, further opening a market, not only for opium but for textiles as well.

The British-led opium trade from India to China had three results. First, it reversed the flow of money between China and the rest of the world: during the first decade of the 19th century, China was still enjoying a yearly trade surplus of 26 million silver dollars; by the third decade, 34 million dollars per year were leaving China to pay for opium. Second, estimates are that by the end of the 19th century, one out of every ten Chinese was addicted to opium. Finally, textile exports from England to India and China increased from 6 percent of total British exports in 1815, to 22 percent in 1840, 31 percent in 1850, and more than 50 percent after 1873.

Cotton, Slavery, and the Trail of Tears

Cotton and the British textile industry also figure into the story of slavery and the removal of thousands of Native Americans from their homeland in the United States. The British were able to sell raw Indian cotton to China, but Indian cotton was not acceptable to European and North American markets. Indian cotton produced a shorter fibre, whereas cotton produced elsewhere, notably in Egypt and the southern United States, produced a longer, more desirable fibre. But cotton production in the Americas was labour intensive, and to be profitable, it required slave labour.

Slavery was not created by the need for cotton— as an institution, it was far more ancient than that. It was never uncommon for groups at war to turn captured enemies into slaves. However, the slave trade grew rapidly between the 15th and 19th centuries in response to Europe's economic expansion and the demands of trade. The Spanish required workers for their silver mines; the Spanish, Portuguese, British, and French required cane cutters and millers for their sugar plantations in Brazil and the Caribbean; and Georgia, Alabama, Louisiana, Texas, and Mississippi required labourers for their cotton plantations. Between 1451

Reliance on slave labour in the United States was closely tied to the rise of the British textile industry. Here, a slave family picks cotton on a plantation near Savannah, Georgia, during the early 1860s.

© Bettman/CORBIS

and 1600, some 275,000 slaves were taken from Africa to the United States and Europe. During the 17th century, 1.3 million slaves were forcibly exported from Africa; between 1701 and 1810, it was around 6 million. Another 2 million were exported from Africa between 1810 and 1870, many destined for Cuba.

The production of cotton using slave labour fuelled the Industrial Revolution in the United States. England had long imported raw cotton from its possessions in the West Indies and from Turkey; by 1807, however, half its supply was from the United States. In fact, between 1815 and 1860 raw cotton constituted half the value of domestic exports from the United States.

The American cotton industry grew so rapidly in part because of Eli Whitney's cotton gin, an invention that efficiently separated the seeds from the raw cotton fibre. The gin allowed a person to clean cotton 50 times more quickly than in the past. American cotton production increased enormously as a result, from 3,000 bales in 1790 to 178,000 in 1810, 732,000 in 1830, and 4,500,000 in 1860. But to be competitive, cotton production required cheap labour, and slave labour was half the price of wage labour. Each plantation required between 50 to 200 slaves, depending on the quality of the soil.

The British demand for American cotton was obviously not the cause of slavery, but it ensured its continuance in the United States into the second half of the 19th century. Between 1790 and 1860, 835,000 slaves were moved from Maryland, Virginia, and the Carolinas to Alabama, Louisiana, Mississippi, and Texas in one of the greatest forced migrations of all time. But this was not the only forced migration spurred by the world demand for cotton. Another was the forced removal in the 1830s of 125,000 Native Americans from their homes in Georgia, Alabama, and Mississippi to the Oklahoma Territory, along the route known as the Trail of Tears (see Figure 2.2).

The story of the forced removal of the Cherokee (and other Native American nations) in the United States does much to explain why some of the world's people enjoy greater wealth than others. The Cherokee had always been viewed as among the more "advanced" Native American groups—the early European settlers had counted them as one of the "civilized tribes" of North America. They were horticulturists, living in large, autonomous villages and, after the American Revolution, occupying large tracts of fertile land from North Carolina into Georgia. In 1802, to persuade the southeastern states to give up claims to territory in the west, President Thomas Jefferson instituted what became known as the Georgia Compact of 1802. The compact called for Georgia and the Carolinas to give up claims to western territories in exchange for land held by southeastern indigenous groups, including the Cherokee. The indigenous people fought the removal, embarking on a modernization

FIGURE 2.2 MAP OF THE TRAIL OF TEARS, ALSO KNOWN AS THE CHEROKEE REMOVAL

THE MEANING OF PROGRESS AND DEVELOPMENT

plan; within a decade the Cherokee had built plantations, were holding slaves, and had their own newspaper, schools, and alphabet. They were also among the soldiers under Andrew Jackson who attacked Canada in the War of 1812.

The Cherokee lobbied the U.S. Congress extensively to repeal the Georgia Compact, but to no avail. Andrew Jackson, who had made Indian removal one of the cornerstones of his presidential campaign in 1828, signed the final order, and the army was sent in to forcibly move the population as land speculators flooded onto what had been prosperous Cherokee farms and plantations. Thousands of additional acres of what had been Indian land were taken over or converted to cotton production by white farmers using black slaves. In this way, white farmers using Native American land and African labour to produce cotton for the British and American textile industries created much of the future wealth of the young country. The political economy of cotton production, slavery, and land alienation during this period of history laid the groundwork for ongoing systemic racism in North America, as we discuss in Chapter 6.

Progress for Whom?

To summarize, the growth of the British textile industry produced great wealth for some people; but in the process, it destroyed textile manufacturing in India, led to the colonization of India, escalated imports of opium into China, extended slavery in the United States while draining Africa of productive labour, and enhanced the wealth of the United States while driving indigenous people from their lands. In addition, the mass production of textiles in Britain and elsewhere in Europe destroyed textile manufacture by artisans in areas of the world where British textiles were sold; and since women were the main textile producers in many societies, we might also speculate that the textile trade led to a decline in the status of women in these societies.

We must also consider that Britain was not the only producer of textiles, nor was it the only country seeking to open and control overseas markets. France, Germany, the Netherlands, and (later) the United States also had thriving textile industries. We must remember, too, that the textile industry was only one among many in Western Europe that required raw materials and new markets. As a result of the growing European demand for sugar, cocoa, palm oil, tobacco, and coffee, millions of hectares around the world were converted from subsistence farming to cash crop farming. This turned self-sufficient peasant farmers into dependent wage-labourers or unemployed poor. Finally, remember that we have examined only a brief period of time. The high point of European colonial expansion came later than the events described here, in the last quarter of the 19th century and the first decades of the 20th. By looking at the bigger picture, we can begin to understand why the problems of the so-called non-industrial nations are due less to their own shortcomings than to the exploitative activities of others, and why a peasant farmer in India in 1400 was significantly better off economically than his Indian counterpart of 1960. In the next section, we explore the manifestations of this kind of economic "progress" on a global scale.

QUESTION 2.3: HOW DO GLOBALIZATION, ECONOMIC DEVELOPMENT, AND CULTURAL DIVERSITY RELATE TO ONE ANOTHER?

The Industrial Revolution radically transformed the lives of people in Western Europe and North America as the vast majority of the population went from being farmers to labourers. Usually, this was not a matter of choice: people began selling their labour not because wage labour offered a better life, but because they no longer possessed land on which to secure a livelihood.

Moreover, the availability of jobs was subject to the whims of the market and the rise and fall in the demand for products. As long as there was a demand for products, jobs were secure; when demand slackened, people were thrown out of work. The development of industry in the 19th century was marked by periodic downturns in economic growth and by economic depressions such as those of 1840 and 1873.

Overall, however, the rate of economic growth and technological advancement was astounding and resulted in a dramatic improvement in the standard of living of most people in Western countries. Nevertheless, many in the industrialized world did not enjoy increased wealth, and people in the Third World often saw their living standards decline as their countries fell under the influence of European powers.

As countries began to achieve independence from their colonial masters, national leaders promised to improve the lives of their people, and the leaders in the rich countries promised to help. Hence the push for what became known as "**economic development**." Yet as John Isbister, whom we cite in this chapter's epigraph, argues in *Promises Not Kept: Poverty and the Betrayal of Third World Development*, these promises were empty.

The ideology of economic development included the assumption that the world's nonindustrial countries were backward and needed to progress or develop, develop being largely a code word for "Westernize." Tania Li, an anthropologist at the University of Toronto, documented how a development project in Indonesia typically began: "First, it is necessary to identify a target group with a deficiency to be rectified ... Second, there needs to be an agency tasked with planning and executing the appropriate development fix" (1999b, 298).

There flourished in the West an unprecedented resolve to know everything about the Third World, which experienced a massive invasion of experts, all of whom were tasked with investigating, measuring, and theorizing about every aspect of Third World

societies. In *Encountering Development: The Making and Unmaking of the Third World*, Arturo Escobar suggests that:

> development fostered a way of conceiving of social life as a technical problem, as a matter of rational decision and management to be entrusted to that group of people—the development professionals—whose specialized knowledge allegedly qualified them for the task. Instead of seeing change as a process rooted in the interpretation of each society's history and cultural tradition ... these professionals sought to devise mechanisms and procedures to make societies fit a preexisting model that embodied the structures and functions of modernity. Like sorcerers' apprentices, the development professionals awakened once again the dream of reason that, in their hands, as in earlier instances, produced a troubling reality. (1995, 52)

Three key assumptions shaped the idea of economic development that emerged: (1) economic growth and development is the solution to national as well as global problems; (2) global economic integration will contribute to solving global ecological and social problems; and (3) foreign assistance to undeveloped countries will make things better. Thus, countries that wished to develop sought foreign loans and investments to create an industrial infrastructure—dams, power stations, ports, roads, and railways, and so on—as well as schools for training local people to operate

economic development
The term used to identify an increase in level of technology, and by some, standard of living of a population. Others view it as an ideology based on three key assumptions: (1) that economic growth and development is the solution to national as well as global problems; (2) that global economic integration will contribute to solving global ecological and social problems; and (3) that foreign assistance to undeveloped countries will make things better.

these. The loans, then, would allow undeveloped countries to produce export goods such as cotton, sugar, palm oil, tobacco, coffee, and cocoa (and other cash crops) and oil, metal ores, and lumber (and other natural resources). This theory of economic development was nothing new; what *was* different was the degree of apparent support that the wealthier nations were offering the poorer. One major Western institution that promoted economic development was the **World Bank**.

The World Bank was founded in 1944 in Bretton Woods, New Hampshire, at a meeting of the representatives of major industrial nations. At the time of this conference, the Allied powers were still at war with Germany and Japan (which, of course, were not invited). The task of those attending was to develop plans for the economic reconstruction of those countries that were being devastated by the war and to develop a postwar plan for worldwide economic and monetary stability. It was decided at Bretton Woods to establish the **International Monetary Fund** (IMF) and the International Bank for Reconstruction and Development (the World Bank). Funds for the bank were to be provided by member nations, largely in the form of loan guarantees. The bank would lend money to governments for specific projects—highways, dams, power plants, factories, and the like; those governments would agree to pay back the loans over a set period of time. The charter also specified that the loans must be made without regard for political or non-economic factors and that the bank must not interfere in the political affairs of any member or debtor nation.

The World Bank began operating in 1946, with the initial loans going to European countries. But soon the World Bank was making huge loans to countries such as Brazil, India, and Indonesia—loans that were supposed to transform their economies, generate wealth, and alleviate poverty. Many people have argued since that however benign their intentions, these loans only *increased* poverty in the Third World, besides leading to environmental devastation. How could this have happened?

The Case of Brazil

Brazil has been one of the major recipients of World Bank loans. In the 1960s the Brazilian government made a conscious decision to industrialize. Using loans from the World Bank and other Western lenders, along with money from private investors, Brazil built dams, roads, factories, and industries. It also modernized its agriculture, becoming a world leader in the export of crops such as soybeans. The economy surged, and Brazil became a model of modern industrialization: factories created jobs, and people flocked to the cities for employment as Brazil's cities began to rival any in the West.

But there was a downside: To repay its debts, Brazil needed to earn foreign income. Consequently, landowners were encouraged to expand their production of cash crops, especially those that could be sold in North America and Europe. Since the West already produced more than enough food (American farmers were being paid by the government not to grow food crops), Brazilian farmers turned to crops with other uses, such as soybeans, sisal, sugar, cocoa, and coffee. To grow more of these products required modern farming techniques and lots of land. Small farmers, forced off their land, had to find farm employment growing cash crops or migrate to the cities in search of jobs that, for the most part, did not exist. Moreover, those who found jobs on the large farms were not paid enough to purchase the food they had once grown themselves on their small plots. Brazil did increase

---

World Bank
One of the institutions created at the Bretton Woods, New Hampshire, meeting in 1944 of Allied nations. The World Bank (or the Bank for Reconstruction and Development) functions as a lending institution to nations largely for projects related to economic development.

International Monetary Fund
Formed in 1944 at the Bretton Woods Conference to regulate currency transactions among countries. The IMF now makes loans and regulates the economies of lending countries.

Between 2000 and 2009, over 150,000 square kilometres of Amazon rainforest was burned down to make room for cattle farms, soybean farms, and roads. That is an area larger than New Brunswick, Nova Scotia, and Prince Edward Island combined.

production of some food crops, notably beef, but because poor Brazilians could not pay as much for beef as relatively wealthy North Americans and Europeans could, most Brazilian beef was exported.

To make matters worse, in the mid-1980s Brazil and other debtor countries discovered that they could not keep up their payments to the World Bank and other Western financial institutions. To help these countries avoid default, the World Bank allowed them to renegotiate their loans. First, though, they had to agree to reduce their government spending—and typically, the targets for spending cuts were public education, welfare, housing, and health. These cutbacks resulted in still greater hardships for the poorest citizens.

In the wake of its program for economic development, Brazil has increased its total wealth. Some people have become very rich, but it is estimated that more than 40 percent of Brazilians are still living in poverty. And Brazil is not unique; most of Central and South America, Africa, and Southeast Asia followed the same formula for development, and most of these countries also experienced increased poverty and hunger for the majority of their people.

Economic development also brought environmental destruction. Between 1981 and 1983, the World Bank began delivering payments on a loan for Brazil to construct a road through the Amazon rain forest and to build new settlements. The economic goal of the Polonoroeste project was to open vast tracts of Amazon rain forest for settlement by displaced peasants, thereby transforming the forest into a cash producer. Nearly half a million settlers flooded into the area between 1981 and 1986. The government, however, was not prepared for that level of migration, and the new migrants were forced to burn forests to grow food to survive. But the poor soil of the rain forests would not support agriculture for more than a couple of years, and people ultimately were left with worthless land. The only activity that proved worthwhile was cattle ranching, and that required the burning of still more rain forest. The area of Rondônia went from 1.7 percent deforestation in 1978 to 16.1 percent in 1991. Furthermore, life-threatening diseases developed, rates of malaria approached 100 percent, and infant mortality rates of 25 to 50 percent were not uncommon. Indian land was pillaged, and epidemics ravaged the population. The pesticide DDT (banned in North America) was used in an attempt to eradicate the mosquitoes that spread malaria, and rural violence broke out between ranchers and rubber tappers.

Do Progress and Development Inevitably Lead to Inequality?

Whether the price of progress through industrialization must be increased poverty, hunger, and environmental devastation is, for many, an open question. Many argue that economic and industrial development takes time and that countries such as Brazil and India are now beginning to see a marked improvement in their economic situation. Some point to the so-called newly industrialized countries, such as Korea and Taiwan, as examples of what can be done. Yet the non-Western countries that have succeeded in emulating the West (and Japan is foremost among these) were never colonized by the West as were the poor countries of Africa and South America.

So, are the world's people better off now than they were before the Industrial Revolution? Obviously, the answer depends on who you are. If you are fortunate enough to be a labourer, businessperson, or professional in a wealthy country, you are likely to be materially better off than your counterpart of five centuries ago, provided that the price you pay in health risks because of a damaged environment does not offset your material gains. If you are a labourer or small farmer in one of the world's poor countries, it is hard to see how you could be better off than your peasant counterpart of centuries past. If you are among the world's landless, unemployed, or underemployed, or one of the billion without enough food, it is difficult to see how your life could be an improvement over that of your counterpart two centuries before.

Globalization and Cultural Diversity

Modern societies have not been kind to groups that have retained or tried to retain a way of life that is thousands of years old. Societies such as the Ju/'hoansi, the Inuit of the Canadian Arctic and Alaska, and the peoples of the New Guinea Highlands have not always fared well when contacted by more complex civilizations. Living in small, scattered groups with little need for complex political structures or technology, they have often been no match for the well-armed, organized, acquisitive people and governments who have coveted their land or labour.

The vulnerability of small, egalitarian cultures has increased in recent years, largely because of what is termed "globalization"—that is, the expansion into virtually all areas of the world of a culture that assumes that economic trade is the source of all well-being (we will discuss globalization in more detail in Chapter 7). For example, in their efforts to pay off debts accumulated over the past three decades, countries have been forced to export goods and commodities to gain cash to repay these debts. Support for small-scale agriculturists or peasant farmers has

been reduced as a result. When Mexico signed the North American Free Trade Agreement (NAFTA) with the United States and Canada, it precipitated a revolt in the State of Chiapas by peasant farmers (the Zapatistas) whose livelihood would be destroyed by the agreement. NAFTA's terms compelled Mexico to allow large-scale corn farmers in the United States to sell their product in Mexico at a price lower than what the peasants could meet. Small Mexican farmers might still have been able to compete except that the Mexican government nullified a portion of the national constitution that gave peasant farmers access to land on which to grow their crops. Also, Mexico's large-scale cattle ranchers needed more land to produce beef to sell to American consumers. As anthropologist James D. Nations pointed out, peasant farmers in Chiapas were faced with a choice of moving to a city to sell Popsicles from a pushcart, working for a cattleman punching cows, or rebelling against a situation that seemed to have them trapped.

Often the same economic forces that are undermining traditional cultures are also promoting environmental destruction. A case in point is that of the Guaraní of Paraguay. There are about 15,000 Guaraní. For centuries their lives centred on the rain forest, where they gathered tree crops, grew food crops, raised animals, and hunted and fished. The first European governor of the area described them in 1541 as "the richest people of all the land and province both for agriculture and stock raising." They quickly entered into trade with Europeans, mostly by gathering and selling a caffeine-bearing plant called *yerba mate*. These trade arrangements did not greatly affect Guaraní life, since they would gather and sell *yerba mate* only when they needed some Western trade item, such as a metal pot. Consequently, Guaraní culture was able to sustain itself and thrive. Just as important, the Guaraní exploited the rain forest in sustainable ways by adapting to it rather than trying to change it. Then in the 1970s, due largely to international trade arrangements, both the Guaraní and the rain forest began to decline.

In the 1970s, Paraguay, like most developing countries, enjoyed an economic boom fuelled largely by loans from the World Bank and other international lenders. Increasing production of crops such as soybeans, wheat, and cotton also fuelled the boom. The "economic miracle" was accomplished by bringing more land under cultivation; this, however, involved cutting down forests, selling the timber, and converting the cleared land into farmland or pasture. The rate of rain forest destruction accelerated rapidly. Between 1970 and 1976, Paraguayan rain forests were reduced from 6.8 to 4.2 million hectares. The country had cleared half its rain forest cut by 1984, and an additional 5 percent a year is being cut. At this rate, the entire Paraguayan rain forest will be gone by 2020.

Guaraní culture has been one more casualty of "economic development." This group's livelihood has been destroyed, and new roads through the rain forest have brought with them thousands of new settlers eager to stake claims to some portion of the forest, clear it of trees, and grow cash crops. Unfortunately, rain forest soil quickly loses its nutrients once the forest canopy that protected it has been destroyed. Furthermore, all the animals and plants that the Guaraní once depended on have been decimated. As a result, they have been displaced to squatter settlements in towns and cities or along the roads that have been built through the rain forests. The wages they can make working for farmers or in other odd jobs are inadequate to support families; illness and disease have increased; and suicide rates in the past ten years have more than tripled.

Finding Hope in the Face of Cultural Devastation

The experiences of peoples such as the Guaraní raise an important question: What does it mean to experience cultural devastation? This question is important, not only for what it tells us about the experiences of other people, but also for how we understand what culture is and what culture change can mean. Clearly, all cultures are vulnerable. People's views of the world, what they count as important, what they value, and what the good life means to them are all subject to sudden upheaval.

One of the best examples is what has happened to indigenous peoples of the Americas. When Columbus arrived in the "New World," there were hundreds of thriving societies. These were quickly devastated by European diseases, which wiped out nearly 90 percent of the population. That devastation continued well into the 19th century as the remnants of these people struggled to adapt to the westward expansion of settlers. However, it is important to note that adaptation is not the only possibility, nor is what counts as "adaptation" particularly straightforward, especially if we recognize that it has generally been the colonizers who have defined the terms of engagement. Dawn Martin-Hill's work with the Lubicon Cree of Alberta provides an instructive example of what it means to go from being an independent hunting society to one struggling for recognition, self-determination, and cultural survival within the Canadian nation-state.

For centuries, the Lubicon Cree have lived, hunted, and trapped within a 110 kilometre radius of Lubicon Lake in northern Alberta. Because of their relative isolation, the Lubicon avoided much contact with white settlers until the end of the 19th century. Then in 1899, Lubicon elders, wanting to secure their territory against the encroachment they saw happening elsewhere, approached the Canadian government about signing a treaty. However, the treaty failed to materialize over the following years. In 1939, the Lubicon were finally recognized as a band under federal law and the groundwork was laid for establishing a reserve of 65 square kilometres. However, the Second World War created a shortage of surveyors, and the required survey never happened. The Lubicon population was decimated by illness in the first half of the 20th century, and in 1942, many remaining Lubicon were removed from the band registry by the Department of Indian Affairs. As a result of that, they were deemed too small a population to warrant a treaty or a reserve (Martin-Hill 2004, 315–16).

The Lubicon elders decided that their young people should learn English in order to pursue their

proposed Lubicon reserve

unceded Lubicon territory

Lubicon Lake

Peace River

Fort McMurray

ALBERTA

Edmonton ✪

Red Deer

Calgary

Medicine Hat

land claims. One of these youth, Walter Whitehead, was elected chief in the early 1970s and began to lay the legal groundwork for the land claim. Unfortunately, he was doing so at the same time that oil exploration was beginning in northern Alberta. Since then, the Lubicon Cree have been embroiled in an unsettled land claim. Meanwhile, oil and gas corporations have been extracting resources from land that the Lubicon have never legally relinquished, all the while contaminating it. In their struggle for recognition, the Lubicon must walk a fine line between trying to work within the Canadian legal system on the one hand, and maintaining their own indigenous knowledge on the other.

As Martin-Hill points out, "from the West's perspective, Indigenous peoples [like the Lubicon] are always standing in the way of progress, development, and civilization" (2008, 153). She also points to the Lubicon's determination to reach a fair

deal with the Canadian government; their resolve "is rooted in their firm belief that good always overcomes bad" (158). They are using their own indigenous knowledge to their advantage (as best they can under the circumstances), "restructuring their damaged traditional system by recreating a modern anti-colonial community" (159). Martin-Hill recounts a conversation, excerpted here, with Albert Laboucon, a Lubicon elder, who explained the transformative possibilities of such a community:

> I met Albert Laboucon [a Cree-speaker in his 70s] during my second trip to Little Buffalo in December 1989 … I asked Albert to tell me about himself, and for his thoughts on the land claim. His answers were short and often direct.

"I was raised in the bush, trapping, hunting, a hard life but a good one. There has been much change. No more animals, no wildlife, everything is disappearing, our ways are. They came in the road and destroyed everything in their path. They cut right through trap lines, right through everything. Everything is dirty, water and animals are not so clean. I want the children, the grandchildren, to have something, that's why I stay with it. I think they are trying to wipe us out. I never thought that really before—to wipe us out … just to get us out of the way. They are greedy, greed like we don't know. There is nothing for me, just doing this for my grandchildren now … This has been going on a long time, since I was young. I thought it would all be okay; we would get our reserve, no big deal. They seem to want to wipe us out instead, don't know why. I think they have money, no word for the money they have. We don't want much … A lot they do doesn't make sense, destroying the land, water, air. No matter, they think they're above all this—they're not. They're needing air, water, food, and they can't see what will happen to us will happen to them too. They don't think about their children either. What will these young ones have to drink if all the water no good? Maybe if we keep hollering they will hear us, if we keep making enough noise. It's good that other Indians like you [Martin-Hill is

Mohawk] come here and help. We need to help one another the way the Creator intended. I feel better when there are other Indians helping."

I asked Albert to tell me what he wanted me to take back to my people, what to tell them from him. He sat quietly for a long time and then said in Cree, "We should put our voices together, our drum, it will be heard across the country." (117–18)*

Albert Laboucon's drumming inspired the Drum Beat Conference, first hosted by McMaster University and the Six Nations community in 1989, which hosted indigenous people from all over North America and was aimed at raising awareness of First Nations issues. The conference laid the groundwork for the creation of the Indigenous Studies Program at McMaster.

The dilemma of peasant farmers, the Guaraní, and the Lubicon is shared by thousands of other societies and groups around the world. Equally involved in the dilemma are the so-called civilized societies that are responsible for driving small-scale societies to the edge of culutural devastation or forcing them to experience development through its dark side of poverty, disease, and forced labour. If we conclude that "progress" from simple foraging societies to modern industrial states is all positive, we may be short-changing ourselves. By systematically destroying small-scale societies, we may be eliminating systems of meaning that hold solutions to compelling world problems such as environmental destruction, intergroup and intragroup conflict, poverty, and sickness.

EXERCISE 2.2

It is 1967. You are members of a task force that the Botswana government has convened to evaluate the living conditions of the Ju/'hoansi. Another group of government officials, distressed over the foraging ways of the Ju/'hoansi, had recommended that they begin to enjoy the benefits of modern technology. Specifically, the group recommended that the government settle the Ju/'hoansi in permanent villages, dig wells to ensure a steady water supply, distribute domesticated animals to ensure a ready food supply, and introduce modern health services. The group had also recommended that jobs be found for the Ju/'hoansi.

You have toured the area and spoken to some of the Ju/'hoansi. Your specific task is to evaluate the recommendations of the previous government task force and make your own recommendations to the government on how the lives of the Ju/'hoansi could be improved. You may agree or disagree with the previous panel, but you must give reasons for your recommendations.

QUESTION 2.4: HAVE PROGRESS AND DEVELOPMENT IMPROVED HUMAN HEALTH?

Illness and Inequality

Even if the economic changes of the past two centuries have not improved many people's lives, can't we at least assume that *some* technologies—notably medical technologies—have done so? To answer this question, we need to consider two things: first, whether we have progressed in our ability to treat disease (using the **biomedical model**); and second, whether we fully understand

---

biomedical model
A term, also known as Western medicine, scientific medicine, or modern medicine, that combines biology with the diagnosis and treatment of illness and that views the body as a machine, independent of social context, that must be repaired periodically.

---

* Source: From *The Lubicon Lake Nation: Indigenous Knowledge and Power*, by Dawn Martin-Hill, © University of Toronto Press, 2008. pp. 117–118. Reprinted with permission of the publisher.

the traditional medical techniques that modern medicine has sought to replace.

One of the supposed triumphs of modern society has been the treatment and cure of disease. Life expectancy has more than doubled in the 20th century. In 1900, world life expectancy was around 30 years; by 2000, it was 63 years. Antibiotics save millions of people from death each year, and modern diagnostic methods and equipment allow medical practitioners to identify the onset of disease more easily. Yet the progress we often take for granted is not available to all. In fact, the single most important determinant of a country's ability to protect its citizens from disease is the degree of economic equality.

In developing countries, infectious disease is responsible for 42 percent of all deaths, compared to just 1.2 percent in industrial countries. Around the world, 40 percent of all deaths are caused by environmental factors, including organic and chemical pollutants. These pollutants are far more deadly in poorer countries, where, for example, 1.2 billion people lack clean, safe water. However, the same contaminants can affect people in wealthy countries such as Canada. On Walpole Island in the St. Clair River, toxins from 52 industrial sources have been found in fish, ducks, and various animals that share the island with the 3,100 people of the Walpole First Nation. This is in addition to a "toxic blob" that was discovered in 1985 (VanWynsberghe 2002). Thus, your income and dwelling place determine your chances of coming into contact with a deadly pollutant. The industrialized countries already ship 20 million tons of waste annually to the world's poorer countries.

We can, perhaps, better judge the extent to which we have "progressed" by examining what it takes for us to die of an infectious disease. At least four things have to happen. First, we have to come into contact with some **pathogen** or **vector** that carries a disease. Second, the pathogen must be virulent— that is, it must be able to kill us. Third, if we come into contact with a deadly pathogen, it must evade our body's immune system. Finally, the pathogen

must be able to circumvent whatever measures our society has developed to prevent it from doing harm. As we will see, our chances of dying are affected at every step by social and cultural patterns, particularly by the degree of economic and social inequality.

Cultural complexity has increased our exposure to infectious agents. Large, permanent settlements attract and sustain vermin such as rats and fleas, which serve as hosts for microorganisms and ensure their survival and spread. Permanent settlements also result in the buildup of human wastes. Sedentary agriculture requires altering the landscape in ways that can increase the incidence of disease. Schistosomiasis, for example, is a disease caused by worms and snails, which thrive in irrigation ditches. The domestication of animals such as dogs, cats, cattle, and pigs increases contact between people and disease-causing microorganisms. Large populations must store and process their food, and this also increases the likelihood that disease-causing agents will survive and spread.

Coming into contact with an infectious pathogen is not in itself enough for death to ensue: the pathogen must be deadly. But this, too, depends on your social and cultural situation, including your income. Generally it is not to the advantage of pathogens—viruses, bacteria, parasites—to kill their hosts; pathogens find it advantageous to allow their hosts to live and supply nutrients. However, if the pathogen does not need its host in order to survive, it can evolve into a more deadly form. This is the case with waterborne infections. Pathogens that spread by contaminated water can survive regardless of how sick their host becomes, and by reproducing extensively in their host, they make it more likely that they can contaminate water supplies—for example,

---

pathogen
An infectious agent such as a bacteria or a virus that can cause disease.

vector
An organism, such as a mosquito, tick, flea, or snail, that can transmit disease to another animal.

through bodily wastes. All of this means that you are far more likely to contract a deadly disease if you do not have access to clean and treated water.

Even if you come into contact with a deadly pathogen, your immune system is designed to prevent it from killing you. However, the strength of your immune system is clearly a function of diet, and diet is determined largely by income level. In this respect, we have not progressed. In 1950, 20 percent of the world's people (500 million) were malnourished. Today some 50 percent (3 billion) are malnourished. Insufficient food is one of the principal causes of immune system failure.

Finally, societies have developed methods to cure illnesses that our immune systems have failed to ward off. There is little doubt that the discovery of cures for infectious diseases is one of the great success stories of modern culture. Unfortunately, access to these cures is determined largely by individual wealth. This suggests why the United States, the wealthiest country in the world overall, ranks 38th in the world in life expectancy. It is no coincidence that the United States has the largest income gap between rich and poor of any industrialized country. Japan, which has the lowest gap between rich and poor, also has the highest life expectancy, even though Japanese are three times heavier smokers than Americans.

In sum, although we have indeed made dramatic progress in understanding and curing infectious disease, we have made no progress—and indeed have gone backwards—in terms of our ability to provide access to these cures. At the same time, we have increased global exposure to environmental pollutants and infectious pathogens.

The Meaning of Illness

Even if we conclude that modern societies are more susceptible to contagious diseases, have they not at least improved their technologies for curing illness? In answering this question, it is important to grasp that the meanings members of different societies give to illness vary as much as the meanings they give to other aspects of their lives. In North American society, illness is viewed as an intrusion by bacteria or viruses. Our curing techniques emphasize eliminating those agents. Death can occur, we believe, when we have failed to do so.

In many other societies, interpretations of illness are completely different. Illness may be attributed to witchcraft—that is, a witch or sorcerer has used magic to inflict illness on another person. Or it may be attributed to soul loss—that is, the soul has left the body. Or it may be understood as being about one's connection to the land, as is the case with the Whapmagoostui Cree (discussed in Chapter 1). Or it may be attributed to spirit possession, the idea that a foreign spirit has entered the patient. These explanations are not mutually exclusive; for example, the soul may flee the body as the result of witchcraft or sorcery.

Those who believe that illness has spiritual or magical causes do not believe that a witch or sorcerer strikes at random, that the soul leaves the body without cause, or that a spirit will possess just anyone. Rather, they believe there must be a social reason for these things to occur. Witchcraft involves relationships between people: the witch voluntarily or involuntarily afflicts someone who has caused offence or who has breached a rule of conduct. Likewise, the soul leaves the body of a person who is having difficulty with others, or a spirit possesses a person who has not honoured social obligations.

The Chewa of Malawi in southeastern Africa contend that illness and death are induced by witchcraft when someone fails to observe some social norm. Whereas Americans react to illness or death by seeking the disease or accident responsible, the Chewa ask what wrong the victim has committed, with whom the victim has quarrelled, or who is jealous of the victim. The Chewa explicitly recognize the connection between sorcery and social tension.

A Chewa who becomes ill consults a diviner to discover the cause of the illness. During the consultation, the patient and the diviner discuss

In a healing ceremony designed to restore the patient to his proper place in the world, a traditional Navajo doctor paints an image of the universe with coloured sand on an earthen floor.

© Paul Chesley/Getty

the social roots of the illness. The diviner needs to know about the patient's relationships with kin and, if ancestral spirits may be responsible, the genealogy of the patient. Thus, Chewa medical theory, although couched in the idiom of sorcery, is a social theory of illness, not simply a supernatural one.

There is a condition in Latin America called *susto* (also known as *pasmo*, *espanto*, or *perdida de la somba*) that is believed to occur when the soul has detached itself from the body. Symptoms of *susto* include restlessness, listlessness, loss of appetite, disinterest in dress or bodily appearance, loss of strength, and introversion. The onset of the illness is said to follow a fright brought on by a sudden encounter or accident, and the cure begins with a diagnostic session between the patient and a healer. After deciding what brought on the disorder, the healer coaxes the soul back into the body. The patient is then sweated, massaged, and rubbed with some object to remove the illness.

Anthropologist Arthur Rubel analyzed specific cases of *susto* and found that all cases share two characteristics. *Susto* occurs only when the patient perceives some situation as stressful and when the stress has been the result of difficulties in social

relations with specific people. In one case, a father was afflicted when he discovered he could no longer provide for his family. In another, a mother was stricken when she was not able to take proper care of her child. In every case, according to Rubel, *susto* resulted when a person did not or could not fulfill an expected social obligation.

These theories of illness—soul loss, spirit possession, sorcery, and witchcraft—have one thing in common: all are expressions of the **interpersonal theory of disease**. Simply stated, in the interpersonal theory of disease it is assumed that illness is caused not by microorganisms but rather by tensions or conflicts in social relations. In this view, witches, spirits, and souls are mediating agents that link a social cause—tension and conflict—to a physical result—illness or death.

If an illness has social causes, then the cure too must be at least partly social. Therefore, a curer attempts not only to remove a spell, return the soul to the body, or remove a spiritual object that is causing illness, but also to repair the social problem. To illustrate, Victor Turner provides a look at one society, the Ndembu, an agricultural society in northwestern Zambia.

The Ndembu believe that a persistent or severe illness is caused either by the punitive action of some ancestral ghost or by the secret malevolence of a sorcerer or witch. The ghosts punish people when they forget to make a ritual offering to their ancestors or when, as the Ndembu put it, "kin are not living well together."

To effect a cure, the Ndembu patient consults a native doctor. The doctor first inquires about the patient's social relations: Has he or she quarrelled with anyone? What is the state of the patient's marital relations? Is anyone jealous of the patient? The doctor asks those with whom the patient has quarrelled to participate in the ceremony, which

> **interpersonal theory of disease**
> A view of disease in which it is assumed that illness is caused by tensions or conflicts in social relations.

is a dramatic affair with chanting and drumming, sometimes lasting for hours. People who have complaints about the patient's social behaviour may come forward, and the patient may report grudges against neighbours. At the climax, the doctor may dramatically extract from the patient's body some object that could have been causing the illness.

The Ndembu recognize, at least implicitly, that social strain and stress may produce physical illness and that one way to treat illness is to treat the sources of social strain. Western medicine also recognizes the negative health effects that stress can have. Events such as the death of a spouse, the loss of a job, relocation to a new home, or even holidays such as Christmas, can increase the chances of illness. These are the same kinds of events that can trigger the need for ceremonial cures in some societies. Thus, rather than viewing the healing practices of traditional societies as inferior, it makes far more sense to recognize that they focus on social stress as a cause of illness.

Furthermore, ethnomedical cures not only can be beneficial but also are affordable. One consequence of biomedical advances is increasing dependence on expensive technology. Consequently, while significant advances have been made in medicine, the cost to patients of many such advances has made them unavailable to all but a small percentage of the world's population. Finally, in societies where healing is everyone's responsibility instead of a commodity to be purchased, it follows the moral values of a social obligation rather than those of business.

EXERCISE 2.3

Can you think of any illnesses that we are familiar with in North America that are currently diagnosed and treated according to the biomedical model, but that might also be explained using the interpersonal theory of disease? How might we treat these illnesses from this perspective?

QUESTION 2.5: HOW CAN WE APPLY A CRITICAL ANTHROPOLOGICAL UNDERSTANDING OF PROGRESS AND DEVELOPMENT OUTSIDE OF ACADEMIA?

As we have seen, efforts by countries such as Brazil to "progress" and modernize have often undermined the lives of indigenous peoples as well as the lives of craftspeople and small farmers. The idea of progress clearly contains some ethnocentric assumptions about what constitutes the "good life." Very often, the idea of "development" simply means the export of Western culture to sometimes willing but often unwilling recipients. That does not mean, however, that efforts should not be made to address economic, social, and human rights problems. In some parts of Brazil, the mortality rate for children under five years is 116 per 1,000; among the wealthiest portion of the population it is 11 per 1,000. Around the world, 24,000 people die every day from hunger or hunger-related causes. Many women around the world have little or no access to education or job opportunities, yet they are responsible for the health and livelihood of their children. In Canada, the 2006 Census found that First Nations peoples who had been forced onto reserves faced unemployment rates of 18 percent, almost triple the national rate. That same year, only 8 percent of First Nations peoples had a university degree, compared to 23 percent of other Canadians, and 40 percent of First Nations peoples over 15 did not have a high school diploma. According to the Indian Affairs ministry, life expectancy among First Nations men is seven years less than for the general male population; for women, the difference is five years. Also, suicide rates are eight times higher for First Nations women and five times higher for First Nations men. The infant mortality rate is 11 per 1,000 live births among First Nations peoples, compared to 6 per thousand for all Canadians. These and other problems need to be addressed by those with the power and money to do so; in the case of First Nations peoples, addressing these problems is a matter of ensuring full and equal citizenship for all Canadians.

Governments, international organizations such as the World Bank, the United Nations, U.S. AID (the official U.S. aid agency), and the Canadian International Development Agency (CIDA), along with nongovernmental organizations (NGOs) such as Oxfam, Amnesty International, and Doctors Without Border/Médecins sans Frontières (MSF), recognize that anthropological perspectives are vital to addressing these problems, and this has created career opportunities for professional anthropologists as well as for people with a background in anthropology. Anthropologists bring cultural expertise to the table, and their critical and ethnographically grounded understanding of what constitutes "progress" (and what does not) can be crucial to ensuring that development initiatives are culturally appropriate.

Anthropologists in Development

The failure of development professionals to understand the cultures and values of the people they are trying to help has had disastrous consequences in the past. The Mackenzie Delta in the western Canadian Arctic has been the home of Inuit, Métis, and Dene peoples for centuries. After the Second World War the Canadian government wanted to develop the area in order to extract oil, gas, and mineral reserves. The government also wanted to prepare indigenous peoples for "modern" life through schooling and wage labour. Planning, however, was top-down, with little or no participation from the people themselves.

The centrepiece of the modernization plan was the construction of a large-scale "science town"

called Inuvik, which was to house a school, a commercial and service centre, and a hospital. The government planners encouraged the establishment of various businesses in the town, including oil companies, hotels, and restaurants.

As Alexander M. Ervin describes it, the town had a profoundly negative impact on the people of the Mackenzie Delta. Of 5,000 inhabitants, only 150 lived off the land. Half the population were "southerners"—transient workers from southern Canada who were paid generous salaries and allowances to encourage them to resettle, if only for a short time, in the Arctic. Few of the indigenous people were employed after the initial building phase, and they were overwhelmed by the social and economic advantages of the southerners. Southerners rarely interacted with the local people, and relations became hostile. School curricula, instead of being designed for

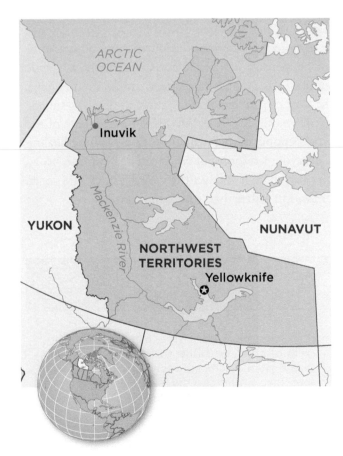

A failure of development professionals to understand the cultures and values of people has had disastrous consequences in the past. A good example is the construction of the town of Inuvik in the Canadian Arctic.

northern youth, were modelled after programs in southern urban schools. This led to high dropout rates, and the alienation of young people was marked by a dramatic increase in petty crimes and assaults. Native women who had children with transient whites were stigmatized, and conflicts arose between families with steady incomes and those who depended on government subsidies. All of this stress was evident in high rates of alcohol consumption and of crimes such as assault, theft, and wife battering, all associated with alcohol. Clearly, the government's optimism that the new town would better the lives of the local people was misplaced.

So what went wrong? There was no consultation with the indigenous people regarding the changes. The entire project had been planned and implemented by outsiders who had pre-existing notions about what would be good for indigenous people. Nobody considered the complex interactions among family structure, cultural values, economics, education, and new residents. No one attempted to integrate local knowledge into the planning process. Furthermore, no one considered the unintended consequences of the changes.

Contrast this with an agricultural project designed by anthropologist Ronald Nigh in Mexico. Like other Central American nations, Mexico has lost vast amounts of its rain forest—more than 100,000 square kilometres since the beginning of the 20th century. Much of the deforested land has been taken over by animal pastures, yet more than half of Mexico's population never consumes animal products. According to Nigh, the destruction of the rain forest was the result of the **factory model** of agriculture, which involves producing a single product in as short a time as possible. This form of agriculture is technologically intensive and environmentally damaging. In Central America, the factory model of cattle raising has required that large tracts of land be cleared with fire and herbicides and then reseeded with grasses that are not well suited to the environment. The result has been degradation of the land by uncontrolled grazing and its eventual abandonment and return to secondary vegetation.

> **factory model**
> An energy-intensive, ecologically damaging form of agriculture intended to grow or raise as many crops or livestock as possible in the shortest amount of time.

THE MEANING OF PROGRESS AND DEVELOPMENT

An agroecological approach produced multiple crops, enhancing the regeneration of land, flora, and fauna.

In his work, Nigh uses an **agroecological approach** that incorporates indigenous farming techniques, which are far more productive and less damaging to the environment than factory farming. An agroecological approach produces multiple crops and animals, rather than a single crop as in the factory model. This approach to production creates a system that helps regenerate land, flora, and fauna.

As an example, consider how the Maya grow corn in the rain forest. The farmers practise swidden agriculture, clearing a site, growing corn there for five to eight years, and then moving on to another site. At first glance, these sites may look identical to land that has been devastated and abandoned by cattle ranchers, but Mayan farmers do not abandon those sites. They continue to work the land so that native plant and animal life will return, eventually creating a highly productive space. The agroecological model, drawing as it does from indigenous systems developed over centuries, creates an ecologically sustainable system of production modelled after natural systems.

Nigh says that a similar model, emphasizing diversity, should be used to rehabilitate lands damaged by cattle grazing. One area of the land would be used for annual crops, such as corn or squash. Another can be used for fruit trees and forage. Yet another can be devoted to intensive

agroecological approaches
Agricultural methods that incorporate indigenous practices of food production along with contemporary agricultural research yet preserve the environment.

EXERCISE 2.4

As an anthropologist, you have been asked to evaluate the mistakes that were made in the modernization of Inuvik. What are some key questions you would want to ask residents of the town? Which residents would you talk with? What specific questions might you ask women in the town? What recommendations would you make to remedy the problems created by the development project?

grazing using selected animal breeds and grasses. Intensive grazing, according to Nigh, frees up rain forest land that should never have been converted to pasture to begin with. He also maintains that by using organic fertilizers and controlled grazing, it is possible to recover aquatic areas and take advantage of water resources such as fish, mollusks, turtles, and birds.

Development projects might begin with good intentions, but they can quickly devolve into ethnocentric, socially damaging institutions. How, then, can development projects provide benefits to everyone involved? As the examples show, an anthropological perspective that carefully considers the cultures and values of indigenous people will go a long way to ease the potential pains of development.

CONCLUSIONS

We began this chapter by noting that over the past 10,000 years, human societies have shifted away from a way of life that had survived for some 100,000 years. Why did so many societies begin to change from nomadic foraging to sedentary agriculture? Some anthropologists, such as Lewis Henry Morgan and Leslie White, have suggested that the need to progress and develop better ways of living might explain the change. However, studies of forager societies reveal that they live quite comfortably and with a minimum amount of effort. Indeed, Marshall Sahlins referred to the foraging way of life as "the original affluent society," characterized by minimal work coupled with ample leisure time.

If we reject the straightforward narrative of progress, how are we to explain the transformation of human societies over the past 10,000 years? It is possible that an increase in population or population density fuelled the transition of societies from foraging to swidden agriculture and then to plough or irrigation agriculture. But although the transition to more labour-intensive forms of agriculture may have been the result of population pressure, other anthropologists have argued that newer forms of agricultural technology may be simply better or more efficient. However, John Bodley's analysis of the energy expenditures of modern agriculture suggests that it is difficult to conclude that it is in fact simply better.

Explanations that equate culture change with progress have influenced the trajectory of global economic development. These explanations, though, fall short when we try to understand the gap between the wealthy and poor nations of the world. We find that we must consider the history of the economic expansion of Europe, as well as the military, political, and social exploitation of the countries of Asia, Africa, and the Americas. We find that hunger is not so much due to a lack of modern agriculture; rather, it is a consequence of poverty and attempts to industrialize. The need to repay bank loans secured for industrialization has led countries such as Brazil to encourage the development of large farms that grow mainly cash crops for export. As a result, people are dispossessed of their land and left without enough money to buy food.

For many small-scale societies, global economic development has led to cultural devastation at the hands of "civilized" countries. This power dynamic is also evident in the colonial history of Canada as a nation-state. The Lubicon Cree, for instance experience cultural devastation at the hands of the Canadian government, and their land claims remain unsettled in part because these claims are seen as "getting in the way of progress." Unfortunately, notions of progress may simply be a convenient rationale for one society to impose its economic and political will on others. Perhaps when we talk about culture change in terms of progress, we should remember to ask: Progress for whom?

In the last two sections of the chapter, we explored the implications of an anthropological understanding of progress for thinking critically and cross-culturally about health, illness, and development. It may seem self-evident that Western standards of health care are higher than those of less developed societies. Researchers have concluded, however, that infectious diseases are more common in industrialized societies and that human behaviours associated with industrialization, modernization, and the unequal distribution of wealth often promote the incidence and spread of contagious disease. Moreover, traditional theories of illness and curing ceremonies can be effective in the diagnosis and treatment of illness or disease. Finally, we examined how an anthropological perspective can aid in planning development projects, and how knowledge of local concerns, the use of local knowledge, and the involvement of segments of the population who are sometimes ignored can mean the difference between helping people or disrupting their lives.

1. In Chapter 1, we discussed the methodological concept of cultural relativism. How might you apply the idea of cultural relativism to the twin concepts of progress and development?
2. Western environmental activists often point to indigenous cultures and modes of livelihood as examples of a more environmentally friendly way to live. What are the possible advantages and disadvantages of this approach, both from the perspective of the environmentalists and from that of the indigenous groups to whom they refer?
3. Given what you have learned about how population, urbanization, agriculture, and technology relate to one another, what predictions might you make about future modes of livelihood and food production?

KEY TERMS:

agroecological approaches   (p. 72)
bands   (p. 43)
biomedical model   (p. 65)
clans   (p. 43)
culture change   (p. 43)
economic development   (p. 59)
factory model   (p. 71)
factory system   (p. 53)
Industrial Revolution   (p. 52)
International Monetary Fund   (p. 60)
interpersonal theory of disease   (p. 68)
irrigation agriculture   (p. 43)
pathogen   (p. 66)
population density   (p. 48)
progress   (p. 42)
"putting out" system   (p. 53)
sedentary   (p. 42)
slash–and–burn (or swidden) agriculture   (p. 43)
state   (p. 43)
vector   (p. 66)
World Bank   (p. 60)

THE SOCIAL AND CULTURAL CONSTRUCTION OF REALITY

Dene artist Alex Janvier's painting, *Morning Star*, as described on the website of the Canadian Museum of Civilization, reflects many common Aboriginal beliefs and values. "Human life, for example, is believed to make a complete circle; a person dies and then life starts again." The Jesuit priest cited in the epigraph would have been incredulous about the spiritual beliefs to which Janvier refers. The difficulties inherent in understanding and respecting others' belief systems is one of the issues we explore in this chapter.

It is amusing to hear them speak of their souls.... They think of the soul as divisible, and you would have all the difficulty in the world to make them believe that our soul is entire in all parts of the body.... God of truth, what ignorance and stupidity!

Jesuit reaction to Amerindian beliefs about life after death

PROBLEM 3

Why do people believe different things, and why are they so certain that their view of the world is correct and that other views are wrong?

INTRODUCTION

The Central Question

How is it that people can believe in a God whose existence cannot be proven? How can they believe in the existence of ancestor spirits, or witches, or devils, or believe in the power of magic to call forth spirits of the dead? Although there is no material proof, people do believe these things, and even take these beliefs for granted. Many North Americans, for example, believe in the existence of God, and some firmly believe in the existence of Satan and the possibility of demonic possession. Such beliefs need not be tied to religion. For example, many North Americans daily consult their horoscope, believing that the position of the stars at their birth somehow affects their destiny.

How to deal with the question of belief has long been a concern of anthropologists. Early anthropological studies of religion sought to explain how people could believe in things that seemed illogical, such as witchcraft. Edward Tylor, considered by some to be the founder of modern anthropology, wrote in *Primitive Culture* (1870) that religion and a belief in the supernatural developed through people's efforts to explain basic phenomena, such as death and dreaming. Tylor imagined early human beings thinking, "What is the difference between a live person and a dead one, between a sleeping person and someone who is awake?" They must have reasoned that there was something, some kind of essence, that left the body at the moment of death or that travelled to distant places in sleep's dreams. According to Tylor, from this reasoning came a belief in the idea of a soul that animated the body but that fled the body in death and sleep. In his view, this was why the word for "breath" and the word for "soul" are the same or similar in so many languages. And it was not unreasonable, said Tylor, for these early philosophers to imagine that other animals and things were animated by souls as well.

Once people arrived at a belief in souls, it was a small step to reason that there were places where departed souls resided and an even smaller step to believe that souls became gods. And it was logical, then, for human beings to appeal to these departed spirits for help in controlling life's uncertainties. For Tylor, then, beliefs in gods and spirits developed through the attempts of human beings to explain certain events, to understand why things happened as they did.

In his classic work *The Elementary Forms of the Religious Life* (1912), French sociologist Emile Durkheim also asked what led to the concept of God. Durkheim, like Tylor, speculated that the secret must lie in the beliefs of early human beings. Durkheim thought that the lives of early human beings could best be studied by looking at societies that were considered simple or underdeveloped. He decided to read about the religious beliefs of the indigenous people of Australia, particularly their beliefs about **totemism**. The totem, said Durkheim, was some element of nature—an animal, an insect, a plant, or some celestial phenomenon—that served as a symbol for a group or clan. The totem was worshipped and was considered sacred and holy by the members of the group. It also served as a concrete representation of the group. If members of the group worshipped the totem and if the totem was a symbol of the group, was it unreasonable to suppose, asked Durkheim, that the group—the clan itself—was the object of worship?

However, what would suggest to people that the totem had sacred power? The answer, said Durkheim, lay in the constraints that people feel are imposed on them by the group and by society and in the special power that people feel when groups come together in celebration and **ritual**. And if in small-scale societies people worship the group through their symbolic representations, as clans worship themselves through their totems, is it not reasonable to suppose that in large-scale societies people worship society through their god or gods? That God is society?

Early anthropologists approached the question of God in particular, and religion in general, with the assumption that such beliefs were essentially in error. Nevertheless, they believed that religious beliefs served some purpose: the beliefs and rituals may have increased group cohesion or provided supernatural sanctions for the violation of group norms.

Recent anthropological attempts to understand belief have built on these early efforts, but as Michael Lambek argues:

> *If many of the nineteenth-century thinkers saw members of smaller-scale societies mired in superstition, ignorance, bliss, or folly, the personal connections forged in decent ethnographic fieldwork immediately deprived westerners of any illusions of intellectual or moral superiority … Theorists began to realize that rather than compare nonwestern systems of thought directly to western science, it was much more sensible to compare religion, common sense, and specialized knowledge about the world within any given society … and to compare western religious practices with nonwestern ones. (2002, 5)*

Today, anthropologists' attempts to understand belief rarely start from the premise that other peoples' beliefs are irrational or incorrect. Rather, they try to understand the nature of belief or religious practice and how it is that people come to believe that their

---

totemism
The use of a symbol, generally an animal or a plant, as a physical representation for a group, generally a clan.

ritual
A dramatic rendering or social portrayal of meanings shared by a specific body of people in a way that makes them seem correct and proper (*see also* symbolic actions).

In examining this problem, we will consider the following questions:

3.1 How does the use of metaphor affect the meanings people assign to experience?

3.2 How does symbolic action reinforce a particular view of the world?

3.3 How does the way we live affect our beliefs and rituals?

3.4 What happened to local world views when they were confronted by the religions of the European colonizers?

3.5 How can people reorder their view of the world if it becomes unsatisfactory?

view of the world is correct. In order to explain and contextualize people's beliefs, we need to examine a number of concepts. Metaphor is one of the tools we apply to make our knowledge meaningful to ourselves and to others; in that regard, it plays a major role in giving us a sense of the universe and ourselves. As we will see, **symbolic actions**—all the rituals, myths, arts, stories, and music that we enjoy or participate in—play a role in organizing and making concrete a particular view of the world. Also, we need to explore how people learn to view the world as they do and how they defend their beliefs against

skeptics who challenge a particular view of the world. What we believe must also be, in some way, a product of our social, economic, and political lives. In addition, we need to ask, and explain, why people sometimes radically change what they believe.

QUESTION 3.1: HOW DOES THE USE OF METAPHOR AFFECT THE MEANINGS PEOPLE ASSIGN TO EXPERIENCE?

Borrowing Meaning with Metaphors

One major characteristic of language is its economy; the same words we use to describe one area of experience can also be used to describe another. This occurs primarily through metaphor. **Metaphors** take language from one **domain of experience**, such as the domain of the body or the domain of animals, and apply it to another domain, such as landscape features or persons. For example, "the shoulder of the road" is a metaphoric extension of a body part used to refer to landscape, while "Jeff is a dog" represents an extension from the animal world to the human world.

When people attempt to make sense of their experiences, they do so by drawing from shared cultural assumptions about how the world works. These shared cultural assumptions create an encompassing picture of reality (which can be religious or secular) called a **world view**. Metaphors are valuable tools for constructing world views. By directing attention to certain aspects of experience, while downplaying or ignoring others, metaphors can reinforce people's beliefs, as well as their understandings of reality, which ultimately come to be taken for granted as correct and true. To put it another way: "Through metaphors we understand the abstract in terms of the concrete" (Lakoff and Johnson 1980, 112).

symbolic actions
The activities—including ritual, myth, art, dance, and music—that dramatically depict the meanings shared by a specific body of people.

metaphor
A figure of speech in which linguistic expressions are taken from one area of experience and applied to another.

domain of experience
An area of human experience (e.g., business, war, science, family life) from which people borrow meaning to apply to other areas.

world view
An encompassing picture of reality based on shared cultural assumptions about how the world works.

Harvey Feit shows how the Cree in northern Quebec used the metaphor "hunting is like gardening" and "hunting lands are like a garden" (2001, 424) as part of their strategy to defend their lands against a hydroelectric project that threatened to flood their land and destroy the habitat of their animals. The garden metaphor countered the view of the Quebec government that the northern areas were uninhabited and unproductive wilderness. The view of Cree hunting lands as a garden produced the image of the Cree as gardeners, who cared for the earth and all that the earth produced and who expected their lands to be treated as other special lands were in the rest of Canada. In the words of a secondary student from Nemaska: "What do you think would happen if you were in Ottawa and saw a garden with a lot of roses and other flowers, and you started picking them? Or if you walked on someone's garden? You'd get a fine of course, maybe we should give Hydro Quebec a fine too" (quoted in Feit 2001, 443–44). The "garden of the Cree" metaphor calls forth an earth that, if protected and nurtured, will sustain Cree life. It also implies that if the Cree "garden" is destroyed, Cree people will be destroyed too.

When language is extended from one domain to another, meaning is also extended. In other words, metaphor involves not only speaking of one experience in terms of another but also *understanding* one experience in terms of another. For example, when those of us who speak English in North America describe an argument, we might say, "His point was right on target," or "Your claims are indefensible," or "She attacked my argument, and I had to defend my position." We might say, "She shot down my argument," or "I think I won the argument." We speak of argument in terms of conflict, taking the language from the domain of war and applying it to the domain of conversation. But we have not only transferred words; we have also transferred meaning. We don't simply talk about argument in terms of war; we actually win and lose arguments.

What would happen if instead of metaphors of war, we borrowed metaphors from the domain of dance to comprehend argument? We might talk about the rhythm of the interaction or the grace of the performance. In fact, this wouldn't be argument at all; instead of two protagonists in a win-or-lose situation, we would have two partners trying to coordinate their movements to arrive at a mutual accommodation.

Alternatively, think about the way the conception of illness is embedded in the language used to describe it. North Americans who speak English take language from the domain of war and use it to talk about health. We build our defences against illness; we get ill because our resistance was low. We fight a cold, destroy germs, wage war on cancer, and have heart attacks. The language that AIDS researchers use is full of metaphors drawn from war. Recent research reports that the AIDS virus weakens the "immune system attack force," and that "killer cells" are meant to "destroy virus-stricken cells." As one researcher put it: "If you want to think of it with a war analogy, it's as though the soldiers are still on maneuvers, but they no longer have their weapons: When they encounter the enemy, they lose their weapons."

Not all societies borrow from the domain of conflict to give meaning to health. The Navaho, for example, see illness as a displacement of the person from his or her proper place in the universe. Illness is a disruption of harmony.

The human body and war, of course, are not the only domains from which North American

EXERCISE 3.1A

North American anglophones often borrow heavily from the domain of sports in their use of metaphor. Create a list of the sports-related metaphors with which you are familiar. How do such metaphors shape your understanding of experiences of romance, success, or failure? Can you think of alternative metaphors that might also describe those experiences? How might a shift in metaphor change your understanding of those experiences?

When North Americans use the term "slam dunk" to refer to ensured success, they are borrowing meaning from the domain of sports to make sense of another domain of experience.

anglophones borrow to assign meaning to other areas of experience. North Americans who speak English borrow also from the domain of economic exchange. In English, time is spoken of not only as if it were a distinct thing, but also as if it were a specific type of thing: "Time is money," "You're wasting my time," "This gadget will save you hours," "I don't have the time to give you," "That flat tire cost me an hour," "You need to budget your time," "He's living on borrowed time," "Is that worth your while?" Time in North American cultures is a valuable commodity, a scarce resource that is quantified, invested, and spent.

Metaphors, then, are not simply verbal devices that we use to make our language colourful and economical. Rather, they are like theories, templates, lenses, or filters that we can use to help us understand one domain of experience in terms of another. When we use language from one domain of experience to describe another, whole domains of meaning are transferred: among North American English speakers, arguments become wars, and time becomes a commodity. Moreover, the metaphors we use to describe experiences may predispose us to seek certain solutions to problems associated with those things and people. A Navaho cure seeks to return the patient to a state of harmony with the social and natural universe. Does our North American anglophone way of speaking of illness in terms of war and battle encourage us to take for granted that it is some kind of war? And, if it does, how does that view determine the kinds of treatment for illness that we devise and seek? Doesn't the language of conflict and war imply the need for cures that destroy the agent of disease rather than return the patient to health?

THE SOCIAL AND CULTURAL CONSTRUCTION OF REALITY

The fact that English speakers in North America borrow so heavily from the domains of war and economic exchange for metaphors suggests another way to understand how language operates to influence people's views of the world. Most societies seem to have one or more domains from which they borrow extensively for metaphor. These domains become **key metaphors** that give to each culture a style or cast that makes the culture distinctive. When a culture's members think and speak of many domains of experience in terms of a particular domain, that culture's meanings achieve a certain coherence, and a coherence of belief is thereby achieved as well.

Kwakwaka'wakw Metaphors of Hunger

Perhaps one of the most spectacular expressions of the elaboration of both a key metaphor and the human imagination is found among the Kwakwaka'wakw (once called the Kwakiutl) of British Columbia. We owe much of our knowledge of the traditional life of the Kwakwaka'wakw to Franz Boas, one of the founders of American anthropology, his Kwakwaka'wakw assistant, George Hunt, and filmmaker and photographer Edward Curtis.

Stanley Walens suggests that the act of eating is a key metaphor for the Kwakwaka'wakw. A fundamental meaning the Kwakwaka'wakw find in their experience is that the universe is a place in which some beings must die so that other beings may eat them and live. Eating gives life in at least two ways: it provides nutrition and it frees souls. The Kwakwaka'wakw believe that when a person dies, the soul leaves the body and enters the body of a salmon. But the soul cannot be freed until the physical body is destroyed. For this reason the Kwakwaka'wakw place their dead on scaffolds where the body can be devoured by ravens and other birds. Once the soul enters the body of a salmon, it remains there, living in a salmon world that socially resembles the human world.

However, when the salmon is caught and eaten by human beings, the soul is once again freed and enters the body of a newborn child. Thus, for the Kwakwaka'wakw, the act of eating becomes a metaphor through which much of their life is understood and described.

The importance of eating as a metaphor that orders experience is evident in the dominance of mouths in Kwakwaka'wakw art, ritual, and **myth**. Their world, says Walens, is replete with the mouths of animals killing to satisfy their hunger. Their art is filled with gaping jaws of killer whales, fangs of wolves and bears, and tearing beaks of hawks, eagles, and ravens. Dancers wear masks of cannibal birds

key metaphors
A term to identify metaphors that dominate the meanings that people in a specific culture attribute to their experience.

myth
A story or narrative that portrays the meanings people give to their experience.

with nine-foot-long beaks that shatter human skulls to suck out the brains. In their myths, wild women with protruding lips inhabit the woods, waiting to rip apart travellers and misbehaving children. It is a world where suckling infants turn into monsters and devour their mothers.

The Kwakwaka'wakw use the eating metaphor to give meaning to a wide range of their experiences. Hunger is associated with greed, for, like unrestrained hunger, greed causes people to accumulate wealth far beyond what they need. Hunger is also associated with immorality, as the Kwakwaka'wakw believe that human desires create conflict and destruction that can quickly get out of hand, so that people must work together to prevent and control conflict before it threatens to destroy the group. People who hoard food are, in effect, hoarding souls, preventing the return of a soul from the spirit world. Consequently, the Kwakwaka'wakw place great emphasis on gift giving and generosity. Hunger is also associated with children, who constantly demand to be fed and who will, if allowed, devour all the family's food.

The full impact of a metaphor lies in the fact that people are trying to impose order on their lives by describing the world according to a particular domain of experience. The Kwakwaka'wakw believe that greed, conflict, and child rearing can be

Courtesy of Library of Congress

Metaphors of eating and being eaten abound in Kwakwaka'wakw life. In this religious ceremony, dancers portray cannibal birds with long beaks, and a totem pole includes faces with gaping mouths.

solved by controlling hunger. Eating is thus highly ritualized and controlled. Food must be carefully handled and generously given to others to avoid accusations of greed. In fact, wealthy persons are said to vomit forth goods, vomit being for the Kwakwaka'wakw a life-giving substance. Animals that regurgitate their food, such as wolves and owls, occupy a special place in the Kwakwaka'wakw world. The socialization techniques of the Kwakwaka'wakw are geared to teaching children to control their hunger. In sum, a single domain of experience—eating—has been elaborated by the Kwakwaka'wakw to give to their world meaning.

The Metaphors of Contemporary Witchcraft and Magic

A metaphor is a theory, a system of interpretation that, once understood in the context of one domain of experience, can then be transferred to others. The metaphors may also be embedded in myth and history as well as everyday experience. Mutually sustaining metaphors work to reinforce belief systems and world views. A good example of that is witchcraft and magic.

Anthropologist Tanya M. Luhrmann details some of these practices in *Persuasions of the Witch's Craft: Ritual Magic in Contemporary England* (1989). Luhrmann joined various covens and groups in

---

EXERCISE 3.1B

There are some interesting parallels between the metaphors of eating and hunger among Kwakwaka'wakw and the metaphors of sexual intercourse and sexual desire in North America. Kwakwaka'wakw art, myth, and stories are filled with mouths and images of eating and hunger. What are some of the images that fill North American expressive culture (advertising, for example)? Vomit is a life-giving substance for Kwakwaka'wakw; what symbolizes life giving in North America? Are there other ways in which North Americans use sexual symbolism that are similar to the ways in which Kwakwaka'wakw use hunger and food?

THE SOCIAL AND CULTURAL CONSTRUCTION OF REALITY

England whose membership consists of middle-class urbanites who situate their magic in "New Age" ideology, the "Age of Aquarius," people who place an emphasis on natural foods, good health, and personal stability and whose magical practices consist largely of conjuring spirits, reading the tarot, and magical healing.

Modern magic is based on the assumption that mind and thought can affect matter without the intervention of the thinker's actions. It assumes that thought and matter are one. Magicians believe, says Luhrmann, that it is a distortion to treat objects as isolated and unique. One manual describes magic as

the world view that sees things not as fixed objects, but as swirls of energy. The physical world is formed by that energy as stalagtites [sic] are formed by dripping water. If we can cause a change in the energy patterns, they in turn will cause a change in the physical world—just as, if we change the course of an underground river, new series of stalagtites will be formed in new veins of rock. (quoted in Luhrmann 1989, 118)

A key metaphor embedded in modern witchcraft and magic is that of stratification, of "planes" and "levels." For the follower of good witchcraft, or magic, or the tarot, the universe is divided into a complex collection of entities and beings, each of which exists on different "planes," "astral planes," or "levels," of which the everyday plane of material life is but the lowest. After death, for example, the soul does not die, but goes to exist on another plane, some remaining in contact with the material world. Other magical forces exist on other levels, but they too can be harnessed by human beings to influence events on the everyday plane of existence. Moreover, the properly trained human mind can actually, simply by imagining it, create forms on the "astral plane" that may in turn affect things in the material world.

Becoming a magician, Luhrmann says, requires the acquisition of specialized and esoteric knowledge; consequently, magicians read books, arrange and attend rituals, go to meetings, and learn the tarot, astrology, mythology, and 17th-century Gaelic cures.

The tarot deck consists of 78 cards that comprise an elaborate and complex system of metaphoric associations linking various domains of experience that range from an understanding of the planets and other celestial objects (sun, moon, etc.), to colours, material elements (e.g., mercury, iron, gold), emotions, personal qualities, and mythological beings. Each of the tarot cards is said to have some meaning that is determined by its association with a specific planet, an element, an emotion or human quality, and so forth. Aleister Crowley, one of the founders of modern magic and witchcraft and a designer of the modern tarot deck, says that each card is, in a sense, a living being.

The magician uses the tarot cards to divine the future, but the cards also provide ways for people to interpret their own lives. The cards, says Luhrmann, provide people with a symbolic map with which to interpret and understand themselves as they transfer the meaning of the cards to their own lives and experiences. Thus, some may associate themselves with the Empress, calm and fecund, or they may say that someone has the temperament of the Magician, mercurial and unpredictable. And in associating themselves with a particular card, people also associate themselves with a specific planet (e.g., Mars—dominant and aggressive) or colour (e.g., red—emotional and passionate). In a sense, one may begin to define oneself in terms of the tarot and actually become the person that the cards delineate. The transfer of meaning creates meaning.

In examining the power of metaphor to define our realities and reinforce our beliefs, we must remember that there is no necessary connection between the domains from which people draw metaphors and the domains to which they apply them. There is no natural connection between commodities and time, war and health, eating and immortality, the tarot's Empress and someone's personality. These borrowings are the products of the human imagination. Many different metaphors can be applied to a specific experience, and one domain can never be the exact replica of the other. No man is really a tiger, no woman really a fox. On some level, then, metaphoric borrowings are intrinsically absurd. Yet we constantly seem to confuse one domain with another; we really do fight disease; we really win arguments. And so, as anthropologists, we need to explore by what cultural means people are convinced that by controlling one domain of experience (e.g., eating), they can really control another (e.g., greed). In the next section, we explore the way that symbolic action acts to reinforce world view.

QUESTION 3.2: HOW DOES SYMBOLIC ACTION REINFORCE A PARTICULAR VIEW OF THE WORLD?

Metaphors are not the only way that we mediate between our senses and the meanings we assign to experience. We also participate in activities that express a particular view of the world and that reinforce particular beliefs about the way the world works. Especially important are symbolic actions such as ritual, myth, literature, art, games, and music. Symbolic actions carry bundles of meanings that represent public displays of a culture. They are dramatic renderings and social portrayals of the meanings shared by a specific body of people. More important, symbolic actions render particular beliefs and views of the world in a way that makes them seem correct and proper. The Kwakwaka'wakw and the Western witches and magicians described by Tanya Luhurman provide good examples of how ritual portrays, reinforces, and provides evidence for a particular view of the world. In addition to rituals, popular stories and myths—such as those about zombies and vampires in contemporary North America—are embedded with meanings that are closely intertwined with a particular world view. Stories about zombies alone are not likely to convince anyone that the world works in the way

it is portrayed in the stories. Instead, the meanings that characterize a culture are repeated again and again in other symbolic actions, particularly ritual.

The Kwakwaka'wakw Hamatsa Dance

The Kwakwaka'wakw view of the world, as we noted previously, rests on the metaphor of hunger and is graphically displayed in their language, myth, art, and ritual. One of the most important Kwakwaka'wakw rituals is the Cannibal Dance.

The Cannibal Dance is a four-day spectacle that serves as the highlight of the Kwakwaka'wakw Winter Ceremonial, a period of celebration and ritual observance in which all worldly activities cease. It is a time when the spiritual world of the Kwakwaka'wakw, filled with powerful beings and animal spirits, intersects with the real world. The dance varies in some detail from group to group, but in all it is the focal point of a youth's initiation into the Cannibal Society, a group responsible for performing certain rituals. In the ceremony, the initiate plays the role of the cannibal dancer, or *hamatsa*. Members of the Cannibal Society and others gather in a ceremonial house to call back the cannibal to the human world from his sojourn in the realm of Man Eater, one of the most important of the supernatural beings in the Kwakwaka'wakw pantheon of spirits.

At the beginning of the ceremony, the *hamatsa* is believed to be in the woods frantically searching for human flesh to devour. Some early ethnographic accounts of the dance report that he would actually eat human mummified remains. Meanwhile, members of the Cannibal Society gather around a fire in the ceremonial house to sing and recite prayers to entice the *hamatsa* into the house, periodically sending men out to see if he is approaching the village. Finally, the prayers and calls of the Cannibal Society attract the *hamatsa*, who arrives, dressed in branches of the hemlock tree, pushing aside roof boards and jumping down among the celebrants. Jumping through the roof is supposed to symbolize descent from the spirit world above to the world of the living below. In a seeming frenzy, the *hamatsa* runs around the fire and then into an adjacent room, leaving behind only the sacred hemlock branches he had worn. During the four days of the ceremony, the celebrants try by various means to entice him back into the house and, in effect, tame and socialize him, convincing him to forsake his craving for human flesh and accept normal food. In one part of the ceremony the *hamatsa* flees the house and a member of the Cannibal Society is sent as the bait to attract him. The *hamatsa* rushes upon him, seizes his arm, and bites it. Each time he bites someone, he dashes into a secret room and vomits, an act that is repeated various times during the ceremony.

During pauses, members of the audience exchange gifts. Later the *hamatsa* appears naked and is given clothes, but he flees again. At another point a woman who serves as a co-initiate appears naked, carrying mummified remains. She dances backward, trying to entice the *hamatsa* to enter the house, but she fails. Finally the group succeeds in subduing the *hamatsa* by bathing him in the smoke of cedar bark that has been soaked in menstrual blood. After the conclusion of the public part of the Cannibal Dance, the initiate and a few members of the Cannibal Society go to another house and eat a normal meal, the final symbol that the *hamatsa* has been tamed.

Ritual can be viewed as a symbolic representation of reality. In another sense, ritual presents participants with solutions to real problems, in the same way as symbolic representations suggest real solutions. For the Kwakwaka'wakw, the *hamatsa* is the ultimate projection of the power of hunger, and his desire for human flesh is a manifestation of the forces that can destroy society. The participants in the ritual, by symbolically taming the hunger of the *hamatsa*, are asserting their moral responsibility to control greed and conflict. The ritual is the acting out of the group's successful efforts to overcome forces that threaten their society. Here is how Walens puts it (italics added):

> The hamatsa's hunger is fearsome; but it is the same hunger felt by every human, and

> thus every human has the power to control it. Ultimately the hamatsa and the bestial ferocity he embodies can be conquered … The winter ceremonials prove that no matter how terrible the power of hunger, no matter how many fearsome guises it assumes, no matter how many masks it wears, and no matter how many voices it speaks with, morality will be the ultimate victor. So long as humans have the knowledge to use food correctly, they need never fear hunger nor its awful accompaniment, death. (Walens 1981, 162)

The Cannibal Dance also contains a powerful message about socialization. Children, like the *hamatsa* come from the spirit world and enter the physical world naked. Like the *hamatsa* children have a female assistant, their mother, who must feed and socialize them. Children come into the world hungry, threatening to devour their parents' wealth. Thus, in the Kwakwaka'wakw view of things, all humans are cannibals who must be socialized and tamed. Through swaddling, ritual fasting, denial of food, and other actions, parents transform their children from cannibals into moral human beings. Through ritual enactment, the Kwakwaka'wakw have made their symbols real.

The Ritual of Contemporary Witchcraft and Magic

> In a witches' coven in northeast London, members have gathered from as far away as Bath, Leicester, and Scotland to attend the meeting at the full moon … The sitting room has been transformed. The furniture has been removed, and a twelve-foot circle drawn on the carpet … Four candlesticks stake out the corners of the room, casting shadows from stag antlers on the wall. The antlers sit next to a sheaf of wheat, subtle sexual symbolism. In spring and summer there are flowers everywhere. The altar in the centre of the circle is a chest which seems ancient. On top an equally ancient box holds incense in different drawers. On it, flowers and herbs surround a

carved wooden Pan; a Minoan goddess figure sits on the latter itself amid a litter of ritual knives and tools. (Lurmann 1989, 42)

This is the setting for one of the rituals that Tanya Luhrmann attended in the course of her fieldwork on contemporary witchcraft and magic. These rituals, she says, were particularly important because they were one of the ways that people became convinced of the validity of their beliefs. Going on to describe the ritual in the above setting, Luhrmann writes:

The high priestess begins by drawing the magic circle in the air above the chalk, which she does with piety, saying "let this be the boundary between the worlds of gods and that of men" … On this evening a coven member wanted us to "do" something for a friend's sick baby. Someone made a model of the baby and put it on the altar, at the Minoan goddess's feet. We held hands in a circle around the altar and then began to run, chanting a set phrase. When the circle was running at its peak the high priestess suddenly stopped. Everyone shut their eyes, raised their hands, and visualized the prearranged image: in this case it was Mary, the woman who wanted the spell, the "link" between us and the unknown child … By springtime, Mary reported, the child had recovered, and she thanked us for the help.* (Luhrmann 1989, 42)

Rituals, like this one, like the Hamatsa Dance of the Kwakwaka'wakw, or like those enacted in thousands of mosques, churches, and synagogues across North America, are special occasions that not only involve the enactment of key metaphors but also serve as special events set aside from everyday existence, events that draw participants into an emotional involvement with the metaphors. Rituals really do produce special feelings; people are carried

---

* Source: Reprinted by permission of the publisher, from *Persuasions of the Witches' Craft: Ritual Magic in Contemporary England,* by T. M. Luhrmann, p. 42, Cambridge, Mass.: Harvard University Press. Copyright © 1989 by T. M. Luhrmann.

EXERCISE 3.2A

The Hamatsa Dance and the rituals of contemporary witchcraft presented by Luhrmann may seem "exotic," but rituals are a key part of more familiar world religions as well (prayer is one example). Rituals can also be secular. What kinds of rituals are you familiar with from your own belief system? How do you feel when you practise your rituals? How would you describe the significance and meaning of these rituals to someone who is not familiar with them? What kinds of meanings are produced through the symbolic actions that comprise the rituals you are familiar with? How?

away with the symbolism, the music, and the social communion with others, and it is easy in this situation to come to believe that it is not the ritual itself that produces these feelings, but the forces or powers that the ritual is believed to summon or embrace.

In contemporary witchcraft and magic there is great emphasis placed on visualization and meditation as part of the ritual. The high priest or priestess may relate a story and ask the participants to imagine themselves in the story; it may be a walk through a moonlit wood or a voyage with Sir Francis Drake around the Horn of Africa. After the ritual, people report actually experiencing the salt spray on their face or the pitching of the sea, and they experience fellow participants as shipmates aboard Drake's ship, *Golden Hind*. In other words, the ritual not only dramatically depicts a metaphor but also teaches the participants how to experience the world as if the forces, gods, and spirits were truly real. Consequently, it is not unusual, in any belief system, for people to claim when participating in ritual to have had a "mystical experience," to experience themselves as "one with the universe" or as being overwhelmed with love or light. Thus, ritual not only teaches us about the world depicted in our metaphors but also teaches us how to feel within the universe we create.

THE SOCIAL AND CULTURAL CONSTRUCTION OF REALITY

Zombies Are "Good to Think With"

Contemporary witchcraft and magic draw heavily from myth and literature for their language, symbols, and metaphors. When anthropologists speak of myth, they are not referring to stories that are untrue. Myths, like histories, are accounts that explain the past from a particular point of view. Luhrmann reports that many of the magicians she came to know were first attracted to their beliefs when they read J.R.R. Tolkien's *Lord of the Rings*, or Ursula LeGuin's *Earthsea Trilogy*, or Marion Zimmer Bradley's *Mists of Avalon*. The themes of many of these books, and of contemporary witchcraft and magic in general, are contained in North American popular culture. These books and movies contain **key scenarios**, stories, or myths that, like ritual, portray certain values and beliefs. In the same sense that people act out and communicate their view of the world in ritual and come to learn how to feel in that world, they can be said to act out the scenarios contained in their myths and histories.

Claude Levi-Strauss, a key scholar of myth and meaning, coined the phrase "good to think with" to refer to the way that humans use aspects of the material world as a reservoir of metaphorical and symbolic meanings. Zombies may not be part of the material world as we know it, but zombie stories and myths are certainly good to think with. The proliferation of zombie movies, books, television shows, and video games in the 2010s in North America suggests that the "zombie apocalypse" genre contains key scenarios that embody how we think about our world today. What is it about zombies that we find so compelling, and why now? Zombies, unlike their popular undead cousins, vampires, are barely recognizably human. Zombies are mindless wanderers; zombies are tireless; and zombies are almost uncontrollably contagious—turning loved ones against one another in an instant, creating a pandemic, producing hordes of relentless consumers with insatiable, never-ending appetites. Anthropologists Jean and John Comaroff

How might we explain the contemporary popularity of zombie and vampire myths and stories?

suggest that contemporary zombie stories have much to do with "the implosion of neoliberal capitalism at the end of the twentieth century" (2009, 451). The Comaroffs were interested in the proliferation of zombie stories in late 20th-century South Africa, but their insights are applicable to the North American case as well. Stories of a zombie apocalypse seem to tap into our fears about what

EXERCISE 3.2B

1. What skills are most valuable in the wake of an imagined zombie apocalypse? In zombie myths, who becomes the hero, and who is zombie fodder? What does this suggest about our anxieties about our contemporary ways of making a living in North America?
2. The vampire genre is as popular, if not more so, than myths and stories about zombies. Why do you think this is the case? What do contemporary vampires tell us about ourselves?

key scenarios
Dominant stories or myths that portray the values and beliefs of a specific society.

they call "millennial capitalism": zombies, like North Americans, consume relentlessly (think of shopping malls during the holidays); zombies "work" without ceasing and for little reward (like "ideal" offshore workers under global capitalism); a zombie pandemic, like the avian flu or SARS or H1N1, makes both intimate contact with and global flows of people and goods dangerous, even deadly. Zombie stories are a metaphorical exploration of our fears and desires in our global, capitalist economy.

QUESTION 3.3: HOW DOES THE WAY WE LIVE AFFECT OUR BELIEFS AND RITUALS?

In answering this question, anthropologist Marshall Sahlins wrote:

> When we were pastoral nomads, the Lord was our Shepherd. We were his flock, and he made us lie down in green pastures ... When we were serfs and nobles, the Lord was our king. Sat regnant on the throne of heaven, His shepherd's crook now a jeweled sceptre ... Finally we are businessmen—and the Lord is our accountant. He keeps a ledger on us all, enters our good deeds in black and debits our sins in red.
> (1968, 96)

It is too easy to say, Sahlins points out, that people create gods in their own image or, as Emile Durkheim suggested, that "God is another name for society." Nevertheless, clearly the way we live, the organization of our social, economic, and political lives, must influence what we believe, how we represent those beliefs, and how we act them out. We need to understand, also, how our beliefs and the manner in which we act them out serve to maintain certain patterns of social, political, and economic relations, and how these beliefs and acts serve to reproduce these relations.

To try to understand how what we believe is related to how we live, let's examine some other ways of knowing that challenge Euro-Canadians' beliefs about the world and their place in it.

In *Ways of Knowing: Experience, Knowledge, and Power among the Dene Tha* (1998), Jean-Guy Goulet writes of his own experience learning about a world view very different from the one he learned as a child. For the Dene Tha in northern Alberta, learning comes only through direct experience. In Chateh, the community where Goulet lived while he was a student of the Dene Tha, an adult cannot teach a child how to hunt or cook or perform a ritual by simply giving verbal instructions, for to replace personal experience with objectified instruction is to turn knowledge into a commodity. All Dene Tha must learn by observing and by doing or imitating what they see when watching others. In the Dene Tha view, the only true knowledge is personal knowledge. This emphasis on firsthand knowledge is common among First Nations peoples; for instance, Richard Preston found that the Cree in Quebec "define certain truth value on the basis of what a man can see with his own eyes" (1975, 144). While Dene Tha stories can also contain knowledge, the narrator is careful to avoid making claims about the truthfulness of the story if it is not part of his or her own personal experience.

Along with the importance of personal knowledge comes the right of every Dene Tha to personal autonomy and the responsibility to respect the autonomy of others, including non-Dene Tha. If one interferes with another's direct experience, she or he is seen to be infringing on the right of the other to gain knowledge properly. This extends to small children as well as adults. Dene Tha children are allowed to explore their world in ways that Euro-Canadian children are not. For instance, setting and enforcing a particular bedtime for a child is considered by Euro-Canadians to be a sign of good parenting, but for a Dene Tha parent, this is a sign of an irresponsible parent who is blocking the child's access to knowledge and personal autonomy.

Dene Tha notions of power also differ from those of Euro-Canadians. In the Dene Tha world view, "when Dene speak of a power, they think of a powerfulness inherent in plants, animals, or other substances, which can affect human beings knowingly or unknowingly" (Goulet 1998, 60). Dene Tha distinguish between two different "lands": *ndahdigeh*, "our land," and *echuhdigeh*, "the other land." Plants and animals in the bush are manifestations of the other land in our land; therefore, Dene Tha must be very respectful of all forms of life, human and nonhuman. This is another part of the Dene Tha world view that is shared by many other First Nations peoples. Harvey Feit explains that the Waswanipi Cree in northern Quebec do not believe that animals are radically different from humans. Hunting is a very important part of Cree life, and the Cree in Waswanipi have a special word that encompasses their beliefs about humans, animals, and hunting. The Cree word *nitao* means "to see or to look at something; to go to get or to fetch something; to need something; to want something; and to grow or continue to grow" (2004, 102). The Cree believe that animals are shy and difficult to see at times. To "get" an animal, in the Cree view, is to receive it. The animal must agree to give itself to the Cree hunter, and the hunter must agree to reciprocate with gifts to other Cree and to the spirits. One way to give a gift of appreciation to the spirits is to burn a small piece of meat in a fire so that the smoke goes up to where the spirits will receive it. Cree hunters reciprocate by providing the conditions for animals to survive and grow. Hunters must never waste the animals they are given and must kill the animal cleanly.

Sometimes our land interacts directly with the other land. An example given by Goulet is that of a young man's violent death producing an angry storm that was said to be the result of the man's feelings. In another example, when the animal helpers of a Dene Tha healer felt let down because a patient did not bring proper gifts, the village was covered with low clouds and drizzle for three days.

Dene Tha communicate with the other world through dreams and gain important knowledge about healing using plants and animal parts. However, like the Waswanipi Cree, one must always show respect by giving gifts or healing will not take place. If a piece of bark is taken from a tree or a plant is taken from the ground for its roots, a small portion of tobacco is placed at the bottom of the tree or in the ground at the spot the plant once grew.

In addition to providing meat for humans, animals are very important because of their ability to share power with humans. This relationship of sharing goes back to a time when animals and humans were not as separated as they are now

A Cree hunter.

and when they married, spoke the same language, and lived together. Although this is no longer the case, the Dene Tha still view animals as superior to humans and believe that animals give to humans only the powers they no longer need.

Like the Dene Tha, the Waswanipi Cree do not see humans as completely separate from other phenomena of the world, such as wind and water. For instance, animals do not act alone when they give themselves to hunters; they are also given by "wind persons" and the Christian Jesus or God. The Cree world is filled with all kinds of spirits that interact with people, and the whole Cree environment is thought of as a "society of persons," all of whom are dependent on one another. God and spirits may communicate with humans in dreams, and humans may communicate with spirits through their rituals.

Dreaming is the way the Dene Tha gain powerful knowledge. When elders travel to the other land, they sometimes return with songs that are used in healing ceremonies. Dreams are also the process by which one can see the future and even take steps to avoid misfortune. Dreams may have a very pragmatic use, as when a Dene Tha hunter learns where to find animals who are willing to give themselves to humans. For the Dene Tha, the mind, or soul, is where one's will, memory, and intellect reside. One's mind receives a power to heal or to cause harm from an animal helper. Although one's body may die, one's mind can choose to return to "this land" and become born again in a new body. This means that while human bodies are only temporary, human minds are permanent. Dreaming is understood by the Dene Tha as a journey in which the soul leaves the body and travels to other places in this land or spends time with relatives in the other land. However, if the soul stays away too long, the body may become ill and a healer may be required to bring the soul back. If the soul doesn't return, the body will eventually die. For the Dene Tha in Chateh, some people (but not all) choose to come back to earth once they die. Reincarnation in Chateh is a process whereby the spirit of a relative

enters a woman's body to be born again. If the spirit was a female in her previous life and is born again as a male, family members may call the boy by female kinship terms such as "my sister" or "my daughter," once the former identity of the child is decided upon by the community. The same happens when a male is reborn as a female.

By exploring the examples of the Dene Tha and the Waswanipe Cree, we can see the mutual reinforcement of their beliefs about the relationships among humans, animals, and the land, and the social, economic, and political relations that are unique to their respective cultures. Many First Nations peoples view themselves as part of their environment, in contrast to the world view of most Euro-Canadians, who see "culture" as separate from "nature." For instance, the most important being in the world of the Mi'kmaq in eastern and coastal Canada is the sun. The Mi'kmaq believe that the sun created the earth and everything on it, and both the Sun and the Moon are considered to be manifestations of the Great Spirit. When a person dies, his or her soul climbs the Milky Way to the land of the dead. Another prominent being of the Mi'kmaq spirit world is Glooscap, who was once on earth and who created the natural features of the Mi'kmaq land. Glooscap also taught the Mi'kmaq how to make tools and weapons, and before he left the earth to become the assistant of the Great Spirit, he predicted the arrival of the Europeans.

In *Do Glaciers Listen?* (2005), Julie Cruikshank explains how First Nations women who lived inland from the Saint Elias Mountains of Yukon told her stories in which glaciers had human-like qualities and interacted with humans: "The women I know portrayed glaciers as conscious and responsive to humans. Glaciers, they insisted, are wilful, sometimes capricious, easily excited by human intemperance but equally placated by quick-witted human responses" (2005, 8). In this world view, the behaviour of humans could have grave consequences for the behaviour of the "natural" world. Cruikshank was told by local women that glaciers had a keen sense of smell and disliked the odour of cooking fat. These women warned against cooking bacon for breakfast when near a glacier because the glacier might react by causing a surge that produced ear-splitting sounds.

Indigenous peoples in other parts of the world have strikingly similar beliefs about their physical environments. For instance, the world view of the Maori of New Zealand contains an origin story in which Sky Father and Mother Earth were joined together and produced many children. These children became the spirit being of the sea, the winds, forests, plants, animals, and humans. Thus Maori do not see themselves as separate from the physical world. As Manuka Henare explains, "the resources of the earth do not belong to humankind; rather humans belong to the earth. While humans as well as animals, birds, fish, and trees can harvest the bounty of Mother Earth's resources, they do not own them" (2001, 202).

These "ways of knowing" about the world and one's place in it differ greatly from the world views of Euro-North Americans, who believe that humans are superior to all other entities in the world and that everything in the world belongs to humans. The Euro-North American notion of human ownership of the earth's resources creates a very different way of interacting with the physical environment and justifies the ways of those who take resources from the earth—minerals, trees, animals, plants—without acknowledging any reciprocal responsibility.

However, not all humans in the world are able to "know," through direct observation, what is happening to the earth's resources. Multinational corporations, national companies, and even local businesses may behave in ways that local people are not able to investigate directly because they do not have access to the information they would need. In the next section, we look at two examples of how people cope with not knowing. The first example explores how people in northern Madagascar speculate on what happens to sapphires that are mined locally and then exported to other places. The second example shows how people in Cameroon use witchcraft to explain the conflicts of modernity.

Sapphire Mining in Northern Madagascar

World views contain a people's understanding of how the world works, based on beliefs that are handed down through generations and tested against experience and knowledge. In the case of those who live on the periphery of the world capitalist system, people often attempt to figure out how the world works without having direct experience or direct knowledge. Andrew Walsh describes this process in Ambondromifehy, a mining and trading town in northern Madagascar. Walsh describes the world view of sapphire miners in Ambondromifehy as a complex process of speculation, deception, and knowledge. Sapphires, when uncut, seem to the Malagasy to be useless stones; prior to 1996, they were sometimes used as slingshot pellets. Based on this direct knowledge and experience, the Malagasy have trouble imagining why these stones are suddenly so valuable to outsiders. In an effort to understand, local miners and traders constantly

EXERCISE 3.3

1. Take a few minutes to think about your own beliefs about the relationship between the cultural life of humans and the natural world. Are they connected to a particular religious or secular world view (or both)? How do these beliefs reinforce the life you live (and vice versa)?

2. If you believed that all the entities of the world are somehow connected and have the same rights as humans, how would this belief change the way you think about resources such as the foods you eat, the gas you put in your car, the disposal of your garbage, and the electricity and water you use in your house?

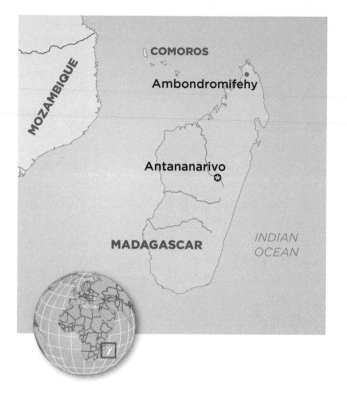

COMOROS

Ambondromifehy

MOZAMBIQUE

Antananarivo

MADAGASCAR

INDIAN
OCEAN

asked Andrew Walsh, "What are sapphires used for?" (2004, 225). Because Walsh was an outsider, his answer to this persistent question—that they were used to make jewellery—was suspect, and many Malagasy speculated that the sapphires must have some other, far more important use. These speculations included the production of electronic parts for CD players or for military vehicles and weapons. The most common speculation was that "sapphires are used, largely by foreigners from the United States, in the production of bombs. Sapphires, this speculation goes, find their way from northern Madagascar to Bangkok to the United States, where they are transformed into arms of the sort that were being used in the U.S.-led coalition bombing of Iraq" (ibid., 233).

The act of speculation about what they are being told is a vital part of the Malagasy experience of the sapphire trade. Individual miners sell their stones to stationary traders who have booths along a strip on the outskirts of Ambondromifehy. The stationary

traders, in turn, sell the stones to *demarchers*, who are mobile traders that run from booth to booth buying stones to sell to foreign traders, who in turn take the sapphires to the Malagasy capital, Antananarivo, and then leave the country. During the four or five trades, deception is often the rule. Because the sapphires are collected by groups of individuals in areas that are protected by the Malagasy state against large-scale mining, there is always the possibility that a miner may hide a stone in his mouth rather than share with the others. Each trader at the stationary booths tries to buy sapphires at a price low enough to make a profit, as does each of the *demarchers* and the foreign traders. But only the foreign traders really know what is happening in the global market, so the local traders are always aware that they do not have full knowledge about the worth of the stones and must continually decide what to believe and what to reject. What the Malagasy do know for sure is that foreigners know something about the value of sapphires that the Malagasy do not know and cannot know.

To complicate matters further, every day several truckloads of tourists pass through Ambondromifehy on their way to the Ankarana Special Reserve, where they claim that the only things they take out of the area are pictures. The Malagasy don't know for sure if this is true, but they speculate that it is a cover for the extraction of something far more important because it is no coincidence that the only places the conservationists and ecotourists are interested in are those that have something valuable in "the belly of the land."

Because sapphires are traded locally and then globally for increasingly higher prices, and foreigners come and go without ever revealing their true purpose, the Malagasy belief that sapphires cannot be used simply for jewellery seems quite logical, given the world events that reach Ambondromifehy through the news media and the reports of foreigners. The Malagasy also know that knowledge is actively being withheld from them and that only foreigners have true knowledge about how the global market works, so they speculate, both *in* and *about* the true value of sapphires, based on their own experience of the intimate connection between world trade and deception.

Using a world view based on lived experience to decipher events that are unfamiliar may produce understandings that appear strange to outsiders. North Americans also do this—for example, when listening to political campaign speeches in which many promises are made but there is no way to verify the "truth" of the messages. North Americans know that they cannot know whether these promises are sincere, and the only choice they have is to speculate on the basis of what seems to be reasonable, given the uncertainty of outside forces such as the global market. In the case of Malagasy sapphire miners, as in the case of North American voters, the lives people live and the forces that shape them come to make sense through those people's world views and beliefs (and those world views are shaped by the lives they live). In Cameroon, the process of evaluating the unknowable by using what is knowable (witchcraft in this case) produces explanations that make sense to those who are living the experience but may seem totally illogical to outsiders who do not share their beliefs. The power of an anthropological perspective is that it gives us methodological and theoretical tools with which to contextualize and understand world views other than our own.

Modern Witchcraft in Cameroon

Peter Geschiere, who has been doing fieldwork among the Maka people in southeastern Cameroon since 1971, found that witchcraft had not decreased with modernization, as had been forecast by development experts. Quite the opposite: Cameroon newspaper reports about the "nightly escapades" of witches had multiplied since Cameroon became an independent state in 1960. In *The Modernity of Witchcraft: Politics and the Occult in Postcolonial Africa* (1997), Geschiere asked himself why. One of his Maka companions repeated a saying that he had heard from a Dutch missionary: "Where there is electric light, witchcraft will disappear" (1997, 2). Yet this man had been threatened by the occult in towns that were very well lit by electricity.

It is perhaps the ambiguity of witchcraft in Cameroon that enhances its connection to politics. In the Maka world view, all events are the result of human action. Nothing happens simply by chance. If someone becomes ill, meets with misfortune, becomes wealthy, or gains a prominent position in politics, the cause is witchcraft. Witchcraft is the process by which inequalities are both created and overcome, because it is through witchcraft that the

Selling sapphires in Illakaka, Madagascar.

© Roger L. Dery

new elites are believed to have gained their wealth. To gain access to wealth and power, a politician must have connections to the occult. This ambiguity extends into the realm of kinship. Witchcraft is said to be "the dark side of kinship." The Maka believe that one's kin are the only people one can really trust, yet it is kin who trade the hearts of their kin for the favours of witches.

The Maka use the term *djambe* to refer to witches. A *djambe* is a small being that lives in the belly of humans. Some say it is like a small grey mouse; others describe it as a crab. Geschiere learned from the villagers that *djambe* used to live in the forest, where they helped hunters find animals to kill. As long as they stayed in the forest and hunters gave them part of the meat from their hunt, *djambe* did not harm humans. But one day a Maka woman became suspicious of her husband's success every time he went hunting. Unable to contain her curiosity, she followed him one day and saw him feed meat to a tiny being at the base of the tree. When her husband left, the woman went to the tree and asked the creature if it would help her the same way it was helping her husband. The *djambe* agreed, and the woman took it home. Once in the village, the *djambe* demanded that the woman feed it meat; when there was no more animal meat to be found, it demanded that she feed it her children. Now that the *djambe* was in the village, it became the source of both fortune and misfortune.

In principle, all humans have a *djambe* in their belly, and as long as it is not activated, it does neither good nor harm. But the Maka say that no one can function without some connection with the occult. The way to activate one's *djambe* is to make it "go out" of one's body—to fly around and meet other *djambe*. To become a witch and be part of the nocturnal feasts held in the forest, one must sacrifice the hearts of one's parents, because witches have an insatiable appetite for human flesh. A highly developed *djambe* also has a second pair of eyes and can see things that are not visible to those who are not witches.

In an effort to control witchcraft, the state justice system now involves itself in accusations of witchcraft. Unlike during colonial times, the state is anxious to prosecute witches to show its citizens that it is legitimate. However, because many of those who are employed by the state owe their good fortune to witchcraft, such prosecutions are themselves paradoxical. As an example of how deep beliefs in witchcraft run in Cameroon, Geschiere tells of a civil servant, himself suspected of having connections to the occult because of his position, who accused villagers of using witchcraft to sabotage government projects.

Witchcraft in Cameroon exemplifies some of the tensions that have accompanied the end of colonialism and the incorporation of newly independent countries into the global capitalist market as individual entities. Beliefs about witchcraft help the Maka explain, in terms they understand, the changes that have taken place now that their own people are filling states positions and capitalism is creating previously inconceivable wealth. The existing world view explains the sudden affluence of the elite that coexists with the poverty of the majority.

QUESTION 3.4: WHAT HAPPENED TO LOCAL WORLD VIEWS WHEN THEY WERE CONFRONTED BY THE RELIGIONS OF THE EUROPEAN COLONIZERS?

In most colonial encounters, some form of Christianity challenged the local world views of the colonized or indigenous peoples. Christianity, with its close links to capitalism, was part of the bedrock of colonial rule. Many early anthropologists assumed that Christianity was such a powerful force that it destroyed all forms of indigenous world views. Recent research has shown that this is not always the outcome, which in turn raises a question: How do indigenous or colonized peoples fit religions such as Christianity into their existing world views?

The Dene Tha and Christianity

Jean-Guy Goulet tells us that the Dene Tha live in a social context that presents many challenges to their world view. Western institutions such as "the school, the police station, the nursing station, and the church" (1998, 193) expect the Dene Tha to absorb the world view of Euro-Canadians. The Dene Tha do accept some Euro-Canadian ways and incorporate them in a complementary fashion within Dene Tha ways of knowing.

Most Dene Tha say they are Christians, usually Roman Catholic or Anglican. But this does not mean that the missionaries and the priests have managed to convince them that their own view of the world is wrong. Rather, it means that some aspects of Christianity make sense when evaluated by a Dene Tha world view. For instance, the Christian figure of Jesus Christ is often incorporated into the category of those who now live in *echuhdigeh*, or "the other land," and who communicate with the living through dreams. The crucifix (or cross) has been accepted, and some shamans use it as a personal symbol, in conjunction with the drum.

An especially powerful role is given by the Dene Tha to the Roman Catholic rosary. A young Dene Tha told Goulet that "they were encouraged by the Elders to carry a rosary on their person as a protection against other Dene who might attack them with their power" (1998, 204). The rosary has a different meaning when used by the Dene Tha and is interpreted according to their own world view, as a prophet explained to Patrick Moore and Angela Wheelock (1990, 62): "Each large bead represents a place where the Son of God came to earth. He walked along the earth and then went back to heaven. He did this many times, and each of the small beads represents his tracks on earth."

When the rosary is used in the Prophet Dance in conjunction with the dominant symbols of the circle and the path, it takes on the meaning of ritual. In the Prophet Dance the circle represents social and cosmic order; it takes its shape from important concepts and objects in Dene Tha life: the sun, the earth, and the drum. Participants dance together in a circle around a fire in three or four rows. The path represents the journey between "our land" and "the other land," and the dancing performed during the Prophet Dance is believed to influence the quality of the journey the dancers will take when they die. The Dene Tha believe that when they dance, *Ndawota* (God) watches their feet and measures their steps; the more steps a dancer takes at the Prophet Dance, the fewer he or she will have to take on the journey to Heaven. The same belief applies to the rosary: each bead of the rosary represents one prayer and one step on the way to Heaven.

At the same time, the Dene Tha refuse to be convinced by some of the most fundamental Christian beliefs. One of the most foreign to the Dene Tha is the belief in original sin and in the Christian "Hell," with its implication that one is never forgiven for some sins and that punishment continues into eternity. The introduction of a Christianity into the cultural world of the Dene Tha did not result in the wholesale destruction of their existing beliefs and world view; rather, they successfully incorporated certain aspects (but not others) of a Christian world view into their own belief system. Christianity was also introduced to the Kwara'ae of the Solomon Islands, but with different results. The difference between existing Dene Tha and Kwara'ae world views helps account for these different practices and beliefs of introduced Christianity.

Christianity in the Solomon Islands

Anglican missionaries first visited the Kwara'ae people in the Solomon Islands of Melanesia in the 1860s. The leaders of local communities met these missionaries with opposition. Ben Burt, an Education Officer at the British Museum of Mankind in London, has been researching Kwara'ae culture and history since 1979. He argues that when the Kwara'ae finally accepted Christianity (albeit with lingering reservations), it was for reasons that had less to do with belief in the Christian message than with the hope that once the Kwara'ae presented the appearance of acceptance, they could learn more about the power of the British colonizers and regain control of their lives under the rule of colonialism.

Before colonization in the 1920s and the arrival of Christianity in the 1860s, the rules for social order in Kwara'ae society were passed down from generation to generation and upheld by ghosts of the ancestors. The Kwara'ae believe that they are all descended from one man who came to the island twenty or thirty generations ago. As his sons and their sons grew, they cleared areas of the virgin forest to plant their gardens and build their villages. In places in these original clearings, Kwara'ae built shrines of stone, where their ancestors stayed in close contact with the land and their descendants.

Ghosts were located at the top of the Kwara'ae social hierarchy. Below them were "Tabu speakers" or priests, who interacted directly with ghosts, followed by men, and finally by women. Burt describes how vital ghosts were to Kwara'ae life: "It was the strength of ghosts which ensured people's health and prosperity, the growth of their gardens and pigs, kept the peace and ensured victory when the peace was broken, guided people's plans and endeavours and made some of them wealthy and successful. Ultimately the ghosts held power of life and death over their people" (1994, 54). The Kwara'ae had to treat ghosts with respect and follow their rules, or the ghosts would cause harm to the living. Making restitution to an angry ghost required sacrifices that ranged from roasting taro to killing the person who had committed an offence.

After colonization and the arrival of Christianity, people were encouraged to give up their ghosts. Some did this quite willingly, because the demands of ghosts were a definite burden. For others, however, life without ghosts just didn't make sense. After the Second World War, a resistance movement arose that called itself Maasina Rul ("Rule of Brotherhood"), which reaffirmed that all are descended from one common ancestor. The name was later changed to Masing Rul (literally "Marching Rule") (1994, 177). Its purpose was to challenge the British colonial authorities. Part of this challenge included a return to some of the pre-Christian values that nonetheless could be supported by the Christian Bible as interpreted locally (1994, 184). The new indigenous Christian theology contained the origin story of common ancestry as well as the laws of correct social behaviour that had been passed on through generations from the original ancestor.

For some, the exchange of ghosts for God has been mainly a change in names. The connection of the pre-Christian world view with the Christian one through reinterpretation of the Bible meant that many of the old ideas simply took on a different validation. As Burt explains, "a person's behaviour affects his relationship with God in much the same way as it affects relationships with ghosts, for God's support and protection is only given to those whose lives are kept clean and pure by following his rules" (1994, 258).

The way the Kwara'ae incorporated Christianity into their existing world view was shaped by that world view but also by the circumstances of their lives under British colonial rule. All reinterpretations of Christianity depend on local histories and local experiences. As discussed in the next example, Jamaicans living in poverty saw the European version of Christianity as intimately linked to colonialism and to the oppressiveness of the capitalist world system. This was then reflected in the reinterpretation of the Christian Messiah in a new religion, Rastafarianism.

Rastafari in Jamaica

In 1834, slavery officially ended in the British West Indies, although there would be four more years of a bondage system known as apprenticeship before ex-slaves were able to leave the plantations. In places such as Jamaica, many of the newly freed people moved away from the sugar estates and began a new life on small plots of land where they could grow their own food and sell the surplus at community markets. In the early 1900s, however, the United Fruit Company moved into Jamaica to start new plantations, employing the small-scale farmers as wage labourers. Within a few years, United Fruit was undercutting the prices of the surplus foods the small-scale farmers had been selling. By the mid-1930s, so many of the rural farmers had lost their lands that a vast pool of landless, unemployed people, numbering in the hundreds of thousands, had left the countryside and moved to the city of Kingston in search of jobs. When they arrived and found that the jobs were not there, they settled on the fringes of the city and tried to survive.

In 1930, Ras Tafari was crowned emperor Haile Selassie I of Ethiopia. The Jamaicans living in extreme poverty on the fringes of Kingston followed the crowning of a black king with great enthusiasm, for this was a clear sign that black men were not always destined to be at the bottom of society. During the coronation ceremonies, Ras Tafari was proclaimed King of Kings and Lion of Judah. To the poor living in Kingston, Haile Selassie was either the Messiah or the living God and a symbol of hope and salvation for all black people. His coronation fulfilled the biblical prophecies that a saviour would come for them and lead them back to Africa. As Rastafari became organized, Rasta leaders founded communities in and around Kingston that emphasized what they understood to be traditional African values: cooperative work efforts, respect for life, and the unity of all peoples of African descent. Through their belief in their messiah, Rasta returned to what they saw as their African beliefs and rejected the values of capitalist society and the capitalist market. By the time Selassie was overthrown in 1974, the Rasta belief system was so widespread that the loss of the messiah did not have much effect. Rasta continued to reject the capitalist world, which they called Babylon, and to create

their own understanding of the Christian Bible, in which they were heroes. Their present oppression (downpression in Rasta terms) comes from the United States, which has taken over the role as the centre of Babylon from Britain. The Rasta, however, believe that eventually Jah (God) will truly set them free (Henry 1997).

The Rastafari response to colonial and post-colonial forms of domination resonated with oppressed peoples around the globe. The continued global popularity of the reggae music of Bob Marley is evidence of this resonance. As discussed in section 3.2 (above), key scenarios, such as rituals, share and perpetuate values and beliefs; popular music often embodies these key scenarios. Bob Marley's extensive discography has been aptly named "Songs of Freedom," and his music remains both relevant and incredibly popular more than three decades after his death (in 1981). According to Jason Toynbee, Marley can be considered the "herald of a postcolonial world" (2007). Toynbee points out that Marley is #12 on *Forbes* magazine's "Top-Earning Dead Celebrities List" (Kafka 2005), with tens of millions of albums sold, and that his music is most popular in the global South, where "most people listen to him on cassettes, generally copied and distributed outside of official music industry channels. No statistics are available for this activity. Nor is there any way to quantify the circulation of images of Marley in the form of posters and drawings, or the spread of stories about him" (2007, 8). How can we explain his ongoing global superstar status?

Marley was among a handful of musicians who challenged the unwritten rules (the "mental slavery") that kept the great masses of the world in bondage to the rich and powerful. As he sang it:

> Today they say that we are free
> Only to be chained in poverty
> Good god, I think it's all illiteracy
> It's only a machine that makes money
> > Bob Marley, "Slave Driver"

*That these lines sound compelling and poignant
is a testament to Marley's extraordinary creative
powers … Marley combined an appreciation of the
embeddedness of oppressive social relations with
affirmation of the autonomy of human beings, and
of their facility to "act back" upon the world in
order to change it. (2007, 27–28)**

The case of Bob Marley's reggae, and of Rastafarianism more generally, provides a powerful example of the often unexpected ways in which people incorporate introduced beliefs into existing belief systems, and of the ways in which one's living conditions shape and are shaped by one's world view. Rather than ask, as some early anthropologists did, how European religions have destroyed the cultures of local people who have lived the experience of colonization, anthropologists are now asking how colonized people have interpreted the colonial religion with regard to their own world view. Although the arrival of colonial religions may change local people's world views, it is rarely the case that the beliefs and values that have worked to explain the ways of the world for a long time will be easily or completely discarded.

Bob Marley.

* Lyrics to "Slave Driver": Words and music by Bob Marley. Copyright © 1972 Fifty-Six Hope Road Music Ltd. and Odnil Music Ltd. Copyright Renewed. All Rights in North American Administered by Blue Mountain Music Ltd./Irish Town Songs (ASCAP) and throughout the rest of the world by Blue Mountain Music Ltd. (PRS). All rights reserved. Reprinted by permission of Hal Leonard Corporation.

QUESTION 3.5: HOW CAN PEOPLE REORDER THEIR VIEW OF THE WORLD IF IT BECOMES UNSATISFACTORY?

The meanings that people assign to their experience do not change easily. We very much take for granted that the view of the world created by the interaction of our own experiences of the world with the mediums of language, symbolic actions, humour, and collective judgments is the right view. But beliefs do change. Changes in the meanings that people assign to their experiences are often triggered by social upheavals, during which old ways of looking at the world, for whatever reason, are no longer satisfactory. Such social upheavals, and the resulting unease, are often the direct result of colonial encounters and subsequent inequalities. If sufficient numbers of people share this unease, they may together try to change both their view of the world and the organization of society.

Anthropologist Anthony F.C. Wallace suggests the term "**revitalization movements**" for these attempts by people to construct a more satisfying culture. The escalating political, economic, and cultural colonization of indigenous peoples over the past few centuries has inspired a multitude of revitalization movements. These movements promise liberation from oppression by foreign powers and tend to incorporate and rework elements of pre-colonial culture. Wallace developed his theory in the context of North American indigenous peoples, but his framework has since been applied to colonial contexts around the world, and enriches our understanding of the effects of colonial contact on existing belief systems.

> **revitalization movements**
> The term suggested by Anthony F.C. Wallace for attempts by a people to construct a more satisfying culture.

Generally, a period of social or economic upheaval or oppression leads to the development of a new or revised belief system that promises to return the society to a real or mythical previous state or that offers a new vision of the world that promises to relieve oppression or frustration. During such social upheavals, the usual explanations for events are unsatisfactory, traditional solutions to problems no longer work, and rituals may be abandoned. Doubts generated by social upheaval are replaced with new certainties born of religious fervour or conversion. Another way that people reorder their view of the world is **syncretization**, in which elements of two or more world views are combined to produce a new way of understanding lived experience. Examples of these two ways people can change their world views are the Ghost Dance among Native Americans and Vodou among Haitians.

Wovoka and the Ghost Dance

As settlers moved west in the 19th century, they came into contact with hundreds of Native American groups. As more and people migrated west, conflicts over land resulted in wars between these groups and U.S. military forces. The Indian Wars covered the period from about 1850 to 1880. During this time, the U.S. government negotiated and signed treaties with Native American groups guaranteeing Indian rights over areas of land, financial compensation, and food and other provisions.

However, as more white settlers moved onto Native American territories, the U.S. government insisted on renegotiating treaties when land that had been given to Native groups was desired by settlers. For example, the Sioux were given rights to the Black Hills of South Dakota; but after gold was discovered there, the government unilaterally insisted on renegotiating the treaties and reduced the Indians' land by more than half in 1889. (In this case, however, the courts later ruled that the government's act was illegal and that the Sioux never ceded their rights.) In addition, the buffalo were virtually exterminated, sometimes in a conscious effort by the U.S. military to destroy the economic basis of native society.

Source: National Anthropological Archives, Smithsonian Institution, Item 659-A-1

Wovoka, the major prophet of the Ghost Dance, is shown here in a photograph taken by anthropologist James Mooney in 1891.

As a result of the Indian Wars, treaty negotiations, government deceit, and the influx of new settlers, Native groups were restricted to reservations, made dependent on government rations, and denied traditional pursuits such as hunting and horse raiding. Government deliveries of food and provisions were often late or did not arrive at all, and diseases brought to the New World by European settlers, to which the indigenous population had little resistance, decimated the population. Children were taken to boarding schools away from the reserves and prohibited from speaking their native languages. Government agents, often at the insistence of Christian missionaries, banned traditional ceremonies and rituals. In brief, the social fabric of indigenous society was virtually destroyed. Those traditional things that help filter

> **syncretization**
> The term given to the combination of old beliefs or religions and new ones that are often introduced during colonization.

experience—language, ritual, and the ability of groups to collectively sustain particular views of the world—virtually vanished.

Revitalization movements usually receive their impetus from a prophet who claims to have received a vision or dream about a new way of viewing the world or a set of moral injunctions governing people's lives. The major prophet for the Ghost Dance was a Paiute named Wovoka. In 1889, Wovoka had a vision in which he was taken up to heaven where he saw God and all the people who had died performing their traditional games and activities. God told him he must go back and tell people to live in peace with whites and with one another. He was also given instructions for a ritual dance. He was told that if this dance were performed for five days and nights, people would be reunited with their friends and relatives in the other world.

Converts to Wovoka's message spread the word from Nevada to Native American groups throughout the United States and Canada. Wovoka's message was sometimes reinterpreted as it spread from Native group to Native group. In some versions, the world would be destroyed and only the Native Americans brought back to life; in others, Euro-Americans and Native Americans would live together in harmony. In some versions, the buffalo would return. In some cases, a specific date was set for the millennium (1 July was one date; another was the time of a major traditional ceremony). In some versions, Wovoka was even said to be the son of God. Whatever the interpretation, the Ghost Dance, as it came to be called, was adopted by many groups who were seeking a revival of a way of life disrupted by Euro-American expansion.

Among the groups that enthusiastically adopted the Ghost Dance was the Sioux. They had sent emissaries in 1889 to visit Wovoka; those emissaries had returned with descriptions of his vision and power. One account of the delegate's report is contained in James Mooney's *The Ghost Dance Religion and the Sioux Outbreak of 1890* (1897). An anthropologist working for the Bureau of American Ethnology, Mooney travelled around the country interviewing key figures, including Wovoka, and collecting firsthand accounts of the dance from Euro-Americans and Native Americans. Here is his description of the report of the Sioux delegates:

> They were gone all winter, and their return in the spring of 1890 aroused an intense excitement among the Sioux, who had been anxiously awaiting their report. All the delegates agreed that there was a man near the base of the Sierras who said that he was the son of God, who had once been killed by the whites, and who bore on his body the scars of the crucifixion. He had now returned to punish the whites for their wickedness, especially for their injustice toward the Indians. With the coming of the next spring (1891) he would wipe the whites from the face of the earth, and would then resurrect all the dead Indians, bring back the buffalo and other game, and restore the supremacy of the aboriginal race. (Mooney 2011[1897], 64)

Based on these messages, the Sioux began to dance in October 1890. However, for the Sioux, the Ghost Dance turned into a tragic reminder of Euro-American oppression. Frightened that the dance might turn into open rebellion, the Indian agent on one of the Sioux reservations called in the military. Some of the Sioux fled the reservation, chased by the Seventh Cavalry, General George Custer's group, which had been decimated by a combined Native American army at the Little Bighorn in 1876. After a promise of a safe return to the reservation, the fleeing Sioux surrendered their arms at a place called Wounded Knee, where they were surrounded by the Seventh Cavalry equipped with Gatling guns. As soldiers rummaged through the Sioux shelters searching for guns, someone fired a shot and the army opened fire, killing hundreds of men, women, and children.

The Ghost Dance virtually ceased among the Sioux after the massacre at Wounded Knee, but it continued among other groups, each of which hoped for the return of their traditional culture. Today it represents one attempt of a people to build a new culture, a new system of meaning after the destruction of a previous one.

Haitian Vodou

Another way people cope with drastic changes in their lives is by developing a different world view. This entails combining elements of a new view with those of an older one—the process called syncretization, described earlier. In Haiti, Africans from many different parts of the continent were forcibly brought together by the slave trade. Having been captured inland, the Africans were taken to the coast, where they were sold to slave traders, loaded onto ships, and taken across the "Middle Passage" to a foreign land, where they were again sold to plantation owners. These Africans could not bring any of their belongings with them across the Middle Passage, but they could bring their beliefs and world views, stored in their memories. After they reached Haiti and were divided among individual plantations, they were unlikely to meet anyone from their own community; as a consequence, much of the initial adjustment they had to make involved learning to communicate with other slaves from other parts in Africa. Once new systems of communication had been established, Africans could create a distinctive Caribbean culture based on their former beliefs and those of the French planters. In this totally new world it must have been immediately obvious to all African slaves that their old world views would not work to explain their new experiences in Haiti.

The new world view that Africans created in Haiti, then, was a **creole** view based on the lived experiences of their new world. That world was filled with work and suffering, first as slaves and then later as peasants living in a country that today is still the poorest in the Western hemisphere. Karen McCarthy Brown explains that Haitians created Vodou to find a way to live in conditions that are among the worst in the world: "Vodou is the system they have devised to deal with the suffering that is life, a system whose purpose is to minimize pain, avoid disaster, cushion loss, and strengthen survivors and survival instincts" (1991, 10).

Although the French introduced Roman Catholicism during the colonial period, the slaves they owned worshipped their Vodou deities in secret. After the Haitian Revolution ended in 1804, free Haitians combined the two religions to produce a third that looks like Catholicism on the outside but is actually something very different. Haitians believe in the Christian God, whom they call Bondye. They believe that this God created all things and that he is supreme. But they also believe that he is a European God who has many Europeans to attend to and is therefore much too busy to bother with poor Haitians. So instead of trying to interact with Bondye directly, Haitians use African spirits, or *lwa*, to intercede for them. These *lwa* have names that connect them to Catholic saints: the Virgin Mary is Ezili, Saint Patrick is Danbala, Saint James is Ogou, Saint Gerard is Gede, and Isidore is Azaka. But this is where the similarities end, for Haitian *lwa* are anything but saintly.

Vodou *lwa* present models for Haitian life and address issues that real Haitians face. Azaka, the poor peasant farmer, teaches Haitians to remember their roots: their land and their ancestors. In the world view of rural Haitians, land, ancestors, and spirits are all the same thing. Azake also reminds people of the importance of their family, and part of what urban Vodou congregations do is provide families for those who have migrated to the cities.

Ezili represents women, and because women play various roles in Haiti, she has various manifestations. Three important Ezili are Ezili Danto, Ezili Freda, and Lasyrenn. Ezili Danto is the hard-working black single mother. She presents and works through the problems that single Haitian mothers face. Ezili Freda is the rich white woman who represents white privilege in Haiti. Freda is usually posed reclining on a sofa, dressed in beautiful clothes, covered with jewellery, and eating chocolates. This image reaffirms

---

creole
A term used commonly to refer to the formation of slave societies in the Caribbean in which elements of African and European cultures were merged, blended, or combined into something uniquely Caribbean.

for Haitians the uselessness of white sensuality, because Freda does nothing except pose. Lasyrenn, often associated with the African "mammy water," is both black and white and lives just below the surface of the water, which Haitians say is "the back of the mirror." If one were to lean over a calm pool, he or she might catch a glimpse of Lasyrenn, but this is a dangerous thing to do because sometimes she pulls people into the water and they disappear; some say she takes them back to Ginen (Africa). Sometimes Lasyrenn will pull women under the water and keep them for several days, or as long as one year. When the women return, they are changed by the sacred knowledge they have learned and may become priestesses. Lasyrenn resembles the carved figureheads that slave trading ships had on their bows. This may mean that she reminds Haitians of the traumatic Middle Passage and slavery.

Danbala, Ogue, and Gede are male *lwa* who represent oppositions in Haitian life. Danbala is the oldest and most respected of the *lwa* and, like Saint Patrick, is associated with snakes. The difference between Saint Patrick and Danbala is that snakes are creatures that have important survival skills. Snakes can curve their bodies to go over obstacles, and if a snake puts its tail in its mouth it becomes a circle with no beginning and no end. Thus Danbala represents life, death, and rebirth in a continuous cycle. He also mediates opposites: as the symbol of the rainbow, Danbala is said to have one foot in the ocean and one in the Haitian mountains. Haitians say that Danbala is becoming angry with politics in Haiti and that he has taken his foot out of the water. People say that Haiti will now wither and die.

Ogue is a warrior who has subdivided into at least seven figures. In one of his manifestations, he is the handsome soldier riding a beautiful white horse who faces battle fearlessly. In another he is a liar and a beggar. In others he is a drunk or a coward. Ogou presents the lesson that while power may liberate, it also corrupts, as has happened to many of Haiti's leaders.

Gede is the master of the cemetery and is said to have one foot in life and one foot in death. Gede is a trickster, always making jokes, and he teaches that one way to overcome misfortune is to make fun of it. It should come as no surprise then that Gede is an important healer.

Haitian Vodou, then, is not just a set of exotic rituals, as it is often portrayed in the media. It is a world view that helps Haitians cope with a life of poverty and hardship. Furthermore, as Brown argues, Haitian Vodou is a system of healing that applies to a variety of areas in the lives of its followers, including troubled social relationships, physical illness, and the pain of the past in which families were torn apart by slavery.

Source: Photo courtesy and property of Anna E. Parmelee of Erzulie's, Inc. and www.erzulies.com

Mama Lola, the subject of Karen McCarthy Brown's (2001) ethnography, *Mama Lola: A Vodou Priestess in Brooklyn.*

CONCLUSIONS

Human beings, as we've noted, live in a world of their own creation. That is, by imposing meaning on experience through the metaphors we select, we construct our own realities and validate them collectively through rituals and myths. Our final example demonstrates how an anthropological perspective on world views and belief systems can help us understand our own taken-for-granted desire to understand our lives as meaningful, especially when faced with seemingly meaningless adversity. Being aware of the ways that people assign meaning to their world relates also to fields such as counselling. Virtually any kind of counselling involves a manipulation of perspective to help people change or cope with the meanings they assign experience.

For example, in *Disrupted Lives: How People Create Meaning in a Chaotic World* (1997), anthropologist Gay Becker studies the ways in which people attempt to create continuity in their lives after some unexpected disruption—an illness, the death of a close one, or even the onset of aging. For Becker, an ongoing interpretation of experiences and events enables people to make sense of their personal world. People create continuity in their lives through ordinary routines or daily repetitive rituals such as drinking a cup of coffee with the morning newspaper. But, says Becker, when expectations about the course of one's life are not met, people experience inner chaos and disruption. Such disruptions represent the loss of the future. As Becker puts it, "restoring order to life necessitates reworking understandings of the self and the world, redefining the disruption and life itself" (1997, 4). She suggests that every culture has its own "cultural life course." This life course can be viewed as a collectively shared image that, through metaphor, provides persons with images to guide their lives. In North American societies, we hear people speak of life as a "journey" or a "life wheel."

Common in the United States, she says, is the view that life is predictable and continuous (the same view is shared by most people in Canada). People develop stories or narratives of how their lives should proceed, what they should accomplish, and what sort of person they will be. But when some unexpected event occurs—illness, death, aging, or infertility—people are forced to redo their narrative. Metaphors not only help people make sense of the disruptions, says Becker, but also enable people to alter their views of reality and restore a sense of coherence.

For example, for many people, having a child is part of their narrative, part of the life course as they expect it to unfold. A diagnosis of infertility disrupts that narrative and requires a reordering of experience and a way of coping with the disruption. In her infertility study, Becker found that people confronting this disruption felt trapped in the present and could not foresee the future. One metaphor that helped them get through this period was seeing it as a period of limbo, a temporary state that preceded a return to normalcy. In her research on how people cope with illness, she interviewed a man of 40 who had been diagnosed with severe asthma but whose identity and life narrative had focused on being active and athletic. In reformulating his narrative, he drew on a military metaphor explaining how "people in midlife are wounded soldiers. And weary soldiers. We've been to the front and back." He thus identified himself with a social condition, extending it to his "war on illness" and redoing his biography to focus on his "fight with asthma." Becker's point is that by recognizing life's disruptions as breaks in a cultural narrative of how life is supposed to proceed, we can better cope with the disruptions. In many ways, of course, Becker is addressing at the individual level the same revitalization processes engaged in by groups when they attempt to construct a more satisfying culture.

We began the chapter by asking how it is that people can believe in things that cannot be proven—for example, why people are convinced of the existence of God, of unseen spirits, or of the powers of witchcraft. As we have seen, to answer

Every culture has its version of how life is supposed to proceed. That is, there are cultural narratives about each person's life course. For this exercise, choose a partner and interview him or her about how they expect their life to unfold. For example, how would they like their life described after they are gone? Ask also whether they have experienced disruptions that they believed might alter their attainment of that life course.

this question requires us to examine the role of such areas of social life as metaphor, ritual, and myth, along with other features of social life that persuade people of the correctness of their beliefs or that convince them to change what they believe.

How does metaphor affect the meanings we assign to our experience? The selection of metaphors has an impact on the meanings we assign to experience. By taking the language from one domain of experience and applying it to another, we carry the meaning of one domain to another domain. Any attempt to understand another culture (or to turn our anthropological analysis on our own culture) requires that we pay close attention to key metaphors.

The social and cultural construction of reality does not happen through metaphor alone. Symbolic actions also reinforce a particular view of the world. Ritual, for example, symbolically depicts a certain view of reality in such a way that it convinces us of the truth of that reality. Recall, for example, the Hamatsa Dance of the Kwakwaka'wakw, which portrays the values of Kwakwaka'wakw society and provides members with a way to control their lives. Recall as well the rituals of contemporary English magic and witchcraft, which convince participants that mental forces can influence the material world.

Relevant metaphors and rituals do not come from nowhere, and not just *any* metaphor or ritual will be meaningful or effective in a particular cultural context. The way we live (including social, political, and economic forces) influences what we believe and how we act out those beliefs. "Ways of knowing" among First Nations peoples differ from the kinds of knowledge that Euro-North Americans take for granted as correct because of the different ways these groups make their livelihood. People tend to act based on what they know about the world around them, which is shaped by their world view. Sometimes, as we have seen in the examples from Madagascar and Cameroon, people are forced to speculate about what they cannot know—for example, what happens to sapphires when foreigners take them out of the country, or why some people are rich while others remain poor. People speculate using the tools provided to them by their existing world view. These explanations may not make sense to an outsider, but knowing what we know, as anthropologists, about how belief systems work helps us begin to take such explanations seriously instead of dismissing them out of hand.

We also looked at three examples (Dene Tha, Kwara'ae, and Rastafari in Jamaica and beyond) of how people reinterpret new European religions using the world views that helped them explain their experiences prior to colonization or slavery. In most cases, people actively select parts of the new religion to incorporate within their own world view. As the global popularity of Bob Marley shows, forces of globalization (see Chapter 7), and local responses to these forces, mean that many people around the world have had to reorient their belief systems in similar ways, despite differences in local histories and local experiences.

Finally, we saw how, under certain conditions, people might be led to radically change what they believe. The experience of social upheaval may lead, as it did among the Plains Indians, to a new system of belief that promises to reorder society—and, in the case of the Ghost Dance, to resurrect the past. In the case of Haitian Vodou, a new world view has been constructed to help people cope with the new conditions of a life they don't believe they can change. Overall, the key significance of understanding how and why people come to believe what they do is that doing so gives us insight into one of the things that makes us human: our desire, and need, to make our lives meaningful.

CRITICAL THINKING QUESTIONS

1. If reality is culturally and socially constructed, can there be such a thing as objective truth? What are the implications of taking a social constructionist approach to reality for the pursuit of knowledge? Is objectivity possible? What obstacles might this present for the anthropological study of culture?
2. Do we need to believe in rituals in order for them to be effective?
3. How have the forces and circumstances of globalization shaped belief systems around the world?

KEY TERMS:

creole   (p. 102)
domain of experience   (p. 79)
key metaphors   (p. 82)
key scenarios   (p. 88)
metaphor   (p. 79)
myth   (p. 82)
revitalization movements   (p. 99)
ritual   (p. 78)
symbolic actions   (p. 79)
syncretization   (p. 100)
totemism   (p. 78)
world view   (p. 79)

PATTERNS OF FAMILY RELATIONS

William Berczy, "The Woolsey Family," 1809. Copyright National Gallery of Canada, Ottawa

In this portrait of a "typical" nuclear family, John Woolsey, the patriarch, is the central figure and dominates the scene; his wife is portrayed much as the good wife in the wedding sermon quoted in the epigraph—comfortably subordinate to her husband. Today, the composition of the nuclear family may be similar, but many would argue that the power dynamic has changed. Can we speak of a "typical" family in contemporary North America? If so, what would it look like?

If ever though purpose to be a good wife, and to live comfortably, set down this with thyself: mine husband is my superior, my better, he hath authority and rule over me; nature hath given it to him … God hath given it to him.

W. Whately, A Bride-Bush, or A Wedding Sermon, London *(1617)*

PROBLEM 4

What do we need to know before we can understand the dynamics of family life in other societies?

INTRODUCTION

Family Relations in North American Popular Culture

In 1973, renowned anthropologist Margaret Mead reviewed a new, genre-defying television show, which aired on PBS, titled *An American Family*. The 12-episode documentary chronicled seven months in the lives of the Loud family of Santa Barbara, California, a "typical" nuclear family comprised of a husband, a wife, and their five children. Why would an eminent anthropologist be interested in a television program? For Mead, the controversial program—an early prototype for today's ubiquitous reality television shows—was "as important for our time as were the invention of drama and the novel for earlier generations: a new way to help people understand themselves" (cited in Ruoff 1996, 270). Ten million people tuned in weekly to "understand themselves." Much of the interest the show generated had to do with the unexpected, soap opera–like plot twists and character developments: Pat Loud, the mother, asked her husband William for a divorce; William's successful business fell on hard times; and Lance, the eldest son, was arguably the world's first openly gay TV "character."

An anthropologist might have learned a great deal about North American family relations in the 1970s by watching *An American Family*, noting the reasons for domestic strife, the choices characters made, and the impact those choices had on family members. Furthermore, an anthropologist would learn much by paying close attention to viewers' reactions to the show: What did they find plausible, scandalous, or relatable? What exactly was it about this family that made its members both typical and compelling?

Although North American viewers no longer find reality television especially groundbreaking, and many would be unfazed by the inclusion of divorced or gay characters, an anthropologist might still want to pay attention to the family structure and dynamics portrayed on popular television shows and the discussions they evoke. For instance, in May 2012, U.S. President Barack Obama publicly declared his support for same-sex marriage (which has been legal in Canada since 2005). In an interview with ABC News, he explained that he had taken his cue from his two young daughters, who had schoolmates whose parents were gay and who could not imagine why they would be denied the right to marry. President Obama's statement echoed the growing public support for same-sex marriage; nonetheless, it generated much controversy. For instance, Bristol Palin, daughter of 2008 Republican vice-presidential candidate Sarah Palin, criticized the president in her blog post titled "Hail to the Chiefs: Malia and Sasha Obama." She suggested that Obama's daughters had watched too many episodes of *Glee*—a popular television show with several prominent gay characters—and that President Obama should be a "proper" father and leader, teaching his daughters what to do and think rather than allowing them to teach him. Palin's critics, in turn, suggested that having become a single mother at the age of eighteen, she was in no position to judge others regarding issues pertaining to the family. Whose version of the North American family is the "correct" one?

The study of kinship, including family composition, descent, and marriage, has long been central to sociocultural anthropology. Franklin and MacKinnon argue that in fact, "the study of kinship is itself symbolic of the anthropological tradition" (2001, 1). Kinship has long intrigued anthropologists because it relates so closely to social organization. Many early anthropologists assumed that kinship was more important in small-scale societies, where it provided the entire basis of social organization, than it was in large-scale societies. But as we will find later in this chapter, contemporary kinship studies have demonstrated that kinship remains a meaningful element of social life in large-scale societies. When we study kinship, we are interested

both in classifications—who is considered a relative and who is not—and in the ways people make particular relationships meaningful. Anthropologists who study family relations often begin by exploring the composition of a typical family and how it is formed and maintained. They examine how the themes of sexuality, love, and wealth are dealt with and what kinds of situations or conflicts can disrupt family life. However, as we can see from the example above, the typical family is just that—an ideal type that may or may not closely align with people's everyday experiences. Questions about what does or does not count as a family, what kinds of rights various members should have, and who should be the head of the household can be contentious. However, by exploring both the typical family *and* the debates about its composition, we can learn much about a given society.

To make the task of understanding patterns of family relations cross-culturally more manageable, we will focus first on family life in three societies: the Ju/'hoansi of Namibia and Botswana, the Trobriand Islanders of the South Pacific, and a rural Chinese farm family in Taiwan. These have been selected for three reasons. First, they represent very different levels of social, cultural, and technological complexity. The Ju/'hoansi are gatherers and hunters living in small, mobile groups; the Trobriand Islanders are horticulturists living in villages of up to 400 people; the rural Chinese in Taiwan represent a large agricultural society. Second, family structure and roles vary significantly among the three, as do notions about the bases of kinship relations and how kinship terms, such as mother, father, sister, and brother, are used. Finally, the three societies have been well studied in the anthropological literature. We will discuss these societies in what anthropologists refer to as the **ethnographic present**; that is, although the actual

---

ethnographic present

Use of the present tense to describe a culture, although the description may refer to situations that existed in the past.

descriptions may refer to situations that existed in the past, they will be described as if they still existed. In reality, the Ju/'hoansi, the Trobriand Islanders, and the rural Chinese are, to varying degrees, very different today than they were when they were studied by the anthropologists whose work we will mention. Then we will look at some of the more recent kinship studies by anthropologists to show some of the problems they have encountered and the new directions they have taken.

QUESTIONS

4.1 What is the composition of the typical family group?

4.2 How are families formed, and how is the ideal family type maintained?

4.3 What are the roles of sexuality, love, and wealth?

4.4 What threatens to disrupt the family unit?

4.5 How has the anthropological study of families changed?

4.6 How can understanding patterns of family relations be relevant outside of academia?

QUESTION 4.1: WHAT IS THE COMPOSITION OF THE TYPICAL FAMILY GROUP?

To understand family composition in different societies, we need certain concepts and tools. One place to begin is by examining how unmarried North Americans would typically respond if asked about the composition of their families. They would likely list their mother, father, brothers, and sisters. If asked, "Who else?" they would likely add grandparents, aunts, uncles, and cousins. If married, they would add their spouse and children. Figure 4.1 shows how this family structure would be diagrammed using genealogical notations.

David Schneider was one of the first anthropologists to study American kinship systematically, and his 1968 study led him to conclude that kinship, in North America and elsewhere, is a cultural system, not a set of biological facts. For instance, although Americans talk about kinship in terms of biological relatedness (often using the metaphor of shared blood), in practice, kinship is not dictated by any biogenetic reality. Often, we call people kin who are not related to us biogenetically; conversely, we often deny kinship status to biogenetic relatives (Feinberg 2001, 8). We employ the language of blood, of love, and of solidarity strategically to determine whom we consider kin and whom we do not.

EXERCISE 4.1

Using the genealogical notations introduced in Figure 4.1, draw a kinship diagram of your own family. Include as many generations and as many lateral kin as are relevant to your own family life. Would you include anyone who is not biologically related to you? Have you left out someone who is a "blood" relative but whom you do not consider kin? How do explain these inclusions and exclusions in your family?

Certain features of some North American families stand out for the anthropological observer. Many North Americans consider themselves equally tied by kinship to both their mother and their father, and to both their maternal and their paternal kin. In other words, North Americans generally reckon kinship **bilaterally**, or through both parents. This, as we will see, is not true of all societies. Second, many North Americans make no linguistic distinction between the mother's siblings and the father's siblings; both are referred to as aunt or uncle, as are the spouses

bilateral kinship
A system in which individuals trace their descent through both parents.

FIGURE 4.1 COMPOSITION AND DEVELOPMENT OF THE CANADIAN NUCLEAR FAMILY

1. The traditional Canadian household generally begins with a husband and wife pair moving from the households of their parents.

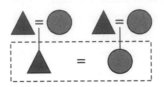

2. The arrangement is formalized with the birth of children, which produces a new nuclear family.

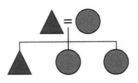

3. At some point the household might be composed of three generations, as married children join the household with their children.

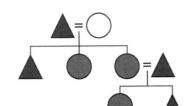

KEY

Female	●
Male	▲
Marriage	=
Blood Tie	⌐
Descent	│

4. At a later stage, the household might consist of the original couple or a single person.

▲=●

of their parents' siblings. Nor do they distinguish linguistically the children of aunts and uncles; all are referred to as cousins. For many North Americans the most important family grouping is the **nuclear family**—the group consisting of father and mother and their biological or adopted children.

Families in other societies may be composed very differently. For example, other societies may place greater emphasis on ties to one parent or the other. In some cases, only people related through *either* the mother *or* the father are considered family. Societies that emphasize persons' ties to their mother are said to have **matrilineal kinship** systems; those that emphasize persons' ties to their father are said to have **patrilineal kinship** systems. However, in few societies is an individual's relationship to one side of the family or the other totally ignored; rather, in most societies, relationships with mothers'

families and fathers' families are viewed differently. For example, North Americans traditionally inherit their surnames from their fathers, thus embracing the patrilineal principle; in cases of divorce, however, North American legal systems usually give priority to the matrilineal principle by awarding custody of the child to its mother.

---

nuclear family
The family group consisting of father, mother, and their biological or adopted children.

matrilineal kinship
A system of descent in which persons are related to their kin through the mother only.

patrilineal kinship
A system of descent in which persons are related to their kin through the father only.

---

112   CHAPTER 4

Each of the three societies discussed in this chapter—the Ju/'hoansi, the Trobrianders, and the rural Chinese—defines the composition of the family and relations among members differently.

The Family Composition of Ju/'hoansi

For most of the year, the Ju/'hoansi live in groups numbering 10 to 30 or 40 people, bilaterally related (through both parents), who hunt and gather in a territory associated with a particular water hole. Camp groups are often organized around a brother-and-sister pair who claim ownership of the water hole. They bring their spouses and children into the group; in turn, the spouses may bring in their brothers, sisters, and even mothers and fathers.

A typical camp might look like the one described by Elizabeth Thomas in her classic work *The Harmless People* (see Figure 4.2). Membership in a camp is fluid. People move freely from camp to camp based on hunting alliances or because conflict develops in the group. Within the camp, however, the basic family group is the nuclear family of husband, wife, and children. Children spend most of their time with their mothers. The Ju/'hoansi

acknowledge that pregnancy results from sexual intercourse (not the case in all societies). They also believe that conception takes place at the end of the woman's menses, when the man's semen joins with the last of the menstrual blood.

A feature of Ju/'hoansi society that figures prominently in the dynamics of family life is the custom of **brideservice** at marriage, which requires that a groom work for the bride's parents for a specified period of time. Among the Ju/'hoansi, when a couple marries, the groom is expected to come and live in the bride's parents' camp and work for her parents for as long as ten years. Tales of Ju/'hoansi family life are often built around the effects of this arrangement on family dynamics.

The Family Composition of Trobriand Islanders

The people of the Trobriand Islands live in some 80 villages, whose populations range from 40 to 400. Each village is surrounded by water holes, fruit trees, palm groves, and cultivated fields of yams, taro, and other crops. Each is further divided into hamlets, and each hamlet ideally consists of a **matrilineage**, or *dala*, as Trobrianders call it—that is, a group of men related to one another through the female line, along with their wives and unmarried children.

The matrilineages are ranked relative to one another, and each village has a chief who is the eldest male of the highest-ranking matrilineage. Since each person is a member of the lineage of his or her mother, neither a man's wife nor his children can be members of his own dala (see Figure 4.3, on page 117).

Trobrianders' mythology and beliefs about procreation dramatically depict the matrilineal element in their lives. Their mythology contains

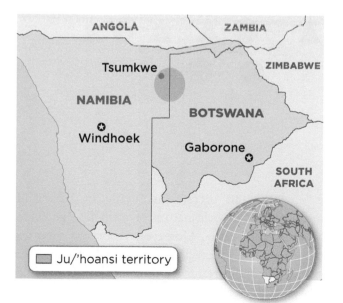

ANGOLA
ZAMBIA
Tsumkwe
ZIMBABWE
NAMIBIA
BOTSWANA
⊕ Windhoek
Gaborone ⊕
SOUTH AFRICA

▢ Ju/'hoansi territory

brideservice
The requirement that when a couple marries, the groom must work for the bride's parents for some specified period of time.

matrilineage
A lineage that is formed by tracing descent in the female line.

PATTERNS OF FAMILY RELATIONS

FIGURE 4.2 COMPOSITION AND DEVELOPMENT OF A JU/'HOANSI CAMP

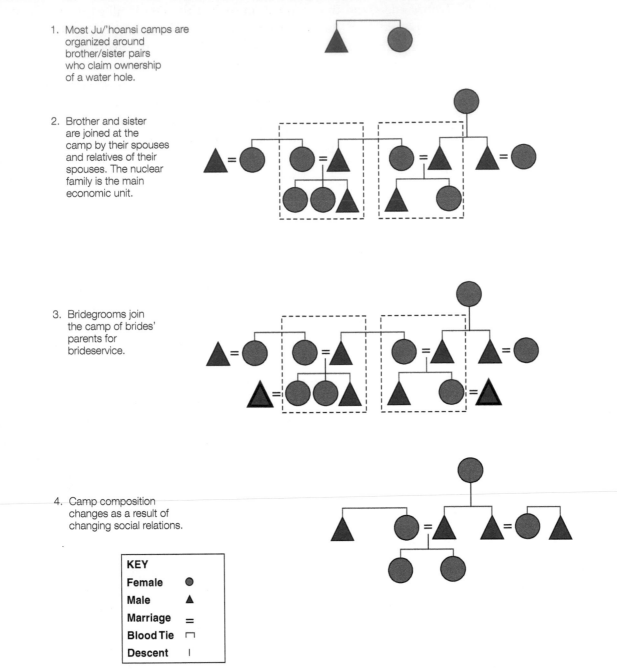

1. Most Ju/'hoansi camps are organized around brother/sister pairs who claim ownership of a water hole.

2. Brother and sister are joined at the camp by their spouses and relatives of their spouses. The nuclear family is the main economic unit.

3. Bridegrooms join the camp of brides' parents for brideservice.

4. Camp composition changes as a result of changing social relations.

KEY

Female	●
Male	▲
Marriage	=
Blood Tie	⌐
Descent	I

stories of how, a long time ago, pairs of brothers and sisters emerged from the ground to begin each *dala*. *Dala* members trace their descent back to their mythological ancestors, and they base their claims to specific plots of land on the fact that it was from there that their ancestors emerged. There is obviously an incestuous theme in Trobriand myth, since the originators of each lineage were brothers and sisters. However, Trobriand theories of procreation ostensibly deny a role to men in conception. They reinforce the matrilineal principle as well as the tie between brothers and sisters.

Trobrianders say that when a person dies, the soul or spirit becomes young and goes to live on an island called Tuma. There the soul ages, but it regenerates itself by bathing in the sea. As the skin is sloughed off, a spirit child, or *baloma*, is created, which returns to the world of the living and enters the womb of a woman of the same matrilineage as itself. In effect, a Trobriand matrilineage exists in perpetuity, as souls and spirits travel back and forth between the land of the living and the island of the dead.

The *baloma* may enter the woman through her head, or it may be carried by water into her womb. In some areas of the Trobriand Islands, if a woman wishes to become pregnant, a pail of water is brought to her dwelling by her brother. In fact, a woman cannot conceive without the "permission" of her brother. Consequently, the act of conception among Trobrianders is a matter of three agencies—a woman, the spirit or *baloma* of a deceased ancestor, and the woman's brother. Sexual intercourse is said to play no role in conception, but it does play a role in the development and growth of the fetus. Trobrianders believe that the man's semen provides food and nourishment for the fetus, and that is why

children physically resemble their fathers. Sexual intercourse is also said to open the womb for the child to emerge.

While Trobriand procreation beliefs may, at first glance, seem strange, in the context of their ideas about descent they make perfect sense. When a person is believed to be descended exclusively from the mother, possible relations and ties to the father are excluded not only socially but physically as well. In fact, we find in strongly patrilineal societies corresponding beliefs about conception. Earlier in this book we examined how Carol Delaney explained how Turkish villagers had a "monogenetic" theory of procreation. "It is the males," she wrote, "who give life; women merely give birth." Turkish villagers use an agricultural metaphor to describe procreation; men provide the seed, women are the soil. It is the seed that contains life, the soil simply nurtures it. The man is believed to plant the seed, and the woman is said to be the field in which the seed is planted. In this way the male role in the patrilineal family system of the Turkish village is emphasized and the female role is diminished.

Trobrianders can rationalize and "prove" their beliefs about procreation very easily. Bronislaw Malinowski, who spent four years studying the Trobrianders, tells of their response when he suggested to them that sexual intercourse plays a role in procreation:

> *I sometimes made myself definitely and aggressively an advocate of the truer physiological doctrine of procreation. In such arguments the natives would quote, not only positive instances of women who have children without having intercourse; but would also refer to the many cases in which an unmarried woman has plenty of intercourse and no children. This argument would be repeated over and over again, with specially telling concrete examples of childless persons renowned for profligacy, or of women who lived with one white trader after another without having any baby. (Malinowski 1929, 185–86)*

PATTERNS OF FAMILY RELATIONS

To what extent Trobrianders really deny a role to men in procreation is a matter of some debate. Annette Weiner, who worked with them in the early 1970s, some 50 years after Malinowski's pioneering work, reported that they no longer denied the direct role of men in conception. However, she also reported a case where a grandmother claimed that she had used magic to make her granddaughter pregnant when the woman conceived while her husband was away.

Regardless of the extent to which Trobrianders recognize the role of coitus, their ideas about descent and procreation reflect important features of the composition of their families. First, the key family relationship for them is not, as it is among the Ju/'hoansi, between husband and wife; it is between brother and sister. Second, the father of the family is an outsider to his children, a member of another family group. His interest, ideally, is in his sister's children, since it is they who are members of his matrilineage. Third, since the matrilineal **extended family** group, the *dala*, is more important than the nuclear family, Trobrianders merge certain people under the same kin term, the same way many North Americans refer to different kinds of kin as aunt, uncle, or cousin. In the Trobrianders case, a person refers to all women of his or her matrilineage of the same generation by the same term; for example, a man refers to his mother, as well as his mother's sisters, by the term *ina*. A woman refers to her brother and to all other men of her matrilineage and generation as *luta*. Thus, a man has many "sisters," and a woman has many "brothers."

Another consequence of matrilineal kinship is that men inherit property not from their fathers but from their mother's brothers, and it is ideally in his maternal uncle's village that a young man goes to live. The fact that these ideal conditions are not always met creates some of the drama in Trobriand family life.

The Family Composition of Rural Chinese

Family life in rural China revolves around the patrilineal extended family household of a married couple, their married sons and daughters-in-law, and their grandchildren and unmarried daughters (see Figure 4.4, on page 118). To understand a rural Chinese family, you have to understand the idea of temporal depth, for in China the **patrilineage** exists as much in time as it does in space, and the family includes a long line of patrilineal ancestors. A patrilineage is a lineage that is formed by tracing descent in the male line. Anthropologist Francis L.K. Hsu notes that the identity of each male is defined by his relations to the dead as much as it is by his relations to the living. His social worth and destiny are but reflections of the actions of his ancestors. He thus exists, as Hsu says, "under the shadow of his ancestors." Likewise, the spirits of the dead are dependent on the contributions of the living. These contributions are ceremonially made

EXERCISE 4.2

The procreation beliefs of the Trobriand Islanders prompted debate among anthropologists about whether the Trobrianders really did believe that men played little or no role in reproduction or whether, to emphasize the matrilineal principle, they pretended not to acknowledge the male's role. In either case, we would expect to find in societies that emphasize the patrilineal principle that a woman's role in reproduction is de-emphasized. What kind of belief about reproduction can you think of that would deny the importance of the female? How does this compare with the biological roles of men and women in North American societies?

extended family
A family group based on blood relations of three or more generations.

patrilineage
A lineage that is formed by tracing descent in the male line.

FIGURE 4.3 COMPOSITION OF A TROBRIAND ISLAND DALA AND HOUSEHOLD

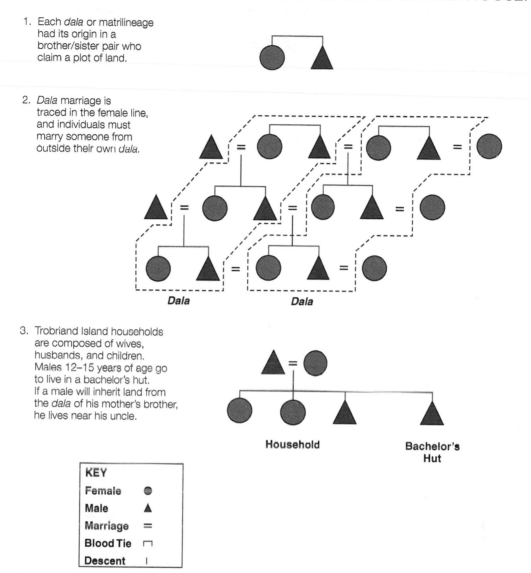

1. Each *dala* or matrilineage had its origin in a brother/sister pair who claim a plot of land.

2. *Dala* marriage is traced in the female line, and individuals must marry someone from outside their own *dala*.

Dala

Dala

3. Trobriand Island households are composed of wives, husbands, and children. Males 12–15 years of age go to live in a bachelor's hut. If a male will inherit land from the *dala* of his mother's brother, he lives near his uncle.

Household

Bachelor's Hut

KEY

Female	●
Male	▲
Marriage	=
Blood Tie	⊓
Descent	I

at altars, prominently positioned in each home, from which people send gifts to their ancestors by burning paper money, paper clothes, or other paper articles.

Given the interdependence between the living and the dead men of the patrilineage, it is apparent why it is essential for a Chinese male to have male descendants to look after his well-being and to provide for him in the afterworld. Male children and grandchildren are living proof to a man that his line will continue. For this reason, unlike the Ju/'hoansi or the Trobrianders, the Chinese express a marked preference for male children. Males are needed to maintain the patrilineal descent group, for if the only children born are daughters whose children will in turn belong to the patrilineage of their husbands, a family line will die out. A son, as some Chinese put it, is a major happiness; a daughter is but a small happiness.

In addition to a long line of male ancestors, an ideal rural Chinese household should include several generations of fathers and sons sharing a common

FIGURE 4.4 COMPOSITION AND DEVELOPMENT OF A RURAL CHINESE FAMILY

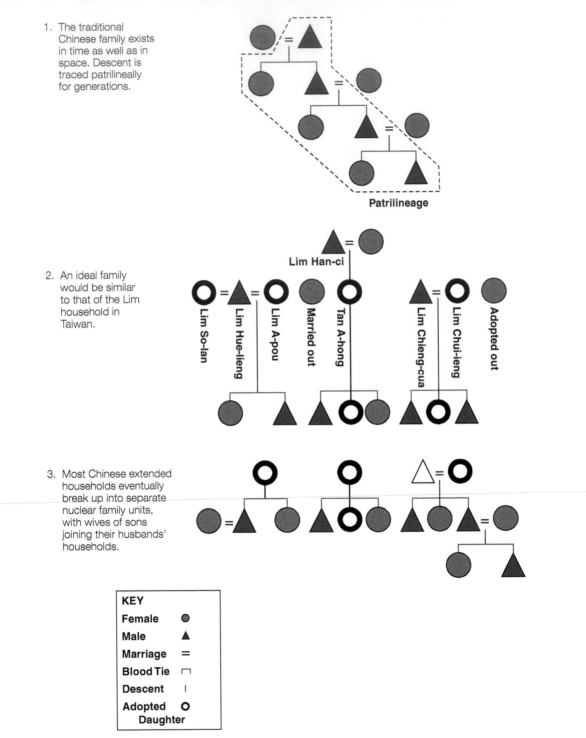

1. The traditional Chinese family exists in time as well as in space. Descent is traced patrilineally for generations.

Patrilineage

2. An ideal family would be similar to that of the Lim household in Taiwan.

Lim Han-ci

Lim So-lan

Lim Hue-ieng

Lim A-pou

Married out

Tan A-hong

Lim Chieng-cua

Lim Chui-ieng

Adopted out

3. Most Chinese extended households eventually break up into separate nuclear family units, with wives of sons joining their husbands' households.

KEY

Female	●
Male	▲
Marriage	=
Blood Tie	⌐
Descent	l
Adopted Daughter	O

hearth or cooking stove and an ancestral altar, the symbols of the household. In the architecture of Peihotien, the village where Margery Wolf did her fieldwork, houses are constructed in such a way that they can easily be extended to accommodate additional sons and grandsons, who bring their wives to live in the family home. In reality it is very difficult to maintain this ideal; most households in villages such as Peihotien are small, consisting of a married couple and several dependent patrilineal relatives.

RESOURCE 4.1

The study of kinship organization and terminology can be highly complex, yet it is essential for understanding the patterns of social organization of many societies. You can find out more about this and engage in some entertaining exercises at Brian Schwimmer's Kinship and Social Organization: An Interactive Tutorial at http://www.umanitoba.ca/faculties/arts/anthropology/kintitle.html

QUESTION 4.2: HOW ARE FAMILIES FORMED, AND HOW IS THE IDEAL FAMILY TYPE MAINTAINED?

Regardless of the size of family units or descent systems, most societies require the socially recognized union of a male and a female (we will discuss the exceptions later in this chapter). Generally, this takes the form of marriage, which is a publicly recognized joining of two people or two families. However, while marriage makes or sustains families, the manner in which such an arrangement comes about varies significantly in different societies. In North American societies, for example, many children begin learning about courtship and marriage at an early age: five- and six-year-olds are teased about their "boyfriends" or "girlfriends," and playing house together is a popular preschool pastime. Most North Americans begin serious courting in their early teens and usually go through a series of relationships before choosing a partner for their first marriage, most often when they are between the ages of 18 and 30. Although the choice of a marriage partner is supposedly based on feelings of love and sexual attraction, other factors also influence it. North Americans, like people in all societies, are prohibited by the **incest taboo** from marrying or having sexual relations with certain categories of kin, such as brothers or sisters, children or parents, or, in some cases, cousins. Preferences (sometimes tacit, sometimes explicit) also exist about choosing one's spouse from an appropriate income, ethnic, gender, and racial group.

The marriage ceremony in many North American societies is often arranged and financed

> **incest taboo**
> A rule that prohibits sexual relations among certain categories of kin, such as brothers or sisters, parents and children, or, in some cases, cousins.

by the bride's family. After the honeymoon, the couple ideally establishes an independent residence. Their relationship based on love expressed through regular sexual intercourse is later transformed by the arrival of one or more children, when a wife becomes a mother, a husband becomes a father. However, the cycles of events that create or sustain the family among the Ju/'hoansi, the Trobrianders, and the rural Chinese illustrate the diversity of such arrangements.

The Family Cycle of Ju/'hoansi

Ju/'hoansi men and women, like most North Americans, begin to learn about courtship, sex, and marriage early in life. Because there is little privacy in a Ju/'hoansi camp and children sleep with their parents, they soon are playing at marriage and imitating the bodily movements of parents making love. Most young men and women have had sexual experiences by the time they are 15. Ju/'hoansi men usually marry for the first time between the ages of 18 and 25, when they are able to hunt and work for their wives' parents. Marriage is important for a man for a number of reasons. It marks him as an adult worthy of taking part in Ju/'hoansi public life; he gains a sex partner; and he gains a mate to provide his food. While men are obligated to share and formally distribute the meat they obtain in the hunt with everyone in the camp, women are not obligated to share what they gather outside their nuclear family group, and women gather from 60 to 80 percent of the food in a camp.

Women often marry as early as 12 to 14 years of age, generally before their first menstruation, which occurs at about 17. Girls have fewer reasons to marry than men. Single or married men are always available as sex partners, and since the product of male labour, meat, is widely shared, a woman need not have a husband to ensure her share of the hunt. However, a girl's parents have good reasons for getting her married as soon as possible. The earlier she is married, the longer she and her husband will

In Ju/'hoansi culture, most marriages are arranged by the couple's parents, and the bride-to-be frequently objects to the chosen spouse or to the prospect of marriage itself.

remain with her parents until she is of age, and the longer her husband will work for her parents. Moreover, the bride's family gains an alliance with another family and is less likely to get involved in open conflict between men over their daughter.

Marriages are almost always arranged by the couple's parents. Typically the mother or father of the male approaches the family of the girl with a proposal for marriage. If the girl's parents approve of the match, the families exchange gifts to indicate their agreement. An appropriate husband for a daughter is a man who is not too much older, is not yet married, is a good hunter, and is willing to accept responsibility. The prospective groom should also be cooperative, generous, and unaggressive.

The Ju/'hoansi not only avoid choosing a spouse who is a close kinsperson, but also are restricted in the choice of a marriage partner by their naming system. There are only about 30 to 40 names that can be chosen for newborns, and people with the same first name consider themselves connected, regardless of their actual kinship relation to one another. For example, if two people are named Toma, then everyone related by kinship to one Toma will be considered related in the same way to the other Toma. Consequently, if a man's name is Toma, all the brothers and sisters of everyone else named Toma would be considered his brothers and sisters, all the sons and daughters of other Tomas would be considered his sons and daughters, and so on. Therefore, a marriage partner should occupy neither an actual prohibited kinship category nor one created by the naming system. A woman, for example, could not marry a man with the same name as her father or a man whose father had the same name as her father, since she and the man would refer to themselves as brother and sister. When Richard Lee was working with the Ju/'hoansi kinship system, he found that interpretations of the naming system varied, and disagreements about the kin connection between people would always be resolved by the interpretation of the older person in the relationship.

Once a suitable match is made, one more obstacle to the marriage remains. Perhaps because they have little to gain or much to lose, young women often object strenuously to the marriage or to their parents' choice of a husband. If they protest long and hard enough, the marriage will be called off; if the protest is not sufficient to call off the arrangements, a marriage ceremony takes place. A hut set apart from the bride's family village is built for the couple by members of both families. Friends bring the couple to the hut, and the girl, head covered, is placed in the hut. Coals from the fires of both families are brought to start the fire in the couple's hut. Friends stay, joking, singing, and dancing, while bride and groom stay apart. Often, especially if the girl is young, a relative stays with them in the hut until she begins to adjust to her new status. These "honeymoons" are often the source of continuing conflict.

Working among the Ju/'hoansi, Marjorie Shostak forged a close relationship with a Ju/'hoansi woman, Nisa, who described her wedding night. Nisa said that she cried so much and objected so strongly to spending the night with her new husband, Bo, that her parents asked a female relative, Nukha, to sleep between Nisa and Bo. She soon discovered that Nukha was having sex with Bo, and after a few nights she told her parents. They took her and moved to another water hole, leaving Nukha and Bo behind.

Typically, half of all first marriages fail among the Ju/'hoansi, who may enter several marriages over the course of their lives. Nisa's second marriage, to Tashay, followed the same lines as her first; on her wedding night she cried and cried and eventually ran away into the bush. Relatives tried to explain the benefits of marriage and to convince her to accept Tashay. When she finally agreed, Tashay took Nisa to his parents' home to live, and Nisa's parents followed. But not until Nisa and Tashay had been living together for a long time did they have sex. Nisa remembers the aftermath of their first lovemaking as being painful, and it was a long time before she allowed it again and began to enjoy it.

The Family Cycle of Trobriand Islanders

Courtship and sexual play begin early in the Trobriand Islands. Children play erotic games at the ages of seven and eight and begin seeking sex partners at ages 11 to 13. Trobriand adolescents are permitted to openly display their affection for each other; girls scratch, beat, thrash, or even wound their lovers, and boys accept this treatment as a sign of love and display their wounds as proof of manliness and success in courtship. They sing about love, both successful and unrequited, and take great pains with their physical appearance. Here is what Malinowski says about adolescent courtship: "An adolescent gets definitely attached to a given person, wishes to possess her, works purposefully toward his goal, plans to reach fulfillment of his desires by magical and other means, and finally rejoices in achievement. I have seen young people of this age grow positively miserable through ill-success in love" (Malinowski 1929, 63).

Because sexual activity before marriage is common and expected among Trobrianders, the couple often has already been living together, and the marriage simply formalizes an existing relationship. Although the couple may take the initiative in arranging a marriage, parents approve or disapprove of the choice of a spouse and sometimes arrange matches. There are certain categories of people a Trobriander may not marry. All Trobrianders belong to one of four clans, groups whose members consider themselves descended from a common ancestor. They must observe **exogamy**, which requires one to marry outside of one's own group—in this case, out of their own clan and into another (other societies practise **endogamy**, which requires marriage into one's own group). In addition, the incest taboo applies to all close relatives, particularly brothers and sisters, who include all members of a matrilineage of the same generation. Trobriand myths tell of disastrous consequences of brother–sister incest that resulted in both parties committing suicide. Sexual relations between a father and daughter are prohibited, although Trobrianders tell stories about it and joke about the idea of a father being overwhelmed by the beauty of his daughter. From a Trobriand point of view, fathers are not related by kinship to their daughters. The best marriage for a man is to a woman from his father's clan, for then his children, who will trace their descent from their mother, will be members of his father's clan. Consequently, the close relationship a man has with members of his father's clan will continue into the next generation.

There is no formal marriage ceremony; the girl simply stays overnight in her boyfriend's house. The next morning the bride's mother brings the couple cooked yams to indicate the bride's family's approval of the marriage. If the girl's parents don't approve, they demand that their daughter return home with them. Significantly, sharing food is considered by Trobrianders to be more intimate than having sex. Later, the wife's mother and maternal uncle bring raw yams for the couple, while the groom's father and maternal uncle begin collecting **bridewealth**—valuables such as stone axe blades, shells, and money—to give to the wife's kin and her father. The requirement of bridewealth makes young men dependent on members of their matrilineage. This differs from the brideservice required of a Ju/'hoansi man, since brideservice

does not obligate a man to members of his family (see Question 4.1).

During the first year of marriage, the couple lives in the hut that served as the groom's adolescent retreat, and during that year the groom's mother brings meals for them to share. At the end of the year, the groom's mother builds a stone hearth for the couple, and at that point the wife becomes responsible for the cooking.

The end of the first year of marriage marks a dramatic change in the husband–wife relationship. They no longer eat together, and the sexuality that bound them together as adolescents must be publicly submerged. After the first year of marriage it is shameful for anyone to refer to the couple's sex life together. In public, a husband and wife never hold hands or display affection. Their lives become segmented into a private domain in which affection and emotion can be displayed, and a public domain in which the meaning of their relationship is dictated by their obligation to help ensure the continuity and honour of their respective matrilineages.

The matrilineal principle in the life of a Trobriand husband and wife requires each to have a continued involvement with others outside the nuclear family. In addition to his ties to and concerns for his wife and children, the husband is also involved in the family life of his matrilineage: his sisters and their children. The wife is continually

---

exogamy
A rule that requires a person to marry someone outside one's own group.

endogamy
A rule that requires a person to marry someone inside one's own group (the group could be a lineage, an ethnic group, a religious group, etc.).

bridewealth
The valuables that a groom or his family are expected or obligated to present to the bride's family.

involved with her and her children's matrilineage—particularly her brothers. This involvement is economic and revolves around wealth, particularly yams, banana leaf bundles, and skirts, all of which are controlled ultimately by women.

One reason men marry is to obtain yams. Yams are more than food in the Trobriand Islands; they are valuable symbols or objects of wealth and are used as gifts to create and sustain relationships among people. They are particularly important in marriage transactions and in the continued tie of a woman to her matrilineage. Trobriand family yam gardens belong to the wife, but they are tended first by her father and later by a "brother." Each year at harvest time the yams grown in her garden by her father or brother are ceremoniously taken to her. The amount and quality of the yams grown by a woman's brother are usually proportional to the bridewealth given to the wife's family by the groom's family when the couple was married. Early in the marriage these yams are stored in the rafters of the couple's hut, and the husband uses them as valuables to be redistributed to those of his kin who contributed the bridewealth. Later—often 10 to 15 years later—if a man is recognized as important by his wife's kin, they construct a yam house for him to store the yams they bring each year. The amount and quality of the yams stored and displayed by a man are indications of the regard in which he is held by his wife's kin and of his status in the community. The yam house is, according to Weiner, like a public bank account.

As a man seeks a wife to obtain the yams grown for him by his wife's brother, brothers seek husbands for their sisters, not only for the children nurtured by the husbands for their wives' matrilineage but also for the brother-in-law's help in obtaining banana leaf bundles. Sisters are obligated, with the help of their husbands, to prepare bundles of banana leaves to be used to finance the funerals of members of their matrilineage. Some are made by the woman, but her husband may have to purchase additional bundles. They are given away at funerals by members of the deceased's matrilineage to people who were important in the life of the deceased. The more important the person was to the deceased, the greater the number of banana leaf bundles he or she receives. In this way, members of a matrilineage uphold their honour and status; to fail to fulfill these obligations would bring dishonour to the matrilineage.

The development of Trobriand family life, then, must be understood in the context of the movement of such goods as yams and banana leaf bundles between husband and wife and members of the wife's matrilineage. It is the successful completion of the cycle of exchanges of yams and banana leaf bundles that ensures the stability of a marriage and a matrilineage.

The Trobriand nuclear family promotes stable bonds between husband and wife, although divorce is both frequent and easy to obtain. The initiative is usually taken by the wife. Most divorces occur in the first year of marriage; they are rare after the couple has been together for a few years.

While fathers are not technically members of their children's family, they are very important in the lives of the children. Once children are weaned they sleep with their fathers, and later the father is responsible for enhancing their beauty with presents of shells, necklaces, and tiny tortoise-shell

© Peter Essick/Aurora Photos

Among the Trobriand Islanders, lineage is traced through the mother, and individuals must marry outside their own clan. Here a Trobriand chief on Kiriwina Island is shown with family members at the home of one of his two wives.

PATTERNS OF FAMILY RELATIONS

earrings. These objects are evidence of a father's presence in the life of his child; in fact, Weiner says, the term for a child with unpierced ears is translated as "fatherless." So important is the tie that develops between a man and his son that when the son marries, the father may try to convince him to remain in his village rather than moving to the village of his maternal kin, as is expected.

The Family Cycle of Rural Chinese

The key relationship in Ju/'hoansi families is between husband and wife, and among Trobriand Islanders it is between brother and sister. In China, the family centres on the relationship between father and son. Marriage in traditional China is less a matter of a man getting a wife than of bringing a child bearer into the household. As Hsu describes it, "a marriage is made in the name of the parents taking a daughter-in-law, not in the name of the son taking a wife."

Since marriage has far less to do with relations between husband and wife than with those between the husband's family and a daughter-in-law, marriages in rural China are almost always arranged, often far in advance, and there is little if any courtship. When a boy is six or seven years old, his parents might hire a matchmaker to find a girl who will eventually be an appropriate bride for their son. Since they believe that the time of a person's birth influences his or her personality and fate, the parents may also enlist the services of a diviner to make the appropriate match. The matchmaker takes a red paper with the time and date of a girl's birth to a prospective groom's family. The boy's mother brings this paper (or papers, if there is a choice of brides) to a fortuneteller, who predicts the compatibility of the boy and girl. If a girl is deemed appropriate by the fortuneteller, the matchmaker tries to convince the girl's parents to accept the match. If she is successful, the bridewealth—that is, the marriage gifts of the husband's family to the wife's parents—is then negotiated.

Another way parents can obtain a wife for their son in rural China is to adopt an infant girl who will be reared in the household and later will marry the son. While this kind of arrangement is not as prestigious as bridewealth marriage, it has two advantages. Since the prospective bride was raised in the household of her future mother-in-law, she is more likely to be obedient, and it is not necessary to pay a brideprice for an adopted daughter-in-law. The major disadvantage is that the prospective bride and groom are raised as brother and sister and often find it difficult to make the transition to husband and wife.

The adoption of a boy to serve as a husband for a daughter is a third way marriages are arranged in rural China. This is done only when a family has no sons. The adopted boy then assumes the family name, so that his sons continue the line of his adopted father. Such marriages are not as respected as others, and a man who is adopted into his wife's family bears the stigma of having abandoned his parents and ancestors. For poor or orphaned boys, however,

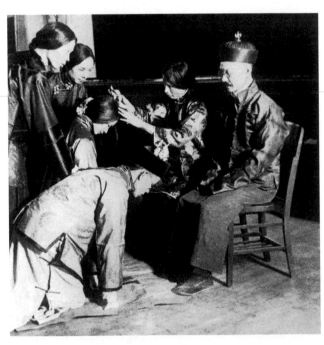

In a rural Chinese wedding, the bride's mother places a rose in the bride's hair and then transfers it to the groom. Then the couple proceed to the household of the groom's parents, where they will make their home.

the prospect of heading a thriving household may outweigh such a stigma.

Compared to Ju/'hoansi or Trobriand marriage ceremonies, the rural Chinese wedding is very formal and, for the groom's family, very expensive. The date and hour of the wedding are determined by a diviner, who even decides the exact time the bride will arrive in her sedan chair. The day before the wedding, the girl's **dowry**—goods and valuables that the bride's family supplies to the groom's family or the couple—is sent to the groom's home in a procession accompanied by a band, drummers, and ushers. The dowry consists of such goods as leather chests, tables, stools, cosmetics, housewares, clothing and cloth, but never land or a house. On the day of the wedding, the groom is carried in a sedan chair to the house of the bride; when he arrives, she shows token resistance, and she and her mother weep. Then she is carried to the groom's house in a red sedan chair decorated to suggest the early birth of sons. Offerings are made at the ancestors' altar to ensure the success of the marriage. Then the couple is taken to pay respect to the boy's parents—the formal introduction of the bride to the groom's household. Feasting and dancing accompany the wedding and sometimes last for three or four days.

After the wedding, there is little time or place for romantic relations between husband and wife. Hsu reports that after the marriage, husband and wife sleep in the same bed for only seven days, and there is no public expression of affection between them. Once the wife enters into her husband's family, she finds herself among strangers, virtually cut off from her parents and siblings. She must treat her mother-in-law with respect and acquiesce to the demands of sisters-in-law or other members of her husband's family. She occupies the lowest place at the table, and she does not acquire full status in her husband's family until she produces a male child. Until then, the husband must show indifference to his wife, addressing her through a third party; after the birth of a son, he can refer to her as the mother of his child. For the groom, marriage is a

continued expression of his duty to his father and his ancestors. Whereas divorce is fairly common among Trobrianders and among Ju/'hoansi, it is virtually unheard of in rural China. A husband can take mistresses with impunity, and in theory, he can murder an adulterous wife. Wives have no rights of divorce. A wife may flee her husband's household, commit suicide, or become a prostitute, but a woman who wishes to leave her husband and in-laws has few other alternatives.

QUESTION 4.3: WHAT ARE THE ROLES OF SEXUALITY, LOVE, AND WEALTH?

Sex, Love, and Wealth Among Ju/'hoansi

Wealth plays no part in the lives of the Ju/'hoansi, but especially for women, according to Nisa, sex, love, and beauty are very important. A Ju/'hoansi woman's sexuality is her major means of negotiating the conditions of her relationships with others. Sexuality is important first for her own well-being. Nisa told Marjorie Shostak that if a girl grows up not learning to enjoy sex, her mind doesn't develop normally; if a grown woman doesn't have sex, her thoughts are ruined and she is always angry. Moreover, a woman's sexuality maximizes her independence. Sex attracts lovers, and a love relationship, being voluntary, recognizes the equality of the participants. By taking lovers, a Ju/'hoansi woman proclaims her control over her social life, because she can offer her sexuality to men as a means of vitalizing them. Nisa talked candidly about sex, male impotence, and the contributions women make to men:

> **dowry**
> The goods and valuables a bride's family supplies to the groom's family or to the couple.

A woman can bring a man life, even if he is almost dead. She can give him sex and make him alive again. If she were to refuse, he would die! If there were no women around, their semen would kill men. Did you know that? Women make it possible for them to live. Women have something so good that if a man takes it and moves about inside it, he climaxes and is sustained. (in Shostak 1983, 288)

There is one trade-off for Ju/'hoansi women who use their sexuality. Men see them as sources of male conflict and consequently as potentially dangerous.

Motherhood, unlike sexuality, is not easily bartered by Ju/'hoansi women. In other societies, parents may stress how much they have sacrificed or suffered for their children, thus using motherhood or fatherhood as a way of creating obligations and ties. It makes little sense for a Ju/'hoansi woman (or man, for that matter) to make such a claim. Children owe their parents little; there is no need for bridewealth or dowries for marriage, and food and kin to care for them are plentiful. The dynamics of Ju/'hoansi families are built on the need of individuals to avoid permanent ties and obligations and to maintain their independence.

Sex, Love, and Wealth Among Trobriand Islanders

The maintenance of sexuality is important throughout life among Ju/'hoansi; among Trobriand Islanders, it is important for women only prior to their marriage. Armed with the magic and bodily adornments contributed by her father, but without the wealth (yams, banana leaf bundles, other valuables) she will later acquire, an unmarried woman uses her sexuality to negotiate her relationships with others. Once married, she ceases to emphasize her beauty and sexual attraction and instead emphasizes her fertility and motherhood. A woman's worth, once measured by her father's concern for her and by her own sexuality and beauty, is determined after marriage by her ability to collect yams for her husband, produce children, and provide banana leaf bundles for her matrilineage.

Men's sexuality is viewed very differently. Since Trobrianders claim that men play no role in reproduction, their sexuality is never very important anyway. Their physical attractiveness, however, is important, for this is what attracts lovers and later a wife to collect the yams by which a man measures his status. Beauty is especially important for chiefs. They must maintain an aura of sexual attractiveness in order to attract more wives, whose fathers and brothers will supply the wealth they need to maintain their influence.

Wealth also forms different kinds of links for Trobrianders. Because Ju/'hoansi have little wealth to contend for, and what there is (e.g., meat) is widely shared, the links that men create with their wives' families are based not on wealth but on their labour. Among Trobrianders, however, men who want to marry must use the wealth of members of their matrilineage as bridewealth payments to their wives' families. They are required to return this wealth to members of their family by redistributing the yams they later receive from their wives' brothers. Moreover, the yams they receive from their brothers-in-law are in some ways payment for the children their wives produce, who are members of the wife's and brother-in-law's matrilineage.

Sex, Love, and Wealth Among Rural Chinese

The themes of sexuality, love, and wealth are played out very differently in Chinese rural families. Whereas Ju/'hoansi and Trobriand adolescents have considerable freedom to utilize their sexuality to attract and influence others, quite the opposite is true in China. If a girl comes from a family that is wealthy and influential enough to make an attractive match for her, she will have little to do with boys. Virginity is both valued and necessary for a Chinese bride; for a Ju/'hoansi or Trobriander woman, it is almost no consideration. In China, if a girl is known to have been mixed up in an affair, her only chance of marriage is to someone in a distant village.

According to Margery Wolf, romantic love and sexuality are irrelevant also in the relations between traditional Chinese husbands and wives. A wife's function is to produce children. A man who can afford it takes concubines. A man who can't afford it, but does so anyway, is criticized not for his infidelity to his wife but for squandering the wealth of his ancestors and descendants.

In fact, sexuality figures very little in the life of a rural Chinese woman either before or after her marriage. Her sexuality is simply not negotiable; instead it is as a mother that most Chinese women establish significant relations. Her value consists in her potential to become the mother of a boy. Becoming a mother cements her relations with her husband, her father-in-law, and her mother-in-law, and it is her motherhood that secures her later life. While a son is obligated to care for his aged mother, the obligation is not so great as it is to care for a father. To compensate, Wolf argues, a woman must establish bonds of emotion and affection with her sons. She may do this with the assistance of her husband. After a boy is six or seven, fathers become aloof and withdrawn in order to assert and reinforce their authority and control over a son. A mother can use her husband's aloofness from his son to strengthen the son's ties to her. Even if she enjoys good relations with her husband, she will try to reserve the son's affections for herself, while preserving the son's respect for his father.

QUESTION 4.4: WHAT THREATENS TO DISRUPT THE FAMILY UNIT?

In the introduction, we briefly discussed contemporary debates about same-sex marriage and teenage and single motherhood in North America. Much of the debate focuses on whether or not these social phenomena pose a "threat" to the typical North American family. There are also threats to the stability and maintenance of traditional Chinese, Trobriand, and Ju/'hoansi families, but these differ from the ones that are perceived to threaten the North American family.

Threats to a Ju/'hoansi Family

The major threat to family stability among the Ju/'hoansi is conflict between husband and wife over infidelity or the efforts of a husband to secure a second wife. Like many societies around the world, the Ju/'hoansi allow **polygamy**, a form of marriage in which a person is permitted to have more than one spouse. Men are allowed to have more than one wife (**polygyny**), and apparently women are permitted to have more than one husband

---

EXERCISE 4.3

In North America, we tend to take romantic love and sexual attraction for granted as central to the development and maintenance of relationships. However, the cases explored above demonstrate that romantic love and sexuality are clearly not universal. Yet there seem to be features of love and sexuality in all three that are similar to life in North American families. Your problem is simply to list those features of conjugal relationships among Ju/'hoansi, Trobriand Islanders, and rural Chinese that resemble those of North American families. Put another way, what features of North American conjugal relationships would be familiar to a Ju/'hoansi, a Trobriand Islander, or someone from rural China?

---

polygamy
A form of marriage in which a person is permitted to have more than one spouse.

polygyny
A form of marriage in which a man is permitted to have more than one wife.

(**polyandry**), though this is rare. In fact, polygamy is the exception rather than the rule. A survey conducted by Lee in 1968 of 131 married Ju/'hoansi men found that 93 percent were living monogamously, 5 percent were living in polygynous unions, and 2 percent were living in polyandrous relationships.

One reason that polygamy is rare, even though having more than one wife is a sign of prestige, is the family difficulties it creates. According to Marjorie Shostak, a popular saying is "There is never any peace in a household with two women in it." Stories of the complications resulting from polygamous unions are an endless source of humour for those who are single or monogamous. Here is how Nisa described polygyny in her society to Shostak:

> When a man married one woman, then marries another and sets her down beside the first so there are three of them together at night, the husband changes from one wife to another. First he has sex with the older wife, then with the younger. But when he goes to the younger wife, the older one is jealous and grabs and bites him. The two women start to fight and bite each other. The older woman goes to the fire and throws burning wood at them yelling "What told you that when I, your first wife, am lying here that you should go and sleep with another woman? Don't I have a vagina? So why do you just leave it and go without having sex with me? Instead you go and have sex with that young girl!" Sometimes they fight like that all night, until dawn breaks. A co-wife is truly a terrible thing. (in Shostak 1983, 172)

While polygamy is rare, marital infidelity is not. At one water hole with 50 married couples, Lee recorded 16 couples in which one or another of the partners was having an affair. The Ju/'hoansi recognize certain benefits in taking lovers. For a woman, extramarital affairs add variety as well as economic insurance. Here is Nisa again:

> When you are a woman, you just don't sit still and do nothing—you have lovers. You don't just sit with the man of your hut, with just one man. One man can give you very little. One man gives you only one kind of food to eat. But when you have lovers, one brings you something and another brings you something else. One comes at night with meat, another with money, another with beads. (in Shostak 1983, 271)

Men say that the emotion and passion of extramarital affairs are wonderful—"hearts are on fire and passions great," as Ju/'hoansi say. When Shostak asked a young married man about his lover, he said they fantasized about running away. She asked what it would be like, and he smiled and replied, "The first few months would be wonderful!" Extramarital affairs are likely to be threatening to a husband, however, and they are the most common cause of conflict and violence among the Ju/'hoansi. Wives are important to Ju/'hoansi men because as long as they have wives they are dependent on no one. Male adulthood requires acquiring and demonstrating a willingness to fight for a secure marital status.

Threats to a Trobriand Island Family

Among Trobriand Islanders it is not threats to the husband–wife relationship that are critical but threats to the matrilineage. Because the matrilineage is the principal social unit, the honour of that family group relative to other groups is a central concern to all members. Lineages among Trobriand Islanders are ranked according to the closeness of their genealogical connection to the founders of the lineage. Each lineage must be able to maintain its position vis-à-vis others through the ceremonial presentation of valuables,

---

polyandry
A form of marriage in which a woman is permitted to have more than one husband.

particularly yams and banana leaf bundles. So important are yams in the relative ranking of matrilineages that groups try to demonstrate their wealth by giving more yams to others than they receive. Since giving may be taken as a claim of superiority, however, it can be dangerous; as Trobrianders put it, "When you give too much, people worry."

While it may seem implausible, yams could become the focus of a Trobriand soap opera or reality television show. For example, a man's political power, measured in yams, is a direct result of the support he receives from his wife's kin—it is her yams, grown for her by her father and brother, that create status for her husband. However, the annual yam gifts received by a husband can also be a source of conflict. If the amount or size of yams harvested does not live up to a husband's expectations, he may be insulted. On the other hand, if a woman's brother is unhappy over the bridewealth he received from the husband's family or the support given by the husband to his sister in collecting banana leaf bundles, he may purposely communicate his unhappiness by not working hard in his sister's yam gardens. Other plots could be devised about unrequited love, about attempts by fathers to convince their sons to remain in their father's village, and even about incest. But a theme that would be sure to attract a Trobriand audience would be about sorcery.

Trobrianders claim to know of spells and magic forms that are capable of killing. Generally only chiefs have this power, but others can seek out a chief and, for a price, convince him to use his power against their enemies. Someone who is believed to have this power is both feared and respected; Trobrianders tell of instances when they were challenged and retaliated with sorcery. Vanoi, an important Trobriand chief, told Weiner about being challenged by a Christian convert who openly mocked Vanoi's knowledge of sorcery. Vanoi offered the man a cigarette, saying that he should smoke it if he doubted the chief's knowledge of sorcery. The man did; he became ill later that night and died a week later.

A person who uses sorcery against another is dominating that person, and since each person's fate is tied to that of the matrilineage, a threat to one is considered a threat to all. That is why any death among Trobrianders is a serious matter. Since all deaths are attributed to sorcery, every death is a sign that the power of a matrilineage is being challenged by someone from another lineage. Each funeral marks an attempt by the members of a matrilineage to reassert its power; at the same time, the mourners assert their innocence of sorcery. The matrilineal kin of the deceased do this by distributing banana leaf bundles and other valuables to those who have come to publicly mourn the passing of the deceased and to assist with the funeral arrangements by decorating and carrying the corpse. In recognition of their contribution to the life of the deceased, they receive gifts. The deceased's matrilineage empties its treasury to announce its strength in the face of the threat to its integrity that is signalled by a death.

Maintaining one's identity and that of the matrilineage is a never-ending process among Trobrianders because death threatens the network by removing someone from it. Here is how Weiner sums up the meaning of death for them:

> *Because of the expanding possibilities in a person's life, each Trobriander represents her or his matrilineal identity—originally conceived through a woman and an ancestral baloma spirit—as well as the accumulation of all the other relationships that parenthood and marriage made possible. Therefore, a death demands attention to this full totality, as the members of a matrilineage seek both to repay all "others" for their past care and to hold on to them now that this death has occurred. (Weiner 1988, 161)*

Threats to a Rural Chinese Family

The biggest threat to the traditional rural Chinese family is, of course, the absence of a son. The lack of a male heir endangers not only the continuance of a household but also the entire patrilineage through time. A man without sons, a spirit without descendants, has no one to offer incense for him and no altar on which his spirit can find refuge and honour. The existence of a son is no guarantee of smooth family relations, however. Fathers have enormous authority and power over sons, and sons are obligated to worship, respect, obey, and care for their fathers. But often fathers become overbearing or use force to assert their authority. Margery Wolf says that Lim Han-ci in the village of Peihotien (see Question 4.3) was unusual in the frequency with which he administered physical punishment to his sons; once he beat them with a hoe handle and left bruises that lasted for weeks. However, regardless of how harshly a person may be treated, breaking away from one's father is considered a violent act. Wolf reports a conflict between Lim Han-ci and his eldest son, Lim Hue-lieng, that illustrates both the dilemma of a father–son split and the difficulties that can arise in adopted marriages. When Lim Hue-lieng was a child, Lim Han-ci adopted Lim A-pou, then nine months old, to be reared as the eventual wife of his son. Growing up in the Lim household, Lim A-pou was a model daughter-in-law. She accepted reprimands and punishment without becoming sullen, she did not complain, and she was a hard worker. However, her relationship with her prospective husband was not a happy one. When Lim Hue-lieng was 19, he committed what in rural China is an act of moral violence: he left home and severed his relations with his father. If a son dies before his father and so is unable to care for the father in his old age, the father ritually beats the son's coffin to punish him. Lim Hue-lieng was able to leave home only because he had become a leader in the *lo mue*, a secret society that is involved in crime and extortion but that also protects the downtrodden and contributes heavily to religious festivals.

Dramatic splits between fathers and sons are rare in traditional China. More frequent is conflict between brothers over the division and sharing of the family wealth at the death of a male head of the household. In most other rural, peasant societies around the world, the male head of the household designates his heirs before his death. He may in some fashion divide his property among his offspring—**partible inheritance**—or he may leave all his property to one or another descendant—**impartible inheritance**. In rural China the ideal is for brothers to continue to live together and share the inheritance, usually under the direction of the eldest son, thus avoiding the division of property. In fact, however, brothers rarely continue to share, and ultimately conflict between them leads to a division of household property.

Wolf documents the ultimate disintegration of the Lim household after the death of Lim Han-ci and the resulting arguments over property by the sons and their wives. When Wolf went to live in the Lim household, Lim Han-ci and his oldest son, Lim Hue-lieng, had already died. The two remaining family units consisted of the family of the second oldest son, Lim Chieng-cua, and the family of Lim Hue-lieng's widow, Lim A-Pou. While Lim Han-ci was alive, his power and influence and his control over the family's wealth were enough to maintain the extended family. Once he died, conflict between Lim A-pou and her son on the one hand and Lim Chieng-cua on the other led to the division of family property. The wealth that had held the extended family together served, finally, to drive it apart. After dividing the property, brothers or their families often continue to live in the same house, but they partition it into separate family units with separate stoves, as did the son and grandson of Lim Han-ci. The once extended household becomes, in effect, a family compound.

---

partible inheritance
A form of inheritance in which the goods or property of a family is divided among the heirs.

impartible inheritance
A form of inheritance in which family property is passed undivided to one heir.

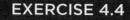

EXERCISE 4.4

An international television production company has hired your company, Creativity Enterprises, to write a pilot episode of a soap opera to be marketed in rural China. The plot of the program you will create will revolve around the Wang family. The Wangs are a relatively well-off farming family in rural China. The characters in the show are to include the following family members:

Wang Zhou: the 55-year-old male head of the family
Wang Lim: the wife of Wang Zhou
Wang Xiao: the eldest son of Wang Zhou
Wang Lao: the wife of Wang Xiao
Wang Jiang: the second son of Wang Zhou
Wang Jane: the wife of Wang Jiang
Wang Sally: the 20-year-old unmarried daughter of Wang Zhou
Wang Nai-Nai: the mother of Wang Zhou
Xiao and Lao have four children, two boys and two girls.
Jiang and Jane have two children, both girls.

You may, if you wish, add other characters to the story. The story line should be simple but clear, and you are free to embellish the characters in any way you want, but keep in mind that the soap must appeal to a rural Chinese audience.

QUESTION 4.5: HOW HAS THE ANTHROPOLOGICAL STUDY OF FAMILIES CHANGED?

As we stated in our introduction, a lot has changed within Ju/'hoansi, Trobriand, and rural Chinese societies since the anthropologists in the previous sections of this chapter did their fieldwork. Culture is never static, and even small changes in both local societies and global politics may affect how different people in different places construct their beliefs about family relations and kinship. For

instance, between the 1930s and the 1970s, China experienced almost constant turmoil: the war with Japan (1937 to 1945), a civil war (1945 to 1949), the Great Leap Forward (1959 to 1961), and the Cultural Revolution (1966 to 1976). Laurel Bossen suggests that throughout this time, women in Lu Village, in the southern province of Yunnan, have gained some benefits, such as "the end of footbinding, greater recognition of women's economic contributions, improved female health and education, lower infant mortality, a wider variety of employment options and family choices, more labor-saving technology and modes of communication, and a greater public voice" (2002, 19). Although patrilineal descent and patrilocality are still the rule, Bossen found families in Lu Village that followed uxorilocal marriage, where the husband leaves his village and moves to the village of his wife. Lu villagers use the term "*zhao guye*" or "seek a son-in-law" to refer to uxorilocal marriage (2002, 229).

After the Cultural Revolution in China, women gained more control over their lives than they had in the 1960s when Wolf did her fieldwork. Ellen Judd (1994) has suggested that legal changes, such as the Inheritance Law of 1985, which allows daughters to inherit their parents' property, as well as the increase in women's access to employment in rural North China, have allowed some women to gain some freedom from previous constraints.

Challenges to Theory in Anthropology

Anthropologists experienced changes in the ways they think about and study family relations when they began to question the origins of some of their main assumptions. The idea that these assumptions might be rooted in Euro-American culture and then used to describe and analyze other cultures gained momentum in the 1970s and 1980s. In Canada, Martin Silverman questioned the relationship between political economy and anthropology as it applies to the ways that European and anglophone North American anthropologists view their own family relationships and those of other peoples in other cultures. Silverman argued that the view of marriage as an exchange of women, for instance, with men directing the exchanges, resembles the model of commodity exchange "in which something is bought and sold ... a thing which has no rights of its own, and in which the direct producer has no rights" (1979, 71).

Linda Stone (2001) has reviewed two important factors questioned by David Schneider in the early 1980s—factors that led anthropologists to re-evaluate some of their underlying assumptions about how different societies establish connections among family members. The first was Schneider's critique of his own work among Yap families in the West Caroline Islands. The more Schneider thought about what he had written, the more he began to wonder how much of what he had described as Yap notions of relatedness were actually projections of his own Eurocentric beliefs about the role of biology in kinship. When he re-evaluated his account of Yap kinship, he found that two of the fundamental kinship terms in Western biological explanations of conception and birth, mother and father, did not apply to Yap notions of producing children. The biological term "father" as anthropologists were using it was only roughly equivalent to the mother's husband at the time she became pregnant in Yap society. Likewise, the term "mother" applied to the woman who gave birth to a child, but this child was placed in her womb by ghosts, not by the fertilization of her egg by the father's sperm.

The second factor was Schneider's critique of the ethnocentric evolutionism in studies that assume kinship is important in small-scale societies only where it provides the basis for social organization. In this argument, kinship loses importance as societies become more complex and disappears as a major institution in modern industrial states. Families likewise change from the large extended size in small-scale societies to the efficient nuclear size that is found in North America. This, according to Schneider, might actually be an anthropological myth, and if the myth itself is investigated, "kinship might ... become a special custom distinctive of European culture" (Schneider 1984, 201).

When Schneider asked, "Is blood really thicker than water?", several anthropologists began to take a closer look at whether groups that used kinship terms for their association were related on the basis of biology or, actually, on the basis of some other factors. Co-residence on the basis of friendships, for instance, may look like kinship from the outside, especially when family terms are used as identifiers. The notion of whether "blood" or some other substance is the basis of how family members are related has also been debated. For example, whereas in the Western science model children are related to their parents through "blood," people in a neighbourhood of Gaborne, Botswana, told Frederick Klaits that husbands and wives become "of one blood" when they have sexual intercourse and produce children.

Food is another substance that may be more important than blood in creating kinship. David and Dorothy Counts tell a very instructive story about their own experience of being defined in kinship terms by the Kaliai people, whom they visited in New Guinea to do their research. They believed that their adoption into a Kandokan family had been basically only fiction, and then learned to their surprise that it was very real: "We learned that when members of our Kandokan family brought us bananas, pineapples, and watermelons, and we gave them rice, fresh bread, and tinned beef, we were not just exchanging groceries. We and they were becoming family ... When they fed us and our children and received food from us in return, we were exchanging the stuff of which substance is made: we were *becoming* Kaliai" (1998, 152).

Another major influence on how anthropologists study family relations is the feminist insight that we must question the ways in which the structure of families and their connections to biology reinforce gender inequalities. For instance, the fact that women give birth is consistently translated into a closer attachment of women to nature and to home, whereas men are more able to take part in the wider social sphere of politics and economics. This assumption tends to see women's place in the home as "natural" and therefore as found in all families. Evelyn Blackwood uses the term "heteronormative" to refer to the way in which anthropologists have described the "normal" family unit as in need of a dominant heterosexual male. She argues that "Patriarchal Man is an artifact of western narratives" (2005, 5) that is firmly embedded in anthropological theories of marriage, families, and kinship.

The feminist critique of family relations has encouraged studies in which a variety of other factors, such as history and power, are taken into account when anthropologists ask how family relationships have formed. A prime example of the influence of the heteronormative concept can be found in the history of colonization and the ways in which European colonizers viewed local family relationships as "primitive" when they differed from the European patriarchal model. In the Caribbean, for instance, family relations were defined as "abnormal" because many households appeared to lack a male figure who acted as the head of the family. Lisa Anderson-Levy, a Jamaican anthropologist, argues that colour, class, and gender work together to structure Caribbean families. Lower-class women tend to be the unmarried heads of their households or to live in extended households headed by their unmarried mothers. Upper- and middle-class women, whose skin colour is lighter, tend to be married and to live in nuclear families. Thus, "marriage was, and to a certain extent still is, something that rich people do" (2000, 195). Even female sexuality is race- and class-specific in Jamaica. Lower-class, dark-skinned women are thought to be unable to control their sexuality, whereas light-skinned, middle-class women are supposed to be fully in control.

Internal colonization, referring to the treatment of indigenous peoples by the state, often follows the same pattern. Anthropologist Max Hedley (1998) has written about how families in the Walpole Island First Nation changed after the Department of Indian Affairs insisted that they reorganize their agriculture. No longer was growing food a community project, as in the past; instead it was a matter of individual household production, with men as heads of the families. Around the same time, band government was imposed on the community, with women excluded from formal participation, unable to either hold office or vote. With the introduction of wage labour and formal education, the status of women within the family decreased as they left to work outside the home. Professional educators then took over important aspects of socializing children. All of this changed the meaning of motherhood.

The study of family relations has expanded to include gay and lesbian families and families produced by in vitro fertilization and by surrogate mothers. Gay and lesbian marriages became legal in Canada in July 2005, making Canada the fourth country in the world to recognize same-sex marriage (the other three were the Netherlands, Belgium, and Spain; since then, Argentina, Iceland, Norway, Portugal, Spain, South Africa, and Sweden have joined the list). As Meg Luxton (1997) points out, when families are formed by gay and lesbian couples, the definition of marriage is changed: both sexuality and child bearing are separated from legal marriage. This separation of marriage and child bearing has been one point of contention in the debate about gay marriage in Canada. Those who

Gay men celebrate the legalization of same-sex marriage in Canada.

© REUTERS/Peter Jones/Landov

oppose gay marriage cite the family as the institution in which children are produced and argue that the purpose of sexual intercourse (i.e., only between a male and a female) is to accomplish this.

Yet this does not mean that gay and lesbian couples cannot include children in their families. Children may be brought into the marriage from a former heterosexual relationship; other options for producing children are adoption, in vitro fertilization, and surrogate mothers. Indeed, all three methods are being used by heterosexual couples as well as by gay and lesbian couples.

QUESTION 4.6: HOW CAN UNDERSTANDING PATTERNS OF FAMILY RELATIONS BE RELEVANT OUTSIDE OF ACADEMIA?

As we've seen, knowledge of family relations helps us understand a whole range of things, from parent–child relations, to marriage and courtship patterns, to ideas about love, sexuality, and wealth. Understanding these relations can help societies address a multitude of issues involving families— for example, spousal abuse, divorce, and parent–child conflicts. The same knowledge can be valuable for those who work in a variety of fields that require an understanding of intimate human relations. Anthropologists, for example, can apply their understanding to prevent sexually transmitted diseases, especially HIV/AIDS.

The major problem in AIDS prevention (and in the prevention of STDs more generally) is how to persuade people who are sexually active to protect themselves and their sex partners. Condom use is one of the simplest and most common measures. Yet even when people are aware of the risk of contracting an STD, they often fail to take this easy precaution. What do medical practitioners and those working in AIDS prevention need to know in order to design effective prevention programs? And what can anthropologists do to help?

AIDS Prevention in Namibia

As noted earlier, we have been using the "ethnographic present" when describing patterns of Ju/'hoansi family relations, though in reality, many aspects of daily Ju/'hoansi life have changed since anthropologists first studied them. Ju/'hoansi territory spans the border of the contemporary nation-states of Botswana and Namibia, and the Ju/'hoansi are being buffeted by the same local, national, and global forces as their fellow citizens. Richard Lee has been doing fieldwork with the Ju/'hoansi since the 1960s and has witnessed the effects of these forces firsthand. One unavoidable force that has shaped, and been shaped by, Ju/'hoansi kinship patterns and practices is the AIDS pandemic.

In the mid-1990s, when Lee and medical anthropologist Ida Susser began conducting research on the epidemic in southern Africa, one in every four adults aged 19 to 44 in South Africa, Namibia, and Botswana was HIV positive, and rates were rising (Lee 1996, 27). On the one hand, governments were making a concerted effort to mount publicity and education campaigns, even in remote areas where the Ju/'hoansi have traditionally lived. On the other, Lee and Susser were surprised by the relative "calm" surrounding the AIDS epidemic in the public sphere. Lee argues that silence and stigma about both sexual practices and AIDS in these southern African countries contributed to this deceptive sense of calm (28). Silence surrounded AIDS-related illness and deaths, and AIDS-related deaths were characterized simply as the result of "a long illness" or "unknown causes." In fact, physicians in Namibia were encouraged to omit any mention of AIDS from medical documentation (28). Such silences were a result of the strong stigma of having AIDS. Often, those who were infected hid their illness out of shame, and many transmitted the disease to their unknowing partners while they kept their secret. At the time, Lee argued that "only when the magnitude of the problem is clear and the terrible stigma overcome will it be possible to make the critical behavioral changes that will prevent the further spread of AIDS" (30).

At first glance, the Ju/'haonsi would seem to be especially vulnerable to the AIDs epidemic. Anthropologists such as Paul Farmer (whose work we discuss in Chapter 6) have shown that poverty, inequality, and marginalization exacerbate the spread of AIDS throughout the world. Susser (2006) points out that contemporary Ju/'hoansi are in an unusual position in terms of poverty and inequality. Poverty is relative, and while the Ju/'hoansi may not have much in terms of material wealth, their relatively egalitarian society has helped them avoid the gap between the rich and the poor that often contributes to ill health. Although the Ju/'hoansi have not lived exclusively as hunter–gatherers for many years, many still gather some berries and nuts and snare small animals, and these unique patterns of subsistence have provided a slight cultural "buffer" against the encroachment of surrounding groups and the incursion of capitalism (206). Ju/'hoansi kinship practices—especially sharing and women's sexual autonomy—are central to this cultural buffer; moreover, Susser suggests that these practices have protected the Ju/'hoansi against the spread of HIV/AIDS.

These protective effects are most evident when we compare those Ju/'hoansi who continue to live in relatively remote areas to those who live in Tsumkwe, Namibia. Once a small Ju/'hoansi village, Tsumkwe has become an administrative centre, populated and visited by Ju/'hoansi, civil servants, tourists, cattle farmers, construction workers, and border guards. Ju/hoansi living in more remote villages engage with capitalism by selling goods or services through community cooperative organizations, which mediate collectively between the villages and the market economy (Susser 2006, 215). However, the Ju'hoansi in Tsumkwe are not protected by the social organization and kinship relations of the (partial) subsistence economy; instead, they enter into most lowest, most exploitative levels of the economy, which revolves around tourism and services. Besides living in poverty in Tsumkwe,

many Ju'hoansi spend a lot of time (and money) at local *shebeens* (makeshift bars that sell home brew), where Ju/'hoansi women often engage in "survival sex" (Susser 2009, 182), often with non-Ju/'hoansi itinerant workers.

Two important differences between life in remote villages and life in Tsumkwe stand out as relevant to understanding the spread of HIV/AIDS. The first is that, according to Susser, villagers "are somewhat protected from the individual risk and insecurity involved in marginal work and the lowest rung of the tourist economy, [and] appear to be less vulnerable to the ravages of HIV/AIDS" (2006, 215). The second is that, as we saw in section 4.3 above, Ju'hoansi women living in small villages continue to exercise a great deal of sexual autonomy and authority, which has limited the spread of HIV infections in those villages. By contrast, rates of infection among Ju'hoansi women in Tsumkwe are much higher. When Susser asked a group of young married women in a small "traditional" village if they would be able to use a box of male condoms, they replied, "Give us some, and we will teach our husbands how to use them" (2009, 171). This self-assuredness is markedly different from that of Ju'hoansi women living in Tsumkwe, and from that of women from other ethnic groups in Namibia, whose experiences of economic and gender inequality, coupled with silence and stigma around sexual practices, make it nearly impossible for them to ask their partners to wear condoms. Anthropologists and others note that the introduction of the female condom appears to be giving women some measure of autonomy and self-protection. Although exact figures are lacking, it is clear that the Ju/'hoansi—especially those *not* living in Tsumkwe—have a much lower incidence of HIV/AIDS infection than their neighbours (between 3 and 6 percent as opposed to the national average of 25 to 30 percent) (Lee and Susser 2010). Clearly, prevention efforts aimed at the Ju/'hoansi will build on the insights of Lee and Susser's fieldwork. Maintaining aspects of a foraging way of life, which allows families to maintain their

Women discuss the female condom. Dobe, 2001.

households and women to maintain aspects of their historic autonomy, will make all the difference in limiting or even preventing the spread of HIV infections among the Ju/'hoansi.

Elsewhere in Namibia we see altogether different links among kinship patterns, sexuality, stigma, and HIV/AIDS. Robert Lorway conducted fieldwork in Windhoek, Namibia's capital, with a gay and lesbian community group, the Rainbow Project. He found that the greatest barrier to successful prevention initiatives in this community was the perception, perpetuated through public health initiatives, that "AIDS in Africa" is exclusively a Pattern II or heterosexual epidemic (Lorway 2007, 276). There are virtually no public health campaigns in Namibia that address homosexual behaviour in their prevention education, and as a result, men who have sex with men are more vulnerable to HIV infection (2006, 435). For example, there was a common (mis) understanding among men who had wives or girlfriends, and who also enjoyed sex with men, that they were practising safer sex when sleeping with men. One of Lorway's informants explained: "Most of the men I know who have girlfriends are saying that they prefer to have sex with us moffies [effeminate males] because they don't want to catch STDs cheating on them, or HIV, or get someone pregnant. Most of them think they can even have sex with men without a condom because they think it is less risky than sex with a woman" (Jason, 21-year-old male from Katutura) (2007, 276).

Lorway's work shows that although heterosexual intercourse *is* the main source of transmission of HIV in Namibia, the exclusion of any information about same-sex transmission was limiting possibilities for education and prevention. These transmission myths were compounded by intense anti-homosexual sentiment (and laws prohibiting homosexuality) in Namibia, which resulted in equally intense stigma, shame, and secrecy. Lorway's fieldwork demonstrated the urgent need for short-term interventions that would work even in a climate of intolerance and fear. During his fieldwork, he was actively involved in precisely this kind of prevention: he helped coordinate community-level education strategies (through the Rainbow Project) that could "move safer sex information through secretive social networks without risking public exposure" (292). Maintaining secrecy may run counter to mainstream HIV-prevention goals, such as raising public awareness about homosexual transmission, and to encouraging acceptance of homosexuality in the public sphere, but Lorway's ethnographic evidence suggests that it is the most culturally appropriate and immediately effective means of prevention. His work, like that of Lee and Susser, demonstrates just how important it is that "intensive ethnography is centrally incorporated within the methodologies of health science projects" (2006, 448).

EXERCISE 4.5

Developing a Program for Prevention of STDs

For this exercise, you play the role of an HIV/AIDS prevention specialist and help design a program for your culture to promote condom use. You need to answer the following questions:

1. What are some of the cultural barriers that might inhibit condom use? Are any similar to those in Namibia?
2. What are some measures that you would suggest to help people who are sexually active overcome these barriers?

CONCLUSIONS

In this chapter we have examined the structure and dynamics of family life among three peoples—the Ju/'hoansi, the Trobriand Islanders, and rural Chinese. Throughout the chapter, you have been asked to think about those aspects of the North American family that we tend to take for granted as natural but that are culturally situated and often unique. As we have seen, each society has different rules about whom a person regards as a family member, and family membership can vary based on variations in descent systems. In each case, we have also thought about how the family is formed and how the ideal family type is maintained in these societies. But it is important to keep in mind that these ideal types are not static and timeless; sometimes the idea of an ideal family type can be a contentious one. Sexuality, love, and wealth each play a key role in family life, although as we have seen, the significance of each varies from culture to culture. Often, the forces that threaten the family unit are those that threaten sexuality, love, or wealth as they are understood in each cultural context.

Although kinship questions have always been central to anthropology, the ways that anthropologists think about and study family relations have changed a great deal in recent decades. Critiques such as those by David Schneider and various feminist anthropologists have inspired some researchers to be more aware of the effects of colonialism and of their own underlying Eurocentric assumptions about what families should look like. Nonetheless, knowledge of family and intimate relations in a society remain an important focus of anthropological research, and, importantly, can be applied to the development of culturally appropriate and effective programs to promote sexual health.

CRITICAL THINKING QUESTIONS

1. What are some common ways in which we use the idea of family as a metaphor for other kinds of social relationships (i.e., in the workplace, or when working in teams). What do we accomplish when we make these kinds of metaphorical comparisons?
2. Debates about same-sex marriage in North America often pit "traditional family values" against "universal human rights." What have you learned in this chapter (and the rest of the text) that might undermine this straightforward dualism?

KEY TERMS:

bilateral kinship (p. 111)
brideservice (p. 113)
bridewealth (p. 122)
clan (p. 122)
dowry (p. 125)
endogamy (p. 122)
ethnographic present (p. 110)
exogamy (p. 122)
extended family (p. 116)
impartible inheritance (p. 130)
incest taboo (p. 119)
matrilineage (p. 113)
matrilineal kinship (p. 112)
nuclear family (p. 112)
partible inheritance (p. 130)
patrilineage (p. 116)
patrilineal kinship (p. 112)
polyandry (p. 128)
polygamy (p. 127)
polygyny (p. 127)

THE CULTURAL CONSTRUCTION OF IDENTITY

© Mark Anthony Jacobson

From the moment we are born, interactions with others are shaped by their perceptions of us. According to Goffman, who we quote in the epigraph, we use our bodies in unconscious and conscious ways to communicate information about ourselves to others. Through our speech, clothing, gestures, postures, and other phenomena, people make assumptions and often judgments about our character and our place in the world. Similarly, we often consciously manipulate our bodies to show others who we think we are. These aspects of what we call identity—including race, class, and gender—form the subject of this chapter.

When an individual enters the presence of others, they commonly seek to acquire information about him or to bring into play information about him already possessed. They will be interested in his general socioeconomic status, his conception of self, his attitude toward them, his competence, his trustworthiness, etc. Although some of this information seems to be sought almost as an end in itself, there are usually quite practical reasons for acquiring it. Information about the individual helps to define the situation, enabling others to know in advance what he will expect of them and what they may expect of him. Informed in these ways, the others will know how best to act in order to call forth a desired response from him.

Erving Goffman

PROBLEM 5

How do people determine who they are and how do they communicate who they think they are to others?

INTRODUCTION

Try to imagine a society in which every person is physically indistinguishable from every other person. How would people in such a society know how to behave toward one another? Whenever we interact with another person, the interaction must be based on some idea of who the other is: Friend? Stranger? Family member? Teacher? At the same time, the other must have some idea of who *we* are, a conception of the relationship that exists between us. The need to know the social identity of others is apparent whenever two strangers meet and, directly or indirectly, seek to elicit information about each other. Each tries to place the other in some identity at some spot on the social landscape.

Imagine next a society in which every person is completely unique. In this case, every interaction would be different, and there would be no way to learn from one situation how to behave in another similar situation. Each person would need to have an infinite variety of behaviours with which to interact with an infinite number of types of people. We avoid this situation by categorizing people, placing them in groups so that not everyone in our social universe is unique. We group them into categories based on criteria such as gender (female, male, or some other gender); ethnicity (Irish, Italian, Chinese); personal characteristics (short, tall, husky, thin), and so on.

Try to imagine, also, a social landscape in which no person acknowledges any other person or communicates in any way who she or he thinks the other is.

This, too, would represent an impossible situation. People would have no way of acquiring from others confirmation that they occupy the social identities they think they occupy. In reality, our social identities are constructed in large part by others, who, by their behaviour toward us, confirm that we occupy the spot on the landscape we claim to occupy. Put another way, nobody is anybody except in relation to somebody.

Finally, try to imagine a social landscape in which everyone communicates to everyone else that they occupy the wrong spot on the landscape. Every person actively disagrees with every other person about who they are. This situation would be, if not impossible, at least chaotic.

To examine how people in a society determine who they are and communicate who they think they are to others, in this chapter we will explore the ways different societies define the person, the ways individuals are differentiated from others, the ways they find out who they are and convey to others who they are, and the ways they form collective identities. Then in Chapter 6 we will continue our exploration of identity with an in-depth examination of how social identities such as race, gender, and class are constructed.

QUESTIONS

5.1 How is identity, and one's sense of self, learned?

5.2 How does the concept of personhood vary from society to society?

5.3 How do societies distinguish individuals from one another?

5.4 How do societies mark changes in identity?

5.5 How do individuals communicate their identities to one another?

5.6 How do individuals form identities through collective struggles?

QUESTION 5.1: HOW IS IDENTITY, AND ONE'S SENSE OF SELF, LEARNED?

Learning Identities

Hugh Brody begins his book *The Other Side of Eden: Hunters, Farmers, and the Shaping of the World* (2000) with a description of a baby Inuit girl:

> *Imagine the darkness of the far north. Not as something in which the adventurous traveller moves in awe. But as a beginning, for those for whom the Arctic is home. Imagine the inside of a skin tent, or a snowhouse, or a government-regulation low-rental prefab. In this home, an Inuit baby girl wakes in the night. She is held, fed, cuddled—and talked to …*
>
> *In these words, the child is given the sounds of love, and can know that she is safe. Not safe just to feed, to sleep, but safe to do these things as and when she wants. For she is a baby who carries atiq, the spirit and name of her late grandmother. She is the adored baby; she is also her mother's mother, her grandfather's wife. Her grandmother is alive again in the baby. This means the baby is doubly and trebly loved. And she must be treated with respect. (2000, 11–12)*

Is this Inuit baby born with an **identity**? Or is her identity something she must learn? It is certainly very clear to others in her Inuit community that she is the reincarnation of her grandmother, but how long will it take the baby to understand what that means?

---

identity
Learned personal and social types of affiliation, including gender, sexuality, race, class, nationalism, and ethnicity, for example.

Learning to Belong

Hugh Brody suggests that the Inuit baby begins to know that she is an important member of her family almost the moment she is born, and that this knowledge expands daily as she interacts with others. As people tell her stories about her land and its creation, she builds up an image of her world and of her place in it. She learns that she is connected to her land and to all the other creatures that share the land with her.

Stories present people of all ages with ways of knowing about who they are and where they came from. Storytelling is also a way of communicating information from one generation to another (Ridington 1990, 14). No one censors Inuit stories, and children's understanding grows as they grow. Brody describes the Inuit child's experiences with stories told by her grandfather and other adults: "The small child listens for as long as she wishes— she is, after all, also her own grandmother. And she discovers that stories are always a mystery, for they have much that cannot be understood, and much that comes from knowledge and experience beyond understanding" (2000, 13).

As this child grows, she recognizes stories that are told over and over, with the same main characters and events. She also learns that no one understands everything in the stories, and she keeps her sense of wonderment about the world.

Brody's example highlights a key point about identity: we are not born knowing who we are or what our places are on the social landscape; we *learn* to be Canadian or Japanese, husbands or wives, Andrea, Gavin, Homa, Natasha, or Sebastian. We learn how we relate to others as sons, daughters, students, friends, or lovers. Both consciously and unconsciously, individuals form various identities so that they can relate to others and cultivate a space for themselves within their social landscape. At the same time, identities are political and collective, formed around struggles against such threats as colonialism or the state. As we become who we are, we learn how we stand in relation to others.

Identities like gender, sexuality, race, ethnicity, and national identity, to name a few, are not natural or biological. We are not born knowing instinctively what it means to "be Canadian," for instance. Our sense of Canadianness, like any other identity, is cultivated and learned through various agents of **enculturation**. These are sociocultural forces and institutions that teach us, consciously or unconsciously, about what it means to be a Canadian citizen. Agents of enculturation may include the mass media, parents, peers, school, and the government, for instance. Think about the ways in which children are enculturated into the norms of "Canadian identity," for example, in many public school systems across Canada. In elementary school, most children learn how to sing the national anthem, and because provincial governments control the content of the school curriculum, they learn a government-sanctioned version of Canadian history. Students must demonstrate their successful acquisition and knowledge of this history on tests and papers in order to advance to the next grade. Even as they graduate and get older, Canadians continue to learn about Canada through participation in Canada Day parades and other public spectacles, or by watching the national news on Canadian television stations like the CBC (Canadian Broadcasting Corporation). In Canada, the mass media play an important role in shaping ideals of Canadianness through media depictions of sport, for instance. Hockey, in particular, has long been promoted as a component of a distinctive Canadian identity. However, hockey's participants and spectators are mostly white, middle-class, and male (Gruneau and Whitson 1993; Hartman 2009). As such, it is a sport that (perhaps unintentionally) promotes a dominant,

---

enculturation
The process through which individuals learn an identity. This can encompass parental socialization, the influence of peers, the mass media, government, or other forces.

Canadians playing hockey.

a shared sense of "Canadianness" is created through mediated experiences: watching and listening to stories about the 2010 Vancouver Olympics; attending Canada Day spectacles and ceremonies; following the national news on television, radio, and the Internet or in newspapers; and so on. Because this process of enculturation often begins when we are young, we often fail to see how various cultural forces shape our identities. Thus, we often view our identities as natural, primordial, or biologically based. Think of the many people who are willing to "sacrifice" themselves or die for their country, for instance. Often, an individual is willing to go to such lengths only if they feel that their identification with their nation is somehow instinctual and, by extension, natural.

Over the past century, anthropologists have engaged actively with precisely these sorts of debates. We live in a pop culture that privileges natural explanations for human behaviours. This has been the case since the late 1800s, with the rise of the **"nature versus nurture"** debate in academia. In 1874 the British naturalist Sir Francis Galton, inspired by the principles of Darwinian evolution, coined the term "nature versus nurture." Galton was a eugenicist who felt that some people, by virtue of their class, race, or other factors, were better suited to reproduce as they were more "fit" to survive in society. Galton believed that many human differences, including intelligence, were rooted in biology, or "nature." His ideas spawned wildly inaccurate assumptions and research on the

or normative, ideal of Canadian identity as white, middle-class, and male. This is a problem, given that Canada is officially a diverse, multicultural nation in which no particular gender, sexuality, or ethnic or racial identity should be privileged as "more Canadian" than any other. In this context, hockey's iconic status as a national symbol is ironic, for it excludes a large portion of the nation's multicultural population and promotes hierarchies of Canadianness. To be "truly" Canadian, we learn, is to consume and participate in hockey. In recent years, the sport has been trying to connect with the nation's increasingly multicultural and multilingual population base. Beginning in 2007, for instance, the NHL began broadcasting hockey games in Punjabi.

Despite the problematical nature of hockey as a "Canadian" identity marker, it is important to note that shared experiences, such as sports and other mediated events, are often used to cultivate a sense of **imagined community**. This term, coined by political scientist Benedict Anderson in 1983, suggests that identities, including national ones, are culturally constructed through shared experiences, even in the absence of face-to-face contacts. So, even though a Canadian living in Halifax may never have visited Toronto, Regina, or Whitehorse,

imagined community
A term coined by Benedict Anderson in 1983. It refers to the fact that even in the absence of face-to-face interactions, a sense of community (e.g., nationalism) is culturally constructed by forces such as the mass media.

nature versus nurture
This phrase, coined by Francis Galton in 1874, references a longstanding scholarly debate concerning whether or not human behaviours and identities are the result of nature (biological and genetic factors) or nurture (learned and cultural factors).

part of academics throughout the late 19th and 20th centuries. At the time, many scholars felt that many of our identities, such as race or class, are acquired, and genetic and thus "natural"—that we are born the way we are.

One of the first anthropologists to engage ethnographically with the nature versus nurture debate was Margaret Mead. In 1926, Mead set out for American Samoa to conduct research that would challenge widespread ideas among scientists that acts of teenage rebellion and experimentation were the result of hormonal or other physical changes brought on by puberty (or "nature"). Such behaviour was commonplace among American teenagers; Mead wondered whether similar behavioural patterns existed in other cultures. Under the direction of her doctoral supervisor, Franz Boas, she travelled to the island of Ta'u to study the behaviour of teenage girls. She observed that their experiences of adolescence were completely different from the experiences of American girls. In Samoa, girls were given a lot of freedom to experiment with their sexuality and did not go through periods of torment with parents. Samoan culture, she argued, did not possess the same Judeo-Christian ideals of sexual morality; this in turn contributed to different behaviours and attitudes toward sexuality. Mead thus argued that the experiences of adolescents varied depending on the culture in which they were raised. She therefore emphasized the role of culture or "nurture" in human behaviour. While Mead's methods and research findings would subsequently be disputed, she continued her ethnographic work on the "nature/nurture" debate in 1935. She visited three tribes along the Sepik river in Papua New Guinea to explore differences in gender roles. She found that in each tribe, men and women took on different responsibilities based on their gender. She was thus able to suggest, once again, that human behavioural differences (in this case, gendered divisions of labour) were the result of culture and not biology.

Research that seeks to link biology with human behaviours and identities is potentially dangerous, for it can provide biological justifications for social inequalities in society. Back in 1968, for instance, Washburn and Lancaster sought to argue that women, for biological and evolutionary reasons, were better "nurturers" of children—an argument that has since been disputed by feminist scholars. But think of the consequences of this type of research. If women can be "proven" to be naturally better "nurturers," then it becomes easy to argue that a woman's place is in the domestic sphere. This information could then inform government policies relating to day care funding, affirmative action, and other social issues.

Anthropological fieldwork in various societies has shed light on the problems associated with viewing all human identities in terms of "nature." Yet the development and widespread valorization of the Human Genome Project continues to link identities with nature. Think of the ways in which scientists are actively searching for specific genes that they believe are the cause of particular behaviours. We live in a society that valorizes the "gene" and that is fascinated by ongoing research on the so-called "gay gene," or the "selfish gene." Such research, however, reduces the diversity of human behaviours to biology, ignores the role of culture in shaping identities like race, gender, and sexuality, and obscures the fact that many individual behaviours, such as "selfishness," may

© Bettmann/CORBIS

American anthropologist Margaret Mead in Admiralty Islands.

THE CULTURAL CONSTRUCTION OF IDENTITY

Some contemporary Tsimshian children continue to follow tradition by wearing traditional shawls and will change their name upon entering adulthood.

be the result of complex interplays of culture and biology.

Now that we have explored how anthropologists tend to emphasize the learned, culturally constructed nature of our personal and collective identities, in the next section we examine in greater detail how a sense of self or personhood is shaped by various cultural forces.

QUESTION 5.2: HOW DOES THE CONCEPT OF PERSONHOOD VARY FROM SOCIETY TO SOCIETY?

The Importance of Self

Of all the products of our culture, the one we most take for granted is our self.

Personal names in all societies are intimate markers of the person, differentiating individuals from others. Names also can reveal how people conceive of themselves and their relations to others. For many North Americans, they are perhaps the most enduring aspect of the self. Assigned at birth, our names remain with us throughout our lives. Some people may choose

to modify them—to shorten Kathleen to Kate, or Phillip to Phil. Whatever form a name takes, it represents the self. How much of the self is revealed by a name varies by culture and situation. University students meeting for the first time exchange personal names, rarely bothering with family names. Theirs is a self independent of any group or past. When North American businesspeople meet, they exchange first names, last names, and business titles. Business people are linked to their organizations. When Moroccans from different towns meet, the names they offer to others include not only the names of their families but the names of the towns they are from. The Moroccan self is embedded in family and place of origin. Among the Tsimshian of British Columbia, the names people use depend on their social position; when they enter adulthood, get married, or assume a higher rank in Tsimshian society, they change their names. The Tsimshian self is inseparable from one's position in society.

Jorge Chimbinda, an anthropology student from Angola, wrote about Umbundu names for his master's thesis at the University of Western Ontario. Among Umbundu people in Angola, there are two ways of naming a child. The most common way is to name a child after a relative who is either alive or dead (an ancestor). The second way is to give a child

a new name that refers to some unusual circumstance that was present during the child's birth. For example, a child born during a severe drought will be given a name that refers to the drought and keeps the memory of the suffering alive. The child of a mother who dies in childbirth will be given a name that keeps the memory of his or her mother's suffering and death. The result of this way of naming is that each child has his or her own last name. At the same time, the Umbundu naming system is a historical version of cultural values, such as identity, kinship, geography, folktales, stories, and proverbs. Therefore, beyond an Umbundu name we can find a proverb and beyond this proverb there is a story. As a consequence, when people hear a name, they remember the wise message that is transmitted through this name.

From the Umbundu perspective, names are tools with which people reward the life they have received from their relatives and their world. Names serve to perpetuate the wide kinship web and stress the concept of extended family. Each child represents one of his or her living relatives or ancestors. All relatives and ancestors on both the father's side and the mother's have equal value, because each of them has contributed with his or her life to the existence of the child. These names also inscribe the imprint of lived experiences on children, so that children named after unusual circumstances embody the meaning of the experiences.

Jorge Chimbinda also explores the effects of colonialism on his people. When Angola became a Portuguese colony, the colonial administrators found it too difficult to keep track of Umbundu people because the naming system did not group people in ways that the administrators understood. For the Portuguese, as for most Europeans, last names were shared among members of families and made family identification orderly. Thus, one of the first ways that the Portuguese colonizers tried to destroy Umbundu identity was to force people to discard their Umbundu names and to use Portuguese names instead. The differences in naming practices among different societies reveal the different ways societies conceptualize what a person is and how that person relates to the group. Many North Americans believe that individuals are stable, autonomous entities who exist more or less independently of whatever situations or statuses they occupy. As they move from status to status or place to place—from student to husband or wife, to employee, to father or mother—they believe themselves to be the same persons nevertheless. Otherwise, each time they changed situations or statuses they would in effect become different people and would have to change their names. In this regard North Americans are highly **individualistic.** This does not seem to be the case in other societies, where individuals are not seen as entities distinct from their social position or group. In societies such as the Umbundu, the relationship between the person and the group, or the person and his or her social position, is **holistic**; the person cannot be conceived as existing separately from society or apart from his or her cultural beliefs and values. The holistic view of the self is expressed in Gandhi's metaphor of individuals as drops in the ocean; the drops cannot survive without the ocean, and the ocean loses its identity without the drops.

EXERCISE 5.2

If you were an Umbundu and lived in Angola, which of your ancestors would you choose for the name of your first child? Why would you make this particular choice? In other words, what are the qualities in your ancestors that you would want to transfer to your child? What about your second child and your third?

individualistic
A view of the self in which the individual is primarily responsible for his or her own actions.

holistic
When an individual's sense of self cannot be conceived as existing separately from society or apart from his or her status or role.

The Egocentric and Sociocentric Self

These differences between the individualistic and holistic conceptions of the self led Richard A. Shweder and Edmund J. Bourne to delineate two distinct ways in which the person is conceived in different societies: the **egocentric** and the **sociocentric** views of self. Note that these terms are generalizations about the nature of self in different societies. There will, of course, be exceptions to these patterns, especially given the increasing influence of globalization in constructing our identities. For example, over the past 40 years or so, individuals have become increasingly mobile, travelling in search of work, for immigration, as tourists, or as refugees. Many people's sense of self is also shaped by relationships and experiences with mediated technologies, such as the Internet, which disseminate new ideas within various societies. So it is important to recognize that there exist multiple definitions and interpretations of self, even within the generalized contexts of the societies described below.

In the *egocentric* view, typified in many ways by the Western view adopted by North American societies, each person is a replica of all humanity, the locus of motivations and drives, capable of acting independently from others. For Westerners, the individual is the centre of awareness, a distinct whole set against other wholes. Social relations are regarded as contracts between autonomous, free-acting beings. Individuals are free to negotiate their places in society, and the dominant idea is that each individual is responsible for what and who he or she is. Moreover, individuals possess intrinsic qualities such as generosity, integrity, or beauty. The egocentric view of the person places a high value on individualism and self-reliance.

Keeping in mind that factors such as poverty and ethnicity may make individualism and self-reliance difficult to achieve, it is worthwhile to explore the beliefs associated with this view of the individual. Robert Bellah and his co-authors of *Habits of the Heart* (1984) examined ideas of the individual in the United States that seem to apply equally to Canada. The self in the United States, they say, seeks to work out its own life plot by individually pursuing happiness and satisfying its wants. Unlike individuals in some other societies, many Americans seek to cut themselves off from the past, especially from their parents. Each wishes to become his or her own person, to find his or her own self. Americans seem to want to give birth to themselves. Young men and women need to demonstrate that they can stand on their own two feet and be self-supporting. This belief in a self-reliant, independent self underpins the belief Americans hold that success is the outcome of free and fair competition among individuals in an open market. Most successful Americans, say Bellah and his associates, claim that they achieved success through their own hard work, seldom acknowledging the contributions made by their families, their schooling, or their position as a member of the upwardly mobile middle class. The only way they can say they deserve what they have achieved is by succeeding through their own efforts.

Because of this dominant perspective of self, many people who were raised within Western, industrialized societies are inclined to view those afflicted with, for instance, eating disorders such as anorexia nervosa or bulimia, as suffering from an individual pathology. It's as if eating disorders were the result of an individual's "problem." Helen Gremillion (2003) conducted fourteen months of ethnographic research at a small inpatient

---

egocentric
A view of the self that defines each person as a replica of all humanity, as the location of motivations and drives, and as capable of acting independently from others.

sociocentric
A context-dependent view of self. The self exists as an entity only within the concrete situations or roles occupied by the person.

eating disorder clinic in the United States. She discovered there that the various cultural forces that have contributed to increases in diagnoses of eating disorders are being ignored in favour of "individualistic" explanations. For example, Gremillion and others often point out that mass media advertising plays a role in constructing normative expectations of an impossibly ideal femininity. Increasingly, the feminine ideal is being defined by physical appearance—in particular, by representations of predominantly white, youthful, slender, "beautiful" women. In this way, advertising on television and the Internet, in magazines, and on billboards is playing a powerful role in shaping Westerners' sense of self. Advertising provides a blueprint, or a measuring stick, for comparing our bodies with others. Yet its images of ideal femininity have themselves been constructed and manipulated by computer technologies, which remove wrinkles or fine lines, minimize fat, and reshape facial features. Gremillion argues that because they fail to recognize the role of culture in shaping the self, many eating disorder treatments replicate Western notions of individualism within their treatment plans, which include the careful daily monitoring of weight and patient "progress." These principles of egocentrism, of the individual monitoring of the body—and, by extension, the self—have led to a proliferation of eating disorders.

In contrast to the egocentric view, the *sociocentric* view of the self is context-dependent. The self exists as an entity only within the concrete situations or roles occupied by the person in much the same way that Tsimshian names are linked to a position in society and not to some autonomous, separate self. From a sociocentric perspective, there is no intrinsic self that can possess enduring qualities such as generosity, integrity, or beauty. These qualities can apply only to concrete social situations. Instead of saying that a man is generous, a sociocentric perspective would be that "he gives money to his friends." Instead of saying that a woman is principled, the perspective would be that "she does not give away secrets."

Personhood in Japan and North America

Some anthropologists attribute a sociocentric view of the self to people in Japan. Anthropologist Christie Kiefer (1976) explained that the Japanese are more likely to include within the boundaries of the self the social groups of which the person is a member. Contrast this with the North American self-concept, which does not extend beyond the physical body. Japanese children are not trained to rely solely on the self, as many North American children are. They are taught that interdependence between the person and the family or group is more important than independence.

Robert Smith (1983) noted that the Japanese view of the self is expressed in their language. For example, Japanese language does not include anything resembling English personal pronouns. In English, children quickly learn to use the two personal referents, I and you; Japanese boys, on the

other hand, must learn six, and girls must learn five. The personal referent used in Japan depends on the speaker's relationship to the listener. It expresses how the self is defined relative to a specific social interaction.

In addition, wrote Smith, the Japanese language contains vocabulary that is very conscious of status. It is characterized by what the Japanese call *keigo*, or "polite speech." *Keigo* has the effect of establishing at the outset of a conversation the relative social standing and degree of intimacy of speaker and listener. Japanese speakers use different forms of address depending on their social position relative to the person to whom they are speaking. Since the Japanese language is status based, people must be careful of the linguistic forms they use in conversations. When conversing with someone in a superior social position, a speaker must linguistically acknowledge the social difference between speaker and listener. Japanese advertisers have a problem with *keigo* because actors should not give imperative commands (e.g., "Drink Coke") for fear of offending people. They solve the problem by using low-status people who are nonthreatening (e.g., clowns, coquettish women, or children) to issue the commands.

The sociocentric Japanese differ also in their approach to social interactions. Most North Americans believe it is desirable to assert themselves; some even take assertiveness training. They believe that it is desirable for people to stand out, to take charge. The Japanese believe that social interactions should be characterized by restraint or reserve, traits they identify as *enryo*. With *enryo*, giving opinions is avoided; this attitude is summarized by the Japanese proverb "the nail that sticks up shall be hammered down."

Yet the Japanese *do* conceive of themselves as separate entities. They are as attached to their personal names as North Americans are, if not more so. Moreover, they believe in self-development. But for them, the autonomy of the individual is established, not in social situations where they actively distinguish themselves from others, but *away from* society, where self-reflection and introspection are legitimate. It is through introspection that the Japanese find their true heart (*kokoro*) and are put in touch with their true nature—their *hara* ("belly") and *jibub* ("self").

In the remainder of this chapter, we will be looking at the self less from an egocentric perspective and more from a sociocentric perspective, as something contingent and relative to the situation. Our focus will be on that part of the self that is defined by social relations and social processes and that is subject to change and redefinition.

EXERCISE 5.3

Young people begin to learn in early childhood what their culture expects of them with regard to appropriate behaviour. Schools in North America are significant environments for learning about self and others. How does the school environment function to help shape the identity of individuals and groups? Are there ways in which individualism is submerged? Might school settings differ in the extent to which the egocentric, as opposed to the sociocentric, self is developed?

QUESTION 5.3: HOW DO SOCIETIES DISTINGUISH INDIVIDUALS FROM ONE ANOTHER?

Differences and similarities among persons are the materials from which we construct our social landscapes. Those materials are what allow us to distinguish individuals from one another or assign them to one group or another. From these similarities and differences we construct our social identities. However, all societies do not use the same similarities and differences to construct a social code, nor do they use these similarities and differences in the same way. Some characteristics of persons—some tools in the "identity toolbox," so to speak—are used almost universally to differentiate people or to group them together. For example, most societies use family membership, gender, and age as categories within a social code. But there are other characteristics that figure prominently only in some societies—ethnic group membership, skin colour, and wealth, for example.

In many societies, the most important characteristics for defining the self are related to kinship and family membership. In these societies, kinship is the central organizing principle—the main determinant of a person's social identity. Anthropologists working with these societies are often "adopted" by a family. This act is a signal of acceptance; but it also serves the practical purpose of assigning an outsider a social identity through which she or he can be approached by others. To have no kinship label or designation in such societies is to have no meaningful place on the social landscape.

Language is another important identity marker, one that is sometimes viewed as essential for the maintenance of group identity. Language is often tied strongly to a national identity, and many countries have established institutions to oversee the "purity" of the national language. The Académie Française has for centuries been charged with keeping the French language free of foreign borrowings, such as "le hot dog" or "le weekend." In some countries, conflicts between groups focus on language issues. In Quebec, for example, efforts of one group to preserve French as the official language of the province, and thus protect what it sees as essential to group identity, have led to a movement for independence from the English-speaking remainder of Canada.

The Québécois, however, argue that Quebec identity is not based solely on language. As they see it, their history in Canada is one of "slights, assaults, yet survival" (Eller 1999, 297). The conflict between anglophones and francophones in Canada has been ongoing since both arrived on North American shores. In 1759, the English drove the French "Acadians" out of eastern Canada; and after the Battle of the Plains of Abraham, outside the walls of Quebec City, the Treaty of Paris gave Canada to the English. In 1791, two separate societies were formed: Lower Canada was French and Upper Canada was English, and each had its own culture, religion, stories, political views, and language. Then in 1841, the Act of Union joined the two societies together, but this was an uneasy union: Canada East was still French, Canada West still English. Canadian Confederation, set out in the British North America Act of 1867, created two provinces: Quebec for the French and Ontario for the English. Even so, the two were part of a single entity, Canada, and that entity was ruled by the English.

In the 1960s, during what is often referred to as the Quiet Revolution, Quebec began building its own sense of nationalism, which saw Quebec as a "homeland" in which the French were "masters in their own house" (Eller 1999, 327). That "house" was no longer inhabited by French Canadians or francophones; rather, it was the house of the Québécois—people who were ready to take control of their own lives and separate from the rest of Canada, if necessary.

© Alain Nogues/Sygma/Corbis

Continuing his support of Quebec's Quiet Revolution, French president Charles de Gaulle declared, "Vive le Québec libre!" in his historic 1967 speech at Montreal's town hall.

THE CULTURAL CONSTRUCTION OF IDENTITY

QUESTION 5.4: HOW DO SOCIETIES MARK CHANGES IN IDENTITY?

Identities are not static, and people are constantly changing their identities as they move through the life cycle. These changes in identity are announced in myriad ways. Many societies have particular ceremonies or rituals that mark a change in a person's status or role in society. Most societies hold religious and/or secular events such as baptisms, confirmations, bat/bar mitzvahs, birthdays, funerals, and graduations to mark significant changes in an individual's status in society. In this section we explore cross-cultural examples of these phenomena.

The Transition to Adulthood

In a 1908 book now considered a classic of anthropology, Arnold van Gennep introduced the concept of **rites of passage**. These rituals mark a person's passage from one identity to another, in the same way that a person's progress through a house might be marked by entering one room after another. Van Gennep identified three phases in rites of passage: separation, liminality, and reincorporation. First, the ritual separates the person from an existing identity; next, the person enters a transition phase; finally, the changes are incorporated into a new identity. These phases of rites of passage are not equally elaborated in all ceremonies. The separation phase, for example, is a major part of funeral ceremonies designed to help the living let go of the deceased; transition is a major part of initiation ceremonies marking the passage of a person from, say, childhood to adulthood; and incorporation is emphasized in marriage ceremonies, which in most societies mark the transfer of a person from one social group to another.

Rites of passage are visible in Canadian society. For instance, a young man or woman who joins the military is required to undergo "boot camp."

Geographically and spatially sequestered from mainstream society, the new recruit lives with other recruits in a dormitory. He or she marks this sense of separation by undergoing physical changes, such as cutting one's hair and wearing a uniform. These acts standardize physical appearances and visually mark an individual as a newcomer/initiate. Recruits then undergo a period of transition or liminality, where they are expected to perform physically and emotionally draining tasks, such as running long distances when sleep deprived, or enduring verbal insults. Finally, a recruit who is able to endure the stresses of boot camp re-enters mainstream society with a new status—soldier. This period of reincorporation is marked by a new uniform and by a ceremony where the initiate is reintroduced to family and friends with a new status.

Prominent in most societies around the world are ceremonies that mark the transition of a male from boyhood to manhood. Most such ceremonies involve a test of courage. According to anthropologist David Gilmore (1990), one reason why so many societies incorporate tests of masculinity and tortuous initiation rituals for males is that the male identity is more problematical than the female identity. For every individual, there is at the beginning of life a subliminal identification with the mother, and men must make greater efforts to differentiate themselves from their mothers. Consequently, societies incorporate rituals that symbolically separate the boy from his mother, while at the same time incorporating him into manhood.

Victor Turner (1967) used van Gennep's model of rites of passage to describe the move from boyhood to manhood among the Ndembu of Zambia. When Ndembu boys reach puberty, they are taken, as a group of age mates, away from their mothers and

> **rites of passage**
> This term, coined in 1908 by Arnold Van Gennep, refers to rituals that accompany changes in status, such as the transition from boyhood to manhood, living to dead, or student to graduate.

out of the village (separation), to live in the forest (transition). There the boys shave their heads and remove anything from their bodies that might identify them as individuals. While in the forest, the young Ndembu are circumcised and taught all of the special knowledge that Ndembu men know. But in the forest, they have no identity; they are no longer boys, but they are not yet men. In Turner's words, they are "betwixt and between." Once their circumcisions heal and the lessons are completed, the young men return to the village (reintegration) as new persons with new identities. These men, who made the transition to manhood together, will remain in close association throughout their lives as age mates, a category that cuts across kinship groups and that has special tasks in many societies, such as herding animals among pastoralists.

QUESTION 5.5: HOW DO INDIVIDUALS COMMUNICATE THEIR IDENTITIES TO ONE ANOTHER?

Both consciously and unconsciously, we make statements about our identity—who we think we are, or who we want to be—with objects and material things. The clothes we wear and the things we possess are used to display an identity that we desire or that we think we have. In North America, think about how designer clothing, shoes, and bags are coveted by some women as markers of class and status. Similarly, we use language, or the way we speak, to communicate our identities. In many societies, for instance, one's accent is a marker of class status, gender, geography, or other phenomena. Think about how accents in Britain are based not only on where an individual lives—Londoners have a different accent from Liverpudlians—but also on class.

Similarly, clothing can express class as well as gender, sexuality, ethnicity, or religious affiliation. In some cases, clothing marks some individuals as

"Other" even within their own society. Women who wear the Muslim veil in North America, for instance, have often been identified as "the enemy within," especially since 9/11. Some Muslims in Canada have dealt with this by changing their names and creating fictitious origins. Others have removed visible signs of their Muslimness, particularly with regard to their dress. Still others have tried to show Canadians that the stereotype that all Muslims are terrorists is not only wrong but completely illogical.

In a study conducted by Homa Hoodfar (2003), young Muslim women in Canada reported that wearing the veil was not something their parents forced them to do. In fact, most of the women Hoodfar talked to said they had had to fight with their parents in order to wear it. This contradicts the claims made by some North American feminists that banning the veil will free women from Islamic patriarchal oppression (2003, 15). When Hoodfar and her research assistants asked young women why they wear the veil, one woman said that doing so "allowed her to be a 'person' rather than an object of male scrutiny" (2003, 17–18). Other women explained that they took up the veil when they started university because wearing it communicated certain values. In Hoodfar's words, "By taking up the veil, they symbolically but clearly announce to their parents and their community that, despite their unconventional activities and involvement with non-Muslims, they retain their Islamic mores and values. They are modern Muslim women who want to be educated and publicly active, but not at the cost of their moral principles" (2003, 21). In the same sense that "a picture is worth a thousand words," they believed that wearing the veil communicated identity in a way that saved them from having to explain why they behaved in certain ways.

While some Muslim women in Canada choose to wear "Islamic dress"[1] to emphasize their modesty

---

[1] There are different interpretations as to what constitutes an "Islamic dress." For example, some women wear a head scarf and a long dress over their clothes to cover the body completely, and sometimes conceal part of the face; others believe that a head scarf suffices to fulfill the requirements of their faith.

and to divert attention from the contours of their bodies and their sexual appeal, people in some societies may want to *highlight* their sexuality so that it is immediately visible to others. Men in some groups in New Guinea, for example, wear penis gourds. And in 17th-century Europe, men wore codpieces to emphasize their male anatomy.

Sexual identification is an important identity marker, but there are other signals that people use to display their identity. In some parts of Africa, people from different villages have different hairstyles; in North America, teenagers encode their schools or teams by the jackets they wear. People signal their connectedness to others by holding hands, by wearing rings, or by feasting and drinking together.

Rituals of Gift Giving and Hospitality

One of the most influential works in the history of anthropology is *The Gift* (1925), by Marcel Mauss. In it, Mauss identifies what he calls the **principle of reciprocity**: the giving and receiving of gifts. His main point is that gifts, which in theory are voluntary, disinterested, and spontaneous, are in fact obligatory. The giving of the gift creates a tie with the person who receives it and who, on some future occasion, is obliged to reciprocate. To Mauss, what is important is not what is given but the relationship that is maintained or established by the gift. The types of things given and received signal the identities of the participants in the exchange and the kind of relationship that exists between them. If the gifts are roughly of equal value, the relationship is one of equality. But if the gifts are unequal in value, the person who gives the more valuable gift is generally of higher status than the receiver.

A well-known example of gift giving in the anthropological literature is the ***kula* ring** of the Trobriand Islanders. The seagoing Trobrianders leave their homes on islands off the eastern coast of New Guinea and travel from island to island, visiting and trading. Noteworthy in their travels is their pattern of gift giving. Each man has trading partners on the islands he visits, and these partnerships are signalled with gifts of red shell necklaces or white shell armbands. As a man travels and trades objects, he gives and receives necklaces and receives armbands. A man who receives either an armband or a necklace does not keep it but passes it along to another trading partner. There is a set pattern to the exchange: necklaces travel from island to island in a clockwise direction, while armbands move counterclockwise. The time between exchanges and the distances between the islands are so great that it may take two to ten years before the necklaces and armbands make a complete circle.

The *kula* ring serves as a concrete representation of ties among individuals. Any change in the pattern of gift giving reflects a change in the nature of the social ties. Special gifts that are individually owned are also circulated, and the owner's status and

EXERCISE 5.4

Suppose you were to travel to an island where no one knows anything about you or the society you came from. Also suppose you could only communicate to people on the island using objects that you carried with you, and you could only take five things to tell people about yourself. What would they be?

principle of reciprocity
According to Marcel Mauss, gift giving involves reciprocity. The idea is that the exchange of gifts creates a feeling of obligation, in that the gift must be repaid.

***kula* ring**
A system of inter-island gift exchange documented by anthropologist Bronislaw Malinowski in the Trobriand Islands. It involves the exchange of shell necklaces and armbands. According to Malinowski, the kula ring serves, among other things, to create alliances and social ties among individuals living on different islands.

Trobriand Islanders define and maintain their social identities by participating in the *kula* ring, a ritualized pattern of gift giving involving the exchange of necklaces and armbands.

© I. DeVore/Anthro Photo

renown grow as the goods he owns circulate along predetermined paths. A successful *kula* operator participates in many such exchanges and can profit from them by keeping items for as long as he can before passing them along. Of course, if he keeps them too long, others will be reluctant to exchange, so a good deal of social skill is required to *kula* successfully.

Anthropologist Margaret Anderson has devoted many years to studying another famous example of gift giving: the **potlatch** ceremony of the people of the Northwest Coast of British Columbia. Among the Tsimshian, the potlatch is typically a feast that legitimates a change in social relations, such as a funeral. Someone who dies is vacating a spot on the social landscape—or, more specifically, leaving a name empty. The Tsimshian are organized into matrilineal clans or houses. Each house has associated with it a fixed number of personal names, and each name has associated with it specific spiritual powers, honours, and objects of wealth. The man with the highest ranking name is recognized as the owner of the house. The name a Tsimshian holds when he dies is vacated until it is claimed by or given to someone else. If the name vacated belongs to a chief, the feasting will begin with his death and end with the acceptance of a new chief, who is usually the eldest son of the deceased chief's eldest sister. A person who disgraces his name by doing something wrong (such as having an automobile accident or being put in jail) must give a feast to "clean the name."

The potlatch feast, however, does more than allow a Tsimshian to obtain a new name and identity. It also serves to symbolically reorder and validate the names, and hence the social positions, of everyone at the feast through the distribution of gifts. Members of the house of the deceased generally serve as hosts to members of the deceased's father's house. The guests are feasted for the services they have performed (preparing the corpse, carving a pole) and as repayment for the gifts they formerly gave the deceased to help him acquire his name. When the guests are seated, the hosts announce the gifts they are giving to the guests, along with the name of the person from the host group who has contributed the gift. Higher ranking guests receive more gifts at a potlatch than lower ranking guests. Consequently, the seating arrangements and the value of the gifts given to guests at the feast serve to announce or publicly notarize the social position or identity of each guest.

potlach
A celebration, usually involving elaborate feasting and the redistribution of gifts, found among many indigenous Northwest Coast groups, such as the Tsimshian. The potlatch is a means of creating a new identity or of reinforcing social status within a group.

Anderson argues that although the potlatch has changed since Christianity was introduced in 1857 (when William Duncan of the Church Missionary Society came to Fort Simpson), its meaning and symbolic value have remained, in part because as long as the feasts began with a prayer, Duncan considered them respectable.

Exchanges that convey recognition of identities need not be limited to material goods. The exchanges also may consist of emotion and sentiment. Hawaiians, for example, define a desired identity in part by expressions of gregariousness and hospitality. The emotional qualities of a person's relationships are one criterion by which others judge, interact with, and respond to that person. For example, if you accept an offer of hospitality in Hawai'i, it is a signal that you recognize the generous nature of the offer and that you wish to maintain the social link. If you reject the offer of hospitality, it is seen as a hurtful sign that you do not recognize the generous nature of the person making the offer and do not wish to maintain the relationship. Hawaiians attempt to keep social pathways open through altruistic exchanges of love (*aloha*), sincerity, feeling (with heart, *na'au*), and warmth (*pumehana*).

Gifts and Commodities

An important characteristic of traditional *kula* and potlatch goods is that they have histories. A Trobriander who receives a necklace or armband can probably recite the history of the object, sometimes from its creation through all the persons who possessed it at one time or another. These goods are similar to heirlooms in our own society, whether it is the family wedding ring that has been worn by brides for three generations, the watch that was owned by a great-grandfather, or the quilt that was made by a great-aunt. The histories of these objects, especially when they are given as gifts, are vital to the identity of the person who gives them. They say something special about the relationship between the giver and the receiver of the gift. The same is true to a lesser extent of gifts that are

produced by the giver: these carry a special meaning apart from the object itself. A lamp made and given as a gift is often far more meaningful than a lamp purchased at a department store. However, we often must choose the gifts that we give from among thousands of mass-produced, largely impersonal goods available in department and chain stores. Herein lies a dilemma.

James Carrier, in his book *Gifts and Commodities: Exchange and Western Capitalism Since 1700* (1995), argues that since the 16th and 17th centuries, the production and distribution of goods has become impersonal, and that the spread of industrial and commercial capitalism has meant the spread of alienated objects and relations. In earlier times, commodities were personalized in various ways. The relationship between the producer and the seller of goods was a personal one between relatives or friends; the buyer knew who made and sold the object purchased. Even when stores replaced home trade and markets, the buyer knew the store owner, who further personalized the goods by buying them in bulk and individually packaging and displaying them. The buyer–seller relationship was further personalized by the extension of credit from seller to buyer and by the customer loyalty expressed by the buyer to the seller. Today the buyer knows neither the producer nor the seller, and if the item is bought on credit, it is through a credit card issued by some distant bank based on the filing of an impersonal application, with the transaction accomplished completely by mail. Eyes never meet.

Carrier labels goods that carry no special meaning **commodities**, to distinguish them from what he calls possessions. Gifts, says Carrier, must be possessions before they can carry meaning in an

---

commodity
Traditionally, commodities are items that involve a transfer of value and a counter-transfer: A sells something to B, and the transaction is finished. A longstanding personal relationship between buyer and seller is not established. This is typical of capitalist market-exchange systems.

exchange. Commodities involve a transfer of value and a counter-transfer: A sells something to B, and the transaction is finished. But in a gift exchange, a more or less permanent link is established between giver and receiver. Gifts are inalienable, that is, they are bound to people after the presentation; commodities are independent of their sellers (or producers). It is easy to return, destroy, or give away a commodity; it is a dilemma to do any of those with a gift. Ralph Waldo Emerson vividly expressed the difference between gifts and commodities when he wrote that "the only gift is a portion of thyself. Thou must bleed for me. Therefore the poet brings his poem; the shepherd, his lamb; the farmer, corn; the miner, a gem; the sailor, coral and shells; the painter, his picture; the girl, a handkerchief or her own sewing. This is right and pleasing … when a man's biography is conveyed in a gift" (in Carrier 1993, 56). Or, as Emerson said again, "It is a cold, lifeless business when you go to the shops to buy me something that does not represent your life and talent" (in Carrier 1993, 56).

As noted, for North Americans the contrast between commodities and gifts poses a special problem. Most of the items we give as gifts are store-bought commodities, often mass produced. Their history is brief and undistinguished: an item of clothing was probably assembled in some factory in Mexico or Indonesia by a young woman earning perhaps a dollar an hour; a sports item was probably assembled in some factory in South America, shipped to a warehouse in Toronto or Chicago, and sold through a mass-produced catalogue; a radio, iPod, or CD player, assembled in Korea, distributed by a Japanese company, was probably sold in a North American chain store. These are commodities, not gifts. Their meaning is contained in their worth or utility, in their materiality. The meaning of a gift is different: the perfect gift is priceless, its materiality is immaterial.

For Carrier the problem is how, in a world filled with impersonal, alienated commodities—goods without history, so to speak—we can turn these things into personal items with meaning and history, into possessions that carry something of the buyer's identity. In gift giving, how do we turn commodities into items that say something about the relationship between the giver and receiver? How do we make commodities meaningful?

We convert commodities into possessions and gifts, says Carrier, through a process of appropriation. For example, when a person takes an impersonal space—a dorm room, say, or a rented apartment—and decorates and modifies it, he or she has appropriated it and given it meaning. When we buy food at the supermarket, we appropriate it by preparing or cooking it. When a person buys an automobile, one that is virtually identical to thousands of others of the same make, model, year, and colour, and comes to think of it as unique, as an expression of his or her identity, that person has appropriated an object and made it a possession. Shopping itself, says Carrier, is a way of appropriating commodities; the "wise shopper" chooses what is "right" for them or what is "right" for the recipient of the gift.

Manufacturers and sellers, of course, try to aid the process of converting a commodity into a possession by themselves stamping their products with a distinct identity. A good example is Harris tweed, which most buyers associate with some Harris Islander weaving on a loom in his shed, creating the item as his ancestors have done for centuries, and even giving each item its own serial number. In fact, the yarn that is used is spun in textile mills and then woven on looms given to the weaver with the frames already warped so that no special skill is necessary to weave the cloth. In actuality, other than the fact that they are narrower, the only difference between the looms they use and the ones used in factories is that the Harris Island weaver supplies the power with a foot treadle rather than a machine.

Endorsements from sports or movie celebrities help consumers transform a commodity into a possession. Also, displaying goods in catalogues in ways that help the buyer appropriate commodities has become a fine art. For example, when Wayne

Gretzky endorses a product, it takes on a Canadian flavour, regardless of where it was manufactured.

Gift Giving and the Christian Celebration of Christmas in North America

The dilemma of converting commodities into gifts is especially acute during the Christian Christmas holiday season, when most gift giving takes place in North America. Christmas as Christians know it did not really emerge until the height of the Industrial Revolution. Its precursors included the traditional end-of-year festivities that took place in England, where gifts consisted of food or feasts given by superiors to their dependants. In the 1770s in New York City, people began celebrating 6 December, the day of St. Nicholas, instead of the New Year. This was actually something of an anti-Christmas celebration; St. Nicholas was Dutch, and the colonists were celebrating things Dutch to protest British rule over what had been New Amsterdam before British colonization. It wasn't until 1809 that the holiday began to spread and that St. Nicholas turned into Santa Claus giving gifts of candy to children. The appearance of Clement Moore's *A Visit from St. Nicholas* in 1823 (or *'Twas the Night Before Christmas*, as it later became known) marked the movement of the holiday to the end of the year. At this point children began to get toys rather than food. Even then, Christmas was celebrated largely on New Year's Day and in the industrial northeast.

The next major step in the evolution of Christmas was the appearance of Charles Dickens's *A Christmas Carol* in 1843. It was an immediate sensation, especially with its victory of Bob Cratchit and Tiny Tim and their world of the home over Scrooge and the cold, impersonal world of work. By 1865, Christmas had been declared a national holiday, and in 1862, the Thomas Nast image of Santa Claus began appearing in *Harper's Weekly*, completing his construction as a fat, jolly,

old man dressed in fur-trimmed robes (inspired, Nast later admitted, by the fur-trimmed clothing of the wealthy Astor family). By the 1880s, writers were beginning to complain about the commercialization of Christmas.

Most social scientists who have written about the Christian celebration of Christmas agree that it is largely a celebration of the family, serving especially to distinguish the world of the family from the outside world of work. Christmas serves to affirm the identity of Christians all over the world as members of specific family groups, and the circle of kin with whom gifts are exchanged defines the boundaries of the family. In one study conducted in a midwestern American city, 90 percent of all

© Monika Graff/The Image Works

In North American societies, the yearly Christian ritual of Christmas shopping provides a means of converting impersonal commodities into personalized gifts that show one's love for family members and close friends.

gifts exchanged at Christmas were exchanged with family members. Christmas heightens a person's sense of family identity, expressing how warm the family is and how cold the world outside may be.

Thus, it is within the family that the Christmas gift is most important. Furthermore, the gift must contain something of the biography of the giver and the history of the relationship—that is, it must be a possession rather than a commodity. The question is how to resolve the problem of using commodities as family gifts, how to transform commodities to make them suitable as statements of the special role that family and family relations play in defining our identity. This problem, apparently, is not a new one. The dilemma of giving gifts that are manufactured and sold in stores apparently existed as early as the mid-19th century, when department stores tried to convince buyers to purchase their gifts in stores by advertising them as "special Christmas stock." Even today, through Christmas decorations, music, and special attractions, such as the ever-present Santa Claus, retailers try to inject the spirit of Christmas into their stock of goods.

But there are other ways that consumers try to appropriate commodities and turn them into Christmas gifts. First, we may simply say that the nature of the gift itself is immaterial, that "it's the thought that counts." A second way is to purchase things that aren't very useful, giving frivolous or luxurious gifts, or items that are Christmas-specific, such as Christmas tree decorations or clothing with Christmas decorations on it. Third, and very important, there is the wrapping rule: Christmas gifts must be wrapped. The wrapping itself converts the commodity into a gift. Difficult-to-wrap presents (a piano, a horse, a bicycle, etc.) must be decorated with a bow. The only categories of things that needn't be wrapped are items made by the giver, such as breads or jams. These items need only a bow and a card.

Finally, says Carrier, there is the shopping itself, the time we spend getting the "right" gift for the "right" person. Why, he asks, do we go through all of this? It is onerous, it is stressful, and it is expensive. Yet one-third of all retail sales are made in November and December, most of them accounted for by Christmas shopping. One-sixth of all retail sales are related to Christmas. People complain about the materialism of Christmas and Christmas shopping. Yet people shop intensely for Christmas.

In the face of this bother and complaint, why do North Americans, even devout Christians, spend so much effort in Christmas shopping? Why not give homemade gifts? Indeed, why give presents at all? Why not give a Christmas card instead? It is true that the giving of purchased gifts reflects a number of motives, ranging from displays of affluence to a desire to shower a loved one with lovely things. However, these more commonly recognized motives do "not explain the intensity of Christmas shopping and people's ambivalence towards it" (Carrier 1993, 62).

Carrier suggests that the answer to this riddle lies in the fact that shopping in itself is a method of appropriation, of converting a commodity into a gift: we exercise a choice from among the mass of commodities presented to us. As Carrier puts it, "Christmas shopping is an annual ritual through which we convert commodities into gifts. Performing this ritual indicates that we can celebrate and recreate personal relations with the anonymous objects available to us, just as it strengthens and reassures us as we undertake the more mundane appropriations of everyday life during the rest of the year" (1993, 63).

Christmas shopping also demonstrates to people, says Carrier, that they can create a world

---

EXERCISE 5.5

These days, gift cards for stores, restaurants, spas, or other goods and services are popular holiday gift items. After reading Carrier's work, discuss how gift cards might fit into his discussion of commodities and gifts. How can gift cards, as commodities, be turned into gifts? Or can they be?

of family, a world of love, out of the impersonal commodities that flood the world "out there." The Christian celebration of Christmas is a time when North Americans make a world of money into a world of family, a time of contrast between the impersonal world of commodities and the personal world of possessions and gifts.

QUESTION 5.6: HOW DO INDIVIDUALS FORM IDENTITIES THROUGH COLLECTIVE STRUGGLES?

As this chapter's epigraph suggests, the formation of identity is a cultural process that involves the lived experiences and everyday practices of people. This cultural construction of identity creates both the individual and the collectivity, which we think of as society. In this section, we focus on the collectivity and ask how identity is produced through collective struggles.

The Meaning of "Indigenous"

After examining **indigenous peoples** of Asia, Africa, Meso- and South America, North America, Eurasia, and Europe, Bruce Miller attempts to arrive at a definition of what "indigenous" means. He concludes his book *Invisible Indigenes* (2003) by looking at the common elements in the various ways the term has been used in different parts of the world. One common factor in all the societies Miller encountered is the association of indigenousness with both the presence and the absence of certain traits. The most critical element in the various definitions is that indigenes are recognized because they live in some clearly identifiable way that maintains their own distinct culture, and that they have been living exactly the same way since they were encountered by the colonizers. Furthermore,

people are defined as indigenous because "broadly, definitions have come to focus on difference—the idea that indigenes are distinct—and the related idea that distinctions show up in many ways. These include self-identification and the recognition of distinction by others" (2003, 213).

Furthermore, people are defined as indigenous because "ancestors of members did not practice one of the world religions and therefore needed to be converted. Or members of a group are indigenous because they or their ancestors were not organized around Western values and practices, in particular Enlightenment values of universalism, secularism, rationalism, and subsequent modernist traits of bureaucratization and the centralization of authority" (2003, 213–14). Finally, indigenes are defined by their relationship to the state, in which they are recognized as having different rights than other citizens.

When indigenous peoples attempt to gain rights to land or to resources that may lie beneath the surface of the land they occupy, the state or some other entity interested in blocking indigenous claims may use the definition of essential difference as a weapon against indigenous claims. For instance, issues such as wearing the same kinds of clothing as other Canadians have been cited by those who are opposed to Aboriginal rights as evidence that First Nations peoples no longer have a separate culture.

Social Movements

Kim Clark (2005) has explored the ways in which class struggles and state legislation created the space in which indigenous social movements could form in Ecuador. The actors in Clark's historical account of the growth of CONAIE (Confederation of

> **indigenous peoples**
> Groups of people whose ancestors pre-date the arrival of European or other forms of colonialism, who share a culture and/or way of life that they often identify as distinct from "mainstream" society, and who often feel that they have a right to self-government.

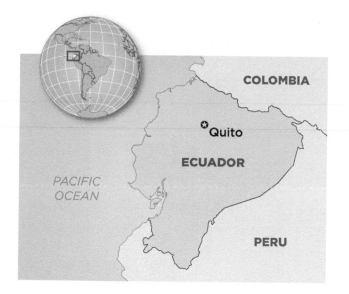

countryside diminished rapidly and indigenous organizations became more autonomous. The result has been that indigenous identity has strengthened rapidly, especially in the countryside. Clark argues that the "rural population of the Ecuadorian highlands is becoming more rather than less indigenous" (2005, 60).

The indigenous leaders of this new social movement now participate directly in negotiations with the state and rural elites over such matters as agrarian reform and the privatization of water. In 2004, representatives of the indigenous movement were appointed to positions in the Ecuadorian government.

Indigenous Nations of Ecuador), and of the eventual amalgamation of small, grassroots social movements, include the state, Ecuador's elites, and Indians. In the early 1900s, the aim of the state, backed by the elite class, was to turn the Indian population into proper "civilized" consumers; however, the indigenous peoples took advantage of this undertaking to promote their own goals. For instance, they started a literacy program in order to be able to check the account books of the haciendas, and they began to form small local groups.

As more grassroots indigenous organizations formed, the state used part of its revenues generated from an oil boom to modernize the Ecuadorian countryside, expecting the indigenous groups to passively accept the state's authoritarian paternalism. But local indigenous leaders were learning to interact with the administrators of the state's development projects and with NGOs from both inside and outside the country, and they were gaining confidence in their ability to express the common identity that was growing among the various groups that belonged to CONAIE.

The debt crisis of the 1980s compelled Ecuador to reduce its spending on social programs. When that happened, the state's influence in the

Palestinian Refugees

The plight of the Palestinian refugees has not had a happy ending. Randa Farah, a Palestinian–Canadian anthropologist living in exile, states: "Palestinians constitute the largest refugee population in the world, and their exile is one of the longest in contemporary history, spanning over half a century" (2003, 1550). In a refugee camp in Jordan, where 120,000 Palestinians live in an area of 1.4 square kilometres, Randa Farah listened to the stories of three generations of Palestinian refugees. Farah's study revealed that the refugees reinforced their collective memory by invoking memories of the land, of original villages, and of shared experiences of exile. This reconstruction of the past cannot be separated from the present political struggles, which counter the plans of host societies to integrate the refugees. At the same time, the refugees reaffirm their hopes for repatriation. The Palestinian refugees also express their collective identity by reproducing symbols of home while they are away from home or, as Farah puts it, "a sense of place while out of place" (2005, 210).

When camps were not overcrowded, as they are today, Palestinian women planted gardens in front of their shelters as they did in their original villages, and they passed on to their children and grandchildren stories and images of what it was like to live in their villages before they had to flee. Public streets and walls in the camp are inscribed with political graffiti featuring Palestinian political history. Within refugee homes and shelters, Palestinian culture is displayed in Palestinian embroidery—especially embroidered peasant dresses—in pictures of the Dome of the Rock in Jerusalem, and in children's diplomas, decorative Koranic verses, and maps of Palestine and its flag.

The notion of prolonged temporary residence, which establishes that exile is not their permanent home, is vital to Palestinian identity. This is evident in the structures of refugee shelters. In the words of a refugee in Jordan interviewed by Farah:

> No one at the time used concrete for their shelters … They used to say this is not our Homeland, we should not build here …
> My father used to say we want to return to our Homeland, if not this year, next year …
> My father, until he passed away in the eighties, believed we shall return. He didn't even want to build a roof using cement, he kept saying we shall return, but we didn't! (2004, 177)

Land and return are at the centre of Palestinian identity, and keeping the memory alive is a form of resistance. As Farah explains, without the "Dream of Return" the older generation would have to concede that the younger generation—those born in the refugee camps—"are stateless refugees, without a past or a future" (2004, 181) and without an identity.

Conflict Within Collective Identity: Telefolmin and Land in Papua New Guinea

Creating a collective identity does not mean that everyone who assumes that identity experiences it in the same way. In Papua New Guinea (PNG), rights to land characteristically overlap and, as

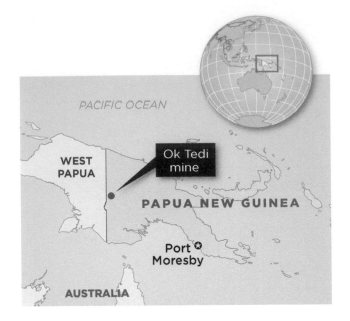

anthropologist Dan Jorgensen documents, are causing all kinds of problems in light of a proposed mining project, the Nena, at the site of Nena Mountain. Mineral exploration has been going on in PNG for quite some time, and the 1980s and 1990s saw a mining boom with four new mines in operation. Although mining brings some benefits to local people, such as employment and royalties, it also causes environmental damage, so compensation is paid to landowners. The Telefolmin people live in an area that has experienced mining since the 1960s, and many men have been employed in the industry.

The Telefolmin identify themselves as "Min," along with many of their neighbours. This identity is based on common descent from an ancestress known as Afek, who travelled through the area in the mythological past. When she came to the present site of Telefolip, she built a spirit house, which became the centre of important rituals for Min people. All Telefomin men must be initiated at Telefolip, and they return at death in order to reach the "Land of the Dead." After Afek built Telefolip, she killed her younger brother, Umoim, and sent him along an underground passage to Mount Fubilan to establish Bagelam, "The Land of the Dead," located west of Telefolip. This place associated with the dead is also a source of wealth, for it is here that Umoim produced stone adzes used to clear gardens, and it is here that *bonang* shells, an important item of exchange in marriage and mortuary rituals, originated. In 1980, copper was discovered at Mount Fubilan and a mine called Ok Tedi was built there. The Telefolmin were hired during the initial construction phase and as wage labourers once the actual mining began. But they had no control over the land and the resources that Afek had given them. With another mine approaching, the connection between place and identity was crucial.

One of the ways the Telefolmin and other Min peoples approached this problem was to propose that a new province be created that would contain all of Afek's descendants. This would give geographic expression to the collective identity that had been established in the story of Afek; it would also give the Min peoples a legal tool with which to assert more control over what was being taken out of their land and how they were compensated for environmental damage. But this would not solve all the problems, for the Min people relate to the land in different ways.

The Ok Tedi mine.

The Telefolmin hold a few basic principles that determine who has first rights to which pieces of land. The principle of first clearance means that whoever clears a plot of land has rights to that land as long as it is in use, and the principle of bilateral inheritance means that land can be passed on through both maternal and paternal connections. A third way that Telefolmin can gain access to land is through being granted permission to use some part of the land of another. While all of this seems fairly simple in theory, when the principles are combined, the actual practice becomes much more complex. For instance, rights in land and rights based on residence may not be the same. The principle of bilateral inheritance may mean that a Telefolmin has rights in lands located in different places and that he or she, or the entire family, may move away temporarily in order to use land in another hamlet, giving permission to a friend to use land in the place they left. When the mining company agrees to pay occupation fees, royalties, or compensation to a landowner for environmental damage, the question becomes "Who and what is a landowner?"

Adding to the complexity is a history of conflict and warfare that has left some villages empty in the area of the mines but that has not destroyed old rights in land. Furthermore, when one group defeated another, women and children were often adopted into the victorious group and their rights in land were passed on to their children. Over the years, this overlapping in land rights has created a vast puzzle that defies solution. When Jorgensen made one of his many return visits to Telefolmin, he landed right in the middle of the conflict:

> *My arrival had been anticipated and people*
> *came forward with a variety of different evidence,*
> *or wisnes (witnesses) prepared. Most of this*
> *came in the form of oral accounts of personal*
> *genealogies and land use histories, with detailed*
> *listings of the marks they or their ancestors had*
> *left on the ground around the proposed mine*
> *site. This testimony was backed up with the aid*

THE CULTURAL CONSTRUCTION OF IDENTITY

of locally recognized collateral evidence in the form of ancestral relics, war trophies and the text of commemorative songs that provide a crucial medium of Telephol oral history. (1997, 611)

The Min conflict over rights to land highlights the connection between place and identity for Telefolmin; it also shows how "a self-conscious Min identity has multiple roots" (1996, 202). Added to the variety of ways that Min people relate to one another through their common descent are colonial and missionary definitions that reinforce the notions of fixed categories and boundaries.

All three examples of how people form identities through collective action (indigenous groups in Ecuador, Palestinian refugees in Jordan, and Telefolmin in PNG) challenge the notion of fixed categories and boundaries. Common ancestry, the sense that people as much as plants and trees are grown from the land, and a sense of self and other all come into play as different facets of identity are reworked in relation to current experiences and events.

CONCLUSIONS

The concept of the self, or personhood, varies from society to society. In the egocentric view, the person is viewed as an autonomous, discrete individual; in the sociocentric view, the self is viewed as contingent on a situation or social setting. The sociocentric view is often taken by social scientists who are interested in the social processes by which social identities are formed and maintained.

Societies distinguish individuals from one another by using criteria such as age, gender, kinship, ethnicity, and language. Differences and similarities in characteristics among individuals are used to construct social landscapes on which each person's place or identity is indicated. The characteristics that determine identity, such as gender, are treated differently in various societies.

People must also be able to communicate their identities to one another. One way to do this is through gift exchange and the principle of reciprocity. The *kula* ring of the Trobriand Islanders is an example. North Americans and other people in modern industrial societies have a special problem with gift giving: somehow they need to convert an impersonal, store-bought commodity into a personal and meaningful gift. We examined how during the Christian celebration of Christmas this is a special problem, and we explored some of the ways in which North Americans solve it.

Another way people form their identity is through collective struggle. Examples of how this is done include the indigenous social movements in Ecuador, the experiences of Palestinian refugees, and land disputes in Papua New Guinea.

CRITICAL THINKING QUESTIONS

1. Even though anthropologists and other scholars view our identities as learned phenomena, we live in a society that privileges biological or "natural" explanations for our behaviour. What are some of the consequences of thinking about our identities as natural?
2. Hoodfar discusses what veiling means for many Muslim women and how they seek to express and communicate aspects of their identity through veiling. But many people use not just clothing but other forms of body modification to communicate their identity. How are tattoos and piercings markers of identity for many people?

KEY TERMS:

commodity (p. 154)
egocentric (p. 146)
enculturation (p. 141)
holistic (p. 145)
identity (p. 140)
imagined community (p. 142)
indigenous peoples (p. 158)
individualistic (p. 145)
kula **ring** (p. 152)
nature versus nurture (p. 142)
potlatch (p. 153)
principle of reciprocity (p. 152)
rites of passage (p. 150)
sociocentric (p. 146)

THE CULTURAL CONSTRUCTION OF SOCIAL HIERARCHY

© Art Resource, NY

This painting of construction workers by the famous French artist Fernand Léger depicts a scene of reconstruction in post–Second World War France. In many ways, it represents the struggles of the working classes; it also serves as a metaphor for the formation of various social hierarchies in conjunction with the rise of capitalism and industrialization in the West. Racism, caste, and gender will also be discussed in this chapter as social hierarchies. As we see in the epigraph, racism operates in a particular way in Canada.

Although it may never be possible to quantify the degree of racism that exists in a given society, the evidence unmistakably reveals that racism widely distorts the attitudes of white Canadians toward Aboriginal peoples. Whether blatantly or covertly, many Canadians still believe that Aboriginal people are inferior; as a result, these people believe that there is a sound, rational basis for discriminating against Aboriginal persons at both the individual and institutional level.

James S. Frideres and Rene R. Gadacz

PROBLEM 6

Why are modern societies characterized by social, political, and economic inequalities? How are certain gender, class, racial, and other identities privileged or marginalized in various social contexts?

INTRODUCTION

The Rationale for Social Inequality

The maldistribution of wealth, status, power, and privilege is a significant problem throughout the modern world. To North Americans it is visible in the starving faces that stare out from our television screens in documentaries and on the evening news, interspersed with advertisements for luxuries such as automobiles, cosmetics, and household appliances. Some people can purchase the finest amenities, while others lack the basic necessities of life, such as food, shelter, and health care. There are few, if any, modern nations in which one portion of the population does not in some way enjoy privileges that other portions do not share.

Anthropologists use the interchangeable terms **social stratification** and **social hierarchy** to refer to the ordering and ranking of individuals within a society. This ranking is normally based on pervasive systems of inequality that privilege particular classes, castes, races, or genders over others.

Social hierarchy is not an inevitable feature of human societies. For example, groups such as the Ju/'hoansi and the Inuit are not totally egalitarian, but people go out of their way not to

> **social stratification/hierarchy**
> The ordering and ranking of individuals within society. Those at the top of the hierarchy are generally afforded more power, wealth, prestige, or privileges in a society. Hierarchies can be based on race, gender, class, caste, ethnicity, national affiliation, or other factors.

appear better than others. Moreover, there does not seem to be a universal inclination to rank people by one criterion or another; in some societies, skin colour makes a difference, while in others it does not. In some societies, men are accorded far greater status than women; in others, there is little if any difference in gender rank. Even the use of age as a criterion of rank varies from society to society. The only general rule seems be that as societies become more complex and more populous, their propensity for social stratification increases.

Some people contend that the hierarchical ordering of people and groups is unavoidable. In their view, scarce resources, occupational specialization, and the power of an elite group to control the behaviour of others inevitably result in some form of social stratification. Others maintain that stratification is not only avoidable but also counter to human nature. According to anthropologist Thomas Belmonte, "since the emergence of stratification, man's history (his changing ways of relating to nature and other men) has stood opposed to his humanity. The emergence of power-wielding elites … laid the basis for a new kind of anti-collective society whose vastly accelerated growth was founded, not on the reconciliation of antagonisms between men, but on their origination and amplification in slavery, caste, and class" (Belmonte 1989, 137).

Those who support Belmonte's view note that in societies such as those of Ju/'hoansi and Inuit, there are no "poor," "rich," "inferior," or "superior" people. This is not to say that these societies are totally egalitarian, or equal; even in small-scale societies, valued statuses are not available to some members. Rather, the question at hand is why modern societies are characterized by extremes of poverty and wealth. It is worth noting here that poverty is not random; indigenous populations, ethnic minorities, and women are the social categories of people most at risk for poverty. In Mexico, for example, over 80 percent of the indigenous population lived in poverty in the early 1990s, compared to 18 percent of the non-indigenous population (Psacharopoulos and Patrinos 1994, 4). In Canada, Frideres and Gadacz found that the average Aboriginal income in 2001 was $17,000; among all Canadians it was $24,000 (2001, 91). Also in Canada, Kazemipur and Halli examined the 1991 and 1996 census data and found that "immigrants were consistently over-represented among the poor, and that this over-representation had a clear ethnic and racial colour, with visible minority immigrants experiencing the most severe conditions" (2001, 217). Finally, in the United States in 1997, women living in poverty outnumbered men by a ratio of 4:3. Furthermore, because women are most often the primary caregivers, children pay an even greater price than women do. In the United States, child poverty rates fluctuated between 18 and 21 percent between 1995 and 2000, but only 5.7 percent of French children and 7.3 percent of British children were considered poor. As Valdas Anelauskas (1999) has pointed out, children in the United States are twice as likely to be poor as Canadian children, three times more likely to be poor than British children, four times more likely to be poor than French children, and seven to thirteen times more likely to be poorer than German, Dutch, and Swedish children. How do we explain the distribution of poverty, power, prestige, status and wealth based on **race**, indigenous status, and gender, among other factors?

In this chapter we examine how societies construct social hierarchies and why some groups erect social edifices based on social dominance and submission, high and low status, and oppressors and oppressed. We examine why most people in stratified societies—both those at the top and those

> **race**
> A culturally constructed form of identity and social hierarchy, race refers to the presumed hereditary, phenotypic characteristics of a group of people. These physical or phenotypic differences are often erroneously correlated with behavioural attributes.

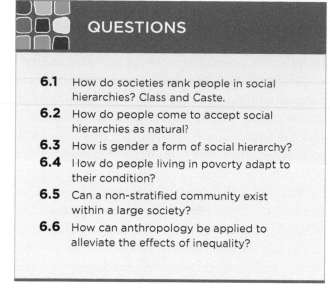

QUESTIONS

6.1 How do societies rank people in social hierarchies? Class and Caste.

6.2 How do people come to accept social hierarchies as natural?

6.3 How is gender a form of social hierarchy?

6.4 How do people living in poverty adapt to their condition?

6.5 Can a non-stratified community exist within a large society?

6.6 How can anthropology be applied to alleviate the effects of inequality?

and upper class). They are classified by cultural or family background into ethnic groups (e.g., Italian, Jewish, Hispanic, or white Anglo-Saxon Protestant), or by physical appearance or skin colour into racial categories or visible minorities (e.g., black or white). They are also classified by gender and age, as well as by standards such as education. People in Canada and the United States may move from class to class, and they may choose to emphasize or de-emphasize their ethnic group membership, but generally, their racial category and gender are perceived as fixed.

EXERCISE 6.1

Remember that social hierarchies are based on people's perceptions of others. Below is a list of personal attributes. Your task is to rank them by number from most to least important to you in judging a person's social or personal worth. No ties are allowed. If there is an attribute not included in the list that you wish to add, do so. What are some of your reasons for your rankings? Why are some attributes more important to you than others? What do your rankings tell us about our society?

Rank

____ Personal appearance

____ Income

____ Gender

____ Age

____ Religion

____ Ethnic or community origin

____ Family background

____ Intelligence (as indicated by school performance)

____ Athletic ability

____ Personal possessions (clothes, car, etc.)

____ Personality (fill in your description of type of personality)

at the bottom—consider social ranks to be "the nature of things." We ask how people at the bottom levels of the hierarchy—those who live in poverty, for example—adapt to their conditions, and we explore whether a nonstratified community can exist within a large-scale society. Finally, we explore how an anthropological perspective can be applied to alleviate the effects of inequality.

QUESTION 6.1: HOW DO SOCIETIES RANK PEOPLE IN SOCIAL HIERARCHIES? CLASS AND CASTE

Social hierarchies in different societies vary along several dimensions: the criteria used to differentiate people into one level of society or another; the number of levels that exist; the kinds of privileges and rights that attach to people at different levels; and the strength of the social boundaries that separate the different levels. In Canada and the United States, for example, people are stratified by income and personal possessions into social **classes** (e.g., lower class, middle class,

class
A form of identity informed by perceptions of an individual's economic worth or status. It is also a form of social hierarchy.

Class as a Form of Social Hierarchy

Social class refers to perceptions of an individual's standing or status in society, normally based on economic criteria, status, or other factors, which may vary from society to society. Max Weber argued that social class can be based on economic wealth and/or "status class": prestige, honour, educational or occupational achievements, or religious or spiritual affiliation. In North American societies, for instance, we tend to place particular value on some occupations that require years of post-secondary schooling over more "hands on" professions such as construction work and trades. While many tradespeople earn sizable incomes, their professions lack the "status" associated with medicine or law. Also, we live in a commodified, consumer-driven society in which material possessions such as cars, houses, clothing brands, and other objects are often perceived as markers of an individual's class background and, by extension, his or her access to wealth, power, and prestige. Unlike social identities, such as race, which is normally perceived as an ascribed (fixed, unchanging) status, class in North American society has long been viewed as a more fluid social identity. In other words, it can be either an **ascribed status** or an **achieved status**. An individual may be born into a life of wealth, power, and high status as a Rockefeller or a Massey; or alternatively, he or she may, through hard work and determination, overcome the odds and achieve a higher class status for themselves. This popular myth that class is an achieved category is enshrined in American fiction (F. Scott Fitzgerald's *The Great Gatsby*) and in real life (Barack Obama). However, these stories overshadow the ways in which class intersects with other identities, such as gender and race. In many ways, stories of opportunity, available for all, privilege a white male perspective. As discussed earlier, ethnic minorities and women, for instance, are often positioned at the bottom of many social hierarchies, making it difficult for them to have the same opportunities or access to tools—such post-secondary education, training, or other resources—that are needed to "achieve" a higher class status.

Caste as a Form of Social Stratification

In India, the population is stratified into hundreds of different **castes**. In a caste system, individuals are assigned at birth to the ranked social and occupational groups of their parents. A person's place in the social order is fixed; there is no mobility from one caste to another. This is one feature that distinguishes the notion of caste from class. Castes are also separated by strict rules that forbid intermarriage and other forms of interaction, such as eating together, speaking to one another, or working together.

In any stratified society, people's access to jobs, wealth, and privilege is determined largely by their position in the hierarchy. Castes in India are based on traditional roles, for example. The Brahmins, priests whose lives were devoted to worship and teaching, occupied the top of the caste hierarchy. Directly under them were the Kshattriya castes, whose members comprised the soldiers, politicians, and administrators. Next were the Vaisya castes, made up of farmers and merchants. At the bottom of the hierarchy were the Sudra castes, which were devoted to the service of other castes. Beneath the religious hierarchy were the Harijans, "untouchable" or "unclean" persons whose occupations were believed to be polluting to others. Members of the Harijans caste have recently changed their name to *dalit*, which means "oppressed" or "ground down." *Dalit* included washermen, tanners, shoemakers, and sweepers, people whose occupations

---

ascribed status
An identity that is perceived as fixed and unchanging because a person is believed to be born with it. In Canadian society, race is often assumed to be ascribed at birth.

achieved status
An identity that is believed to be in flux and that is dependent upon the actions and achievements of an individual.

caste
A form of social stratification and identity in India where individuals are assigned at birth to the ranked social and occupational groups of their parents.

required them to come into contact with animal or human wastes. The Indian government has outlawed discrimination against *dalit* based on caste membership, but it persists nevertheless.

QUESTION 6.2: HOW DO PEOPLE COME TO ACCEPT SOCIAL HIERARCHIES AS NATURAL?

Race as a Form of Social Stratification

Sociocultural anthropology is about seeing behind the façade of everyday appearances to what lies behind those appearances. Understanding how societies construct rationales to justify and legitimize social discrimination is one of the most important and, to some extent, the most difficult tasks in anthropology. Franz Boas, a founder of anthropology, was among the first social scientists to discredit racist and sexist theories and ideologies that sought to legitimize the marginalization of people based on race, religion, gender, and ethnicity. Part of the problem is that racist and sexist theories exist not only in popular culture but also in science. It will be useful, then, to examine how such theories are constructed and often taken for granted, and how they are used to justify the ranking of people within the social hierarchy.

Constructing the Ideology of Racism

As discussed earlier, in Canada and the United States the ideology of class is based on the assumption that a person's position in the class hierarchy is determined largely by achievement or individual effort; that is, individuals who work hard and dedicate themselves to their work will succeed. Yet

Franz Boas (1858–1942), was one of the founders of anthropology and one of the first anthropologists to challenge racism and sexism in popular culture.

there is also the attempt to justify social position by a person's innate, biological makeup—largely by race, innate mental ability (intelligence), and other factors. This hierarchical ordering of society is seen as an expression of a natural law that some people are born more fit to lead and succeed.

The term *race* is used here to refer to the presumed genetic, natural, heritable characteristics of a group of people, normally based on physical attributes like skin colour, eye colour, or hair type. We live in a society that views race as a natural, ascribed category; it is something we believe we are born with. Unlike class, then, race in many industrialized societies (such as Canada) is seen as a fixed, unchanging form of identity.

Anthropologists and other scholars, however, maintain that there is no scientific basis for positioning different groups of people into discreet "races" on the basis of physical features. This is because there is no population of individuals anywhere in the world that is morphologically distinct. In other words, for a "race" to scientifically exist, a certain physical feature (e.g., skin colour) would have to be demonstrated as occurring consistently and uniformly within a particular population. But there is no group of people, anywhere in the world, that fits this criterion. Simply put, there is too much physical diversity within specific populations. The Executive Board of the American Anthropological Association, the largest professional association of anthropologists in the world, sums up this argument:

> Both scholars and the general public have been conditioned to viewing human races as natural and separate divisions within the human species based on visible physical differences. With the vast expansion of scientific knowledge in this century, however, it has become clear that human populations are not unambiguous, clearly demarcated, biologically distinct groups. Evidence from the analysis of genetics (e.g., DNA) indicates that most physical variation, about 94%, lies within so-called racial groups. Conventional geographic "racial" groupings differ from one another only in about 6% of their genes. This means that there is greater variation within "racial" groups than between them. In neighbouring populations there is much overlapping of genes and their phenotypic (physical) expressions. Throughout history whenever different groups have come into contact, they have interbred. The continued sharing of genetic materials has maintained all of humankind as a single species. (American Anthropological Association 1998; http://www.aaanet.org/stmts/racepp.htm)

These days, most academics view race as a culturally constructed form of identity. In other words, they view race as a byproduct of cultural beliefs, not biology. Race may not exist from a strictly scientific perspective, but that does not mean it is not an important topic for anthropologists to explore. In Canada, we live in a society in which the myth prevails that race is a natural category (i.e., as a biological, ascribed category). Because of this, race has had a variety of social consequences. Over the years, for instance, race has been conflated with behavioural characteristics, resulting in **racism**, or systems of prejudice based on the stratification of physical differences, which are erroneously thought to correlate with behavioural, physical, or intellectual differences in certain populations. The book *The Bell Curve*, discussed below, is a problematical example of how science is often used in an uncritical manner to foster racism, classism, and social stratification.

For centuries, European and North American societies have been characterized by racial stratification. In these societies, membership in certain racial or ethnic groups has been enough to place people in particular positions in a hierarchy that defines their social, political, and economic worth. In the United States, for example, one's position in the racial hierarchy has often determined whether a person can vote, hold political office, pursue a particular occupation, live in a certain area, use certain public facilities, attend certain schools, or marry a particular person.

Although most Canadians consider themselves to be far less racist than their southern neighbours, racism has a long history in Canada, and groups have been formed on the basis of white supremacy in both countries. The Ku Klux Klan, for instance, was founded in Tennessee in 1865 to terrorize newly freed slaves who questioned white supremacy. By the 1920s, the Klan was well established in Canada. When it arrived from the United States, it added French Canadians and Catholics to its list of inferior

---

racism
Refers to the discrimination and mistreatment of particular "racial" groups.

peoples. In the 1960s, the Canadian Nazi Party and the Edmund Burke Society, the forerunner of the Western Guard, openly supported racism. Ten years later, the Nationalist Party and the Aryan Nations took their place among the radical right. The common belief shared by these groups was that the "white race" was superior and that it was on the verge of being "wiped out" by the "dark-skinned races." As Stanley Barrett put it, "according to white supremacists, interracial mixing, or as they preferred, mongrelization, was more dangerous to humankind than the atomic bomb, because without the genetic purity of 'the master race' the world could not survive" (2002, 92).

African Canadians are not the only ones to experience racism in Canada. Racist beliefs about Aboriginal peoples are deeply rooted in Canadian history. James Frideres and Rene Gadacz call this structural racism (as opposed to prejudice and discrimination by individuals), because it is embedded in Canadian social institutions. Frideres and Gadacz argue that the Indian reserve is "an internal colony" in which "Canadians are seen as the colonizing people, while Aboriginal persons are considered the colonized people" (2001, 4).

Stratification by race has existed for a number of reasons. It was certainly economically profitable to people who could buy black slaves or obtain workers from among groups legally or socially barred from anything but low-paying jobs. It was advantageous, also, to those who did not have to compete for jobs with people who were socially or legally barred from them. However, stratified societies often claim that the ranking of people by race and ethnicity is natural and that social hierarchies are not socially constructed. In the case of racial stratification, some proponents claimed that it was the Christian God's will that some persons were inferior to others; others claimed that God created different races as He created different species of animals, and, furthermore, that the Christian Bible says the species are to be kept apart. Others claimed that members of one race or another were intellectually or morally superior to members of other races. Generally, of course, it was the race of the person making reference to the Christian God or the Bible that was somehow superior.

Most people had little trouble constructing an ideology to justify racial stratification, especially since it was reinforced by state and religious authorities. Even the supposedly objective findings of scientists assisted in building a racist ideology. In the 19th century, reputable scientists devoted much time and energy to proving that the racial stratification of society was "in the nature of things." Indeed, many contemporary forms of racism emerged out of 19th-century scientific studies of race. Both misguided and ethnocentric by today's standards, they functioned to maintain what Peggy McIntosh refers to as **white privilege**—the positioning of "white" individuals at the top of racial hierarchies. Science thus became a tool for naturalizing the power, authority, and privileges afforded to individuals with white skin. Their research findings supposedly proved that members of one race (usually whites or Europeans) were intellectually superior to members of another race (usually blacks or Asians).

Canadians assisted fugitive slaves, as depicted in the Charles T. Webber painting *The Underground Railroad*.

© Bettmann/CORBIS

---

white privilege
Refers to the fact that in many societies, "white" people have access to greater power, authority, and privileges than non-white people.

Samuel George Morton was a respected scientist and physician who began in the 1820s to collect and measure skulls from all over the world. When he died in 1851, he left a collection of some 6,000 skulls. Like many in the 19th century, Morton believed that a person's intelligence was related to the size of his or her brain; the larger the brain, the more intelligent the person. Since the size of the brain could be determined by the size of the skull, he believed that a ranking of the races could be objectively achieved by a ranking of skull size.

Morton first measured the size—more specifically, the cranial capacity—of skulls by filling them with mustard seed and then pouring the seed into a container to measure the skull's volume in cubic inches. Dissatisfied with the inconsistency of measurements obtained with mustard seed, he later used 1/8-inch-diameter lead shot. He concluded from his measurements that "white" skulls had a mean value of 92 cubic inches, "American Indian" skulls 79 cubic inches, and "black" skulls from America, Africa, and Australia 83 cubic inches. Among "white" skulls, the largest were those of Germans and English people; in the middle were those of Jews; and at bottom were those of Hindus. Thus, the social hierarchy of whites at the top, with the English and Germans at the top of the top and blacks on the bottom, was said to be supported by the evidence of brain size and intelligence.

Morton concluded from all this that "whites" (specifically, northern European "whites") were not only socially superior but also biologically superior. He believed he had provided objective evidence that the distribution of status and power in 19th-century North America accurately reflected not merely social but biological merit.

When Stephen Jay Gould, a Harvard paleontologist, re-examined Morton's published data in 1977, he concluded that Morton's summaries were a "patchwork of fudging and finagling" to reach conclusions that supported the socially constructed hierarchy. Gould found no evidence of conscious fraud. He concluded that Morton had simply selected or rejected certain data to ensure that the results confirmed what he and most other Americans "knew": that whites were naturally more intelligent than the people they called Indian or black.

Working with the same skulls Morton had used more than 150 years earlier, Gould discovered that the sample of 144 Native American skulls included proportionally more small-brained Inca skulls from Peru and fewer large-brained Iroquois skulls. This naturally produced a lower mean cranial capacity for indigenous Americans than would have occurred had Morton correctly adjusted for this discrepancy. Moreover, Gould discovered that Morton's failure to include the small-brained Hindu skulls with his "white" skulls had produced a higher average cranial capacity for white skulls. When Gould corrected for Morton's sample biases, he discovered that there was no difference between

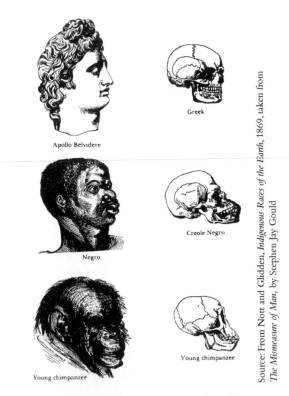

Apollo Belvidere

Greek

Negro

Creole Negro

Young chimpanzee

Young chimpanzee

Source: From Nott and Glidden, *Indigenous Races of the Earth*, 1869, taken from *The Mismeasure of Man*, by Stephen Jay Gould

Nineteenth-century scientists attempted to "prove" that whites were naturally superior to other races. In this illustration from an 1868 racist tract, the proportions of the skulls were distorted, giving the impression that blacks might even rank lower than the apes.

Euro-American and indigenous American cranial capacity. As for comparisons between "white" and "black" skulls, Gould discovered that Morton had ignored the facts that brain size is related to body size and that male skulls are larger than female skulls. Examination of Morton's black skulls indicated that the group included proportionally more female skulls and fewer male skulls. When Gould remeasured the "black" and "white" skulls, he discovered that the mean cranial capacity of black males was slightly higher than the mean for white males, while the mean for white females was slightly higher than that for black females.

Gould did not believe that Morton consciously manipulated his skull measurements to prove that whites were intellectually superior to Native Americans or blacks. Rather, he thought that Morton had simply assumed that this is what his measurements would prove and that he set about achieving the results he expected. For example, Gould observed that when Morton used mustard seed to measure cranial capacity, he obtained even greater differences between his "white" and "black" skulls than he had obtained using lead shot. Gould concluded that because mustard seeds are smaller and lighter than lead shot, Morton, probably unconsciously, packed more mustard seed into "white" skulls to obtain a greater difference in cranial capacity between "blacks" and "whites." Unfortunately, while Morton's measurements were obviously in error, as was his assumption that cranial capacity reveals intelligence, and though his conclusions were dictated by the socially constructed hierarchy of his day, they were used well into the 20th century to support the ideology that the racial ranking of persons in society could be justified on natural rather than social grounds.

Class, Race, and the Social Construction of "Intelligence"

Morton's experiments were just one example of the efforts in North America and Europe to show that people somehow deserve their ranking in society,

that it is not the result of chance or family privilege but, rather, the result of innate attributes. To believe otherwise would threaten a key assertion of North American ideology: that everyone in Canada and the United States enjoys an equal opportunity for success. Moreover, there are serious political and economic consequences to believing otherwise. If poverty and a low ranking in society are not the fault of the poor, then they must be the result of some failure of society. Such an admission provides a strong reason for governments to enact social and economic policies (such as affirmative action, programs of economic redistribution, and laws barring racial and other forms of discrimination). However, such changes might lead to a loss of privilege for those who benefit from present policies, so there is strong motivation to find some concept that legitimizes inherited privilege while still placing the blame for poverty or lack of success on the poor themselves.

The concept of intelligence neatly solves this problem; if people accept the idea that intelligence can explain how well people do, then the fiction that people's rank in society depends solely on their own innate ability can be maintained. Moreover, if it can be shown that intelligence is inherited, then we can explain why it is that the children of successful people tend to be successful, and why certain groups, notably people of colour and certain immigrant groups, are disproportionately poor.

The failure of the thesis that cranial capacity, and hence brain size, reveals intelligence did not end all attempts to link intelligence to success and to race and ethnic class membership. There has been, instead, a continuing effort on the part of some members of the scientific establishment to marshal evidence that intelligence is inherited and that it varies among racial groups. These efforts have included the work of Arthur Jensen in the 1960s and 1970s and, more recently, the publication in 1994 of *The Bell Curve* by Richard J. Herrnstein and Charles Murray. Missing from most of these accounts is any acknowledgment that intelligence itself is a social construct, an invented idea. We need, then, to look closely at our concept of intelligence. How did it evolve?

To begin, anthropologist Allan Hanson notes that the concept of intelligence contains a number of questionable assumptions. First, intelligence is assumed to be a single entity. Second, it is assumed to be measurable and unequally distributed in the population. Third, the amount people have is assumed to be relatively fixed throughout life. Fourth, the amount people have is assumed to largely explain their degree of success in life. Finally, it is assumed to be largely inherited.

Each of these assumptions is critical to the intelligence construct as most people think of it, and each has been the subject of enormous scientific attention and criticism. The first assumption requires that we accept the idea that if someone is intelligent in one way, they will be intelligent in other ways, rather than believing that some people can be intelligent in some ways but not in others. The second assumption implies that we can somehow measure innate intelligence, as opposed to achievement, and the third presumes that we can show that whatever is measured does not vary throughout a person's life. The fourth is built on the idea that people who have more measurable intelligence are more likely to be successful, while the fifth assumption requires us to show that the children of people with high measurable intelligence also have high measurable intelligence.

In spite of the number of assumptions that lie behind the notion of intelligence, and in spite of the studies that illustrate how questionable each of these assumptions really is, most North Americans take the notion for granted. Yet it is an almost unique idea, one that is not shared by many other societies. Indigenous maritime navigators of the South Pacific, for example, learned to read wave patterns, wind direction, celestial constellations, and other signs and find their way thousands of miles from one island to another. Yet others in the same society who are unable to duplicate this feat did not view the navigators as somehow being smarter; they saw them as people who could navigate. The Japanese view what we call intelligence in much the same way as we view health—except in certain (and generally temporary) circumstances, we all have enough of it.

This book is not the place to summarize all those works that call the concept of intelligence into question. Nevertheless, we might learn something about the social construction of ideologies of class by looking briefly at the early history of the intelligence construct and by reviewing how reputable scientists proceeded to develop it. Three pioneers—Francis Galton, Karl Pearson, and Charles Spearman—supplied the basic ideas and experimental proofs for the classic concept of intelligence as a fixed, "mental" entity that is differentially distributed in the population, is measurable, largely explains a person's educational and occupational success, and is inherited.

Francis Galton was one of the leading intellectual figures of the late 19th century. He was the founder of modern statistics as well as the founder of eugenics, which is the attempt to identify the most desirable human traits, specify the individuals who possess them, and, through selective reproduction, enhance the number of people possessing those desired characteristics. In his best-known work, *Hereditary Genius* (1867), he sought to demonstrate that the "genius" of selected eminent men was linked to the fact that they had eminent parents and, it followed, that their "genius" was largely inherited. In his sample of 997 eminent British men, he found that 31 percent had eminent fathers, that 48 percent had eminent sons, and that 41 percent had eminent brothers—far higher percentages than one would expect by chance. For Galton, this illustrated the power of heredity in the distribution of "genius." He was, of course, rightly criticized for ignoring the impact of environment. But he did something else that was more interesting, something that went largely unchallenged: he selected the eminent men from the British upper and upper middle classes, ignoring the "captains of industry and finance" and, of course, women. That is, for him, eminence was eminence only within a select range of activities and occupations. Galton, a nephew of Charles Darwin and of upper-middle-class background, was faithfully reproducing the judgments of his own status as to what constituted intelligence.

Much of Galton's later research was devoted to arguing that what he called "genius," "mediocrity," and "imbecility" were analogous in their statistical distribution within a society to certain physical characteristics. He developed a number of tests for cranial capacity and for sensory capacities—the ability to discriminate between colours or smells, for example. He was not the only one trying to do this; in Germany, the United States, and England, other researchers were trying to measure intelligence, largely by measuring sensory and reflex activities, such as reading aloud rapidly, rapidly giving the colours of named objects, naming and classifying plants, animals, and minerals, and other tests of memory and spatial judgment. Around 1900, however, there was a move away from these kinds of measures, because they weren't showing any correlations with one another and, more important, because they showed only a low correlation with teachers' estimates of the mental capability of their students. Regardless, by 1900 the classic intelligence construct had been laid out, although its proof was somewhat wanting.

The next figure in our story is Karl Pearson, one of the most fascinating figures of the late 19th and early 20th centuries, whose published works included more than 400 articles on mathematical physics, statistics, and biology, as well as poetry, a passion play, art history, studies of the Reformation and Medieval Germany, and political essays. In 1901, Pearson published a study in the *Proceedings of the Royal Society* of London in which he concluded that "the mental characteristics in man are inherited in precisely the same manner as the physical. Our mental and moral nature is quite as much as our physical nature, the outcome of hereditary factors" (Pearson 1901, 155).

It is instructive to look at how Pearson reached this conclusion. He took pairs of brothers and measured specific physical characteristics, such as stature, forearm length, hair colour, eye colour, and cephalic index. He found, not surprisingly, that there were high correlations among brothers for these traits, as well as a mean correlation of .5171. He then asked teachers, using a separate sample, to rank brother-pairs on seven "mental characteristics": intelligence, vivacity, conscientiousness, popularity, temper, self-consciousness, and shyness. Thus, under "conscientiousness" teachers were asked to rate each child as "keen" or "dull" and to choose among six subdivisions of intelligence. When the teachers' evaluations of brother-pairs were tabulated, Pearson found a strong correlation between brother ratings, and a mean correlation of .5214, thereby proving the power of inheritance.

Much about this study is questionable, but of particular note is the role of teachers' judgments. Clearly, teachers were evaluating selected behaviour patterns and personal characteristics—patterns and characteristics that they judged to be evidence of various "mental characteristics." In other words, the teachers' judgments were highly subjective and, at best, questionable. But Pearson's work marked an important development in the construction of our concept of intelligence: he claimed to be showing that whatever intelligence was, it was obviously inherited at least as much as physical characteristics.

Let's move forward a couple of years to the next important stage in the construction of the intelligence construct: Charles Spearman and "general intelligence." Spearman's research, published in the *American Journal of Psychology* in 1904, was designed to prove that there were different degrees of correspondence between an individual's performance on different types of tests. Thus, one would expect a high correspondence between one's performance on geometrical tests and tests of spatial perception, and a low degree of correspondence between one's performance on, say, tests of musical ability and tests of weight discrimination.

If there were some degree of correlation between all the test results, this would point to some general factor, "g," that affected performance on all tests. Thus, tests that resulted in a high correlation (e.g., geometrical ability and spatial perception) would be heavily saturated with g, while tests with little correlation would not be. For example, to use an athletic analogy, if someone hits both a baseball and a golf ball a long way, we might assume that there exists some general factor for athletic ability accounting for both skills.

Spearman was suggesting that the g factor underlay all mental operations and that if it could be found, it would approximate true intelligence. This was a major claim, for if the existence of g could be proved, it would dismiss the idea—widely held at that time—that different people can be intelligent in different ways and that each person has a unique contribution to make. With g, people would be intellectually different in only one way, and people with lots of g would have more to contribute than people with only a little g.

To experimentally prove the existence of general intelligence, Spearman isolated four kinds of intelligence that, he claimed, when correlated would show a high degree of correspondence: "present efficiency," "native capacity," "general impression produced upon other people," and "common sense." "Present efficiency" referred to the "ordinary classification according to school order" in subjects such as Greek, Latin, and mathematics. "Native capacity" was arrived at by taking the difference between a child's rank in school and his age, while "general impression produced on other people" was obtained by asking the teacher of a class who was the brightest pupil, the next brightest, and so on. "Common sense" was arrived at by asking the oldest child in a class to rank her school fellows on the basis of "sharpness and common sense out of school." As Spearman said, she seemed "to have no great difficulty in forming her judgments concerning the others, having indeed known them all her life." As a check on the reliability of judgments, he also asked the rector's wife to rank the children, although as Spearman notes regretfully, she did not know some of them. Spearman, not surprisingly, found that children who ranked high on one kind of intelligence tended to rank high on others, thereby validating the existence of g.

Obviously, the methodology of these classic studies was seriously flawed, relying as it did on subjective judgments as to who was intelligent and who was not—judgments that were bound to be biased by such factors as the social class of teachers and students. From Galton's first major work on hereditary genius through Spearman's work on general intelligence, members of the professional middle class were selecting as intelligent those people whose behaviour patterns and appearance most conformed to their own. Moreover, little effort was made to conceal the fact: subjective judgments of members of the professional class were the principal means for defining intelligence. Regardless, the intelligence construct as we know it was generally complete and was perceived by reputable scientists as having been validated experimentally: intelligence was a singular trait, represented by "g," that was inherited and that was differentially distributed in the population.

Much more was to come, of course, in the social construction of intelligence. Most notable in this regard was the development of the Stanford-Binet IQ test, and later the Scholastic Aptitude Test (SAT; recently renamed the Scholastic Assessment Test). Additional and more sophisticated experiments were performed that some claimed supported the conclusions of Galton, Pearson, Spearman, and other early researchers. But the most interesting feature was the continued part played by the social judgments of people—largely teachers, psychologists, and school administrators—in determining what did or did not constitute intelligence. As late as the 1960s, intelligence test results were still being cross-checked with teachers' judgments and students' ranks in class; if the test scores failed to correlate with the teachers' judgments, the tests were changed.

Race, Class, and Social Hierarchies in Brazil

Despite the efforts of some scientists to find a biological basis for racial hierarchies, it should now be clear that race is culturally constructed, as is class. We can now turn our attention to an ethnographic example of how categories like race and class are negotiated in Brazil. Anthropologist Alexander Edmonds has explored the ways in which race and class converge in Brazil to form social hierarchies. While conducting his doctoral dissertation fieldwork in Rio de Janeiro, Edmonds noticed that plastic surgery clinics proliferated in urban areas of Brazil. Furthermore, while access to plastic surgery had once been a marker of middle- or upper-class status (due to the high cost of such surgeries), the attainment of physical "beauty" was regarded as a necessary means of achieving social mobility. In Brazil, plastic surgery rates are among the highest in the world, and the government subsidizes plastic surgeries for the working classes. There are even plastic surgeons who practise "charity" surgeries on behalf of the urban poor. "Beauty" is thus a marker of class status, and is increasingly viewed as a "right" that should be available for everyone.

Plastic surgery, however, is also a means by which non-white Brazilians can seek to "whiten" their appearance by correcting what some of Edmonds's informants viewed as an undesirable—a "Negroid" nose, for instance. In Brazilian society, race exists along a continuum, and white skin and stereotypically "white" facial features are associated with power, privilege, and prestige. Indeed, many of Edmonds's informants, especially young women, did improve their employment prospects, and ultimately their class status, by undergoing plastic surgery. In this context, plastic surgery represents a means by which some Brazilians can "whiten" their bodies and, by extension, improve their social standing in Brazilian society. Interestingly, Brazil has been mythologized as a multicultural nation, and while its citizens are encouraged to celebrate diversity, there exists enormous social pressure to emulate the powerful (i.e., white, upper class) in Brazilian society. Racial identity is also understood to be malleable, and linked to one's social class—according to a popular Brazilian adage, "money whitens." Ultimately, this ethnographic example highlights the fluid and interconnected nature of social hierarchies such as class and race, as well as the ways in which the conscious manipulation of

EXERCISE 6.2

In Canada, we tend to pride ourselves on being an accepting, multicultural nation. However, there are many examples of embedded/institutionalized racism in our society. Select a recent (published within the past two years) Canadian newspaper or magazine article that offers an example of embedded racism. Provide a brief overview of the article and outline how institutionalized racism is at work.

features like "attractiveness" are viewed as a means of achieving a sense of individual fulfillment, well-being, and status.

QUESTION 6.3: HOW IS GENDER A FORM OF SOCIAL HIERARCHY?

Constructing Male and Female

We often assume that gender, like race, is biological. But there is an academic distinction between the terms "**sex**" and "**gender**." Sex refers to biological, hormonal, and chromosomal differences between males and females; gender, by contrast, is cultural. In other words, gender is the cultural interpretation of sex. Cross-culturally, different standards apply to being male, female, and (in some societies) a **third gender**. As such, there is no cross-cultural, universal understanding of what is considered to be "appropriate" dress, demeanour, behaviours, occupations, or roles for men or women; rather, these understandings must be learned in their respective cultural contexts.

In North America, this process of gendered learning begins at birth with the announcement: "It's a girl" or "It's a boy." However, these commonsense proclamations conveniently ignore the 4 percent of births in which the infant has various combinations of male and female characteristics (e.g., an infant with one testis and one ovary, an infant with one testis and aspects of the female genitalia, or an infant with ovaries and some aspect of male genitalia). Once the announcement of gender is made (or after a surgical procedure in which the infant is "corrected" to fit into either the male or female category), the infant is given a gender-appropriate name, dressed in properly designed and coloured clothing, and spoken to in gender-appropriate language. Parents and other caregivers then teach male children that it is manly to endure pain, to be strong and tough. Male children are discouraged from expressing discomfort and encouraged when they can withstand it. Female children, on the other hand, are comforted when they hurt themselves. Although gender stereotypes are changing, many North American male children are still encouraged to be aggressive and competitive; they learn to compete in games and play with toys that require aggressive behaviour. Females are still taught to be caring and helpful; they are given toys such as dolls that encourage "feminine" behaviour.

Also, societies vary in the number of gender categories they recognize. For example, many Native American societies recognize a third gender, such as that of the *two-spirit* among the Cheyenne and Lakota. The *two-spirit* is a biological male who does not fill a standard male role. Such individuals are not seen as men, nor are they defined as women. They occupy a third role, one that is culturally defined, accepted, and in some cases revered. Male children among the Lakota and Cheyenne thus can choose from two gender categories, rather than learning that gender roles are defined by physiology. Among the Lakota, male children learn that if they desire, they can adopt the dress and work roles of women and have sex with men, although the *two-spirit* role does not necessarily involve sexual behaviour. The *two-spirits* do not play only women's roles, however; some are noted for their hunting skills and exploits in war. In North American societies, in contrast, individuals who do not assume the gender roles associated with their anatomy are most often

---

sex
Hormonal, chronosomal, or physical differences between men and women.

gender
Culturally constructed ideals of behaviour, dress, occupations, roles, and comportment for particular sexes.

third gender
A gender role given to someone who does not fit within strictly masculine or feminine gender roles in a given society.

defined as deviant, abnormal, or nonconformist, unless the reversal of gender roles is framed as play.

One way to learn about how a society constructs gender differences and relationships is to explore theatrical and ritual transvestism, as Michael Taft did on the Canadian Prairies when he studied mock weddings. The principal feature of a mock wedding is role reversal: men dress and act like women and sometimes women dress and behave like men. These mock figures are often as much caricatures as stereotypes, reflecting some feature of the identities of the actual wedding pair.

Taft's study focused on men who dressed as women in these rituals of reversal, which were filled with ludic (i.e., playful) behaviour. He repeatedly asked men why they did this, and the most frequent answer he received was that they were just being "good sports." As good sports, men do not attempt to become women in their role in the mock wedding. In Taft's words, "they play clownish and distorted women. They exaggerate the female physique with over-large breasts and behinds. They mince and wiggle in mockery of femininity" (1997, 135).

Thus, these men are expressing their views of women to one another. Taft suggests that one

In this photograph of a mock wedding ritual on the Canadian Prairies, transvestism represents a form of gendered social commentary on notions of power, equality, and the position of women in this community.

reason men do this may have something to do with the economic conditions of farming on the Prairies. Although farmers or ranchers may *seem* to be independent, in reality they are dangerously dependent on government bureaucrats, subsidies, and the world market. In contrast, women have considerable power on farms and often do the same work as men, besides working part-time off the farm in order to pay the bills. By making fun of women, men may be reasserting their own importance. Whatever the men's motives, Taft argues that "wherever it is found, theatrical transvestism acts as a sounding board for commentaries on gender relations" (1997, 137).

Constructing Stratification by Gender

As discussed earlier, the biases that falsely linked race to biology and intelligence to class also led to the belief in the "natural" (as opposed to socially constructed) superiority of men over women. Many people believed that women's bodies defined both their social position and their function, which was to reproduce, in the same way that men's bodies dictated that they manage, control, and defend.

The view that the biology of females makes them lesser persons than males is embedded in North American cultures, sometimes in very subtle ways. An example is the language used by professionals to describe women's bodily processes of menstruation and menopause. Anthropologist Emily Martin says that during the 19th century, Americans regarded the female body as if it were a factory whose job was to "labour" to produce children. Menopause was viewed negatively because it marked the end of productive usefulness, and menstruation was described as a sign of the failure of the implantation of a fertilized egg. Medical writers of the time such as Walter Heape, a Cambridge zoologist and militant antisuffragist, described how in menstruation the entire epithelium (cellular tissue) is torn away, "leaving behind a ragged wreck of tissue, torn

THE CULTURAL CONSTRUCTION OF SOCIAL HIERARCHY

glands, ruptured vessels, jagged edges of stroma, and masses of blood corpuscles, which it would seem hardly possible to heal satisfactorily without the aid of surgical instruments."

According to Martin, the same attitudes toward female reproductive functions that existed in the 19th century persist today, encoded in contemporary medical and biology textbooks. Menstruation is likewise described even today as a breakdown in the reproductive process. When an egg is not implanted, the process is described in negative terms as a disintegration or shedding. Here is one example Martin found:

> The fall in blood progesterone and estrogen "deprives" the "highly developed endometrial lining of its hormonal support," constriction of blood vessels leads to a "diminished" supply of oxygen and nutrients, and finally "disintegration starts, the entire lining begins to slough, and the menstrual flow begins." Blood vessels in the endometrium "hemorrhage" and "the menstrual flow consists of this blood mixed with endometrial debris." The "loss" of hormonal stimulation causes "necrosis" (death of tissue). (in Martin 1987, 45)

Another otherwise objective text states that "when fertilization fails to occur, the endometrium is shed, and a new cycle starts. This is why it used to be taught that 'menstruation is the uterus crying for lack of a baby.'"

In yet another textbook, menstruation is depicted as a sign of an idle factory, a failed production system, a system producing "scrap" or "waste." However, Martin notes that very different language is used in the same textbooks to describe male reproductive functions. For example, the textbook from which the above description of menstruation is taken describes the production of sperm as follows: "The mechanisms which guide the remarkable cellular transformation from spermatid to mature sperm remain uncertain. Perhaps the most amazing characteristic of spermatogenesis is its sheer magnitude: the normal human male may manufacture several hundred million sperm per day" (in Martin 1987, 48).

This text, which describes menstruation as "failed production," fails to mention that only about one of every 100 billion sperm ever makes it far enough to fertilize an egg. Moreover, other bodily processes that are similar to menstruation are not spoken of in terms of breakdown and deterioration. Seminal fluid picks up shredded cellular material as it passes through the male ducts, and the stomach lining is shed periodically. Why are these processes not also described in the same negative terms as menstruation? Martin says the reason is that both men and women have stomachs, but only women have uteruses. The stomach falls on the positive side, the uterus on the negative.

Rather than describing menstruation as failed production, Martin suggests that it might be more accurate to describe it as the successful avoidance of an egg implant. If a couple has done anything to avoid the implantation of an egg, is it still appropriate to talk of the reproductive cycle in terms of production?

Emily Martin's analysis reveals that in contemporary North American societies, the ideology of gender stratification remains embedded in our language and in our ideas about the bodily functions of males and females. Describing the bodily processes of women in negative terms makes women seem to be lesser human beings. Moreover, describing menstruation and menopause in negative terms leads women themselves to believe that their bodily functions are less clean and less worthy than those of men.

Gender Stratification and the Privileging of Hegemonic Masculinities

All societies have particular images and stereotypes of masculinity and femininity that are privileged as normative—that is, as societal ideals. These ideals of masculinity, for instance, are referred to as **hegemonic masculinity**. Industrialized societies, for example, often view traits such as athleticism, courage, rationality, and heterosexuality as markers of an ideal "manliness."

Hegemonic masculinities are often used to construct gendered hierarchies in societies. For instance, those individuals who fall outside hegemonic gendered ideals are often labelled as "less masculine" than others, which leads to the proliferation of homophobia and/or the objectification of women. Canadian anthropologist David Murray, for instance, has studied how performances of a hegemonic masculinity on the Caribbean island of Martinique are dependent on "proving" one's heterosexuality through the aggressive pursuit of women, cat calling, and flirting with the opposite sex. Men who fail to pursue women aggressively are often labelled *macumé,* a derogatory word in Martinique that is equivalent to "sissy." In a society marked by intense homophobia, all men, whatever their sexual orientation, go to great lengths to uphold the norms of hegemonic masculinity in public settings. To be labelled *macumé* is a social liability, and a man risks physical and verbal abuse if he does not conform to societal ideals of gender.

Hegemonic masculinities are also constructed, performed, and maintained within societies through sports, competitions, and rituals. Fraternities, for instance, are a means of constructing hegemonic masculinities; they are also a way to promote often dangerous gendered hierarchies within university settings. This leads to the objectification, abuse, and marginalization of women.

Peggy Reeves Sanday, in her study of college fraternity gang rape, provides a vivid portrait of how male identity is defined and reinforced in American society. Gang rape, or "pulling train," as it is called in fraternities, begins with the coercion of a vulnerable young woman who is seeking acceptance. The ritual incorporates the man into a group whose activities reinforce a male identity, which is defined largely by the degradation of female identity through sexual conquest and physical abuse of women. Pulling train is both an expression of male sexuality and a display of the brotherhood's power to control and dominate women. In other words, gang rape is but one instance of the abuse and domination that begin during the initiation and that are continued later in relations with women and new pledges.

When she is too weak or intoxicated to protest, a "train" of men have sex with her. Gang rape is not limited to college campuses; it is also associated with sports teams, street gangs, and other groups of men for whom the act often serves, according to Sanday, as a male bonding ritual.

Sanday and her associates interviewed fraternity members, women who were associated with them, and victims of rape, seeking to explain what it was about male identity that encouraged these actions. Three things seemed to stand out in her account. First, there is a heavy emphasis in fraternities on male bonding and male-bonding behaviour, to the extent that a college man's self-esteem and social identity depend on gaining entry to a fraternity and being accepted by the brothers. Fraternities confer status; on most college campuses they are recognized as places "where the action is." They also provide reassurance, security, and a ready-made identity. Membership in a fraternity transforms outsiders into insiders.

Second, sex constitutes a major status and identity marker. Masculinity is defined and demonstrated by sexual conquest. In the fraternity in which the gang rape occurred, a major activity was persuading a woman to have sex. Men who had more success gained status, while those who often failed were in danger of being labelled "nerds" or, worse, "fags." Sex in this case is a public thing. Men in the fraternities that Sanday interviewed bragged publicly about their sexual conquests and arranged for brothers to witness them. Some fraternities posted weekly newsletters listing brothers' sexual conquests.

> **hegemonic masculinity**
> Refers to ideals and norms of masculinity in a society, which are often privileged over others.

A third element in the identity of fraternity men concerns their attitudes toward women. Many of the fraternity members in Sanday's study implied that women were sex objects to be abused or debased. A woman's identity among fraternity men was determined largely by her sexual interactions with them. Women who were sexually unresponsive were "frigid," women who allowed advances only up to a point were "cockteasers," and women who had sex with many men were "sluts" or "cunts." Such labels indicate that the role of girlfriend is virtually the only role with no negative connotations that a woman can play. In one fraternity, brothers marked women who attended their parties with "power dots," black, red, yellow, white, or blue stickers they attached to a girl's clothing at parties to indicate how easy the girl was to pick up.

For fraternity men, the debasement of women is interwoven with the themes of male bonding and sexual conquest. Part of the reason men bond in college, says Sanday, is to achieve the domination and power they think is owed to males. One fraternity man explained how verbally harassing a girl increases male bonding. "I mean, people come back the day after a party and say, 'You should have seen me abuse this girl.' They're real proud of it in front of everyone."

Sanday uses the term phallocentrism, "the deployment of the penis as a concrete symbol of masculine social power and dominance," to describe the use of sex and the debasement of women to demonstrate masculinity. Phallocentrism as well as the themes of male bonding, sexual prowess, and the debasement of women are all manifested in the act of pulling train. It is a form of bonding, it publicly legitimizes a male's heterosexuality, and it makes women an object of scorn and abuse.

Sanday is quick to emphasize that not all college men subscribe to the ideology of phallocentrism and that not all fraternity men measure their masculinity by sexual conquest. In the case that initiated her study, all the women who knew them described the six men charged with gang rape as "among the nicest guys in the fraternity."

Individually, probably none of them would have committed the act they were charged with. In the context of the fraternity, however, gang rape was the credible outcome of a process of identity formation manifested in fraternity life in general and in the fraternity initiation ritual in particular.

Gender Stratification and the Feminization of Poverty

Throughout the world, gender and age are significantly related to whether a person lives in poverty. In *Women and Children Last* (1986), Ruth Sidel draws an analogy between the doomed ship *Titanic* and society in the United States at the end of the 1980s. Both, she says, were gleaming symbols of wealth that placed women and children at a disadvantage. When the *Titanic* went down, women and children were indeed saved first, but only those who were travelling in first- or second-class accommodations. Women and children in third class and steerage were not saved. Although only 8 percent of the women and 3 percent of the children in first and second class drowned on the night the *Titanic* sank, 45 percent of the women and 70 percent of the children in steerage died. As with the *Titanic*, Sidel says, certain women and children in the United States are not the first to be saved; instead, they are the first to fall into poverty.

Most of the world's poor are women and children. As Michael Todaro, an economist, explains: "[Women] are more likely to be poor and malnourished and less likely to receive medical services, clean water, sanitation, and other benefits" (2000, 172). Female-headed households make up the poorest segments of Third World populations. For instance, as of 2000, 40 percent of all households in Kenya and 20 percent in India had no male wage earners. The percentages have increased since then. Women's potential earnings are far below those of males. Women have less access to education and government employment programs and are more likely to be employed in the informal sector, where neither wages nor working conditions are regulated. Even in households where there is a male wage earner, women may not have access to the household income. In countries where there is a strong male bias—such as India and China—household resources may be distributed very unevenly. In India, it is estimated that "girls are four times more likely to suffer from acute malnutrition and boys are 40 times more likely to be taken to a hospital when ill" (2000, 173–74). This not only results in more female infant deaths, but also contributes to an extremely high female child mortality.

When gender is combined with other factors that contribute to poverty, such as indigenous status, women face a combination of risks. Linda Gerber argues that in Canada, Métis, Inuit, and "Indian" women face "multiple jeopardy"—first as women, then as members of a "visible minority," and finally "as residents of uniquely dependent communities" (1990, 72). In the area of education, 7.7 percent of all Canadian females have not completed grade nine, but the percentages are much higher for Métis women (34.8 percent), Inuit women (62 percent), and "Indian" women (35.9 percent) (1990, 75). Moreover, Métis women have an average income 70 percent that of Métis men, Inuit women earn 76 percent of what Inuit men earn, and "Indian" women have an average income 73 percent of the average income of "Indian" men (1990, 79).

Body Image and Gender Hierarchies

One of the most important identity features for many North Americans is body shape. Although desired body shapes vary cross-culturally and across historical periods, in the West today a thin person is judged to be superior to a heavier person. When researchers asked children aged six to nine to examine three body silhouettes and to describe the kind of person represented by each body type, the children described the "thinner" figure as friendly, kind, happy, and polite, while they described the heavier figure as lazy, lying, and cheating. When

ten- and eleven-year-olds were shown drawings of other children, they consistently ranked heavier figures lowest, even below drawings of children with missing limbs or a child in a wheelchair.

Weight is a handicap also in the educational system, where teachers perceive heavy children as having more behavioural problems than others and as being less well liked by their classmates. Later in life, people who are overweight face hostile work environments and job discrimination. Workers judged unattractive by their peers—especially women—are consistently described in more negative terms.

The relationship between self-image and body shape is particularly relevant for female adolescents, as anthropologist Mimi Nichter discovered during a three-year study among high school girls in Arizona. Adolescent girls are particularly vulnerable to body image issues because during adolescence girls will gain up to 11.5 kilograms of body fat and thus are likely to be more critical of their own bodies. Young girls, says Nichter, are embedded in a morality play in which thinness is good, fatness is bad, and dieting is the way to get in shape. Nichter found that most of the girls in her study were thinking about their bodies either "all of the time" (24 percent) or "a lot of the time" (31 percent) and that 90 percent of white girls in the study were dissatisfied with their weight.

The adolescent girls in Nichter's study formed their idea of the "perfect" body largely from television, films, and magazines, and, of course, Barbie. The ideal woman was tall (170 centimetres) and had long hair (preferably blond), long legs, a flat stomach, a clear complexion, and "good" clothes. However, weight was the key factor: being "thin" was believed to be the ticket to happiness and popularity. As with many adult women that Nichter knew, the girls seemed to see the world in terms of fat and thin.

The girls rarely talked about weight with classmates whom they judged to be "fat"; nevertheless, they made moral judgments about them, believing that if someone who was overweight

really wanted to lose weight, they could. Not losing weight implied that the girl was unconcerned about her personal appearance or was lazy. The lack of respect for overweight girls, says Nichter, was a theme that repeatedly emerged in discussions with the students. One girl explained:

> I have a friend that's overweight and I feel that she should—I mean, I don't have anything against her 'cause she's overweight—but I guess it makes me mad that she doesn't do anything about it. She could do something about it and she doesn't. It's like her responsibility … like last night I went over there and right when I walked in she had a bag of Doritos—she was just, I mean, it's just like she's constantly eating. She's addicted to food. She just can't stop.
> (Nichter 2000, 42)

Language, Gender, and Racial Hierarchies

Societies provide a social landscape along with the symbols or codes through which a person's place on the landscape is conveyed to others. For individuals these symbols or codes serve as toolboxes from which to fashion an identity. Societies may vary in the extent to which people are allowed to negotiate their place on the landscape, but all allow people some leeway.

Language, as we mentioned, is one of the tools that people have to signal how they want to be placed in society. Voice pitch, for example, does tend to differ because men's vocal tracts are longer, thus giving men a deeper voice. But children, whose voice tracts do not yet differ in size, will unconsciously lower or raise their pitch to conform to gender expectations; that is why you can usually tell from their voice the gender of a child. As Penelope Eckert and Sally McConnell-Ginet point out in *Language and Gender* (2003), people use language to present themselves as a certain kind of person, to project an attitude or a style, along with gender. All parts of language can be used in this way. The phonology, that is, the sounds, of a language can convey gender. For example, the /s/ sound can be made by pressing the tip of the tongue against the teeth. When pressed against the teeth it is still recognized as /s/, but this creates a slight lisp associated among English speakers in the United States and Canada with femininity in women and gayness in men.

Grammar can signal gender. Thus in French, there are male and female forms of nouns; in English, the third-person singular he and she force us to differentiate gender. In Japanese there are sentence-final particles that add to or soften the force of an utterance, with so-called women's language characterized as more mild. Thus "I am going" can be said as a mild assertion (*iku wa*), as a neutral assertion (*iku*), or as an emphatic assertion (*iku ze/iku zo*), with the latter being characterized as more masculine.

Whether or not to speak can convey gender. Children, for example, are encouraged to speak or to remain silent. Among the Araucanians of Chile, men are encouraged to talk since it is a sign of masculine intelligence and leadership, while the ideal woman is submissive and silent in her husband's presence.

Conversational styles may also convey gender. Linguist Robin Lakoff was one of the first to draw attention to the way a woman's identity in society influences how she speaks. Women, said Lakoff, are constrained to minimize their expression of opinion with various linguistic devices such as tag questions ("This election mess is terrible, **isn't it**?"), rising intonations on declaratives ("When will dinner be ready? **Six o'clock**?"), the use of hedges ("That's **kinda** sad" or "It's **probably** dinnertime"), boosters or amplifications ("I'm **so** glad you're here"), indirection (e.g., saying "I've got a dentist's appointment then," to convey an inability or reluctance to meet at that time and asking the other to propose another time).

The general thrust of Lakoff's argument has to do with the relative powerlessness of women stemming from their relatively weak social position. Speaking "as a woman," suggests Lakoff, requires avoiding firm commitment or expressing strong opinions and, in general, being restricted to using a "powerless" language.

Language can also be used to construct others, groups from which people want to separate themselves. In a classic work, *Racism in the English Language* (1976), Robert B. Moore discusses how judgments about race are coded into the way we speak. Reference to the colour black is scattered throughout the English language, generally with negative meanings: having a "black" outlook, to "blackball" or "blacklist" or "denigrate" someone, or being a "black sheep." The word "tribal" is often applied to discussions of African politics but not to European affairs. Thus rivalries between Ibo and Hausa and Yoruba in Nigeria or between Hutu and Tutsi in Rwanda are referred to in the press as "tribal conflicts," but not conflicts between Serbs and Croats in the Balkans, between Protestants and Catholics in Northern Ireland, or between Basques and Southern Spaniards in Spain.

Ward Churchill discusses the consequences of naming sports teams the "Braves," "Chiefs," "Redskins," "Seminoles," and "Savages," names that he suggests are deeply demeaning to Native Americans. Since apologists claim that this is just "fun," with no harm intended, Churchill suggests that we spread the fun around and use nicknames from other groups to name sports teams, such as the Kansas City "Kikes," the Hanover "Honkies," the Dayton "Dagos," Wisconsin "Wetbacks," and so on. Churchill draws attention to the way we use language, often unknowingly, that stigmatizes the identities of others.

QUESTION 6.4: HOW DO PEOPLE LIVING IN POVERTY ADAPT TO THEIR CONDITION?

The position in a social hierarchy occupied by each person is like a window through which she or he sees the world: different windows, different worlds. Furthermore, in order to survive in the impoverished conditions that exist in the lower tiers of society, people adopt specific adaptive strategies. Anthropologist Oscar Lewis coined the term **culture of poverty** to describe the lifestyle and world view of people who inhabit urban and rural slums. Some anthropologists object to that term, since it implies that poverty is somehow rooted in the subcultural values passed on from one generation to another, rather than in the social and cultural values of the larger society of which the poor are only a part. The implication is that if it weren't for the culture of poverty, the poor would have no culture at all.

Modifying that view, some anthropologists maintain that the behaviour of people in poverty represents their adaptations to their socioeconomic condition—no money and no jobs. These conditions are the result of inequality, usually reinforced by racism, and further buttressed by an economic system that requires a source of cheap labour. Moreover, descriptions of poor families as broken, fatherless, or female-centred are misleading.

> **culture of poverty**
> A term coined by anthropologist Oscar Lewis to describe the lifestyle and world view of people who inhabit urban and rural slums.

THE CULTURAL CONSTRUCTION OF SOCIAL HIERARCHY

Many of the behaviours of the poor that are viewed negatively by the dominant society are actually resilient responses to the socioeconomic conditions of those living in poverty.

Kinship as an Adaptation to Poverty

One of the classic studies of how families cope with poverty was conducted by anthropologist Carol B. Stack in the late 1960s. She worked closely with a predominantly black community she called The Flats, a section of a small, midwestern city in the United States of 55,000 people. Unemployment in The Flats was over 20 percent, and 63 percent of the jobs held were in low-paying service occupations such as maid, cook, and janitor. While only 10 percent of the whites in the city lived in housing classed as deteriorating, 26 percent of blacks did. Moreover, blacks had inadequate access to health care, and their infant mortality rate was twice that of whites.

Stack's interest was in how the residents responded to their impoverished conditions. She discovered that they fostered kinship ties and created fictive kinship links to form close, interlocking, cooperative groups that would ensure economic and social support in times of need. Few people earned a sufficient amount to provide them or their families with enough to eat or a place to stay on a regular basis; even welfare payments could not always guarantee food and shelter for a family. Accordingly, people in The Flats regularly "swapped" food, shelter, child care, and personal possessions. In this respect, the community resembled societies such as the Ju/'hoansi, in which a person shares with others but expects them to reciprocate at some later time. Anthropologists call this type of sharing **generalized reciprocity**, as distinguished from **balanced reciprocity**, in which items are exchanged on the spot; a direct trade of items would be an example. **Negative reciprocity** is an attempt to get something for nothing or make a profit. The advantage of generalized reciprocity is that widespread sharing ensures that nobody lacks

the basic needs for survival. People in The Flats cultivated diffuse kinship and friendship relations by giving when they could, so that others would give to them when they were in need. These networks were often framed in a kinship idiom, even when no biological kin ties existed.

Another adaptation to poverty in The Flats involved child care. Given the unpredictability of employment, the sometimes young age at which women had children, and the need to respond to unpredictable living conditions and substandard housing, a child might reside with three or four different adults. Often different people performed the roles of provider, discipliner, trainer, curer, and groomer. Stack points out that those who provided child care did so because they considered it a privilege as well as a responsibility. Children were valued, but they were considered the responsibility of a wide network of kin and friends.

Male and female relations were most affected by the difficulty that men had in finding steady employment. Generally a couple in The Flats would not marry unless the man had a steady job. Men in The Flats had accepted the mainstream model in the United States of the male provider, and being unable to find regular employment prevented their assumption of that role. Moreover, marriage removed people from the widespread sharing network, since after marriage their major obligations belonged to their husbands or wives. In addition, because a woman was cut off the welfare rolls if she married, kinship networks and welfare benefits offered a woman more security than a

generalized reciprocity
A form of exchange in which people share what they have with others but expect them to reciprocate later.

balanced reciprocity
A form of exchange in which items of equal or near-equal value are exchanged on the spot.

negative reciprocity
A form of exchange in which the object is to get something for nothing or to make a profit.

husband could. Nevertheless, men and women in The Flats did form intimate relationships out of which children were born. Moreover, the fathers took considerable pride in their children, as did the paternal grandparents, to whom the children often went for help. However, the mothers often regarded the fathers as friends who had failed to fulfill their paternal obligations. Thus, the conditions of poverty drew people into kinship and friendship networks, rather than nuclear family patterns valued by the larger society.

QUESTION 6.5: CAN A NON-STRATIFIED COMMUNITY EXIST WITHIN A LARGE SOCIETY?

Many people who are convinced of the harmful effects of social stratification believe nevertheless that in a modern, industrial society, the system is inevitable. It may be possible for the Inuit or the Ju/'hoansi to have a relatively egalitarian society, for example, but it is not possible in a modern, industrial state. Yet for thousands of years there have been attempts by some groups in stratified societies to create classless, egalitarian, utopian social settings. Christianity began as a utopian dream of universal equality, and the idea of a real-life utopia emerged with the idea that man, under God, has the power to create an earthly paradise. Among the earliest expressions of this idea was Christian communalism, which led to the founding of Catholic monastic orders: isolated, virtually self-sufficient communities in which the work was collective and egalitarian. In the 19th century, industrialists such as Robert Owen attempted to build utopian factory communities, and Karl Marx's goal was to build a national-utopian society. In the middle of the 20th century, psychologist B.F. Skinner outlined a utopian society based on scientific technology in *Walden Two*, a controversial novel that inspired an attempt to translate his fiction into a real-life utopia at Twin Oaks in Virginia. All of these attempts to construct utopian societies are evidence of the long history of the search for an egalitarian social order.

Anthropologist Charles Erasmus examined hundreds of utopian communities in an effort to discover why most failed but some succeeded. He concluded that the main problem for these communities is trying to motivate community members to work and contribute to the common good without the promise of individual material rewards, status, or prestige. Of the successful utopian communities in North America, the most notable are those of the Hutterites, a Christian Protestant sect that originated in Moravia in the 16th century. Why did the Hutterites succeed while so many others failed? Is it possible to use communities such as theirs as models for modern egalitarian communities?

The Hutterites and the Colony of Heaven

"If there will ever be a perfect culture it may not be exactly like the Hutterites—but it will be similar." These words of a member of a Hutterite colony express the feeling that the group has succeeded in building utopian communities. In fact, the Hutterite colonies are among the most successful products of the Christian communal movement, which also includes Mennonites and Amish.

The Hutterites originated during the Protestant Reformation. In 1528 they began to establish colonies throughout what are now Germany, Austria, and Russia. Their pacifism and refusal to perform military service brought them into conflict with European governments, and in 1872, to avoid conscription, they immigrated to the United States and established colonies in South Dakota. During the First World War, a confrontation over military conscription with state and federal authorities in the United States resulted in the imprisonment of Hutterite men in Alcatraz, where some of them

Cooperation is valued in Hutterite society, where community members worship, work, and eat as a group. Here, women are shown preparing a meal for the entire community.

© World Illustrated/Photoshot

died from abusive treatment. As a consequence, many colonies moved to Canada and settled in Alberta and Saskatchewan. Although a significant number of Hutterites returned to the United States after 1920, many remained in western Canada. By the early 1970s there were more than 37,000 Hutterites in the United States and more than 21,000 in Canada. Peter Stephenson, a Canadian anthropologist, has conducted long-term fieldwork among Hutterite communities in western Canada.

The goal of Hutterites is to create a "colony of heaven." Drawing their inspiration from the Old and New Testaments of the Christian Bible, the Hutterites believe in communal living and the proper observance of religious practice. They reject competition, violence, and war and believe that property is to be used and not possessed. They respect the need for government but do not believe they should involve themselves in it or hold public office. A Hutterite colony is governed by an elected board that includes the religious leaders and the community teacher, so authority is group-centred. It is a family-based, agricultural community in which everyone is expected to contribute to the work and to share equally in the bounty. Unlike the Amish, whose beliefs they in essence share, the Hutterites accept and use modern technology; they are acknowledged to be among the most successful

agriculturists in North America. Hutterite colonies in Canada are often million-dollar farm enterprises, and because there are no labour costs involved in their farming expenses, the colonies are able to maintain a competitive edge on other farmers in Canada.

Hutterites are not totally egalitarian. Their society is ranked by age and gender; members do not participate in decision making until they are baptised and married. Baptism is a very important event in a Hutterite community because it marks a person's entry into adulthood. Until a member is baptised, he or she is not thought to be "morally accountable for his or her actions and thoughts" (Stephenson 1991, 127). Although women are considered intellectually and physically inferior to men, Hutterites reject the unequal distribution of wealth as well as competition among members for status, prestige, or personal possessions. Hutterites minimize competition by renouncing private adornment and ostentatious displays of wealth and by practising collective consumption. There is little difference in dress, and adornment is usually frowned on. All the housing is plain and utilitarian. And, as in most Christian communes, they are careful to indoctrinate their children against competition within the colony. Children are taught to avoid seeking honours or placing themselves above others. They are taught never to envy others.

One way Hutterites build commitment to the group is through frequent face-to-face interaction. Members eat together in a communal dining hall, work together, and meet frequently to discuss the affairs of the community. Almost every evening the entire community gathers for church service. Although the Hutterites have no formal means of punishing those who violate group rules, they do practise a form of ostracism called *den Frieden nehmen*, "taking away the individual's peace of mind." An ostracized man is not allowed to talk to other members, including his own wife. He may also be assigned a special room in which to sleep apart and may be required to eat alone.

In addition, the practice of "branching," or community fission, functions not only to adjust community size, reduce friction, and settle other colonies, but also to build internal commitment and reduce competition. Stephenson points out that social movements have difficulty maintaining long-range goals, especially as wealth accumulates. The Hutterites address this problem by dividing the communities, or branching, every fifteen years. During a fifteen-year period, each community saves a portion of its earnings to purchase additional land, build houses and barns, and accumulate necessary machines and livestock to start a new colony. When the new physical facilities are complete, members of the community draw lots to determine which families will relocate. Branching provides each Hutterite community with a tangible goal. Wealthier colonies that delay branching are often disrupted by internal quarrels and become examples of the danger of failing to branch on schedule. Branching also has a built-in renewal factor; new communities reproduce the founding enthusiasm and ideals. If there is competition, it is between colonies, rather than individuals.

In sum, the Hutterites, by a collective effort, have created within the larger societies of Canada and the United States a community without poverty, without economic classes, and with little or no crime, where each person, without the promise of material reward, contributes to the common good. There are, however, some negatives: the Hutterites are a Christian Bible-based religious community that teaches male supremacy and severely limits individual freedoms. The question is whether these negatives outweigh the benefits of creating nonstratified communities within the larger stratified society. There is also a question of whether cooperative communities, such as Hutterites, can serve as a model for the poor in the larger society; that is, does the establishment of closed, collective communities offer a solution to the endemic poverty of those at the bottom level of modern society, and does the success of Hutterites suggest that it is within our means to build societies without poverty?

QUESTION 6.6: HOW CAN ANTHROPOLOGY BE APPLIED TO ALLEVIATE THE EFFECTS OF INEQUALITY?

In Charles Dickens's *A Christmas Carol*, Marley, in his ghostly form, descends on Ebenezer Scrooge to tell him to expect a visit that night from three ghosts. As he disappears he leaves Scrooge with the sound of wailing and lamentations coming from outside the window; as he looks out, Scrooge sees

phantoms, wandering hither and thither in restless haste, and moaning as they went. Every one of them wore chains like Marley's Ghost; some few (they might be guilty governments) were linked together; none were free. Many had been personally known to Scrooge in their lives. He had been quite familiar with one old ghost, in a white waistcoat, with a monstrous iron safe

attached to its ankle, who cried piteously at being
unable to assist a wretched woman with an infant,
whom it saw below, upon a door-step. The misery
with them all was, clearly, that they sought to
interfere, for good, in human matters, and had
lost the power for ever. *(emphasis added)*

The phantoms' dilemma might very well serve
as a metaphor for the wealthy in the world, who
seem resigned to helplessness when it comes to
permanently alleviating poverty and oppression.
Inequality, as we discussed earlier, is striking and is
growing worse both within wealthy countries and
between the rich and the poor countries of the
world. Worse yet, inequality produces differential
access to life's necessities—food, water, shelter,
health care, and protection from torture and cruel
punishment and polluted environments. The
question is, of course, what can be done to alleviate
these problems, and what role might anthropology
play in addressing them?

There are various ways that a background in
anthropology is relevant for dealing with problems
stemming from inequality. Anthropology prepares
people for careers in (for example) delivering
health services, administering treatment programs,
counselling dysfunctional families, and finding
the connections between old age and depression.
We have already examined in previous sections
anthropological work in the areas of economic
development, HIV/AIDS prevention, and
counselling for adolescent girls. But perhaps some
of the most significant contributions that can be
made by people with a background in anthropology
are in the design and implementation of measures
to protect people from human rights abuses.

Anthropology and Human Rights

The idea of individual rights comes to us from the
17th- and 18th-century Enlightenment, as codified
most notably by Thomas Jefferson in the U.S.
Declaration of Independence. That idea, however, is
clearly biased by the notion of the egocentric view

of society (discussed in Chapter 5). However, some
of the rights outlined in the Universal Declaration
of Human Rights, adopted on 10 December 1948
by the General Assembly of the United Nations,
could be extended across cultures.[1]

These might include the right to be free of the
threat of torture or cruel, inhuman, or degrading
treatment or punishment, and the right to freedom
of opinion and expression. Besides these legal
rights, the UN declaration also includes the right
to a standard of living adequate for health and
well-being, which encompasses the rights to food,
clothing, housing, medical care, and necessary social
services along with the right to security in the event
of unemployment, sickness, disability, widowhood,
old age, or other lack of livelihood in circumstances
beyond the person's control.

Similar rights have been incorporated into
various other international treaties and conventions.
Unfortunately, most of the rights outlined in these
agreements are largely ignored or unenforceable.
For example, the member countries of the UN
that were signatories to the Convention on the
Prevention and Punishment of the Crime of
Genocide all stood by in 1994 while more than
800,000 Rwandans were slaughtered by their
countrymen. These countries avoided taking action
simply by refusing to define the killing as genocide
until it was over. Amnesty International and Human
Rights Watch, two of the major NGOs addressing
issues of human rights, have documented violations
of individual rights in at least 150 countries of the
world. In those countries, nonviolent dissidents
have been held without trial, imprisoned, tortured,
killed, raped, or "disappeared" by police or military
or paramilitary forces. When the UN instituted the
post of High Commissioner for Human Rights,
the position was allocated only $700,000, small
even by NGO standards. In his first year on the job,
the High Commissioner did not criticize a single
government anywhere in the world.

---

[1] You can access the Universal Declaration of Human Rights at http://www
.un.org/Overview/rights.html.

Furthermore, as we have seen earlier in this chapter, the economic and social inequality that creates the conditions for human rights violations continues to grow. Billions of people are living in conditions of poverty and oppression while the top 358 global billionaires had a combined income equal to that of the 2.3 billion poorest people in the world.

Anthropologists Carol Nagengast and Carlos G. Vélez-Ibáñez suggest that anthropologists are, of all social scientists, the best prepared for human rights work. This is because they are the best prepared to deal with cultural variation and to understand complex community struggles. They are trained to understand the workings of official bureaucracies and global processes, and they have "a strong penchant for supporting the underdog." The issue, say Nagengast and Vélez-Ibáñez, is that while anthropologists often discover and reveal human rights abuses, they must also find a way to predict such abuses and do something about them, be it indirectly through participation in the design of public policy or directly in the delivery of services. As Canadian General Roméo Dallaire explained, regarding conflict resolution in Rwanda: "What you need now are people who can not only fight—because they may need to protect and defend—but people who have a whole new set of skills You need them to have more intellectually based skills like anthropology, sociology and philosophy" (*Toronto Star*, 13 February 2005, A14).

In their edited book *Human Rights: The Scholar as Activist* (2004), Nagengast and Vélez-Ibáñez suggest also that the human rights agenda, besides addressing individual and political abuses such as land grabs, torture, murder, rape, and disappearances, must include collective rights, including economic, social, and cultural ones. There are, they point out, no binding or enforceable laws or guidelines to constrain the power of corporations and their support agencies, such as the World Bank and IMF, to set working conditions or wages or to impose development projects that displace persons or leave them worse off than before. Basically, all internationally written and customary law has left it to nation-states to enforce the recognition of rights. But nation-states, which claim the right to self-determination, are also the major violators of human rights either directly through the operations of the military or the police or indirectly, by allowing extra-state or paramilitary groups to violate human rights.

Nagengast and Vélez-Ibáñez then ask, "What can scholars do?" First, they say, anthropologists, who among all social scientists most often work with the poor, can publicize human rights abuses. The development of a global communication network, they say, has allowed human rights information to be disseminated quickly. When Augusto Pinochet, former president of Chile, was arrested in London in 1998 following a request from Spain and Belgium for acts of genocide, torture, and "disappearances" committed during his presidency of 1973–1990, his defence of immunity because he was a head of state was rejected by the British High Court largely because of the widespread publicity that followed his case.

Anthropologists can also work with groups whose rights have been violated to help them develop the means to defend themselves. Terence Turner, for example, has been working with the Kayapo of central Brazil since 1962, to prevent development projects that threaten their land. Turner, a founding member of the American Anthropological Association's Committee on Human Rights, has also been directing the Kayapo Video Project, during which the Kayapo have been shooting and editing their own videos about their lives and culture and their relations with Brazilians.

Anthropologist Robert Hitchcock has worked with the San peoples of Botswana and Namibia to map their homelands, institute land claims, and stave off settler takeovers of their land. Hitchcock has ensured that the San participate actively in these efforts. As a result, San communities have created their own human rights and development agencies.

The Kayapo video project.

People with anthropological training have helped service providers alleviate the plight of refugees. As of 2004, the UN High Commission on Refugees (www.unhcr.org) counted over 17 million refugees, with "refugee" defined as a person who "owing to a well-founded fear of being persecuted for reasons of race, religion, nationality, membership of a particular social group, or political opinion, is outside the country of his nationality, and is unable to or, owing to such fear, is unwilling to avail himself of the protection of that country." In addition to these 17 million, over 100 million people are displaced internally—that is, within their own country.

These are just a few examples of how anthropological skills and perspectives can help protect and restore human rights. A description of such efforts would not be complete without the

story of Paul Farmer and his efforts, according to one author, to "cure the world."

Anthropology and Medical Rights: The Work of Paul Farmer

In his Pulitzer Prize–winning book, *Mountains Beyond Mountains* (2003), about the work of anthropologist and physician Paul Farmer, Tracy Kidder described how Farmer's background in anthropology and his experiences in Haiti moulded his view of the links among anthropology, medicine, and human rights. While at Duke University and studying anthropology as an undergraduate, Farmer met and began visiting with Haitians working on tobacco farms and became fascinated with Haitian history and culture. Consequently he visited Haiti in 1983, when the country was still controlled by the U.S.–supported dictatorship of the Duvalier family. Haiti, a country of some 7.5 million people, is the poorest country in the Western Hemisphere; 80 percent of Haitians live in poverty.

Farmer began to work with local and international agencies that were delivering health and social services to the local population and conducting a health census on infant and juvenile mortality, the results of which he characterized as "horrific." He watched a young pregnant woman with malaria die because even after he had helped to raise the $15 needed to purchase

Anthropologist Paul Farmer has worked intensively with a variety of local and international agencies to help plan, implement, and deliver health and social services to local communities.

blood, he couldn't raise enough for the inexpensive equipment needed for the transfusion.

Among the lessons that Farmer drew from his initial experience in Haiti was that a knowledge of anthropology was critical for addressing the health problems of that country's poor. In one instance, a mother permitted a Vodou priest to treat her child for malaria, while at the same time agreeing to let Farmer treat the patient with chloroquine. It was critical, Farmer says, to appreciate the role of Vodou, a religion that combines traditional Catholicism with traditional African beliefs, in the life of most Haitians. A doctor who knew nothing about local beliefs might end up at war with Vodou priests, mistaking patient complaints for bizarre superstitions. However, a doctor with a background in anthropology could find a way to work with the priest. For example, a female patient might complain of something Haitians call *move san, lét gate*. The condition is brought on by *sezisman*, a surprise of some sort or a frightening action. The result is "bad blood," in which a nursing mother's milk stops flowing. While such a description might be dismissed by someone without knowledge of local culture, Farmer notes that, metaphorically, the explanation turns two vital fluids, blood and milk, into poison, thus serving as a symbolic warning about the abuse of pregnant women, particularly those who are nursing.

A second defining lesson that emerged from Haiti for Farmer touched on liberation theology. In the 1960s in Latin America, during heightened periods of human rights abuses by often dictatorial states, Catholic churches became centres for the defence of human rights and attacks against government repression. Church leaders in Latin America attacked inequality and injustice and began to participate in forming organizations and social movements to give the poor a political and economic voice. This was an attempt, as some put it, to apply the Gospel to everyday life in the hope that these efforts would ultimately replace the old order of things. Farmer considered liberation theology to be, as he put it, "a powerful rebuke to the hiding away of poverty." Reacting to the poverty and repression he witnessed in Haiti, Farmer thought that

someone is witnessing this horror show? ... I know it sounds shallow, the opiate thing, needing to believe, palliating pain, but it didn't feel shallow. It was more profound than other sentiments I'd known, and I was taken with the idea that in an ostensibly godless world that worshipped money and power or, more seductively, a sense of personal efficacy and advancement ... there was still a place to look for God, and that was in the suffering of the poor. (in Kidder 2003, 85)

Farmer was attracted to liberation theology because it was driven by a need to accomplish something concrete in the lives of the poor and was characterized by what he called "pragmatic solidarity" with the communities that it sought to assist. Liberation theology argued for giving the poor, not equal treatment, but preferential treatment.

Farmer also gained an understanding of the context in which poverty and oppression occurred. He understood that, as he put it, "a minor error in one setting of power and privilege could have an enormous impact on the poor in another." For example, in the 1950s, with money from the U.S. Export–Import Bank, the U.S.

THE CULTURAL CONSTRUCTION OF SOCIAL HIERARCHY

Army Corps of Engineers built the Péligre dam, which displaced thousands of Haitian farmers, who were forced either to rebuild on the sides of mountains that were unsuited for growing crops or to move to cities such as Port-au-Prince to look for jobs as housekeepers or as low-paid labourers in American-built assembly plants. The most valuable asset for the remaining farmers was their Creole pigs, but an outbreak of swine fever in the Dominican Republic led the United States to destroy all the Haitian pigs in order to protect the American pork industry. The pigs were replaced with pigs purchased from Iowa farmers, but these were delicate and most of them died, leaving the peasants with little. These are examples of what Farmer refers to as **structural violence**, actions of remote government or international agencies that result in denial to the poor of basic rights of food, shelter, and livelihood.

After his initial experiences in Haiti, Farmer enrolled at Harvard University in both medical school and the Ph.D. program in anthropology, completing both programs while spending much of his time travelling back and forth to Haiti, where he worked to build a public health program in the village of Cange. That effort included vaccination programs, protected water supplies, and sanitation. He also trained people to administer medicines, treat minor ailments, and recognize symptoms of serious ones such as TB, malaria, and typhoid. He received both his Ph.D. in anthropology and his M.D. in 1990, writing his Ph.D. thesis, *AIDS and Accusation*, on HIV/AIDS in Haiti. Since that time, Farmer has applied his expertise with infectious diseases to problems of drug-resistant tuberculosis in Russian prisons and in impoverished communities in Peru; and he has worked to help develop health services in Chiapas, Mexico. All the while he has continued to work in Haiti.

Health as a Human Right

Based on his experiences in Haiti, Farmer became convinced that health is a basic human right and that medical workers, along with social scientists, are uniquely situated, both in temperament and in profession, to address the problems of structural violence and to engage with the poor in the spirit of pragmatic solidarity. In *Pathologies of Power: Health, Human Rights, and the New War on the Poor* (2003), Farmer outlines a rationale and a strategy for addressing human rights abuses.

Farmer offers as an example the case of Russian prisons, where multi-drug-resistant tuberculosis (MDRTB) emerged. In Russia, prisoners are crowded together in cells where the air is thick with tubercle bacilli. As a consequence, tuberculosis is the leading cause of death among Russian prisoners. Clearly, says Farmer, the situation is rife with human rights abuses. The first set of abuses begins with pre-trial detention and the violation of the human right to a speedy trial. The Russian court system is backlogged for months, and people who are being held for trial must live in deplorable conditions that are ripe for the contraction of TB, even before it is determined that they have committed a crime. The second set of abuses occurs if they are convicted and are held in a prison in conditions that guarantee exposure to MDRTB. Next, they are denied adequate food and medical care. As one of the Russian physicians put it, "I have spent my entire medical career caring for prisoners with tuberculosis. And although we complained about shortages in the eighties, we had no idea how good we had it then. Now it's a daily struggle for food, drugs, lab supplies, even heat and electricity" (Farmer 2003, 215).

Finally, of course, prisoners are dying because of ineffective treatment, a clear violation of Article 25 of the Universal Declaration of Human Rights, which states that everyone has a right to "share in scientific advancement and its benefits."

Farmer points out that people are dying not because there are no effective treatments (in the vast

> **structural violence**
> Actions of remote government or international agencies that result in denial to the poor of basic rights of food, shelter, or livelihood.

majority of cases, there are combinations of drugs that can cure MDRTB), but because they or the agencies responsible for their care lack the money to pay for the medicine. "Untreatable" has become a euphemism for "too expensive." And the case of MDRTB in Russia is mirrored in the cases of HIV/AIDS and malaria in Africa and HIV/AIDS and TB in Haiti, as well as in most of Latin America. Worldwide, 32 percent of all deaths are caused by infectious disease; but in the poor countries, infectious disease is responsible for 42 percent of all deaths, compared to 1.2 percent in industrial countries.

Once we have defined health as a human right and recognized the structural violence that either creates conditions for disease or that denies the afflicted access to medicine, what can anthropologists, other social scientists, and medical professionals accomplish?

First, says Farmer, they can place human rights violations in their proper contexts so as to identify their structural causes. Russian prison doctors, for example, lack the medicines to cure their patients because international financial agencies, such as the IMF, require most countries, including Russia, to cut government services as a condition for receiving loans. Another example: pharmaceutical companies, which often receive sizable government subsidies and support for research, refuse to waive patent rights to allow poor countries to supply generic forms of drugs that could help HIV/AIDS patients in poor countries. Anthropologists can do a great deal to place human rights abuses in these broader perspectives. As Farmer puts it: "Social inequalities based on race or ethnicity, gender, religious creed, and—above all—social class are the motor force behind most human rights violations. In other words, violence against individuals is usually embedded in entrenched structural violence" (2003, 219).

But, says Farmer, it is not enough to understand the context for violations of health rights. Russian penal codes already prohibit overcrowding in prisons, long pre-trial detentions, and the exposure of patients to malnutrition and disease. Prison officials already recognize the problem of MDRTB—that is why they sought Farmer's help. Physicians in Haiti already know that poverty generated by oppression and corruption drives people to become sex workers in Port-au-Prince, where they are exposed to HIV/AIDS; and doctors in Peru know that a lack of sanitation facilities has exposed the population there to various gastrointestinal disorders.

Consequently, says Farmer, we need a strategy to confront structural violence. The problem, he says, is that traditional government agencies and NGOs are restricted when it comes to addressing rights issues. International institutions such as the UN and organizations such as Amnesty International and Physicians for Human Rights are constrained by the fact that they must work through governments; and often, the major violators of rights are the governments themselves. For this reason, Farmer suggests that independent groups such as First World universities, hospitals, churches, and health care professionals can best serve local communities. If healing and health care can become the "symbolic core," as he puts it, of a new human rights agenda, we will be able to tap into an almost universal concern for the sick, while at the same time involving persons in medicine, public health, and the natural and social sciences.

Farmer's own efforts provide a model for the approach to addressing human rights abuses that he is suggesting. On one of his trips back to Boston from Haiti, he tried to raise money to build a bread oven in Cange, the village where he was working. He approached a local charity that gave him the money and that also put him in contact with one of their regular donors, Tom White, a local contractor. White became so interested in what Farmer was doing in Haiti that he founded a public charity called Partners in Health, as well as a corresponding organization in Haiti called Zamni Lasante on which Farmer could draw for his work in Cange. White began by donating $1 million. Soon Farmer expanded the membership of Partners in Health, adding a fellow anthropology and medical student, Jim Yong Kim, along with Ophelia Dahl, then Farmer's fiancée, to Partners in Health. Partners in Health has since provided funds to develop various public health projects in Haiti, such as the HIV Equity Initiative to complement prevention efforts with antiretroviral drugs for those for whom treatment has failed. Health workers visit patients each day and administer the drugs. Although funds from standard health organizations such as the World Health Organization are limited for expensive drug treatments, Partners in Health can provide them from private donations. After the 2010 earthquake, Partners in Health and Zamni Lasante designed and implemented the Stand With Haiti Fund, and a 2.5 year, $125 million plan to help to rebuild the country. They focused on strengthening the country's health infrastructure, particularly in specialities such as mental health and rehabilitative medicine, which had been weak even before the earthquake.

Summarizing his approach, Farmer (2003, 238) says that "we have a long way to go in the struggle for health and human rights. We cannot merely study this topic without proposing meaningful and pragmatic interventions; but to succeed, we must distinguish between our best analysis and our best strategies. The focus on health offers a critical new dimension to human rights work and is a largely untapped vein of resources, passion, and good will."

CONCLUSIONS

The problem underlying this chapter is why extremes of poverty and wealth exist in modern societies. The criteria customarily used to rank people in social hierarchies include wealth or income, occupation, ethnic group membership, personal appearance, race, gender, and age. The consequences of such rankings, especially in the creation of poverty and the gap between the rich and poor, have raised some of the most challenging questions in modern societies.

People come to accept social hierarchies as natural because they believe that hierarchy is a biological principle. Some people are thought to be naturally more or less intelligent than others or otherwise more or less worthy. Females' biological functions, for example, have been described in terms that make women seem less worthy than men.

People at the lowest level of the social hierarchy, those who live in poverty, adapt to their conditions in various ways. Blacks in The Flats of a midwestern city adapted by building kinship ties; but for some, poverty and rejection by family and friends may mean that the streets are the only places left to live.

A few groups have demonstrated that it is possible to build egalitarian, nonstratified communities within a larger industrial society. Perhaps the most successful in North America have been the Hutterites, a religious group that emphasizes communal ownership of property and equal distribution of production, while rejecting competition, violence, and war.

Finally, we have examined various areas in which persons with a background in anthropology can help address the poverty and oppression that often arise from inequality. We focused largely on human rights abuses, since most of these arise from differential access to wealth. Here we highlighted the work of people like Carol Nagengast and Paul Farmer.

CRITICAL THINKING QUESTIONS

1. In this chapter, we have discussed how most people tend to perceive their identities as natural, or biological. What might be some strategies for getting people to think differently about their identities, and for recognizing the culturally constructed nature of identity? Furthermore, why is it important to understand the role culture plays in shaping social hierarchies?

2. Think of some examples of "white privilege" in our own society.

3. In section 6.6, we discuss how anthropologists can help alleviate the effects of inequality. On reading the examples of Terence Turner and Paul Farmer, both of whom work in non-Western contexts, can you apply any of these ideas to our own Canadian society? What can we as anthropologists and anthropology students do in Canada to make a difference in people's lives and confront the issue of social inequality?

KEY TERMS:

achieved status (p. 168)
ascribed status (p. 168)
balanced reciprocity (p. 186)
caste (p. 168)
class (p. 167)
culture of poverty (p. 185)
gender (p. 178)
generalized reciprocity (p. 186)
hegemonic masculinity (p. 181)
negative reciprocity (p. 186)
race (p. 166)
racism (p. 170)
sex (p. 178)
social stratification/hierarchy (p. 165)
structural violence (p. 194)
third gender (p. 178)
white privilege (p. 171)

GLOBALIZATION, NEOLIBERALISM, AND THE NATION-STATE

© Mark Tansey. Courtesy Gagosian Gallery. Photography by Robert McKeever.

Mark Tansey's *The Invisible Hand* evokes Adam Smith's metaphorical description of a free market governed only by the "natural" principles of capitalism (see section 7.1). Here, the hand shields a cavernous stock exchange, evoking the flow of wealth, money, and power under neoliberalism—a flow that David Harvey highlights in this chapter's epigraph.

The incredible concentration of wealth and power that now exists in the upper echelons of capitalism has not been seen since the 1920s. The flows of tribute into the world's major financial centres have been astonishing. What, however, is even more astonishing is the habit of treating all of this as a mere and in some instances even unfortunate byproduct of neoliberalization. The very idea that this might be—just might be—the fundamental core of what neoliberalism has been about all along appears unthinkable.

David Harvey, The History of Neoliberalism *(2005)*

PROBLEM 7

What are the economic and cultural effects of globalization? What is the relationship between globalization, the nation-state, and national identity?

INTRODUCTION

On 26 June 2010, political leaders from around the world gathered in Toronto, Ontario, for the fourth meeting of the G-20 heads of government. Here, the leaders of twenty of the wealthiest nations in the world convened to discuss the future of global economies, international aid and development strategies, measures for promoting open markets, and means of stimulating economic growth in the wake of a worldwide recession. The two-day event was the most expensive security event in Canada's history, costing $868 million. A 10-metre-high fence was erected in the downtown core, and 10,000 uniformed officers were brought in to protect the delegates. In many ways, however, the actual content of the conference was obscured within the mass media. Much of the national and international media attention afforded to this event focused on the various protests. During the event, more than 1,100 protesters were arrested. The mainstream media homogenized and sensationalized the protesters as young, selfish, violent criminals and emphasized their role in the destruction and vandalism of storefronts, cars, and other public spaces, inciting fear among the general public. Few media outlets stressed that most protests were peaceful, and even fewer focused on what, specifically, the protesters were protesting against. While there is no question that a handful of them used the G-20 as an opportunity for mayhem, the vast majority were peacefully voicing the underrepresented perspectives of marginalized populations around the world—populations directly affected by decisions made by the G-20 leaders. Indigenous groups, gay rights activists, environmentalists, and anti-poverty groups were among the protesters. Specifically, these groups were questioning the ways in which globalization, as a social and economic force, had benefited the wealthiest and most powerful segments of society.

The term "globalization" has been bandied about by academics and the mass media and within our popular culture over the past three decades. Anthony Giddens (1990, 64) defines **globalization** as "the intensification of worldwide social relations which link distant localities in such a way that local happenings are shaped by events occurring many miles away and vice versa." Globalization can have both economic and cultural effects on various populations. The worldwide spread of large multinational companies such as Walmart

and Starbucks has been documented as having deleterious economic consequences on local communities. Walmart, for instance, may seem like an attractive option for shopping because of its low price points. But because of its size and buying power, it can sell products more cheaply than most small, local businesses, effectively driving them out of business.

In many ways, globalization is not a new phenomenon. As we saw in Chapter 2, Europe's colonization of the world was a global phenomenon. But as Roxana Ng (2002, 74) points out, "what is new in this era of globalization is the ability of capital to move sites of production across national borders with relative ease." The production, circulation, and consumption of a common

> **globalization**
> Defined by Anthony Giddens as the intensification of worldwide social relations that link distant localities in such a way that local happenings are shaped by events occurring many miles away, and vice versa.

Protesters at the 2010 G20 meetings in Toronto.

© ZUMA Wire Service/Alamy

commodity, the T-shirt, provides an instructive example of the mechanisms and consequences of economic globalization. Many protesters at the G-20 sported T-shirts emblazoned with anti-globalization slogans, or with the logos of the protest groups with which they were affiliated. By examining what Igor Kopytoff calls the biography of a commodity (in this case, the T-shirt), we can understand much about the global processes that the protesters were criticizing.

For instance, economist Pietra Rivoli wanted to understand the impact, on workers and on the environment, of the policies of multilateral institutions such as the World Trade Organization (WTO), the International Monetary Fund (IMF), and the World Bank. Rivoli assumed that globalization was a good thing, that the increased production and sale of commodities such as T-shirts were helping create jobs in poor countries as well as supplying inexpensive goods to consumers. To convince herself of the benefits of trade, she wanted to trace the chain of production and distribution of a T-shirt, from the growing of the cotton to the delivery of the final product to a chain store in Fort Lauderdale, Florida. She began by locating the company that printed and distributed the T-shirt, Sherry Manufacturing of Fort Lauderdale. Sherry Manufacturing had purchased the shirt from China, one of about 25 million cotton T-shirts shipped from China that year. Rivoli then travelled to China to visit the factory that had assembled the T-shirt, the place where the fabric had been knit, and finally the factory where the yarn had been spun out of raw cotton. The cotton, she was surprised to discover, had been grown in Lubbock County, Texas. The unexpected (yet increasingly typical) biography and global itinerary of her T-shirt—purchased in Fort Lauderdale, printed and distributed by a Florida textile manufacturer, assembled, sewn, and spun in Chinese factories out of cotton grown in Texas—can tell us much about globalization and our role in it as T-shirt consumers in North America. The aspects of neoliberalism and economic globalization that underpin the biography of the T-shirt are the focus of the first half of this chapter.

In the second half of this chapter, we examine the often ambiguous cultural effects of globalization. For some societies, the process has been empowering—a means to strengthen cultural identity as a society's arts, material culture, and values and beliefs circulate around the world. To understand these effects, it is first necessary to understand the relationship between the nation-state and globalization, and between nation-states and national identity. Think, again, about T-shirts and how often they communicate not just political slogans or brand names, but sentiments of national pride and affiliations of national identity (as we saw when Canada hosted the 2010 Winter Olympics in Vancouver, for example). When we wear T-shirts purchased in popular tourist destinations, we demonstrate our own global itineraries while simultaneously conveying a carefully crafted message about the locale in which we purchased the T-shirt. To understand both the forces of economic globalization that make it possible for us to buy cheap T-shirts produced elsewhere, and the forces of cultural globalization that compel us to wear our identity and our global itineraries, literally, on our sleeves, we need to explore the four questions that comprise this chapter.

QUESTIONS

7.1 What is neoliberalism and what role does it play in economic globalization?

7.2 What role do nation-states play in market economies? What is the relationship between nation-states and neoliberalism?

7.3 What is the relationship between the nation-state and identity under globalization?

7.4 What are the cultural effects of globalization?

QUESTION 7.1: WHAT IS NEOLIBERALISM AND WHAT ROLE DOES IT PLAY IN ECONOMIC GLOBALIZATION?

The "Great Transformation"

To understand the various economic effects of globalization, we must explore what we mean by an "economic system." **Economic systems** are about the distribution of goods and services—that is, the rules, mechanisms, institutions, and systems of relations through which people get what they want. This process can be as simple as the borrowing of a cup of sugar or a pair of shoes, or as complex as the production, distribution, consumption, and disposal of automobiles, houses, or military weapons.

Markets go back thousands of years. Communities would set up areas where merchants, farmers, and artisans could bring their goods or services for sale or barter. But as new modes of transportation and manufacturing developed, markets were no longer only places to trade, but entire networks whereby silk manufactured in China, for example, could be sold in Paris. At some point 200 to 300 years ago, technological changes led to what economist Karl Polanyi termed "the great transformation," or the Industrial Revolution.

States have always played a major role in the economy. Some 18th-century economists, however, argued that the state should play as small a role as possible. Ideally, they argued, people will supply only those goods and services for which there is demand; and generally, a balance will be established between what is demanded and what is supplied. In his classic treatise *The Wealth of Nations* (1776), Adam Smith saw the workings of the market as an "invisible hand" by which a benevolent God administered a universe in which

human happiness was maximized, an ideal system in which each person, seeking his or her own ends, contributed to the betterment of society as a whole. Thus, by seeking money and wealth, each person would work toward supplying what others needed or demanded. For Smith, the market represented a utopian vision in which wealth was perpetually created for the benefit of all.

The problem was that an unregulated market, in which the generation of wealth was the only goal, resulted in abysmal working conditions, environmental degradation, and wild economic fluctuations that saw people plunged into poverty. In *The Great Transformation (1944)*, Polanyi addressed the tension between the need to allow the market—that is, the mechanisms for buying and selling—to operate freely without government interference and the need to somehow minimize the social and natural damages inflicted by the market. Polanyi suggested that the market, if allowed to operate unhindered, would soon destroy the very foundations of society. It would disrupt social relations through the operations of the labour market; it would destroy the environment; it would reduce freedom. Yet regulating the market by enacting laws on pollution, land use, and working conditions could destroy the market. Polanyi saw the working out of this dilemma as one of the driving forces of history since the early 19th century.

When it comes to the market's workings, governments have tried to maintain a balance between regulation and noninterference. At one extreme are the almost completely state-run economies of Cuba and North Korea; at the other are capitalist economies such as that of the United States. Economic systems are generally categorized as market-driven or state-run; in practice, though, almost all represent some mix of the two. North Korea is one of the last of the state-run economies,

---

economic systems
The rules, mechanisms, institutions, and systems of relations through which goods and services are distributed and people get what they want.

---

with the government controlling virtually every economic activity; yet the North Korean government also sponsors the Kaesong Industrial Region, a development zone that welcomes foreign investment and that encourages market principles. The United States, by contrast, is a hallmark example of a market economy. Nevertheless, during the recent global recession, there was significant government intervention in the form of corporate bailouts and promises of stricter financial controls. Rarely are even the most capitalist economies free of significant state involvement, and the tension between the state and the market that Polanyi wrote about results in ebbs and flows of regulation.

The British economist John Maynard Keynes called on governments to regulate their economies through spending, tax policies, interest rates, and so on. Government involvement in the economy, support of labour unions, and a progressive tax system in which marginal tax rates ranged as high as 90 percent resulted in rapid economic growth in the United States and Canada through the 1960s.

This was followed, in the 1970s, by a period of slow economic growth, which generated pressure to change economic policies. Economists began to abandon Keynesian economics, arguing that the state should withdraw from any involvement in regulating the economy. This economic philosophy, known as **neoliberalism**, is often synonymous with globalization. Since the application of neoliberal principles may determine your career path as well as what goods and services you can acquire for what price, not to mention the natural, political, and social environment in which you live, it is useful to understand where it came from and what it is trying to accomplish.

The Emergence of Neoliberalism

Neoliberalism emerged from a group of economists, historians, and philosophers who gathered around political philosopher Friedrich von Hayek to establish the Mont Pelerin Society (named after the Swiss spa at which they first met in 1947). Prompted by their concerns about the spread of totalitarian societies and religious and racial intolerance, they argued that totalitarian philosophies not only endangered freedom but also threatened private property and the free market, without which, they argued, freedom cannot be preserved. They called themselves "liberals" because they adhered to ideals of freedom, and "neo" because they adhered to neoclassical economic theory, which was opposed to the Keynesian ideas about state involvement in the economy.

Well-being, neoliberals argued, is best served by liberating individual entrepreneurs to operate within a framework of strong property rights, free markets, and **free trade**. The state's role should be limited to safeguarding the integrity of money and maintaining military, police, and legal structures to secure property rights and protect markets. The state should also open markets in areas such as education, water, land, health care, and social security. Other than that, state intervention should be kept to a minimum, because states can never have enough information to second-guess markets on matters such as prices, and because their involvement allows special interest groups such as unions, environmentalists, and trade groups to distort the operations of the market.

One of the first applications of neoliberalism was in New York City in the 1970s. By the start of the decade, industry was fleeing New York and people

---

neoliberalism

An economic philosophy that argues for minimal government involvement in the economy and greatly accelerated economic growth. Well-being, neoliberals argue, is best served by liberating individual entrepreneurs to operate in a framework of strong property rights, free markets, and free trade.

free trade

The removal of barriers to the free flow of goods and capital between nations by eliminating import and export taxes as well as subsidies paid to farmers and business people. It may also mean reducing environmental or social laws when they restrict the flow of goods and capital.

who could afford new housing were moving to the suburbs. This left the city with a diminished tax base and an impoverished and socially restive inner city— what became known as the "urban crisis." The initial solution was typical Keynesian economics: expand public employment and public assistance. But when President Richard Nixon declared the urban crisis over in the early 1970s, he also reduced federal aid to the city. The economic slowdown of the 1970s that hit New York, combined with a reduced tax base and reduced federal aid, drove New York City to the brink of bankruptcy. Financial institutions were unwilling to negotiate the city's debts unless it met strict conditions that included severe budget cuts. They also required unions to put their pension funds in city bonds, which meant that if the city went bankrupt, workers would lose their pensions. The overall result was a diminished standard of living for New Yorkers, particularly the poor. But ultimately, the city became financially solvent and represented to neoliberals what could be done through free market principles.

This soon became the pattern for countries in trouble. The economic stagnation of the 1970s impacted developing countries that, encouraged by banks, had borrowed heavily but could no longer repay their debts. As a condition for restructuring their loans, multilateral institutions such as the World Bank and the IMF imposed neoliberal economic policies on these countries. These included privatizing state-run enterprises; reducing the value of their currency, thus making goods produced in the country cheaper for foreign buyers (and thereby encouraging exports); and making foreign goods more expensive for citizens (thereby discouraging imports). Other conditions included reducing state funding for education, welfare, and health and imposing user fees for school attendance. These neoliberal policies had few positive results. Only a small number of countries were able to escape debt, and more than $4.6 trillion flowed from poorer to wealthier countries. According to financier George Stiglitz, the poor countries ended up subsidizing the richest.

Removing government involvement in the economy is central to neoliberal economic philosophy; when such involvement ends, so the theory goes, business can be more profitable, create more jobs, and so on. One way that less government involvement can help economic growth is by allowing costs that are involved in the production, distribution, consumption, and disposal of goods and services to be externalized. All along the commodity chain, from the production of goods to their transport to their sale and disposal, there are **market externalities**, costs that are not included in the prices that people pay, such as environmental degradation, health risks, and waste disposal. In the next section, we discuss the relationship between the nation-state and market economies under neoliberalism, and look at the market externalities of Twinkies and T-shirts.

QUESTION 7.2: WHAT ROLE DO NATION-STATES PLAY IN MARKET ECONOMIES? WHAT IS THE RELATIONSHIP BETWEEN NATION-STATES AND NEOLIBERALISM?

Although neoliberal philosophy is the driving force behind what we call globalization, there is a basic contradiction in how it is applied. The central idea behind neoliberalism is to keep governments from interfering in the functioning of the market; yet the nation-state still plays a vital role in how the economy functions.

> **market externalities**
> Costs that are not included in the prices people pay, such as health risks and environmental degradation.

What do we mean by a nation-state? The concept of **nation-states**, or countries, is a relatively recent one, dating back in its present form to the 19th century. Furthermore, the terms **nation** and "state" do not mean the same thing. Most states have more than one nation, as in Canada, where there are many First Nations; moreover, one nation can be scattered across many states, either by choice or by force (for instance, the Palestinian refugees discussed in Chapter 5).

Nation-states keep public order, maintain armies, collect tribute or taxes, and so on. The main difference between earlier states and the modern nation-state concerns the extent to which the modern state influences and controls trade. In historical terms, the increasing importance of trade gave governing elites a greater interest in creating conditions to accumulate profits from trade. Of course, ruling elites have always been interested in the economic lives of their subjects. Early states protected the privileges of the elites by regulating the production of goods from resources, offering protection from other elites, and extracting surplus wealth in the form of tribute and taxes from a largely peasant population. The state also issued coins and paper money, established standards for weights and measures, protected the movement of merchants and goods, purchased goods, and created and maintained marketplaces where merchants could sell their products.

In 13th- and 14th-century China and, later, in 16th- and 17th-century Europe and Japan, states began to actively promote and regulate trade. By the 18th century, rulers were beginning to view trade as the ultimate source of well-being. Consequently, states regulated money. They also passed laws to protect their manufacturers and merchants by imposing taxes and tariffs on goods coming from other states. They used military force to open markets in other places and granted trading monopolies to their own groups. They granted charters to trading companies, such as the East India Company and the Hudson's Bay Company, giving them exclusive rights to trade in specific areas. These were the forerunners of today's transnational corporations. States also created and maintained the infrastructure that made trade possible. They developed and maintained ports, built roads and canals, and, later, subsidized railway construction. In Canada, for instance, the Canadian Pacific Railway was completed in 1885. Connecting a vast expanse of the nation from east to west, the railway facilitated trade and economic links between provinces that would otherwise have been impossible to maintain. States also became important customers.

In brief, nation-states began to develop into partnerships between ruling elites and the merchant classes. As Eric Wolf put it:

> The state bought arms and ships. Goods won by force of arms paid for the hiring of mercenaries, for the manufacture of guns and cannon, and for the construction of more ships. The armed merchants foraging overseas needed the state to shield them against competitors and to provide the officialdom capable of holding and consolidating the newly won areas. At the same time the state needed the merchants to lend money to the Crown or to the captains of expeditions; to collect, ship, and sell the goods obtained abroad; and—increasingly—to acquire and export the goods needed in the far-flung outposts of the realm. (1982, 109)

In these ways, states became the building blocks of an emerging global economic network. Each state was now the guardian of its own "national economy," functioning largely to advance the economic lives of its own citizens. In

nation-state
A political community that has clearly defined territorial borders and centralized authority.

nation
A collection of people who share a common language, world view, and ancestry.

fact, it is accurate to say that the modern nation-state created the conditions that made business profitable, while at the same time ensuring that its citizens could afford the things they wanted to buy. But as we will see, this is possible only if manufacturers do not have to pay the full production costs of what they make and sell, and only if consumers don't have to pay the real costs of things. One need only examine the real costs of even the most basic commodities to appreciate the role that nation-states played in making possible their production and purchase. Take, for example, the cost of a Twinkie.

The Nation-State and the Cost of a Twinkie

Twinkies are described by their producers as "golden sponge cake filled with creamy filling." More precisely, the Twinkie has some 26 ingredients, the main ones being sugar, enriched bleached wheat flour, water, eggs, corn syrup, high-fructose corn syrup, partially hydrogenated vegetable shortening, and dextrose.

In Canada, a package of two Twinkies sells for around $1.00. But that is only the store price. To arrive at the real price, we need to examine the hidden costs, owing to market externalities, of each ingredient; in other words, we need to calculate the additional monetary and nonmonetary expenses that go to produce and distribute each ingredient in a Twinkie, expenses that are not reflected in the store price. In fact, without the intervention of the nation-state, the real cost of a Twinkie would probably be $10 or higher. It is only $1.00 because of the various ways the nation-state functions to keep costs accessible and sales profitable.

To illustrate, let us examine just one ingredient that goes into a Twinkie—cane sugar. Environmentally, sugar is not a benign crop. Its production is responsible for dying coral reefs in Hawai'i, water pollution in Buenos Aires, and damage to river estuaries in Brazil and waterways

One function of the nation-state is to ensure that businesses and corporations profit and that commodities are affordable to consumers. Thus, laws and regulations are written (or not written) that permit corporations to externalize costs so that rarely, if ever, do consumers pay the real prices for things. Even a package of Twinkies, which might sell for $1.00, would likely cost far more if externalized costs were included in the purchase price.

in the Philippines. Florida's sugar cane industry, centred just south of one of North America's largest freshwater lakes—Lake Okeechobee—dumps phosphorus-laden agricultural runoff that destroys native species and results in the growth of non-native species. As a result, almost $8 billion will be spent over the next two years to fix the Everglades. Although sugar producers will pay some of that cost, most of it will be passed on to taxpayers.

Sugar production is heavily subsidized by the U.S. government, which, through import quotas, limits the amount of sugar that can be imported from other countries. This raises the cost of sugar for consumers, but it also makes sugar production more profitable and has resulted in the conversion of more than 200,000 hectares of Everglades wetlands to sugar cane production.

The nation-state also manipulates the prices of things by regulating the price of labour. For example, paying sugar workers less than a living wage minimizes the price of sugar. Thus, though the United States has a "minimum wage," it does not apply to agricultural workers, many of whom come from the English-speaking Caribbean and are permitted to enter the country temporarily only for the purpose of work.

Indirect subsidies for sugar include government funding of the infrastructure for sugar production and processing. This includes, among other things, roads, power systems, water and sanitation systems, and waste disposal. The entire water management infrastructure that supports the Florida sugar cane industry, for example, was built with federal tax dollars. Finally, the tax policies of the nation-state are constantly being adjusted to ensure the maintenance of corporate profits and low prices. Thus in the 1950s the tax bill of corporations in the United States accounted for 39 percent of all federal tax income; by the 1990s the corporate tax bill had been cut to 19 percent.

These are only some of the hidden costs of one ingredient in a Twinkie. To arrive at a real cost, we would need to examine each of the other ingredients and then add the hidden costs of processing, packaging, delivery, and waste disposal. The energy and pollution costs of distribution alone would be considerable. In Europe and North America, a typical food item travels 1,600 kilometres before it reaches consumers' meal plates. A head of lettuce in the local supermarket has travelled an average of 1,900 kilometres from where it was grown. The shipment of foods, while sometimes necessary, is further encouraged by energy subsidies that allow North Americans to enjoy some of the lowest fuel prices in the world. Economists estimate that if tax subsidies, government program subsidies, and environmental damage were calculated and if other externalities of vehicle use were discontinued, the price of gasoline would be as high as $16.40 a gallon in the United States and about $4.00 a litre in Canada.

In brief, then, the nation-state develops tax laws, financial policies, environmental regulations, labour laws, and the like, that help corporations and consumers avoid paying the real costs of production and consumption. And besides all this, the nation-state maintains a standing army, ostensibly to protect us all from foreign invaders, but more realistically to guarantee the maintenance of foreign governments with policies that are friendly to businesses and multinational corporations. The costs of these measures are then passed on to future generations or to people in other countries in the form of low wages, a polluted environment, health risks, and the like. Yet this is, of course, what citizens want. Corporations look to nation-states to further their interests; to ensure this, they spend billions of dollars each year to elect office holders who are sympathetic to their interests. Consumers look to the nation-state to keep the prices of things (e.g., Twinkies and gasoline) within their reach. And workers expect the nation-state to enact policies to enhance job and wage growth. None of this would be possible without nation-states to enact and enforce rules and regulations that allow their citizens to pass on the real costs of things in the form of environmental damage, health risks, and poverty to people in other countries and to marginalized people in their own countries or to future generations.

EXERCISE 7.1

Calculating the Real Cost of Things

Each morning, most students begin their day by brushing their teeth, washing their face, and using the toilet facilities. Then, perhaps, they have a glass of orange juice and maybe a cup of coffee. But what are the hidden costs of these activities? That is, what sort of environmental, health, and economic costs are involved in these activities that we don't pay for directly?

Activity or Product   **Hidden Cost**
Brushing teeth:
Flushing the toilet:
Orange juice:
Coffee:

What Is the Role of the Nation-State in an Increasingly Neoliberalized Global Economy?

Nation-states are currently the political building blocks of the modern world. All individuals derive whatever political rights and privileges they enjoy from their nation–state. Each person is educated, is given or denied permission to travel, and is bound by the laws of his or her state. Yet some people, such as David Korten, claim that the nation-state is a thing of the past, that in an increasingly globalized world, national boundaries are no longer relevant. Millions of people migrate from their home countries in search of jobs, further blurring national boundaries. Around 2 percent of the world's population—120 million people—currently live and work in countries of which they are not citizens. Some say that new **transnational** institutions, such as transnational corporations and transnational treaty organizations like the WTO, are rapidly replacing nation-states. Is the nation-state a thing of the past?

The major candidate to replace the nation-state is the transnational corporation. Currently, half the richest institutional entities in the world are not nation-states, but transnational corporations. Walmart is the 24th-richest financial entity in the world, well ahead of Venezuela (26th), Saudi Arabia (29th), and Hong Kong (46th). Five petroleum companies (including Exxon Mobile and British Petroleum) are included in the top 50 (dstevenwhite.com/2011/08/14/the-top-175-global-economic-entities-2010). One of the reasons why nation-states emerged was to integrate national economies. However, the expansion of the modern global economy requires global, not just state, integration, and transnational corporations have not only a vested interest in expanding across national boundaries but also the power and financial resources to accomplish that end. One consequence of this development has been that corporate interests, as opposed to human interests, now dominate the policy agendas of nation-states and the international agencies they create, support, and control.

A good example of how international agencies have begun to "escape" nation-states' strictures involves the role of the World Trade Organization. The WTO was established in 1995 by international treaty. Its stated goal was to reduce trade barriers among its 140 member nations. Its proponents argued that when these barriers were reduced so that goods and services could flow freely across national boundaries, citizens of all countries would benefit.

But despite its apparently high-minded goals, the WTO has been the focus of mass public protests. In Seattle in 1999 and in Quebec City in 2001, thousands of protesters representing hundreds of labour, environmental, and human rights groups organized to demonstrate against the inequalities resulting from world trade. What were these protests against the WTO all about? Why does it matter that you know? And what does this have to do with anthropology?

Basically, anti-WTO protesters are demanding to know how an unelected body that makes decisions behind closed doors with no provisions for appeal can force sovereign countries to dismantle environmental, health, labour, and social laws that it deems to be "unfair restrictions on trade."

In brief, when a member country, generally acting for a domestic corporation, feels that the laws and/or regulations of another country constitute an unfair restriction of trade, it can ask the WTO to investigate. If a WTO panel, appointed by the member countries, agrees with the claim, the complaining country can then impose trade taxes and tariffs on goods imported from the offending country. See Table 7.1.

---

transnational
Involving more than one nation-state; reaching beyond or transcending national boundaries.

TABLE 7.1 PROPOSED BENEFITS OF THE WORLD TRADE ORGANIZATION

The system helps promote peace
Disputes between nations are handled constructively
Free trade rules make life easier for all
Freer trade cuts the costs of living
Free trade provides more choice of products and qualities
Free trade raises incomes
Free trade stimulates economic growth
The basic principles of free trade make life more efficient
Governments are shielded from lobbying
The system encourages good government

Source: See http://www.wto.org/english/thewto_e/10ben_e/10b00_e.htm. Reproduced courtesy of The World Trade Organization.

An example follows. Most European countries impose a tariff on bananas imported from Central America but not on those from some Caribbean countries, such as Jamaica, Dominica, St. Lucia, and St. Vincent. This policy favours Caribbean countries, since it makes Central American bananas more expensive for European consumers. The rationale for these tariffs dates back to when Caribbean countries were colonial outposts of Britain and France.

The United States appealed the European tariff on Central American bananas to the WTO, claiming it constituted an unfair trade barrier. The Americans acted largely because most Central American banana plantations are owned by U.S. corporations, some of which had contributed considerable amounts of money to the election campaigns of both Republican and Democratic politicians. The WTO ruled that the tariffs imposed by European countries on Central American bananas did, in fact, constitute an unfair restriction on trade. The WTO does not have the power to force countries to change their trade rules; but it can permit offended countries (the United States in this case) to impose tariffs on selected goods of offending countries. The WTO permitted the United States to impose import tariffs on such things as British cashmere and French cheeses, thus increasing their costs to American consumers and likely reducing the profits of British wool producers and French cheese makers.

Some of the WTO's rulings have deeply disturbed health, labour, and environmental advocates, because the WTO can pressure countries to change their health, labour, or environmental laws if its dispute panel rules that these laws constitute an unfair restriction on trade. For example, when a country has banned a product from another country because of health risks, the country in which the product was manufactured or produced can accuse the banning country of creating an unfair barrier to trade. The country passing the law then has to prove to the WTO panel that the ban was "scientifically based." If it cannot, then trade sanctions and penalties can be applied to the banning country. A prominent case here involves the European ban on hormone-treated beef produced in the United States and Canada. Injecting hormones into beef cattle is legal in the United States and Canada. However, some research suggests that treated beef may be harmful. Europeans are especially sensitive to health threats in meat because of the emergence of mad cow disease (Creutzfeldt-Jakob disease) in Great Britain, which is spread by eating meat from animals that had been fed infected feed, the subsequent ban on British beef by European countries, and fears about cancer-causing dioxins in meat and egg products in Belgium.

The United States, at the request of its ranchers and beef processors, brought the case to the WTO, claiming that the ban on beef was an "unfair restraint of trade" and that there was no clear scientific evidence of health risks. The WTO ruled in favour of the U.S. corporations, thus forcing European consumers to accept American hormone-treated beef or accept restrictive tariffs on selected European products sold in the United States. So far, Europe has refused to overturn the ban, and the United States has been permitted to impose tariffs on selected European imports, including truffles from Italy.

Disputes such as these threaten the "precautionary principle," which states that if a product or process poses risks to health or the environment, scientific certainty is not necessary in order for other countries to prohibit or control that product or process. The Europeans reason that while there is no absolute scientific proof that hormone-treated beef is harmful to health, enough research has been done to raise real health concerns. Yet the WTO has rejected the precautionary principle in the case of North American beef, ruling that the Europeans must

either let it in or allow Canada and the United States to impose penalties on European products.

Thus, some critics claim, "free trade" has less to do with trade and with helping citizens of WTO countries than it does with allowing global corporations to force nation-states to change or erase environmental, health, and social regulations that interfere with their business. Critics claim that international agencies are being controlled and manipulated by corporate powers that determine not only what we buy but also the conditions under which our goods are produced and how they are distributed.

Globalization, Free Trade, and the Canadian Garment Industry

An ethnographic approach to studying the Canadian garment industry can yield insights into the local, everyday effects of economic globalization and international trade. First, recall the example at the beginning of this chapter, of Pietra Rivoli's T-shirt—purchased in Florida, made from cotton grown in Texas, but spun into cloth and assembled in China. One important chapter in the biography of this particular commodity is the one about the garment workers. The young women working in the Chinese factories visited by Rivoli were happy to have the work. However terrible the conditions in the factories, they told her, "it sure beats work on the farm." Roxana Ng (2002) has done similar research on the Canadian garment industry. Her findings with respect to the effects of free trade have led her to ask, "Freedom for whom?" From the perspective of Canadian garment workers, longer hours, lower wages, and job loss have been the concrete, everyday results of the neoliberalization and restructuring of the garment industry under free trade. The industry has always relied on low wages to be competitive and has always used immigrants as a pool of inexpensive labour; 50 percent of workers in the garment industry are immigrants, and 76 percent are women (Ng 2002, 75). Since the mid-1990s, control within the garment industry has shifted away from manufacturers, first towards large retail chains such as the Hudson's Bay Company, but increasingly towards transnational retail chains such as Walmart. At the same time that control over the industry has been centralized, production has become fragmented. This fragmentation takes the form of subcontracting. According to Ng, manufacturers have responded to their loss of control by reducing plant sizes and sending work to subcontractors or "jobbers," who increasingly are using home workers or sweatshop operations to maximize their profit margins and reduce their operating costs (2002, 77).

The implementation in 1993 of the North American Free Trade Agreement (NAFTA), which enabled the movement of production and goods more freely between the United States, Canada, and Mexico, also played a major role in the restructuring of the garment industry. Canadian companies such as Gildan, the largest T-shirt manufacturer in Quebec, have since opened plants in Mexico (and throughout the Caribbean). Wages are much lower than Canadian wages, and when labour costs go down, these companies' profits go up. Unfortunately, the direct result in Canada has been job losses, the depressing of wages, and deteriorating working conditions. One garment worker that Ng interviewed demonstrated the unpredictability of wages in this sector:

The lowest salary I earned was about $3 per hour, with the same employers I'm now working. [I asked why she didn't complain about the low rate]. I didn't say anything at the beginning. I dared not. But now I start to talk to them about this. This kind of pocket-cover sewing I'm doing now also requires me to cut certain fabric before I can start sewing. But the employers don't count the cutting time. I told the employers about this. But they said that almost every homeworker asks them for a raise. But they get no raise from their contractor who gives them the fabric. I don't know other homeworkers who also work for them. It would

be better if I know. Their factory is very small. They only have two workers in their factory, plus some part-timers, and the two owners.

The highest salary I earned was around $8 per hour. That was at the beginning when I first worked for these employers, when they let me know the piece rate before I sewed. But now they don't tell me the piece rate before I sew. (Ng 2007, 197)

One effect of economic globalization has been the movement of capital, production, and goods around the globe. There has been a corresponding movement of people around the world as well. People migrate in search of a better livelihood or because they have been displaced by the lack of economic and social opportunities in their home country. As mentioned earlier, the Canadian garment industry has always relied heavily on immigrant labour; to this, Ng adds that illegal migrants and undocumented workers now represent a larger and larger portion of Canada's garment sector workforce (necessarily, the official data are scarce). Undocumented garment workers—indeed, all undocumented workers—are among the most vulnerable participants in the global economy. The anti-sweatshop movement has increased awareness of the poor working conditions for garment workers in parts of the developing world. In 1999, students at the University of Toronto successfully lobbied for a Code of Conduct for Trademark Licensees. The code now ensures that suppliers of school-trademarked merchandise (including T-shirts) have met minimum employment standards. Gildan, one of the university's suppliers, was forced to directly address allegations of unethical treatment of its workers in the developing world (Ng 2002, 79). So it is important to note that free trade regulations in particular, and neoliberalism in general, have not only sent manufacturing jobs to the developing world, but also led to sweatshop conditions for Canadian workers. "In other words, globalization has created Third World working conditions within the geographical boundaries of the so-called First, or developed, world" (Ng 2007, 204).

EXERCISE 7.2

Biography of a Commodity

Take a look at the label on your shirt, T-shirt, sweatshirt, or whatever article of clothing you are wearing. What company made it? Where was it made? By whom? Try and find information online about clothing manufacturing practices (location of factories and labour policies) for your particular label.

QUESTION 7.3: WHAT IS THE RELATIONSHIP BETWEEN THE NATION-STATE AND IDENTITY UNDER GLOBALIZATION?

The integration and maintenance of the national economy is, then, one of the most important tasks facing the modern nation-state. But there are others. The state must be recognized by its citizens as the legitimate source of authority. And it must establish and uphold its own citizenship rules.

To achieve these ends, the state must create a nation out of groups who share (or who believe they share) a common culture, language, and heritage and who willingly identify themselves as members of the nation (review the discussion of the "imagined community" in Chapter 5). Given that almost all of the world's nation-states are composed of peoples with different cultures, languages, and heritages, creating a nation is no easy task. Somehow, these diverse entities must come to see themselves as sharing a common culture, tradition, and heritage; only when they do can state leaders claim to represent "the people," whoever they might be. Furthermore, when people can be persuaded to identify themselves

as members of a common political entity, they more easily accept integration into the national economy—the same wages, the same currency, and the same goods.

But how does one go about constructing a national identity? This involves creating the *Other*—that is, persons or groups who, having been somehow excluded from or pushed to the margins of the nation-state, accent those persons or groups who are more legitimate. The Others may be citizens of rival countries who are thought to embody characteristics that are mocked or feared by members of the nation-state. Thus for centuries the British could pride themselves on not being Irish or French, and Canadians could take pride in not being "American" (citizens of the United States). Colonial empires established by the Germans, French, Dutch, and British substantiated each of those countries' claims that God or providence had chosen them to rule over "inferior" peoples. In Canada, as in many other nation-states, we maintain our sense of "nationhood" by drawing boundaries and by making Others of migrants who enter the country, legally or illegally, to work.

The Other may be constructed out of largely arbitrary criteria, including physical characteristics, religion, or language. In Canada, for example, the Meech Lake Accord, a constitutional amendment that was debated in 1990, attempted to make English and French the only "official languages" of the nation-state, thereby implying that anyone who did not speak one of those languages did not quite belong. The accord was vigorously challenged and defeated by First Nations leaders, including Elijah Harper, a member of the provincial legislature in Manitoba, who argued that the denial of First Nations languages was a denial of Aboriginal existence. People who are immigrants, refugees, or non-Christian, or people whose skin is a darker colour, often experience negative reactions from those who claim to be "authentic Canadians." In this way, Canadians heighten their sense of exclusivity; by creating boundaries, they more clearly define for themselves their membership in the nation-state.

Political scientists, anthropologists, and political philosophers have generally assumed that membership in the state is voluntary and contractual. In exchange for protection against enemies and the enforcement of rules of behaviour, the idea goes, citizens agree to cede to the state the power to use force. Yet the idea that citizens make voluntary contracts with the state is not entirely true. Rather, people are born into nation-states much as they are born into their families; they assume the citizenship of one or both of their parents.

Another way to obtain citizenship in a nation-state is through immigration, which is a prime location for policies of racism. Canada has a long history of immigration policies based on race and ethnicity. Examples include the special head taxes imposed on Chinese immigrants between 1885 and 1923, the setting of quotas for different "racial" groups, and the refusal to allow Jewish refugees into Canada during the Second World War. During the decades when Canada was trying to populate its territory, British and American immigrants were actively recruited, northern Europeans were welcome, and other Europeans were accepted if they were the only ones available. "Peoples of colour," such as Chinese, East Indians, and blacks were the least welcome. However, the Canadian state found ways to admit Chinese workers when labour was needed to build the Canadian Pacific Railway; and in the 1970s, a program was written into the Immigration Act to allow non-Canadians into Canada on a temporary basis as agricultural workers and domestics. For example, the Foreign Agricultural Resource Management Services (FARMS) was created to allow Ontario growers to import workers from Mexico and various Caribbean countries to work on Ontario farms during planting and harvest. In 1967, Canada introduced the "point system," based on a match between the country's labour needs and applicants' education and skills, to accommodate a growing need for skilled workers from outside its borders.

In the same way that the nation-state creates membership rules, it creates rules for categorizing people. In the case of "race," the nation-state again uses notions of birth tempered by geography. According to Statistics Canada, there are three "races" in Canada: "visible minorities," Aboriginal peoples, and Caucasians or "whites." "Visible minorities" include the following: West Asian, South Asian, Chinese, Filipino, Southeast Asian, Arab, and Black. These classifications group people in very strange ways: Filipino is based on a specific nationality, whereas others are based on geographical region; "Black" is based completely on skin colour, with no geographical specification. Besides being imprecise, these classifications create ready-made target groups for hatred, as people of "Arab" descent found after the 9/11 attacks on New York City in 2001. Police in Toronto reported an increase in hate crimes from 1 in 2000 to 121 in 2001. Police in Ottawa, Montreal, and Calgary reported similar increases.

Nation-states carefully define the places occupied by various groups they contain. Through these definitions, they clearly privilege some groups over others and some individuals over others. One of the ways this is done is by creating official accounts of history. As Eva Mackey (1999, 23) argues, "nationalism often depends upon mythological narratives of a unified nation moving progressively through time—a continuum beginning with a glorious past leading to the present and then onward to an even better future. These mythical stories ensure that specific versions of history are highlighted, versions that reaffirm the particular characteristics ascribed to the nation" (1999, 23).

In Canada, that "glorious past" was filled with "nature," and First Nations people were part of the natural landscape. In settler narratives about the creation of the Canadian nation, Aboriginal peoples play the role of helpful "children" who join with the "adult" Euro-Canadians in bringing prosperity to the land. While Canadians pride themselves on being tolerant of ethnic differences, these differences are very carefully managed through the

GLOBALIZATION, NEOLIBERALISM, AND THE NATION-STATE

policy of **multiculturalism**, defined by Fleras and Elliot as an official policy that "involves a process of engaging diversity as different yet equal" (2002, 16). Prime Minister Pierre Elliott Trudeau announced Canada's multicultural policy on 8 October 1971. However, multiculturalism has not been accepted by all Canadians. Himani Bannerji (2000, 44) argues that its ultimate purpose was to sidestep the real issues that were becoming more and more obvious among many new Canadians, such as poverty, unemployment, and racism. According to Eva Mackey, Canadian multicultural policy has not lived up to its promises. It has produced a core of "Canadian Canadians," with tiny segments of ethnic cultures that contribute to the value of the core. "Ordinary Canadians" are the *unmarked* category of the population, the ones who set the standards from which ethnic groups differ. The history that children read in Canadian public schools describes Canada as much kinder to its First Nations peoples than the United States was to its Native population, but even in this gentle version of history, "real Canadians are, by definition, not 'Native' or not from those 'other cultures'" (1999, 89). Furthermore, the meaning of "culture" changes within the policy of multiculturalism. Culture becomes merely a collection of fragments, such as "folklore, food, dancing, music, and customs," when it is used to refer to ethnic groups, whereas Canadian national culture is "conceived of as a whole, entire, way of life" (1999, 90). The Multiculturalism Act was in part an attempt to defuse Quebec's threat to separate from Canada, yet Quebec has rejected the implication that it is just another "ethnic" group. Although Canada claims to have two founding nations, French and British, many of the French in Quebec believe they will never attain equality with the rest of Canada until they separate and form their own nation-state.

Education and the Nation-State

The creation and cultivation of inferior Others through such means as religion, racial classifications, and empire building and the marginalization of peoples based on their geographic origins is not in itself enough to build identity, loyalty, and devotion to the nation-state. A nation-state also requires institutions that integrate all of its members. For example, it needs to impose some sort of common language on its citizens; facilitate travel from one part of the state to another; establish national media to disseminate information from the state; and create a bureaucracy for collecting taxes and revenues, as well as a judicial system through which to maintain authority. It must establish a military and, perhaps most important, build a national educational system to train and socialize children to be "good citizens."

Ernest Gellner (1983) has suggested that the control of education is today even more important than the control of armed force. In order to regulate the national economy, a nation-state must build education systems that enable people to exchange communications with others in a common standardized language. People must be taught to deal with meanings rather than with things such as shovels or ploughs, and they must learn the complex processes through which buttons and other controls activate machines. In a complex industrial society, people cannot be taught in the family; they must be instructed by specialists operating within a national education system. Most important, students must be trained to identify themselves as members of a nation-state as well as to learn the identity of Others. They must be taught loyalty to their nation-state and be instructed in patriotism.

In Canada, the state sponsored residential schools in order to teach First Nations children how to become Canadians. In *Victims of Benevolence:*

> **multiculturalism**
> A term that Eva Mackey defines as a Canadian policy in which all hyphenated cultures, such as African-Canadians and French-Canadians, are described and celebrated as part of a "cultural mosaic." Contrast with the "cultural melting pot" image that is used in the United States.

Discipline and Death at the Williams Lake Indian Residential School, 1891–1920 (1992), Elizabeth Furniss tells the stories of two young boys who died as a result of their experiences in a residential school in British Columbia. One ran away and was found dead at the side of a road; the other committed suicide. Residential schools, which were operated by churches, lasted in Canada for about a century. First Nations children were removed from their homes and sent to these schools, where they were taught Christian beliefs and morality and were trained in agriculture, trades, and domestic skills. They were also taught that the beliefs of their elders and their parents were wrong and immoral. The underlying assumption of the residential schools was that First Nations peoples were inferior to Euro-Canadians and that they needed the guidance of Euro-Canadians in order to survive. Through the residential school system, First Nations children became wards of the Canadian state, and corporal punishment was used on children who made the mistake of reverting to their own languages or religious beliefs. Although some students made the best of their time in the schools, others actively resisted, and this resistance was typically interpreted as confirmation that Aboriginal peoples did not know what was best for them.

EXERCISE 7.3

Creating Citizens of the Nation-State

Students are experts on the role of education in the formation of the nation-state. They are expert because they are the ones most directly involved in the process of creating state citizens, or "patriots." Turn yourself momentarily into an anthropological fieldworker examining the role of education in creating the nation-state. What are some of the activities and the programs that contribute to your identifying with your nation-state?

The First Nations' Challenge to the Canadian State

Thus far we have discussed the nation-state only from the perspective of its power over the people who live within its territory. Tania Li, whose work we also discussed in Chapter 2, argues that development projects carried out by the state are not simply neutral acts of concern by the state for the less fortunate; they are also a way for the state to manage its population. The state typically defines the people it wants to bring under its control as "primitive," "backward," and in need of "proper" housing and education. The critical focus of Li's study was "the ways in which meanings and outcomes are negotiated, albeit within an uneven field of power" (1999, 297). She wanted to learn more about "categories that manifestly do not fit, plans that fail, and compliance withheld or withdrawn [that] expose the fragile nature not only of government agencies promoting this or that development program but of the very idea of 'the state' as knower, arbiter, and provider for 'the people'" (1999, 297).

Li's focus challenges those who would see the state as a source of unquestioned power and its citizens as mindless victims. People who become victims of the state's efforts to create a nation rarely accept their fate quietly. A good example of how marginalized peoples challenge the power of the state is happening right now in Canada.

Canada's history is laced with demonstrations of the power of the colonizers over the colonized. The first step was to define the indigenous people as Other in a way that allowed Europeans to take possession of the land, which they declared "empty" in the sense that no Europeans were living on it. Dara Culhane (1998) points out that from the first moment of contact, the position of the British colonizers was based on an assumed hierarchy wherein the British Crown asserted its will simply by declaring its sovereignty over First Nations peoples and land and then supported that assertion through armed force whenever necessary.

At first, the French and the British *needed* the Aboriginal peoples; it was they who trapped fur-bearing animals and transported their skins to the trading posts, which brought great wealth to the European traders. Also, the British and French recruited the First Nations peoples to fight their battles for them as they struggled to determine which European power would control Canada. Because they depended on Aboriginal peoples in these matters (and in others), the Europeans had to show them some respect, at least initially. The first treaties were signed in order to ensure peace and friendship between Aboriginal nations and Europeans. These early friendship treaties were between the French and the Mi'kmaq, Maliseets, Montagnaix-Naskapi, Huron, and Abenake; those same treaties were then transferred to the British under the Treaty of Utrecht in 1713. When Canada became a British colony, the Colonial Office issued the Royal Proclamation of 1763, which declared that Aboriginal lands could be surrendered only through a legal treaty signed by a representative of the Crown and a representative of the appropriate First Nation. After Confederation, "numbered treaties"—which focused on land far more than on friendship—were signed by the British and various First Nations. The meaning of these treaties is still being debated, and this has led to confrontations between First Nations and the Canadian state. (Also, some First Nations never had treaties at all; this is the case with the Lubicon Cree, discussed in Chapter 2.) Because the treaties were modelled more on agreements that First Nations had negotiated among themselves than on European models of legal contracts, the Aboriginal leaders who signed them did not believe they were surrendering their land or their rights; also, they expected the agreements to be renewed periodically through the exchange of gifts. From the viewpoint of the Colonial Office, the treaties were intended to protect the "primitive" Aboriginal peoples while they were being "civilized." From the viewpoint of the European settlers, the point was to get rid of the "obstacles" that were hindering progress. As the population of European settlers

grew and land became more important than people, the Canadian state began to deny the few promises it had made in the treaties.

First Nations have been refusing more and more often to surrender any more of their rights. When Clifford White and David Bob, members of the Saalequn First Nation in Nanaimo, British Columbia, went deer hunting in the spring of 1963, they were arrested and charged under the Game Act (passed by B.C. in 1960) for hunting out of season. White and Bob argued that they were exercising their Aboriginal right to hunt and fish on unoccupied Crown lands throughout the entire year, a right guaranteed in an 1853 treaty and protected by the Indian Act. The matter went to court and became the first modern Aboriginal rights case in B.C. A British Columbia court found White and Bob guilty; however, the Supreme Court of Canada overturned that verdict and supported the Aboriginal right to hunt and fish on unoccupied Crown lands. Legal tests for Aboriginal rights continue to come before the courts. Some of the most important have involved the Nisga'a, the James Bay Cree, and the Inuit of Nunavut.

In 1969, Frank Calder, a member of the Nisga'a Nation in B.C.'s Nass Valley, argued before the courts that his people had never signed a treaty surrendering Aboriginal title to their lands. In 2000, after years of struggle, the federal Parliament ratified a final agreement with the Nisga'a. The agreement-in-principle gave the Nisga'a 1,900 square kilometres of land, the right to self-government with the power to tax Nisga'a citizens, a Nisga'a court with jurisdiction over Nisga'a laws on Nisga'a lands, $190 million to be paid over a period of years, and the return of Nisga'a artifacts from Canadian museums.

The James Bay Cree have fought for years against the Quebec government and developers that want to build dams on Cree land (see Figure 7.1). By the time Harvey Feit began his work among the Cree in the 1960s, railway and road networks had already expanded into Cree territory and logging and mining had already been established. The position

FIGURE 7.1 MAP SHOWING APPROPRIATION OF CREE LAND FOR QUEBEC GOVERNMENT HYDROELECTRIC PROJECTS

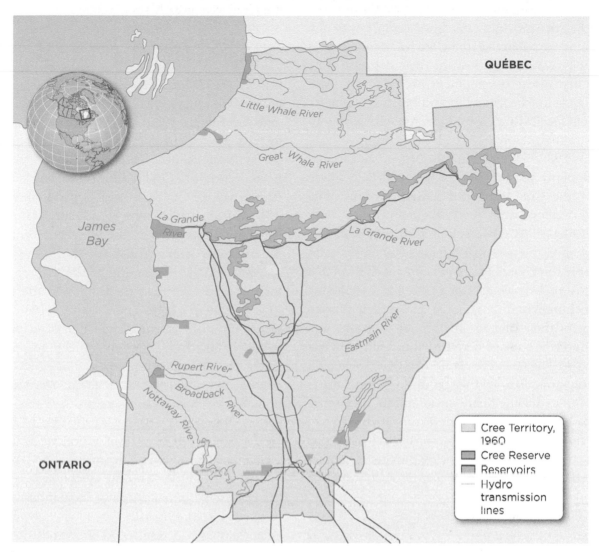

of the Quebec government was that the Cree didn't need all their land because hunting was no longer a viable way of making a living and any "rational" person would much rather have a steady job. When the Quebec government set out to build a series of hydroelectric dams in the region, it did not involve the Cree in the planning, nor did it make any attempt to assess the effects the project might have on the Cree. As soon as the government announced its plans, several young Cree leaders met and came to a consensus that the project would cause severe damage to their land and to the animals they

hunted. Joined by the Inuit of northern Quebec, who would also be affected by the project, the Cree initiated a legal injunction in 1972 to stop construction. The burden was now on the Cree to prove that they had a claim to the land and that the project would cause irreversible damage. They argued, among other things, that flooding the wetlands would destroy the habitat of many of the species of animals they hunted. The government argued that the Cree no longer lived primarily off the land; they had houses, clothing, and food that they bought from stores, and many had jobs. In

November 1973, Judge Malouf ruled that the Cree and Inuit people did have Aboriginal title to the land, that hunting was still very important to them, and that the province was "trespassing." Although the ruling was appealed, the Cree had demonstrated that they would hold firm in their demand to be consulted before development projects took place on their land. The James Bay and Northern Quebec Agreement (JNBQA) gave the Cree some power to back up their resolve.

In 1989, Hydro-Québec began the second phase of its project, on the Great Whale River. Again, the Cree went into action, only this time their strategy went beyond negotiations with the Quebec government. Cree representatives approached the potential buyers of Quebec hydro power in the United States and convinced them that Hydro-Québec would not make good economic or environmental sense. Cree spokesmen showed videos of their land to environmental groups and explained the damage that the hydroelectric project would do. The Cree even conducted their own polls to show politicians that voters in the United States favoured reducing their consumption of electric power over importing power from Quebec. When the New York State power company cancelled one of its contracts with Quebec, the province's premier conceded that the Great Whale project would be cancelled. While the conflict between the James Bay Cree and the Quebec government has not ended, the Cree have greatly strengthened their position.

Global Challenges to the State

Canada's First Nations are not the only marginalized people who have challenged the power of the state. In March 1990, the Huaorani of Ecuador formed an organization called the Organizacion de las Nacionalidades Huaorani de la Amazonia Ecuatoriana, or ONHAE, to challenge Texaco, Petroecuador, Unocal, Petro-Canada, and other oil companies that were conducting large-scale exploration projects in the Amazon. When the oil companies built roads into the forest, settlers followed and began clearing the land in preparation for agriculture. Tourists then followed the settlers. One of the first steps taken by ONHAE was to secure title to Huaorani lands. The main problem in this was that the government retained all rights to subsurface minerals. The government immediately divided the Huaorani territory into numbered "blocks" and auctioned them off to the oil companies. Although ONHAE has signed contracts permitting oil exploration, it has secured a Huaorani voice in negotiations.

Then in January 2000, the Huaorani joined with the powerful Confederation of Indigenous Nations of Ecuador (CONAIE) to block government cutbacks that had resulted in thousands of people losing their jobs and in an increase of 400 percent in the price of water. When the government tried to repress the resistance, CONAIE and other protesters blocked the roads to the capital city, Quito, and seized the Congress, proclaiming a new government. Without support from the urban labour movement, however, the protest came to an end. Then in early July of 2000, joined by labour unions and community organizations, the protesters closed the international airport, the banks, and government offices for two days. Clearly, when indigenous peoples and urban workers join together, the state must pay attention.

Grand Chief Stan Beardy and Chief Glenn Nolan of Missanabie Cree First Nations with Treaty No. 9 Scroll.

Source: Jenna Young/Nishnawbe Aski Nation

In 1999, the government of Bolivia sold its water system in its second-largest city, Cochabamba, to Bechtel Enterprises, based in San Francisco. The price of water immediately rose by 100 percent, and the "water war" began. Indigenous groups joined with Bolivia's Federation of Workers and began to block the streets and hold public meetings to plan strategy. The protesters set 4 April as the date by which the government had to cancel the sale. The government held out until April 10, but finally had to admit defeat.

Ronald Niezen (2003) examines the concept of "Indigenism," a term he uses to "document the international movement that aspires to promote and protect the rights of the world's first peoples." Indigenous peoples such as the Cree and the Huaorani are part of a much larger phenomenon that includes indigenous peoples everywhere who are pursuing the right of self-determination through human rights standards. For most indigenous peoples, this includes a rejection of state legal systems but not necessarily a rejection of the law, as the Nisga'a and Cree examples show.

QUESTION 7.4: WHAT ARE THE CULTURAL EFFECTS OF GLOBALIZATION?

Globalization is having a variety of cultural impacts, both positive and negative. The transnational flow of ideas, commodities, and images can help groups cultivate a sense of collective identity. Some commentators worry that globalization will challenge and perhaps even destroy the autonomy of nation-states and that it will homogenize the world's cultures. There is a pervasive worry, for example, that companies like McDonald's and Starbucks will destroy local food cultures. These fears are not completely unfounded; however, many globalization theorists point out that such fears are essentialist and that they fail to take into account the unique ways in which cultures adapt to and transform new ideas.

Nuxalk Identity in an Age of Globalization

The Nuxalk are a First Nations community in the Bella Coola Valley in central B.C. Nuxalk artists are renowned within their communities—and indeed, internationally—for their intricately carved and painted spirit masks, as well as for other forms of art: totem poles, paintings, jewellery, murals, and so on. Canadian anthropologist Jennifer Kramer (2007) conducted participant observation and interviews with Nuxalk artists, elders, and art school representatives. She also spent time in museums and galleries in Vancouver talking to art

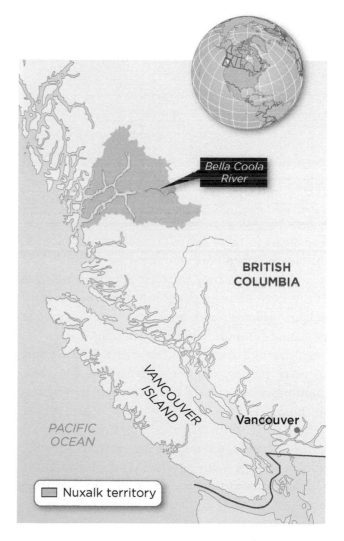

Nuxalk mask.

dealers and curators about the display and sale of Nuxalk art to national and international audiences. She also talked to Nuxalk individuals with the goal of understanding how they felt about seeing their art displayed in national and international museums and art galleries, and how they interpreted the increasing commodification of their art.

More and more Nuxalk artists, in an effort to earn money for themselves and for their community, are putting images of spiritual figures on mugs, T-shirts, jewellery, and other tourist commodities. Others are selling their art to art dealers. Kramer set out to understand how the Nuxalk engage with the forces of globalization, which include tourism as well as increasing exposure for their art on the Internet and in the international art market.

When she entered the remote Bella Coola Valley by car for the first time to conduct fieldwork, Kramer was struck by the number of dangerous mountain switchbacks that face motorists. Often inaccessible in winter except via ferry or boat, the Nuxalk have historically been proud of their geographic isolation from mainstream Canadian society. Throughout her research, Kramer adopted the metaphor of "switchbacks" to explain how her Nuxalk informants felt about the commodification and global flow of Nuxalk art. She argues that most Nuxalk oscillate between feelings of theft and those of pride. Many people felt that they were "selling out": that the commodification of their culture and heritage was devaluing local meanings and interpretations of art. Many were opposed to seeing important Nuxalk spiritual figures on mugs or T-shirts and were upset that most Westerners interpreted the images differently. Tourists, for instance, often buy T-shirts as souvenirs and as proof to friends and family that "I was there," or for their aesthetic value. Because tourists and art dealers map new meanings onto Nuxalk art and have different interpretations of its "value," many Nuxalk feel that the global flow of their art has resulted in a loss of cultural heritage.

Yet many of the same Nuxalk individuals that Kramer spoke with who were upset about the potential loss of Nuxalk traditions were also filled with pride at seeing their art displayed in national and international museums, and with the level of interest expressed by tourists. Many felt that the global flow of their art outside their small community was a form of external validation for their culture as a whole. A sense of Nuxalk national identity was being cultivated through the flow and positive international consumption of their art.

Figure Skating, Globalization, and Canadian Identity

The ambiguous cultural effects of globalization can also be explored in the context of elite, high-performance sport. Karen McGarry (2005) conducts fieldwork among national and Olympic-level

Canadian figure skater Kurt Browning.

Canadian figure skaters, coaches, choreographers, journalists, corporate sponsors, and others involved in the production of Canadian figure skating. In Canada, figure skating is the second-ranked sport behind hockey in terms of television sponsorship and spectatorship. One of the reasons for its popularity is that Canada has a long history of producing top world- and Olympic-level figure skaters, especially in the men's division. Skaters like Kurt Browning, Elvis Stojko, and Jamie Salé and David Pelletier, to name a few, have become household names. These celebrity figures derive much of their power as "national symbols" not simply by winning medals, but by circulating their bodies in international arenas of influence.

Canada has historically had an ambivalent relationship with the United States. On the one hand, Canadians live in a world saturated with American popular culture, from television shows to American-based retail outlets, food chains, and other cultural phenomena. Canada's geographical and social proximity to America has resulted in a

pervasive fear of American economic and cultural influences, or what Kieran Keohane (1998) refers to as a "theft of national enjoyment." In other words, Canadians construct themselves as victims in relation to America. Economically, we see this in contemporary debates and concerns relating to American appropriation of natural resources such as oil, water, and lumber, and in concerns over the impact of NAFTA. Yet at the same time, Canadians yearn for the approval of Americans to evaluate their sense of self-worth as a nation on the international stage. So, for instance, Kurt Browning has become a symbol of "Canadianness" not simply because he won four world championships, but also because his image has been circulated in America—he has appeared in the United States on television shows, in magazines, and in ice shows and other pop culture venues. The positive international (especially American) reception and consumption of his image has boosted Canadians' national pride. The global flow of commodities (like Nuxalk art) and bodies (like athletes) provide countries like Canada with a means of constructing and promoting a sense of national identity.

Intersections of Nationalism and Economic and Cultural Globalization in Vanuatu

As the Nuxalk example suggests, tourism is an aspect of contemporary life in which the simultaneous impacts of economic and cultural globalization are most obvious. The recent growth of tourism has been staggering. In the mid-1990s around 7 percent of the world's entire workforce was employed in tourism, which generated $3.4 trillion for the world's economy.

Tourism is a relatively new phenomenon. Lofgren (2002, 5) describes it as a mode of consumption "based on the idea of leaving home and work in search of new experiences, pleasures, and leisure." To some extent, our society is obsessed with the need for "experiences." We constantly ask

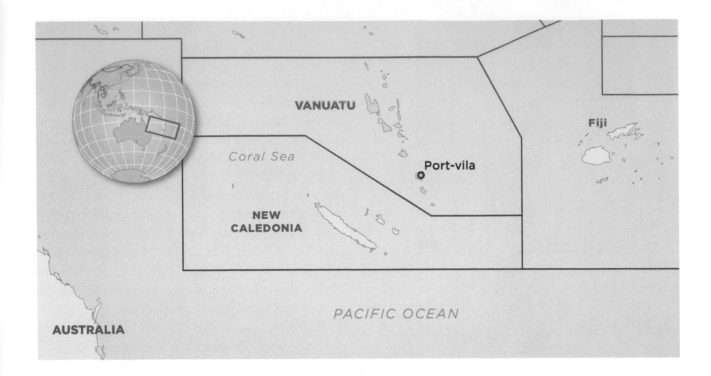

one another, "How was it? How did it feel?" We are also entranced by the thought of being "on holiday," especially as its opposite, being "at work," becomes more and more burdensome. We often display our experiences as tourists and convey our ability to consume other cultures by buying a souvenir T-shirt. Given what we have discussed earlier in this chapter about T-shirts as global commodities, the centrality of the T-shirt (and other inexpensive souvenirs) to the tourist experience begins to hint at the fact that tourism is more than simply a leisure practice: it is an important indicator that globalization is linking us all together economically and culturally. By examining the local impacts of the global tourist economy on Vanuatu, we can begin to understand some of the ambiguous—that is, simultaneously positive and detrimental—effects that global forces are having on local cultures.

Vanuatu (formerly the Anglo-French condominium of the New Hebrides) is an archipelago in the southwest Pacific. In terms of climate, geography, and culture, Vanuatu has all of the "assets" required of the ideal tropical tourist destination: dense rain forests, swaying palm trees,

warm turquoise seas, accessible coral reefs, and so-called "primitive" cultures. The tourism industry in Vanuatu has its roots in the 1960s, which the United Nations declared the "Decade of Development." During that decade, Vanuatu's first international resort, the French-owned Hotel Le Lagon, was built on a former plantation. Between 1970 and 1990, tourism arrivals by air grew from 5,000 to 25,000 per year (Douglas 1996, 216); today, around 7,000 tourists arrive by air each month, and every month another 15,000 tourists arrive by cruise ship for day visits. Tourism is the key economic sector in Vanuatu, accounting for 40 percent of the gross domestic product (GDP). Some observers suggest that tourism revenue is still insufficient to meet the needs of the growing population, especially as Vanuatu struggles to meet the 2015 Millennium Develop Goals set by the UN.

In its efforts to entice foreigners to visit, the Vanuatu Tourism Office has employed various slogans that draw from its imagined status as a land of idyllic, simple pleasures and the easy life: "The Untouched Paradise," "The Friendly Face of the Pacific," "Vanuatu: Discover What Matters." At the same time, many of the attractions and activities geared toward tourists highlight the "darker" aspects of traditional culture, such as cannibalism, tribal warfare, and sorcery. Tourists flow into Vanuatu with particular expectations about the local people and their culture. At the same time, ni-Vanuatu (the local name for indigenous citizens) have their own expectations about what tourists are like, as well as their own sense of national identity, which has been forged at least in part by encounters with foreigners.

If, as a tourist in Vanuatu, you want to purchase an "Untouched Paradise" T-shirt as a souvenir, you will likely do so at one of the market stalls on the seafront in Port Vila, the national capital. You will find a vast array of cheap T-shirts (made in and imported from China), but few if any of the women working in the stalls will be wearing T-shirts themselves. Rather, they will be wearing what they refer to as the "island dress," a long, loose, floral-patterned dress—similar to the Hawaiian *mumu*—which they consider to be both their "national dress" and the most culturally appropriate and modest clothing for women. Maggie Cummings conducted fieldwork in Vanuatu on gender, dress, and national identity and found that women—especially single, childless young women living in the capital—embody a range of ambivalent and contradictory sentiments about national pride, the commodification of culture for tourist consumption, and the global flow of goods and fashions. The island dress was first introduced in Vanuatu during the colonial period by British missionaries, who were scandalized by the scantily clad natives they were trying to convert. Wearing an island dress became a visible sign of one's conversion to Christianity—and to British gender norms, according to which women wore dresses while men wore the pants, both literally and figuratively. Most ni-Vanuatu today are devout Christians, and on achieving independence in 1980, ni-Vanuatu women took up the island dress with pride as a symbol of their uniquely Melanesian Christianity and of their difference from white foreigners. In this context, it makes sense that the island dress, as a symbol of cultural authenticity, would be the appropriate choice

The island dress is considered the "traditional" dress for women in Vanuatu, but many younger women prefer to wear shorts and T-shirts.

for women selling souvenirs to tourists, for whom consuming cultural authenticity is one of the most significant parts of the trip.

The young women Cummings worked with were too young to remember the struggle for independence. They acknowledged the symbolic significance of the island dress (and the importance of wearing it in tourist encounters), but they were also drawn to the kinds of clothing they saw tourist women wearing—T-shirts and shorts rather than skirts. However, young women who chose to wear shorts were often chastised and even fined by their elders, pastors, and chiefs for trying to look "like foreigners." Furthermore, chiefs often accused young women of turning their backs on tradition and destroying *kastom* (traditional culture) when they chose to wear even long, modest surf shorts. Cummings's *The Trouble with Trousers* (2008) highlights the ironies of ni-Vanuatu national identity in the context of increasing globalization. As Vanuatu attempts to increase visits (and revenues) from tourism, more and more ni-Vanuatu are moving to the capital, leaving behind—at least temporarily—their traditional subsistence horticultural livelihoods in search of wage labour in the tourist economy. Yet within the tourist industry, they must perform "ni-Vanuatu-ness" that is perceived as culturally authentic—including wearing the island dress, and sometimes grass skirts as well. However, as ni-Vanuatu women admire and appropriate tourist fashions for themselves (and the availability of cheap imports from China is what makes this possible), they are less and less inclined to wear the "authentic" island dress in their daily lives. One of Cummings's informants neatly summarized the ironies of trying to dress authentically in contemporary Vanuatu, ironies that have their origin in the uneven intercultural encounters in the context of decades of global contact and movement:

> When the missionaries came, they told us we were practically naked when we were wearing grass skirts, and that we had no shame. So we put on the island dress to show that we were good Christians, and now we wear it to show our respect for God and for our kastom. Now all these tourists, whose grandparents told our grandparents to cover up, they come and they flaunt themselves, half-naked on the beach in their bikinis and shorts. Meanwhile, we young women are told, now by our own elders, we have to cover up in the island dress to show our national pride!

Cultural policy in Vanuatu (created in part by a former head of the Vanuatu Cultural Centre, Ralph Reganvanu, a ni-Vanuatu with a degree in anthropology) demands that all foreign anthropologists create a product or provide a service that will benefit the nation. Cummings therefore worked with local fieldworkers (who were trained in ethnographic research skills by the Vanuatu Cultural Centre) to produce a video for local audiences about the dress conundrum. One intention of the video was to bridge the gap between chiefs and young women, one that seemed to be widening in the face of increased tourism and globalization. The Vanuatu Cultural Centre has created many important and innovative programs and policies based on ethnographic insights and collaborations with anthropologists (and historians and archaeologists). For instance, the Vanuatu National History Curriculum Project led to the publication of the three-volume *Histri Blong Yumi Long Vanuatu* (Lightner and Naupa, *Our History*, 2005), which aimed to provide a core high school history curriculum. One effect of the curriculum project, and related projects and policies, has been to ensure that young ni-Vanuatu are able to participate meaningfully in and contribute to the ongoing vibrancy and viability of *kastom* in a global world.

EXERCISE 7.4

Although the context and consequences of tourism and globalization are obviously very different in Vanuatu and Canada, we might find some similarities as well. For example, what similarities do you see between the case of the Nuxalt and that of the indigenous peoples of Vanuatu? Think, as well, about the various ways that different Canadian communities market themselves as tourist destinations. What similarities (and differences) do you see with the situation in Vanuatu?

CONCLUSIONS

How might we use an anthropological perspective on neoliberalism, economic globalization, and the nation-state outside of academia? What might we gain by taking an anthropological perspective on neoliberalism, globalization, and the nation-state? How can this perspective be put to use in the development of public policy? As we saw in section 7.4, one important contribution that anthropologists have made to globalization studies has been to extend the ethnographic focus not just to the economic impacts of globalization but also to the cultural ones. As a cultural force, globalization is far from uniformly negative and homogenizing; in fact, transnational flows of ideas, images, and commodities often *activate* and *animate* new local cultural meanings and practices. In the cases of Nuxalk art, Canadian elite figure skaters, and the tourism industry in Vanuatu, an anthropological perspective enables us to observe how collective identity can be reshaped in response to global forces. These ethnographic examples illustrate how many cultural groups cannot always be understood as passive victims of the economic or cultural effects of globalization. Indeed, people often actively engage with the forces of globalization in an effort to revitalize and reconstruct a sense of collective identity. In the process, as the Nuxalk example highlights, they often selectively appropriate elements of "global" culture to redefine a sense of self in the face of change. As anthropologists, we learn and experience firsthand how culture is both dynamic and shifting in the process. Furthermore, in Vanuatu, anthropological insights have been used to create public policy and educational programs that further mitigate the possible threat of cultural homogenization.

As we saw in section 7.2, nation-states exist in part to regulate and promote the growth of national economies. In fact, economic growth is very clearly the primary directive of market-based industrial societies such as the United States, Canada, and Japan. We measure our economic progress by the growth of GDP (i.e., the sum total of all goods and services transactions in a country in a given year). Failure to maintain GDP can have dire economic, social, and political consequences, including job losses, bank failures, and general political chaos.

So, governments devise economic policies to achieve economic growth. Often forgotten, however, is that market activities have effects that economic policy makers do not consider. We saw some of these effects in section 7.2, when we examined the real cost of a Twinkie and the externalities relating to the cost of sugar, which included underpaid labour and environmental pollution. Yet policy planners rarely consider these externalities. As we saw with the effects of NAFTA on the Canadian garment industry, the local and everyday effects of international trade agreements are unlikely to be taken into account when trade agreements are being drafted. Unfortunately, many organized forms of resistance to neoliberalism and globalization, including the G-20 protests discussed in the opening of this chapter, receive negative media portrayals. In the case of the Toronto G-20 summit, the protesters were homogenized and represented as young, rebellious, and violent. Images of smashed windows on storefronts and masked protesters became the norm within mainstream media outlets. In many ways, these representations overshadow the politics behind such acts of resistance.

One goal of the G-20 protesters in Toronto was to draw attention to the gaps between economic policies, market externalities, and public policies. A major contribution of anthropology in the area of public policy and planning is that it makes people aware of market externalities and of the need to craft policies to eliminate or at least minimize those externalities. As we saw in section 7.3, challenges to the state, both from within and from outside, are always possible, and an anthropological perspective can strengthen those challenges.

CRITICAL THINKING QUESTIONS

1. In section 7.1, we noted how neoliberalism manifests itself in the context of various nation-states. Think of three ways in which neoliberalism impacts Canadian politics, economics, and/or social life differently than in the United States.

2. From a student's perspective, can you think of examples of how principles of neoliberalism affect your education at university? How does it operate on your university or college campus?

3. Section 7.3 includes examples of the ways in which First Nations peoples have resisted state control. Think of two other cultural or ethnic groups in Canada that have resisted the state's homogenizing tendencies. How do they seek to define their sense of identity against that of "mainstream" Canadian society?

KEY TERMS:

economic systems (p. 202)
free trade (p. 203)
globalization (p. 200)
market externalities (p. 204)
multiculturalism (p. 214)
nation (p. 205)
nation–state (p. 205)
neoliberalism (p. 203)
transnational (p. 208)

THE CULTURAL CONSTRUCTION OF CONFLICT AND VIOLENCE

© Bilderbuch/Design Pics/Thinkstock

Canadian memorials to fallen soldiers, such as the Canadian National War Memorial, often evoke the sentiment "Lest We Forget." In the second half of the 20th century, Canada saw itself as a peacekeeper nation, striving to prevent or diminish violent conflict. However, as Richler notes, Canada has more recently become a "warrior nation," especially since it has taken on a combat role in Afghanistan. How do Canadians make sense of our ambivalent relationship with war?

Often it is illuminating to see how history puts on different disguises even as the underlying habits of a place are fundamentally unaltered. This is to say either that Canada today is a "warrior nation"—that the peacekeeping version of Canada was a fifty-year aberration and a public that believes otherwise genuinely has ignored Canada's long military history—or that the Canada with an innate disposition toward "soft power," "making a difference" and the sort of peacekeeping work that is now so disparaged is the underlying constant and the "warrior nation" is the fiction.

Noah Richler, What We Talk About When We Talk About War *(2012)*

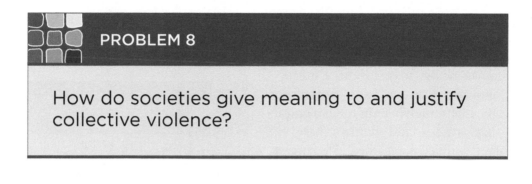

PROBLEM 8

How do societies give meaning to and justify collective violence?

INTRODUCTION

The Justification of Violent Conflict

When the Spaniards invaded the New World in the 16th century, they met fierce resistance from the Carib. A warlike people, the Carib inhabited the northeastern part of South America around what is now Venezuela and Guyana. The neighbours of the Carib recognized their ferocity by calling them "sons of the tiger's teeth." Moreover, the Carib were cannibals. To prepare for war, a Carib chief would hold a feast during which women urged the dancing warriors to be fierce and avenge their dead. The dancing was intended to encourage the tiger spirit, Kaikusi-yuma, to take possession of the warriors, and when they went to war, it was the spirit of Kaikusi-yuma that killed, not them. A warrior could rid himself of the possession only by tasting the blood and flesh of a dead enemy.

From our perspective, the acts of the invading Spanish, like the acts of the Carib, were horrific. The Spanish invaders murdered and enslaved thousands of indigenous people, and the Carib devoured human flesh. But both the Europeans and the Carib considered their acts to be moral and proper: the Spaniards justified their killing and enslavement as the work of God; the Carib defined their killing as the act of an animal possessing a human body. Both peoples constructed meanings for their acts that distanced them from the consequences of their violence. Although we may condemn these acts, we live in a world in which governments construct systems of meaning that allow them to plan and contemplate the use of weapons that are much more deadly than the clubs, spears, crossbows, and primitive firearms of the Carib and Spaniards—weapons capable of incinerating millions of people.

Violence, "a category in between peaceful disputing, and major planned warfare and fighting" (Stewart and Strathern 2002, 1), seems to be an intrinsic feature of human societies. In fact, it is difficult to find societies that do not sanction violence for one reason or another. But why is collective violence so universally sanctioned? Some suggest that human beings have an innate instinct toward aggression and that the roots of war and collective violence lie somewhere in the biological mechanisms that animals and humans have in common. Violent conflict is regarded as a part of human nature. Others reject this explanation as simplistic; collective violence, they say, is above all a cultural construction whose roots lie in the human mind, not in the genes. Although there may be some innate aggressive impulse, human beings can choose whether they will give meaningful form to that impulse.

The fact that human beings construct systems of meaning to justify violent conflict and to distance themselves from its consequences suggests that it has little to do with a natural aggressive impulse. Acts of collective violence are rationalized as purposeful, noble, or inevitable, not as evidence of wanton cruelty. The problem is to discover how societies construct meanings for violent conflict that mask its consequences and that convince people it is right and proper.

To evaluate this issue, the first question to be addressed is how societies create a bias in favour of collective violence. That is, what kinds of meanings are constructed to encourage people to commit violence against others? Then, if there are societies without collective violence, how do they create a bias against it? If violent conflict is not natural and inevitable but culturally constructed, it may

be possible to learn from societies in which there is little if any violence. The question is, are there significant social, economic, or political differences between violent and peaceful societies? And also, what is the relationship between violence and the nation-state? Since collective violence is sanctioned in North American societies, it is instructive to ask how we have created a bias toward violent conflict and constructed meanings that allow us to contemplate, plan for, and pursue the destruction of millions of people in other nations. Finally, we will explore the potential pitfalls and possible insights to be gained by conducting participant observation of, and during, violent conflicts.

QUESTIONS

8.1 How do societies create a bias in favour of collective violence?

8.2 How do societies create a bias *against* violent conflict?

8.3 What are the economic, political, and social differences between peaceful and violent societies?

8.4 What is the relationship between violence and the nation-state?

8.5 How is it possible to justify the construction of weapons of mass destruction?

8.6 How do anthropologists do fieldwork in the midst of violent conflict?

QUESTION 8.1: HOW DO SOCIETIES CREATE A BIAS IN FAVOUR OF COLLECTIVE VIOLENCE?

Horses, Rank, and Warfare Among the Kiowa

One way societies create a bias toward collective violence is by rewarding it. Among the Native

Americans of the western plains, for example, raiding other groups for horses was a means by which a man gained status. Horses symbolized wealth, and in many groups a man's importance was measured by the number of horses he owned and gave to others as gifts.

Horses are not indigenous to North America; they were brought to the continent by the Spaniards in the 1500s. Native American groups such as the Kiowa captured some horses and acquired others in trade with the Spaniards. The Kiowa also obtained horses by attacking other Native American groups with horse-raiding parties of as many as thirty men. The objective of these raids was to secure as many of the enemy's horses as possible and, as well, to demonstrate bravery. Among the Kiowa, rank was determined in two ways: by the number of horses a man possessed and by the honours accruing to him in warfare.

Kiowa society was divided into four ranks or grades. In the top rank were *ongop*, men who were generous, who held considerable wealth, and, most important, who had distinguished themselves in war.

In the second rank were *ondeigupa*, men who had property (especially horses), who were generous, but who had not yet distinguished themselves in war. The lower ranks of Kiowa society were occupied by *keen* or *dupom*, people who were poor, propertyless, or helpless. To rise in status, a young Kiowa male needed to acquire a horse. Often he began his climb through the ranks of Kiowa society by borrowing a horse from a kinsperson to go on a raid, hoping to repay the loan with another horse he had captured. With a horse of his own, he could participate in more raids, gradually obtaining enough horses to rise to the rank of *ondeigupa*, or, as the Kiowa put it, "rise out of the bush of *keen*." Several years of raiding might bring him twenty or thirty horses, at which point people would begin speaking of him with respect.

To rise to the top rank of *ongop*, however, also required the accumulation of honours won in war. The Kiowa had a very elaborate system of battle honours divided into three groups of brave deeds, with group I being the most honored (see Table 8.1). Counting first coup, for example,

TABLE 8.1   KIOWA RANKING AND HONOURS

Group I	Group II	Group III
Counting first coup	Killing an enemy	Dismounting, turning horse loose, and fighting on foot
Charging an enemy while the party is in retreat, thus covering the retreat	Counting second coup	Counting third and fourth coup
Rescuing a comrade while the party is retreating before the enemy	Receiving a wound in hand-to-hand combat	Serving as raid leader
Charging the leading man of the enemy alone before the parties have met		Success in stealing horses
		Efficiency in war camp life

Source: Information from Bernard Mishkin, *Rank and Warfare Among the Plains Indians* (Seattle: University of Washington Press, 1940).

involved charging the enemy alone and striking one of them with a stick. The number of feathers a man wore in his headdress was a measure of his heroic exploits.

Anthropologist Bernard Mishkin (1940) estimates that approximately 10 percent of the men would rise to the top rank of Kiowa society by obtaining a significant number of horses and accumulating sufficient battle honours. In this way, the Kiowa rewarded aggressive behaviour and bravery in battle.

Good Hosts Among Yanomamo

Another way societies create a bias in favour of collective violence is by making it a necessary means for protecting valuable resources. As we discussed in Chapter 1, a classic (but contentious) example is the Yanomamo of Venezuela. The Yanomamo live in villages of from 40 to 250 people and practise slash-and-burn (swidden) agriculture, living primarily on the crops they grow in their gardens.

Warfare between villages is endemic among the Yanomamo. Anthropologist Napoleon Chagnon, who has worked with them since 1964, reports that one village of 200 people was attacked twenty-five times, and that ten people were killed during a period of fifteen months, representing a loss of 5 percent of the village population. He estimates that 20 to 25 percent of all male deaths are the result of warfare.

For the Yanomamo, women and children are valuable resources. The men believe that to protect themselves and their resources, they must be fierce, and raiding another village is one way for them to demonstrate their ferocity. Raids may be conducted to avenge the death of a village member at the hands of an enemy village or as the result of an act of sorcery by an enemy. Raids may also be made to capture women or children. Violence can also take the form of inviting members of another village to a feast and—usually with the aid of allies from another village—killing the guests and abducting their women. Raiding by other villages forces them to move fairly frequently, and sometimes they take refuge from their enemies in the villages of their allies. This practice is risky, however, because host villages generally expect sexual access to the wives of their guests or expect unmarried female guests to marry men of their village. These expectations often lead to open hostilities between hosts and guests.

Expressions of ferocity may be directed among village members as well. For example, men often vent anger and demonstrate their ferocity by beating their wives. A man who accuses another of cowardice or of making excessive demands for goods or women may challenge his opponent to a chest-pounding duel in which they take turns hitting each other in the chest as hard as they can. The duel generally ends when one of the contestants is too injured to continue. Fights with clubs are another form of settling disputes between men, although these generally result in free-for-alls—which can be deadly.

In this environment, where each man strives to acquire women from others, it is necessary to

adopt an antagonistic stance toward others. This in turn encourages the development of what the Yanomamo call *waiteri* (ferocity). The *waiteri* complex, as Chagnon calls it, is evidenced in ways other than direct conflict. The Yanomamo express it in their origin myth, which tells how the original people were created from the blood of the moon, which had been shot with an arrow by beings who believed their children's souls were being devoured by the moon. The first Yanomamo born of the blood of the moon were exceptionally fierce and waged constant war on one another.

The Yanomamo also socialize male children to be aggressive and hostile. Boys are teased to strike tormentors and to bully girls. At one gathering of two villages attended by Chagnon, men were to satisfy their grievances against each other with a chest-pounding duel. Prior to the duel the men gathered all the boys between the ages of eight and fifteen and forced them to fight each other. At first, says Chagnon, the boys were reluctant and tried to run away, but their parents dragged them back and insisted that they hit each other. At the first blows the boys cried, but as the fight progressed, fear became rage, and they ended up pounding each other while they screamed and rolled in the dirt, to the cheers and admiration of their fathers.

Constructing Religious Justifications for Violence

Another way to justify violence is by framing it as a cosmic struggle between good and evil. Most modern religions contain sacred texts describing violent confrontations between the forces of good and the forces of evil. The Book of Revelation with its description of the forces of Satan and the ultimate battle between good and evil provides one of the most powerful (and most violent) metaphors of war and redemption in Western literature. As Elaine Pagels notes, the characterization of one's enemies as "Satanic" and of oneself as God's people has long been a formula for justifying hatred and mass slaughter.

So it should not be surprising that people use religious rhetoric to justify violent acts. But when devout adherents to Christianity, Judaism, Sikhism, Buddhism, or Islam commit violent acts in the name of God or some spiritual mission, they are often responding also to social, political, or economic grievances as well. Osama bin Laden sought the establishment of an Islamic caliphate, but he was also protesting the Israeli occupation of Palestinian territories, the stationing of U.S. troops in Saudi Arabia, and the American support for oppressive governments in the Middle East.

All major religions have their violent militants. On 20 March 1995, five members of the Aum Shinrikyo movement, all of whom had scientific training, walked into the Tokyo subway and, with sharpened umbrellas, punctured plastic bags filled

Aftermath of Tokyo subway Sarin attack in 1995.

© Noboru Hashimoto/Sygma/Corbis

with deadly sarin gas, killing 12 people and poisoning more than 5,500. The group's members explained to Mark Juegensmeyer that Aum Shinrikyo represented for them a critique of Japanese religion and the "hierarchical" Japanese social system. The movement was founded by Shoko Asahara based on the idea that a world catastrophe would occur, a Third World War or "Armageddon," in which the forces of good and evil would confront each other and members of Aum Shinrikyo would survive.

Asahara justified his acts by reference to Tibetan Buddhism and the concept of *phoa*. Instead of focusing on the effect that killing has on the killer's moral purity, this doctrine focuses on the one who is killed and on the merit that comes after death. According to Asahara, if a person is a scoundrel or is part of an evil social system, he or she is accumulating negative karmic debt. Killing such people represents a mercy killing that allows their souls to move to a higher plane than if they continued to exist in sin.

Juegensmeyer (2004) asks under what conditions people are likely to use religious justifications for violence. He suggests that by locating a struggle on a cosmic scale, aggressors elevate its importance beyond local concerns and, instead, invoke legendary battles between good and evil. Osama bin Laden justified violence by projecting the struggle as one between the forces of Islam and those trying to destroy it. The rhetoric of wars of good versus evil is even part of the U.S. political mainstream, with terms such as "axis of evil."

There is real power, suggests Juegensmeyer, in elevating a political conflict to a cosmic war. To live in a state of war, he writes,

> *is to live in a world in which individuals know who they are, why they have suffered, by whose hand they have been humiliated, and at what expense they have persevered. The concept of war provides cosmology, history, and eschatology and offers the reins of political control. Perhaps most important, it holds out the hope of victory and the means to achieve it. In the images of cosmic war this victorious triumph is a grand moment of social and personal transformation, transcending all worldly limitations. One does not easily abandon such expectations. To be without such images of war is almost to be without hope itself. (2000, 154–55)*

There is real power in elevating a political conflict to a cosmic war.

EXERCISE 8.1

Examples of group-sanctioned conflict are readily available in reports in newspapers and on the Internet. To examine the justifications for such conflict, follow a daily newspaper or news website for a couple of days and document the instances you find of group-sanctioned violence and the reasons attributed for it.

QUESTION 8.2: HOW DO SOCIETIES CREATE A BIAS *AGAINST* VIOLENT CONFLICT?

Anthropologist Thomas Gregor (1990) suggests that since war is so widespread in human societies, the task of the social scientist is not so much to explain war as to explain peace. Peaceful societies, he says, are difficult to find. By peaceful, he means a society that is not involved in internal collective violence and in which there is little interpersonal violence. A peaceful society has no special roles for warriors and places a positive value on nonaggressive behaviour and the peaceful resolution of conflict. Societies that have been characterized as relatively peaceful include the Ju/'hoansi, the Semai of Malaysia, and the Xinguano of the Amazon.

Characteristics of Peaceful Societies

Peaceful societies avoid conflicts over material resources through a strong emphasis on sharing and cooperation. It is understood that everyone in the group has a legitimate claim to what the group possesses. Among the Ju/'hoansi the person whose arrow kills an animal is considered to be the owner of the game, but he is obligated to distribute it. The Ju/'hoansi will share arrows with the understanding that if they kill an animal with an arrow given to them by someone else, they will give the owner the game to distribute. This also works to spread out the responsibility for meat sharing and the glory (and perhaps the hostility) that accompanies meat distribution.

The Semai of Malaysia are known for their nonaggressiveness and avoidance of physical conflict. The approximately 15,000 Semai live in hamlets of fewer than one hundred people each. Understanding Semai nonviolence, says anthropologist Clayton

Robarchek (1990), requires understanding the Semai notion of *pehunan*, a state of being in which a person is unsatisfied in regard to some need or want, such as food or sex. The Semai believe that to refuse a request and deny a person a need intensifies the danger to both the individual and the group; for that reason, the group is obligated to help. The idea of *pehunan* encompasses a depiction of the community as nurturant caregivers. Instead of saying that it is each person's obligation to meet his or her own needs, the Semai believe that it is the obligation of all members of the community to help and give nurturance to others. Thus, Semai values stress affiliation, mutual aid, and the belief that violence is not a viable option for settling disputes.

Another way that people in peaceful societies create a bias against violence is by condemning those who boast or who make claims that can be interpreted as a challenge to others. Among the Ju/'hoansi, for example, no one is praised for gathering food or making a kill, and people go out of their way to minimize their accomplishments. Those who make boastful claims are ridiculed. Anthropologist Richard Lee painfully learned this lesson himself when, to show his appreciation to the Ju/'hoansi for the help they had given him, he brought a fine ox to be slaughtered and distributed at a Christmas feast. The Ju/'hoansi, much to Lee's chagrin, ridiculed the ox, claiming it was thin and unappetizing. Lee later realized that they were acting toward him as they would have to one of their own. They were letting him know that he wasn't as important as the gift and the killing of the ox made him think he was.

Thomas Gregor says that villagers in the Xingu basin of the Amazon maintain harmony by purposely sanctioning village monopolies in the production of certain goods such as shell belts, stone axes, salt, cotton, fish spears, and ceramic pots. In this way, each village has something that other villages need. The villages therefore maintain good relations, since to alienate another village might deprive one's own village members of a desired good. Moreover, trade is positively valued in itself. When villagers are asked why they don't make the goods they need themselves, they reply that this might anger those who do make them. Or they may claim that they do not have the knowledge to produce the items, although when they are temporarily cut off from a supply, they seem to learn how to make or acquire them very quickly. Gregor says it is unlikely that any village could not produce the goods desired, since marriage between groups is common so that each village contains people with the skills of other villages.

The Xinguanos place a strong negative value on aggression and on things that symbolize aggression. Killing is wrong because it produces blood; even animal blood is considered defiling. Most game animals are considered inedible, and even fish must be well cooked so that there is no blood. The Xinguanos also hold strong negative stereotypes of aggressive groups. They consider non-Xingu Indians to be "wild Indians" who are violent; they beat their children, rape their women, and shoot arrows at white men's planes. The wild Indian has almost the status of an animal and represents everything a Xinguano doesn't want to be. When Xingu villages have been the object of aggression by others, they have defended themselves, but successful warriors take no trophies and are given no special honour. In fact, they have to take special

This Xinguano will ensure that his catch is well cooked, to ensure there is no blood.

© Ueslei Marcelino/Reuters

medicine to cleanse themselves of the defilement of the blood of their victims.

Peaceful societies also minimize violence and conflict through ceremony. The Ju/'hoansi believe that everyone has "medicine" or power. In the same way that nearby Bantu tribes have witchcraft and sorcery, and Europeans have pills and syringes, the Ju/'hoansi have *n/um*, a substance they say lies in the pit of the stomach. *N/um* has the capacity to keep people healthy and to help cure people who are sick. Most important, *n/um* can be transferred from someone who is acting as a healer to others through the medium of the trance dance, their most common ceremony. The idea of the dance is for a person to "heat up" his or her *n/um* by dancing; as the person dances, the *n/um* in the stomach is vaporized and travels up the spinal cord into the brain, which causes the dancer to go into a trance. The dancer then goes from person to person laying on hands and transferring power to those who are touched, thereby enabling them to ward off sickness and death. Anyone can be a healer among the Ju/'hoansi; in a lifetime, each person is likely to serve as a healer at one time or another.

The trance dance has meanings that go beyond the power to heal, however. Some Ju/'hoansi are thought to have special powers that allow them to see the ghosts of dead ancestors who hover around the fires, to see distant scenes, to see through things, and, in special cases, to change themselves into lions and stalk the veldt in search of human prey. Trance dances are most frequent when large numbers of people come together (from about once a month in small groups, up to four times a week in large camps) and during certain occasions such as the arrival of visitors to a camp, the presence of meat, or sickness. The congregation of large numbers of people, the presence of meat, and the arrival of new people are all occasions that in one way or another create the potential for interpersonal conflict. The fact that trance dances are more frequent during such times seems to indicate that they may serve to heal social conflict as well as individual maladies. By bringing people together in the ceremony, by the sharing of *n/um* and the ritual recognition of common threats, the trance dance unites people and symbolizes the relationship between group harmony and individual well-being.

In sum, peaceful societies create a bias against violence by sharing, by valuing nonaggressive behaviour, by building relations of dependence between individuals and groups, and by engaging in collective behaviours that promote harmony. They are not, of course, always successful, and even among some so-called peaceful societies, there is violence. Lee collected accounts of twenty-two homicides among Ju/'hoansi groups during a thirty-five-year period from 1920 to 1955, for example, but found little if any sanctioned group violence.

QUESTION 8.3: WHAT ARE THE ECONOMIC, POLITICAL, AND SOCIAL DIFFERENCES BETWEEN PEACEFUL AND VIOLENT SOCIETIES?

Thomas Hobbes, a 17th-century philosopher, proposed that human beings in their natural state, without government or laws, are driven by greed and the quest for gain. Without some common power to keep them in awe, Hobbes said, they live in a state of war, with every person against every other person. Here is one of the more famous passages from *Leviathan*, in which Hobbes describes his vision of life before civilization:

Whatsoever therefore is consequent to a time of warre, where every man is enemy to every man; the same is consequent to a time, wherein men live without other security, than what their own

strength and their own invention shall furnish them withall. In such a condition there is no place for Industry; because the fruit thereof is uncertain; and consequently no Culture of the Earth [agriculture]; no navigation, nor use of the commodities that may be imported by sea; no commodious Building; no Instruments of moving, and removing such things as require much force; no Knowledge of the face of the Earth; no account of Time; no Arts; no Letters; no Society; and which is worst of all, continual feare, and danger of violent death; And the life of man, solitary, poore, nasty, brutish, and short. (Hobbes 1881[1651], 94–96)

Hobbes saw human beings as having a natural inclination to be violent, an inclination that can be controlled only by some form of centralized authority. However, as anthropologists have discovered, societies with little formal government, such as the Ju/'hoansi and the Semai, are among the most peaceful in the world (as discussed earlier). Also, these peaceful societies are small in scale and make their living primarily by hunting and gathering or by swidden agriculture. Most are relatively isolated and lack formal mechanisms for resolving conflict once it begins. There are no courts, no police, no jails, and no formally sanctioned threats of violence, even against wrongdoers. Since there is little that people in these societies can do once violence begins, they go to great lengths to avoid it.

Had Hobbes known the Yanomamo, however, he might have found that his vision of a stateless society, "where every man is enemy to every man," had been verified. Their social and economic life closely resembles that of the Semai, and they live in virtually the same environment and are neighbours of the peaceful Xinguano. But Yanomamo society creates attitudes favouring collective violence in order to protect its women and children, which suggests that Hobbes may have been correct, at least in part. In this case, the lack of any centralized control or formal mechanisms for putting an end to conflict results in unrestrained violence rather than the avoidance of conflict.

The Need to Protect Resources

In societies without any form of centralized control and a bias toward collective violence, such as that of the Yanomamo, individuals must protect their own resources through force. Because the Yanomamo, for example, do not effectively control intravillage conflict, men of their own as well as other villages are constantly seeking to seduce one another's wives. Consequently, the men, individually or in groups, must build a reputation for fierceness in order to protect themselves and their families. Failure to control conflict and the need for men to build a reputation for aggressiveness in order to protect their resources combine to produce a society that places a positive value on violent behaviour.

The conditions that give rise to violent conflict among the Yanomamo are not unlike those that promote violence in street gangs in the United States. When Lincoln Keiser worked in the 1960s with the Vice Lords, a Chicago street gang (or "club," as they preferred to call themselves), he concluded that boys joined gangs because alone they could not protect themselves from shakedowns or safeguard their interests in girls. Where the Yanomamo encouraged *waiteri*—fierceness—the Vice Lords valued heart—a willingness to follow any suggestion regardless of personal risk. Where a Yanomamo demonstrated fierceness through chest-pounding duels, axe fights, and raids against enemy villages, members of street gangs in Chicago confirmed their heart in gang fights, or "gangbangs." Street gangs even formed alliances against other gangs, as do Yanomamo villages with each other. The similarities in the dynamics and values of violent conflict among Yanomamo and among street gangs in Canada and the United States illustrate how under certain conditions individuals form groups to protect themselves against other groups. To discourage attacks from others in the absence of protection from other agencies, these groups cultivate a reputation for violence.

The gang violence that Keiser observed in Chicago during the late 1960s has escalated since, and weapons more typical of armed soldiers in the military are now being used. Alex Kotlowitz, in *There Are No Children Here* (1991), reported how the Vice Lords, one of three gang factions in Chicago in the early 1990s, made use of an arsenal that included Uzis and grenades. The purpose was the same, although the stakes were higher. Drugs have become the major source of contention among Chicago gangs (the head of one Vice Lord faction grossed $50,000 to $100,000 a week). When drug wars erupt over territory, the violence reflects the increased stakes and more massive firepower. A couple of years ago, four members of the Vice Lords came upon a rival gang member in the lobby of a housing project and shot him five times with an Uzi, two sawed-off shotguns, and a .25-calibre automatic handgun to establish their dominance in the neighbourhood.

The social and political conditions that characterize the societies of the Vice Lords and

One reason for gang warfare may be a lack of other ways to protect valued resources or to settle disputes, but innocent bystanders may also be killed. Here, spokespeople for Toronto youth groups plead for help from municipal politicians to combat unchecked gang violence.

the Yanomamo are such that in each of them, individuals must mobilize and use force to protect or acquire desired resources. In neither case is there any effective centralized authority to guarantee the safety of resources or to stop violence once it begins. There is a centralized force in Chicago—the police—but they rarely intervene in gang violence, because they are unwilling or do not have the resources to do so, or because local residents are afraid or reluctant to report violence.

Creating the Conditions for Violence

Napoleon Chagnon characterized Yanomamo warfare as a "truly primitive cultural adaptation … before it was altered or destroyed by our culture." It was, he said, the normal state of affairs before it was suppressed by colonial governments. However, there is considerable evidence that Yanomamo warfare and aggression were less a product of their existence or nature than it was a consequence of Western contact.

Brian Ferguson (1995) maintains that the period of Chagnon's fieldwork (1964 to 1972), on which he based his best-selling ethnography, *The Fierce People* (1968), was one of the most turbulent in Yanomamo history. Violence and aggression, writes Ferguson, were a product of three major changes: (1) the presence of new outpost settlements of government agents, missionaries, and researchers; (2) competition for Western manufactured goods, particularly steel cutting tools, and (3) a breakdown of social relations brought about by epidemics and the depletion of game and other food resources.

The Yanomamo, Ferguson points out, had been in contact with outsiders for centuries. Europeans began raiding Yanomamo villages for slaves as early as the mid-17th century and continued to do so until around 1850. In the late 19th century, the rubber boom in the Amazon—a horrendous period for indigenous groups, who were forced to collect rubber under the threat of torture and death—brought the Yanomamo into increased contact and

conflict with other indigenous groups. After the Amazon rubber boom collapsed in the 1920s as a result of competition with Asian rubber plantations, the area in which the Yanomamo lived was relatively peaceful until the 1950s and 1960s, when influenza and measles epidemics swept the area, leaving only one-quarter of the children with both parents. But more disruptive yet was the presence of new, Western outposts.

The new outposts made available manufactured items desired by the Yanomamo (such as steel knives, machetes, aluminum pots, and shotguns). Steel cutting tools, for example, were ten times more efficient than the stone cutting tools they had long been using. Shotguns were effective both for hunting and for raiding. The Yanomamo could obtain these items in various ways. They could relocate their villages near the outposts, they could send trading parties on long voyages to get them, or they could raid other groups for them. But the greatest advantage went to what Ferguson called "anchor villages," those that relocated near outposts. The result was a hierarchy of settlements ranging from anchor villages whose members were able to monopolize the new desired goods to more isolated settlements whose members had fewer and lower quality goods.

Yanomamo in anchor settlements traded Western items to distant groups for local handicrafts such as cotton hammocks, spear points, or manioc flour. But trading parties were also targets of raids by groups desiring Western goods. To protect themselves and their monopoly on Western trade goods and to discourage raiding, Yanomamo groups found it advantageous to cultivate reputations for violence and aggression. A reputation for fierceness was also an advantage in negotiating for desired goods. Thus one man told of the number of people he had killed on raids just before demanding a machete.

Proximity to Western outposts incited violence in other ways. For example, once people relocated their village near an outpost settlement, they were reluctant to move. One way that small-scale, mobile societies such as the Yanomamo avoid conflict is by moving villages away from enemies when conflict is threatened. But since moving would mean giving up access to and a monopoly on Western goods, members of anchor villages were reluctant to move, and hence needed to protect themselves and the goods they obtained from Westerners. In addition, more permanent settlements quickly depleted game resources, resources that had been used in reciprocal exchanges with other people and groups. Thus sharing patterns, which as we noted ealier are crucial for maintaining peaceful relations, began to break down, leading to more conflict.

In these ways, deaths from disease and war disrupted traditional social relations, the depletion of game weakened traditional patterns of sharing and cooperation, and access to Western technology provided new sources of conflict. Furthermore, the new technology introduced a new way of ordering society and enhanced the ability of people in anchor villages to make war.

Access to Western goods also explains the aggressive attitudes of Yanomamo men to women. Traditionally, Yanomamo practised brideservice; grooms were obligated to work for their bride's family from one to four years. But families of grooms in anchor villages were able to substitute Western goods for brideservice, one result being a movement of wives to villages with greater access to Western goods. This, combined with the Yanomamo practice of female infanticide and polygamy, resulted in a shortage of and greater competition for females and the more frequent raiding of other villages for women. In addition, Yanomamo wives go to live in their husband's family villages, particularly where Western goods take the place of brideservice. The result is that women are removed from the protective influence of their families and are more likely to be victims of abuse.

In sum, many of the patterns of Yanomamo warfare, violence, and aggression cannot be understood without knowledge of their history of contact with Western society and the contact conditions that increased the likelihood of violence and war. Even the power of chiefs, whose feast giving played such an important role in Chagnon's descriptions of alliance formation and aggression, was largely a function of Western contact. Outsiders, following traditional customs, brought gifts to local leaders. But the gifts that outsiders brought were far more valuable. Thus Chagnon gave one chief a gift of twenty-five machetes, providing him with items that he could use to enhance his power. And thus, as Ferguson says, "if villages were not anchored to outposts but were able to move freely, if long-established marital alliances were not disturbed by massive mortality, if communal sharing of meat were still the norm, and, above all, if necessary technology were widely and equally available, my theoretical expectation is that there would be little collective violence among the Yanomami" (1992, 225).

Sexism and Violent Conflict

Another difference between peaceful and violent societies that has been suggested has to do with gender roles. Among the Ju/'hoansi, the Xinguano, and the Semai, men and women are relatively equal and there is little institutionalized violence against women. In contrast, the Yanomamo and the Vice Lords are characterized by male dominance, and both sanction violence against women. Several reasons have been advanced to support the link between sexist values and violent conflict. First, it is men that make war, though women may fill certain positions in the armed forces. While there have been societies in which women engage in armed combat, these instances are the exception rather than the rule. During the Sandinista rebellion in Nicaragua in the 1980s, women took an active role in combat, but they were banned from active combat once the Sandinistas gained power. Second, there is a strong cross-cultural link between patriarchy and violent conflict. After examining information on more than one thousand societies, William Tulio Divale and Marvin Harris (1976) concluded that the intensity of collective violence is significantly higher in societies characterized by a strong male bias—patrilocal residence, patrilineal descent, polygyny, postmarital sex restrictions on females, male secret societies, and men's houses. Finally, there is evidence that societies characterized by sexual violence against women tend to be more warlike and prone to collective violence. Peggy Sanday's 1981 study of 95 societies in which there was evidence of frequency of rape supports this conclusion. The question is, does a sexist ideology promote violent conflict, or does the incidence of violent conflict promote sexism?

Those who claim that sexism promotes violent conflict make that connection in various ways. Betty Reardon (1985) and Leslie Cagan (1983) suggest that societies that relegate women to an inferior position explicitly or implicitly sanction violence against women. Moreover, violence toward women serves as what they call a "primal" paradigm for violent warfare against other peoples. That is, once violence is allowed as a means of domination of one group such as women, it can serve as a model for dominance and violence against other groups.

For Peggy Sanday, and for many others, sexism and violent conflict both have their roots in competition over scarce resources. During periods in which resources are not scarce, males and females are valued equally. When there is an imbalance between food supply or distribution and needs, or when groups are competing for resources, males become of greater value, females become objects to be controlled, and sexual violence becomes one way that men demonstrate their dominance. Among cattle-herding people in East Africa, for example, raiding for cattle was common and sometimes led to violent conflict between groups. Violence was defined as a manly activity, leading East African societies to place great emphasis on masculinity and manliness. Manliness, however, was tested not only in battle but in male–female relations as well, for sex was a way of demonstrating strength.

In sum, factors such as a lack of centralized control, competition over scarce resources, private

EXERCISE 8.3

There is some suggestion of a link between militarism and competitive sports; that is, societies that are prone to collective violence are more likely to value games in which men aggressively compete against other men. How does this apply to North American societies? Which sports in North America most closely resemble or promote the values of militarism and war? Does the language of these sports reflect militaristic values? Do gender roles reflect these values? In what ways does Canada differ from the United States on these issues?

property, and sexism may lead societies to construct an ideological bias toward violence. Examining the effects of violent conflict to see if they produce changes in societies may provide insights into the factors that promote violent conflict.

QUESTION 8.4: WHAT IS THE RELATIONSHIP BETWEEN VIOLENCE AND THE NATION-STATE?

The Evolution of the Nation-State

Anthropologists suggest that violent conflict may encourage certain forms of political organization. Robert Carneiro argues, for example, that in the course of human history violent conflict has been the primary agent that has transformed human societies from small-scale, autonomous communities into vast, complex nation-states. He reasons that war has promoted the consolidation of isolated, politically autonomous villages into chiefdoms of united villages and into states. At first, war pits village against village, resulting in chiefdoms; then it pits chiefdom against chiefdom, resulting in states; then it pits state against state. War, he says, began as the effort to oust a rival from a territory but soon evolved into an effort to subjugate and control an enemy. As the process continued, warfare became the mechanism by which the number of political units in the world began to decline. Carneiro predicts that if the number of political states continues to decline as it has in the past, by the year 2300 there should be only a single world state.

The rise of the Zulu state in Africa illustrates Carneiro's theory. The Zulu state took form in southeastern Africa in the early 19th century. Prior to that time, the region was inhabited by small, sometimes warring groups. About 100,000 people lived in an area of about 80,000 square miles by practising agriculture and cattle herding. While there were separate entities that Westerners labelled tribes, the largest political unit was the clan. Warriors from these clans raided one another for cattle, but there was no conquest of land.

Warfare increased between 1775 and 1800 as the population of southeastern Africa increased. The strongest groups were those that could muster the most warriors and organize and discipline them effectively. The process of state formation whereby these separate groups combined into a larger political unit was begun by a leader of the Mtetwa tribe named Dingiswayo. He developed new ways to organize his troops and began to take control of the lands of those he defeated. After he conquered an area, he appointed a person from the head family of the group he had conquered to rule for him. Using new techniques of war and political control, he achieved dominance over a wide area. His reason for extending his control, according to one 19th-century writer, was to make peace among warring groups. Dingiswayo, it was said, "wished to do away with the incessant quarrels that occurred amongst the tribes, because no supreme head was over them to say who was right or who was wrong."

By the early 1800s, Dingiswayo had conquered and united some thirty different groups. He was aided by a young officer named Shaka Zulu, the son of the chief of the Zulu clan. When the Zulu chief died, Dingiswayo installed Shaka as the head of the clan, and when Dingiswayo was killed by a rival, Shaka took over the army and established his Zulus as the dominant clan. By 1822 Shaka had defeated every rival and was master of all of the present South African province of Kwa-Zulu Natal.

Violence and the Nation-State

As we discussed in Chapter 7, the symbolic barriers of excluded Others, infrastructure, and education are essential for nation building. The use of violence or the threat of armed force is another key instrument in creating and maintaining the nation-state. Killing is the ultimate tool of nation-states. In fact, some anthropologists, among them Pierre van den Berghe, Leo Kuper, and Carol Nagengast, view the nation-state as a genocidal or ethnocidal institution, one that conspires to kill or remove those citizens who fail to (or refuse to) conform to the dictates of the imposed national culture. "Ethnic cleansing" is not a phenomenon of the late 20th century. For example, the United States, through policies of either aggressive extermination or benign neglect, attempted to kill all indigenous peoples and assimilate those who remained. Between 1975 and 1979, the government of Cambodia, the Khmer Rouge, systematically murdered two million of its seven million citizens, and in 1994 the Rwandan state slaughtered 800,000 of its citizens. According to Carol Nagengast,

> the numbers of people worldwide subjected to the violence of their own states are staggering. More than a quarter of a million Kurds and Turks in Turkey have been beaten or tortured by the military, police, and prison guards since 1980; tens of thousands of indigenous people in Peru and Guatemala, street children in Brazil and Guatemala, Palestinians in Kuwait, Kurds in Iraq, and Muslim women and girls in Bosnia have been similarly treated. Mutilated bodies turn up somewhere everyday. Some 6000 people in dozens of countries were legally

shot, hung, electrocuted, gassed, or stoned to death by their respective states between 1985 and 1992 for political misdeeds: criticism of the state, membership in banned political parties or groups, or for adherence to the "wrong" religion; for moral deeds: adultery, prostitution, homosexuality, sodomy, or alcohol or drug use; for economic offenses: burglary, embezzling, and corruption; and for violent crimes: rape, assault, and murder. (1994, 119–20)

Pierre van den Berghe contends that what is euphemistically called nation building is nothing but a blueprint for **ethnocide** (an attempt to destroy the culture of a people) at best and **genocide** (an attempt to exterminate a people) at worst. Social scientists, he writes, tend to ignore the genocidal character of the nation-state because of the widespread assumption that nation-states are necessary for maintaining peace and economic stability. Instead, he says, nation-states are, in effect, mafias or gangs that, through the use or threat of violence, extract booty for themselves or their elites from rival "gangs" and extract "protection money" from their own citizens.

Other anthropologists share van den Berghe's view of the nation-state as an instrument of force and violence. Nagengast examined not only state killing but also the use of torture, rape, and homosexual assault to draw the boundaries of the nation-state. State-sponsored violence, she says, serves not only to inflict pain but also to create "punishable categories of people"—that is, people whose existence creates and maintains an Other. These punishable individuals represent an ambiguous underclass believed capable of undermining the accepted order of society. Arrest and torture, she says, stigmatize people and mark them as people no one would want to be. Arrest and torture provide a way to symbolically mark, discipline, and stigmatize categories of people whose existence or demands threaten the idea, power, and legitimacy of the nation-state. Because torture and violence are committed only against "terrorists," "communists," or "separatists," these methods become legitimate. "We only beat bad people," said a Turkish prison official in 1984. "They are no good, they are worthless bums, they are subversives who think that communism will relieve them of the necessity of working." He described with apparent pride the order that he had given that "all prisoners should be struck with a truncheon below the waist on the rude parts, and warned not to come to prison again." "My aim," he said, "is to ensure discipline. That's not torture, for it is only the lazy, the idle, the vagabonds, the communists, the murderers who come to prison" (Nagengast 1994: 121).

One of the most recent instances of state violence against its own citizens occurred on the island of Timor on the southern edge of Indonesia. East Timor had been colonized by the Dutch and the Portuguese and was granted its independence by the Portuguese in 1975. Five days after a state visit by then U.S. Vice-President Gerald Ford and

---

ethnocide
The attempt to destroy the culture of a people.

genocide
The attempt to exterminate a people.

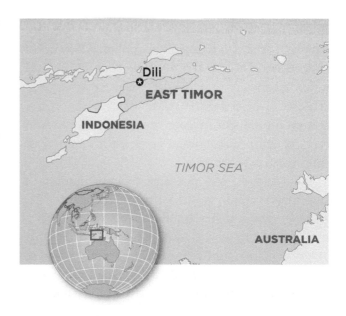

Secretary of State Henry Kissinger, Indonesia invaded East Timor. Over the following two decades, Indonesians, especially members and friends of the ruling family, invested millions of dollars in various enterprises there. And, as many other countries have done, Indonesia embarked on a campaign of violence and terror in its attempt to integrate the East Timorese into the Indonesian nation-state.

Indonesian anthropologist George Aditjondro, who faced an indefinite jail term for criticizing Indonesian leaders, described the campaign of terror, violence, and torture embarked on by the Indonesian state against its most recent citizens. It included, among other things, a "pacification war" that lasted from 1975 to 1979 and repression that continued even after a 1999 UN-sponsored referendum in which 80 percent of the population voted for independence from Indonesia. Torture, says Aditjondro, was a standard method of subjugation. Techniques included physical beatings, the use of cigarette butts to burn holes in the skin, electric shock, crushing victims' hands and feet with chair or table legs, poking the victim's mouth with bamboo sticks, inflicting pain on the genitals (including raping females), and immersing victims in metal tanks filled with water charged with electricity. Torture was used for five reasons, according to Aditjondro. First, to obtain information from victims. Second, to crush the fighting spirit of freedom fighters. Third, to weaken the political power of the Catholic Church by obtaining "confessions" of church complicity in pro-independence politics or in sacrilegious or criminal acts. Fourth, to protect the business interests of Indonesians in East Timor. And finally, to minimize critical press reports from East Timorese newspapers.

But torture was not the only technique of state terror used by Indonesia. There was, for example, physical terror, including mass killings of guerrillas along with women and children that took place during the first decade of the Indonesian occupation. Some 200,000 people—around one-third of the population—were killed or died of deprivations brought about by the terror. Prisoners were thrown to their death from helicopters; people were killed by napalm bombings that also destroyed crops, and thousands died from resulting famines. Many people died in overcrowded prison barracks, some of which were covered with black canvas to turn them into human ovens.

Then there was a campaign to "depurify," as Aditjondro calls it, the bodies of Indonesian women through rape and forced fertility control. Rape was often committed against the wives or daughters of men suspected of being involved with the resistance. In other cases, rape was committed against women who failed to produce identity cards or who refused to accompany or submit to the sexual demands of soldiers. Other women were forced to spy on resistance forces while serving as sex slaves of Indonesian troops. In still other cases, East Indonesian women were forced into brothels for use by Indonesian troops. Rape, says Aditjondro, was also a way to destroy the East Timorese resistance by biologically depurifying their ethnic constituency.

Another way to biologically depurify the population was through forced contraception. Family planning programs were used as means to discipline the population; they symbolically represented state control over human bodies. Thus high school girls were injected with Depo-Provera, a birth control drug, without being told of its function.

Other forms of symbolic violence included erecting pro-Indonesian monuments and forcing citizens to participate in Indonesian political rituals (flag raisings, parades, and parties), subjecting them to arrest, interrogation, and physical torture if they resisted. Language itself was modified, with new linguistic expressions for torture and execution becoming common. *Jalan-jalan ke Jakarta* ("taking a trip to Jakarta") and *Berangkat studi lanjut ke Jawa* ("going for further study in Java") were euphemisms for executions. *Mani laut* ("taking a sea bath") referred to the practice of weighting the bodies of people with rocks and dumping them

The brutalization of East Timor by the Indonesian military and by Indonesian-supported militia from 1975 to 1999 is but one example of how nation-states use force to control their citizens. Here, East Timorese youth are staging a drama portraying the killings of some 271 unarmed protesters by Indonesian troops at the Santa Cruz cemetery on November 12, 1991.

© Supri Supri/Reuters

from a helicopter into the sea. *De-Santa Cruz-kan* ("Santa Cruz-ified") was an expression used by mothers to threaten their children with the sinister connotations of a notorious massacre of Indonesian high school students in 1991 who were protesting Indonesian occupation. Finally, 200,000 people were taken from East Timor and relocated to other parts of Indonesia.

Many East Timorese became **refugees**—forced to flee their home country to seek protection in another. Refugees living in **diaspora**—that is, dispersed and living outside their homeland— escape direct violence and harm; however, the effects of living through sustained, everyday violence are long lasting. Amanda Wise (2006) conducted fieldwork with the refugee diaspora in Sydney, Australia. She found that the experience of shared violence and trauma was a key element in the collective identity of the refugees, who came together to create what she called a "community of suffering." The embodied memories of pain and suffering drew the community together. The Indonesian military inflicted violence on the East Timorese, and "such practices symbolically and affectively bind the pain of the individual to the fate of the ethnic collectivity." The shared memory and common suffering became the foundation of solidarity among her informants (2006, 15).

East Timor finally regained its independence from Indonesia in 1999 after a UN–sponsored referendum in which 80 percent of the population voted for independence. But before they withdrew from East Timor in September 1999, the Indonesian military and military-trained and -supported militias laid waste to virtually the entire country, killing thousands of people and driving 200,000 people out of East Timor and into Indonesia, where many remain under the control of fleeing militia members. For Wise's informants, living in exile in Australia, independence opened up the possibility of a return to their homeland. But many of them, having spent so many years in Australia, had mixed feelings about where they belonged. They had developed a sense of identity based on collective suffering. An exiled journalist described these mixed feelings: "Perhaps the worst condemnation of all is to watch our country recede from our reach like a foreign, distant, indecipherable tide and to witness how indecisively our bodies begin to seek stability after many precarious years; our bodies, unconsenting and perhaps irremediably, grow accustomed to a country which they did not choose of their free will" (in Wise 2006, 163).

Canada's part in the tragedy of the East Timorese is documented in the video *Bitter Paradise: The Sellout of East Timor,* by Elaine Brière. Probably the last tourist to visit East Timor while it was still a peaceful, welcoming society in 1974,

refugees
Groups of people who have been forced from their homeland due to warfare, forced expulsion, acts of terrorism, or other factors.

diaspora
A population whose members are dispersed and living outside of their homeland.

Brière dedicated her life to making the genocide public. The video followed Brière's journey into the business world, where she was told that Canadians who were commercially involved in Indonesia did not know about the genocide or believed that it was an exaggeration; to the world of the media, where she was told by the host of a talk show that Canadians didn't "connect" with the killing of East Timorese; and to Ottawa, where her questions were completely ignored by the External Affairs Minister. Canada continued to give enormous amounts of economic aid to the Suharto regime in spite of the killings and in spite of cutbacks in social programs at home, and Canadian businesses, such as Inco and Bre-X, continued to see Indonesia as a haven for international investment.

The tactics used by Indonesia to subdue people who resisted integration into the Indonesian nation-state are not unique. In fact, virtually all these tactics have been used by most, if not all, nation-states at one time or another. You can get some idea of how nation-states today sponsor violence against their citizens by going to the Internet, where information is readily available from organizations such as Amnesty International and Human Rights Watch.

EXERCISE 8.4

Protesting the Genocide in East Timor

Many Canadian students protested Canada's continued financial support of Indonesia with international aid. What do you think would have happened to Canada's ability to do business in Indonesia if Canada had stopped the aid? Do you think Canadian businesses should have continued to operate in Indonesia in spite of the genocide? Do you thank that if Canada had taken a stand against the genocide (stopped the aid, withdrawn all businesses), the rest of the world would have followed?

QUESTION 8.5: HOW IS IT POSSIBLE TO JUSTIFY THE CONSTRUCTION OF WEAPONS OF MASS DESTRUCTION?

Anthropologist Hugh Gusterson, who had been an antinuclear activist, wanted to know how nuclear weapons scientists could justify conducting research on and testing of weapons of mass destruction. What could create a world view that enabled people to justify performing that kind of work? To answer that question, he set out to study the culture of the Lawrence Livermore National Laboratory in Livermore, California.

Gusterson (1995) suggests that those who justify nuclear weapons and who question nuclear disarmament make four assumptions about the world. First, they claim that anarchy characterizes international relations. Second, they assume that states must rely on self-help since no one else is going to offer them protection. Third, they assume that nuclear weapons are the ultimate form of self-help, because they vastly increase the cost of aggression against them. And fourth, they assume that relatively little can be done in the short term to change the anarchistic nature of the international system.

Critics of nuclear weapons make very different assumptions. They argue that international relations are not as anarchistic as they are made out to be and that rules and norms that control aggression exist. Many critics see the nuclear arms race as "objective social madness." People who work in the area, they assume, must be in denial and must demonize the Other to justify their work.

Gusterson wanted to find out not so much who was "right," but rather how people came to hold such divergent opinions. When he began his research, he was surprised by the variety of political and religious viewpoints of people working at

Livermore. Political views ran the gamut from conservatives to active environmentalists, civil rights supporters, and women's rights advocates. How, he asked, could such a diverse population all agree on the value of nuclear weapons development, an agreement so profound that "they often asked me in puzzlement to explain why antinuclear activists were so afraid of nuclear weapons"?

Nuclear weapons scientists did not, says Gusterson, avoid the ethical concerns of their research. Most, however, accepted the central axiom that nuclear research is necessary to make the world safe. To some, working on nuclear weapons was more ethical than working on conventional weapons, since conventional weapons were more likely to be used. Nuclear weapons, the scientists assumed, were simply symbolic chips in a game, the goal of which was to avoid using them. When asked if he could ever foresee a circumstance in which nuclear weapons would be used, one scientist said, "No, even if we were under attack." In other words, deterrence was the only reason to develop nuclear weapons; if you were attacked, the whole enterprise had failed. Others rationalized their work more baldly, saying they were not responsible for how what they designed would be used. "Are automobile designers," they ask, "responsible for deaths caused by drunk drivers?"

When Gusterson asked people why they chose to work at Livermore, most cited the intellectual freedom they enjoyed working in a weapons laboratory. Almost all compared Livermore favourably to working in universities (which they characterized as "stodgy," "cutthroat," or "high-pressure") or in private organizations. Some also cited the challenges of weapons research and the opportunity to work with state-of-the-art equipment. Also, Livermore paid about twice as much as a university position.

Once a person was hired, secrecy played a major role in forging a person's identity. Livermore employees were investigated before being given security clearance to laboratory facilities. Personnel were divided into different security categories and given coloured badges indicating their level of clearance. "Q" clearance (a green badge) was necessary for classified research; "L" clearance (yellow badge) allowed access to classified areas but not to classified information. The labs themselves were divided into areas of lesser and greater security. As Gusterson put it, the laboratory was "an enormous grid of tabooed spaces and tabooed topics."

Without a green badge, a weapons scientist was not considered a full adult in the lab. The process of getting "Q" clearance was elaborate and could take six months to two years. Virtually every aspect of a person's life was subject to investigation in search of clues that he or she was unfit to handle classified material. But most people passed, and because secrecy was not that well guarded in practice, the security clearance process functioned mostly as a rite of passage that added to the mystique of weapons research and that disciplined the initiate.

Secrecy was one of the principal ways that the lab's diverse population was brought together. Knowing secrets, regardless of how mundane they might be, marked a person as a member of a special group and lent an air of drama and importance to one's work. Secrecy also served to limit discussion that could change a person's view of the work that they were doing. As Gusterson put it, "the laboratory's culture of secrecy does tend to produce certain effects in its scientists: it segregates laboratory scientists as a privileged but somewhat isolated elite; it inculcates a sense of group loyalty; and it thrusts on laboratory scientists an amorphous surveillance, which can become internalized" (1995, 68).

The process of testing nuclear weapons was in many ways the critical step in creating the nuclear scientist. Any Livermore scientist could propose a weapons test, but reviewers (senior scientists at the laboratory) selected only about one out of twenty ideas for testing. Approval of an idea for testing reaffirmed the scientist's membership in the group. Nuclear tests had elements of myth and ritual. Rarely in the narratives that Gusterson collected on testing did anyone note the importance of testing nuclear reliability. Instead, people spoke of the fulfillment of personal ambition, the struggle to master a new technology, the drama of creating something new, and the experience of community that each test created.

Testing produced not only weapons but also weapon designers. It was a way of producing the elite. The more tests one participated in, the greater the prestige and power that accrued. A successful test validated status and credentials and brought forth congratulatory support and reinforcement. Test provided a symbolic simulation of the reliability of the entire system of deterrence: "Each time a nuclear test is successfully carried off, the scientists' faith in human control over nuclear technology is further reinforced. Seen in this light, the 'reliability' the tests demonstrate has an expandable meaning, extending out from the reliability of the particular device being tested to the entire regime of nuclear deterrence" (1995, 161).

The Language of Nuclear Destruction

Carol Cohn (1987, 1991) spent one year studying the culture of a strategic studies institute, or "think tank," for government defence analysts who plan nuclear strategy. She began her study with this question: How are people whose job it is to plan nuclear destruction able to do it? One of her conclusions was that the planners used language to distance themselves from the consequences of the actions they were planning. The language they used obfuscated and reassembled reality in such a way that what was really being talked about—the destruction of human lives—was hidden behind metaphors and euphemisms.

During her first weeks at the centre, as she listened to the participants talking matter-of-factly about nuclear destruction, she heard language that she labelled *technostrategic*. This language included terms such as *clean bombs* (fusion bombs, which release more energy than fission bombs), *penetration aids* (technologies that help missiles get through enemy defences), *collateral damage* (human

deaths), and *surgical strikes* (bombing that takes out only military targets). Domestic metaphors were common in the technostrategic language: missiles were based in *silos*, piles of nuclear weapons in a submarine were *Christmas tree farms*, bombs and missiles were *re-entry vehicles* or *RVs*, and massive bombing was *carpet bombing*. According to Cohn, the domestic images were more than a way for people to distance themselves from the grisly reality they were discussing. Calling the pattern in which a bomb would fall a footprint removed the speakers from any position of accountability for the acts they were contemplating.

Cohn also discovered that the language and metaphors of those working at the institute seemed incapable of expressing certain realities. The aftermath of a nuclear attack was described in technostrategic language as "a situation bound to include EMP blackout, brute force damage to systems, a heavy jamming environment, and so on" (1987, 707). She contrasted this with eyewitness accounts of the bombing of Hiroshima (see the photo and description above). There was, Cohn wrote, no way of describing this experience in technostrategic language. It removed the speakers

This sketch of the effects of the U.S. bombing of Hiroshima was drawn by eyewitness Sawami Katagiri, who recalled, "I was walking among many dead people ... It was like hell ... This picture shows only a part of Hiroshima. The whole city was just like this at that time." Sawami Katagiri, from *The Unforgettable Fire*, NHK Publishing (Japan Broadcast Publishing Co., Ltd.).

from having to think about themselves as victims of nuclear war.

Cohn also discovered that she could not use ordinary language to speak to the defence analysts. When she tried, they acted as if she were ignorant or simpleminded. To communicate at all, she had to use terms like *subholocaust engagement* and *pre-emptive strike*. The word *peace* was not a legitimate part of the vocabulary; to use it was to brand oneself as a softheaded activist. The closest she could come to *peace* in the language of technostrategic was *strategic stability*.

Cohn encountered descriptions of nuclear situations that made little sense until she realized that different realities were being discussed. For example, the following passage describes a nuclear exchange in a situation in which missiles with more than one warhead are mutually banned: "The strategic stability of regime A (a scenario) is based on the fact that both sides are deprived of any incentive ever to strike first. Since it takes roughly two warheads to destroy the enemy silo, an attacker must expend two of his missiles to destroy one of the enemy's. A first strike disarms the attacker. The aggressor ends up worse off than the aggressed" (1987, 710).

By what type of reasoning, asked Cohn, could a country that had dropped a thousand nuclear bombs ten to one hundred times more powerful than the one dropped on Hiroshima end up "worse off" than the country it dropped the bombs on? This would be possible only if winning depended on who had the greatest number of weapons left.

To an anthropologist, the fact that people are limited by their culture, their language, and their point of view is, of course, no surprise. All cultures give a characteristic meaning to violent conflict, whether it is viewed as the act of an animal in possession of a human body, or as the will of God, or as a game. The more serious implication of Cohn's observations is that scientists, academics, and nuclear planners give weight to their claim that their perspective is "objective" and therefore has greater truth value than other perspectives.

Moreover, says Cohn, if one can speak to defence analysts only in the language of technostrategic, and if the language is constructed in such a way as to be incapable of expressing different realities, then there is no way for these analysts to appreciate or understand the other realities involved in the use of nuclear weapons.

QUESTION 8.6: HOW DO ANTHROPOLOGISTS DO FIELDWORK IN THE MIDST OF VIOLENT CONFLICT?

As often as possible, anthropologists try to learn about and understand various social and cultural phenomena through fieldwork and participant observation. However, attempting to understand violent conflict first-hand can be difficult at best and dangerous at worst. Often it is contentious as well. Should anthropologist place themselves in danger in the name of fieldwork? What if, through our very presence, we put others at risk or promote the conditions for further violence? Can we use ethnography to understand war from a soldier's perspective? Below, we discuss three different examples of the possibilities and pitfalls of studying violence and conflict, either directly or indirectly.

The Endangered Anthropologist

The risk of injury, disease, or hostile reactions has always been a feature of anthropological fieldwork. As anthropologists increasingly work in areas where human rights violations are common, these risks are intensified. At least four anthropologists have been murdered because of their fieldwork: In 1982, South African anthropologist and anti-apartheid activist Ruth First was killed by a mail bomb in her office at Maputo University in Mozambique. In 1984, Melanesian anthropologist Arnold Ap was tortured and killed by the Indonesian army, his body dumped by helicopter into the sea. In 1989, South African anthropologist David Webster was shot and killed by members of a pro-apartheid death squad. And in 1990, Guatemalan anthropologist Myrna Mack was stabbed to death by a soldier, ostensibly for her work with Mayan refugees and their experiences in the government's counterinsurgency war of the early 1980s, which killed hundreds of thousands of people. In addition, at least two anthropologists, Ricardo Falla and George Aditjondro, are in exile and under threat of assassination because of their work. These real dangers that anthropologists face may provide insights into how the people with whom they are working experience the threat of violence.

In 1989 and 1990, Linda Green was doing fieldwork in the Guatemalan community of Xe'caj. Like many similar communities, Xe'caj was only beginning to recover from some 35 years of violence. Beginning with a military coup orchestrated largely by the CIA against a democratically elected government in 1954, Guatemala experienced regular violence as the militarized state tried to suppress attempts to overthrow the military regime. Hundreds of thousands of Guatemalans were killed, mostly by the government, in an attempt to suppress the revolt. The late 1970s and early 1980s were particularly brutal as the government embarked on a campaign to destroy peasant villages and relocate people to government-controlled towns. In addition, paramilitary groups, largely supplied and supported by the regular military, embarked on campaigns of terror and torture in an attempt to control the peasant population.

The people of Xe'caj lived in a state of constant surveillance from the military encampment located above the town. Many of the residents had husbands, fathers, or sons taken away by the military. There were rumours of death lists. People had difficulty sleeping and reported nightmares of recurring death and violence. Soon, said Green, "I, too, started to experience nighttime hysteria, dreams of death, disappearances, and torture."

Green interviewed women who had been widowed by the conflict. Without prompting, the women recounted in vivid detail their stories of horror, the deaths and disappearances of husbands, fathers, sons, and brothers, as if they had happened last week or month rather than six to eight years ago.

Then one day when Green arrived to continue the interviews, the women were anxious and agitated. When she asked what had happened, they told her that the military commissioner was looking for her and that people were saying she was helping the widows and talking against other people in the community. When Green told the women she was going to go and see the commissioner, they pleaded with her not to do so, telling her that they knew of people who had gone to the military garrison and never returned. Green decided to visit the garrison alone, and that visit would provide a vivid experience of the fears confronted by the villagers. As she approached the garrison,

> I saw several soldiers sitting in a small guardhouse with a machine gun perched on a three-foot stanchion pointed downward and directly at me. The plight of Joseph K. in Kafka's *Trial* flashed through my mind, he accused of a crime for which he must defend himself but about which he could get no information. I didn't do anything wrong, I must not look guilty, I repeated to myself like a mantra. I must calm myself, as my stomach churned, my nerves frayed. I arrived breathless and terrified. Immediately I knew I was guilty because I was against the system of violence and terror that surrounded me. (1995, 116)

Fortunately the *commandante* said he knew nothing about why she was being harassed. He assured her that she could continue with her work, and everything went smoothly from there. But Green had gained a fuller understanding of the experiences of people who must live under the constant threat of violence.

Is There a Place for Anthropology/Military Collaborations?

In 2005, Montgomery McFate, a military adviser with a background in anthropology, published an article in *Military Review* arguing that there was a "culture gap" in our understanding of the conflict in Iraq caused by "the almost total absence of anthropology within the national-security establishment." She argued that successful counterinsurgency requires a total understanding of local culture. To achieve victory, the United States needed to understand Iraq's traditional authority structure and the competing interests of different groups such as the Shia, Sunni, and Kurds. In a second article, co-written with Andrea Jackson, McFate outlined a proposal to establish an "Office for Operational Cultural Knowledge," which would train teams to provide battlefield commanders with knowledge of local culture, or as it was being called, the "human terrain."

The need for cultural knowledge was echoed by retired Major General Robert H. Scales, Jr., who argued that these new conflicts required not technological superiority but "an exceptional ability to understand people, their culture, and their motivation."

One outcome of this interest in cultural knowledge was the development of Human Terrain Systems (HTSs). The centrepiece of the program was Human Terrain Teams (HTTs), each of which had a staff of five: an army officer serving as team leader, a cultural analyst, a regional studies analyst, a Human Terrain (HT) research manager, and an HT analyst. Each team studied the local culture, interviewed local people, and provided valuable information to the battalion commander. In 2008 the Canadian Forces began a similar program of "white situational awareness teams" (WSAT). In military terminology, white refers to the civilian population (as opposed to the "red" and "blue" of enemy and friendly forces, respectively). Each WSAT team included two military intelligence officers and three civilian Department of Foreign Affairs employees, and aimed to provide a more nuanced understanding of the cultural terrain for military leaders and advisers (Fenton 2010).

Anthropologists who joined the HTS project explained their service as an attempt to do something meaningful. Marcus Griffin wrote: "I have an obligation to use my skills to learn about people and to share what I learn." Working as a member of an HTT in Iraq, Griffin saw his job as finding out what Iraqis needed and helping them meet those needs.

Not everyone, however, shared this positive assessment of HTS. The American Anthropological Association issued a formal statement in 2007 condemning the project, arguing that it would lead anthropologists to violate ethical standards and that it posed a danger to both anthropologists and the people they were studying. Another notable critic, Roberto Gonzales, pointed out a number of dangers of HTS. First, was it possible for informants to *consent* to their participation? Second, what type of information was being gathered by anthropologists, and how would it be used? Third, how well would informants be protected from retaliation from hostile groups or political

U.S. Army photo by SSG Michael Castell

A U.S. soldier takes notes as he talks and drinks tea with local Andar District Special Needs School administrators during a cordon and search of Nani, Afghanistan, in June, 2007. Can anthropological expertise be put to (good) use in a war zone?

rivals? Maximillian Forte, an anthropologist at Concordia University, also expressed concerns about HTS, WSAT, and the potential militarization of anthropology in general: "Their [WSATs'] job seems to be no different from that of HTS, except that for now the civilians they use are government employees, not academics. They have breached a barrier however: the idea that social and cultural knowledge can be useful for counterinsurgency, at least that door has now been opened in Canada" (in Fenton 2010).

What bothers many critics of HTS is that regardless of the efforts of the military and others to put a humanitarian face on the contributions of social scientists, the information gathered by HTTs is clearly going to be used for military purposes. HTS advocates want to make whatever information is gathered available to other agencies and to the governments of Iraq and Afghanistan, to "enable them to more fully exercise sovereignty over their country" (Gonzalez 2009, 74). This reminds many anthropologists of the disastrous CORDS program, implemented during the Vietnam War. Like HTS, CORDS was designed to gather cultural knowledge in order to win "hearts and minds." Using information from social scientists, military personnel exploited Vietnamese superstitions and religious beliefs to frighten and terrorize civilians. When CORDS data were given to the South Vietnamese government, they were used to target political opponents and dissidents. What precautions are being taken to ensure that the Iraqi and Afghan governments do not use HTT information to target political rivals or to create blacklists for personal vendettas?

The use of social scientists for HTTs in Iraq and Afghanistan raises a larger issue: the responsibility of anthropologists and other social scientists to be aware of how their data may be used. The Pentagon, for example, is using information collected by social scientists to help identify dangerous neighbourhoods in Baghdad and Kabul. This allows the military to predict which neighbourhoods are at risk for riots, gun violence, or bombings; it also helps them develop lists of possible participants and their relatives, friends, and associates.

Perhaps more ominous, the military is awarding grants to social scientists to forecast human behaviour. The U.S. Department of Defense is developing a project called Human Social and Culture Behavior Modeling (HSCB). Much of this work will be contracted out to private corporations eager to secure lucrative government contracts. One corporation, Aptima, in conjunction with Carnegie Mellon University, has developed "Social Network Analysis" (SNA) software. SNA has been used by the U.S. military "to predict a state's potential for instability or civil unrest in terms of nine key factors," which range from "lack of essential services" to "corruption level" to "tension."

One danger, of course, is that the philosophy of HTS, and the development of elaborate surveillance technologies using vast quantities of information now available on citizens, will move from military applications in places such as Iraq and Afghanistan to domestic uses that seriously undermine democratic freedoms. Gonzalez concludes his critique of HTS as follows:

What comes across from the accounts of many social scientists supporting counterinsurgency initiatives in Iraq and Afghanistan is a fundamental acceptance of modern warfare in general and the U.S.-led occupations in particular. Furthermore, they generally accept the false notion that counterinsurgency—the "graduate level of war" to quote one military enthusiast—is more antiseptic, more humane, less damaging than conventional warfare. As technicians of power, some adhere to Machiavellian principles: do not question the prince or his war, but instead use the most efficient means to help him achieve victory. War's inevitability is taken for granted. Basic assumptions are left unquestioned. Missing from these accounts is the question of whether war is appropriate at all today. (2009, 123–24)

Making Sense of Combat: Canadian Soldiers in Kandahar

Throughout this chapter, we have explored the ways in which people in various societies and cultures make sense of violent conflict. As we have seen, language and ritual are both employed, quite successfully, to make nuclear proliferation and the subsequent possibility of mass destruction seem both feasible and meaningful. As noted at the outset of the chapter, until recently, pride in peacekeeping was a key part of Canadian national identity. For the first time since the Korean War, however, Canada now has soldiers in active combat (in Afghanistan). In her work with Canadian Forces soldiers stationed in Kandahar, Anne Irwin analyzed the ways in which they use storytelling and ritual to make sense of their experiences in combat.

A former member of the Canadian Forces herself, Irwin spent many years studying Canadian soldiers, both while they trained for peacekeeping operations (Irwin 2002) and, more recently, with a unit that would undertake "full-spectrum operations," including combat (2012, 61). Irwin spent several months with the unit during its tour in 2006, living with them both at Kandahar's air force base and "outside the wire," on patrol and in combat. Irwin found that whereas time and routine on the base were quite structured, time outside the wire was completely disrupted— "there was no day-to-day routine for sleeping and eating, not even predictable shifts" (64). Even when there was no engagement—"troops in contact," in military parlance—the soldiers experienced all time outside the wire as being in combat, not least because of the omnipresent danger of IEDs (improvised explosive devices). Soldiers who spent time outside the wire together seemed to go through a rite of passage, and shared a liminal period together during combat (69). However, Irwin is reluctant to cast combat as a rite of passage that turns boys into men. Indeed, she argues that although combat has some of the elements of a rite of passage, soldiers who return to Canada seem to be both permanent adolescents (referring to themselves and their fellow soldiers as "the boys") and, at the same time, old men: prematurely aged, grief stricken, and often scarred or disabled (76).

Irwin has also collected and analyzed soldier's narratives about the war in Afghanistan. Often these address and link individual morality to social and political debates about Canada's combat role. One

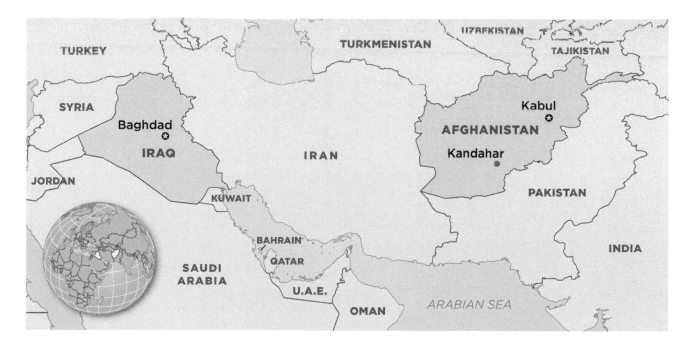

soldier, in telling the story of his experiences, said that "a lot of people in Canada think that we should not be here in Afghanistan, but those people don't see the remarkable changes happening here. One interpreter told me, 'Because Canada is here, our people are happy again.' So to all those Canadians who continue to harp about what they don't know—here's your straw, suck it up" (Cpl Sanders, in Pengelly and Irwin 2011, 52).

Here, the soldier has turned his combat experience into a morality tale, one that takes the qualities of a good solider—responsible, tough, and uncomplaining—and transposes them onto the Canadian public. Moreover, he is attempting to show the moral justness of the war by drawing on "the moral character of a helpful and caring Canada" (2011, 53). By examining these kinds of narratives, we can see how their circulation helps soldiers understand and justify their participation in this violent conflict. Moreover, when such combat narratives draw on a sense of national identity and pride, of Canada as "helpful and caring," we can begin to make sense of the rather rapid (though contested) shift, at the turn of the 21st century, of Canada's role from peacekeeper to warrior nation.

CONCLUSIONS

To examine how people give meaning to and justify collective violence, our first question had to do with how societies create a bias in favour of collective violence. Violent conflict is justified in some societies as a way of achieving status or acquiring or protecting possessions, or as a means of revenge. In peaceful societies, violence is avoided by widespread sharing of resources, building relations of dependence among groups, devaluing or discouraging aggressive behaviour, and emphasizing collective behaviours that promote intragroup and intergroup harmony.

There are economic, political, and social differences between peaceful and violent societies. One difference is that violent societies encourage competition over resources, leading to a situation in which individuals are required, because of a lack of central authority, to protect their own property by violent means. The conversion of communal property to private property, which results in the disenfranchisement of peasant farmers, has been linked to revolution, and sexist ideologies in violent societies may promote violent behaviour against other groups.

War, according to some, has served throughout human history to promote the centralization of authority and the growth of state-level political structures. While violent conflict may increase national solidarity in some cases, nation-states also use violence to punish nonconformity among their citizens or to destroy internal "Others." Despite the obvious ill effects of collective violence, especially with the existence of weapons of mass destruction, we find that people can easily justify even the manufacture and testing of these weapons. Furthermore, the language of defence analysts masks some of the realities of nuclear destruction, keeps them from viewing themselves as potential victims, and turns nuclear planning into a game. It is no easy task to conduct fieldwork in the midst of violent conflict. As we have seen, the insights gained during such fieldwork can be very telling but could lead to increased violence if left in the wrong hands.

CRITICAL THINKING QUESTIONS

1. Is world peace possible? Given what you have learned in this chapter, what are the barriers to world peace in the contemporary world? Can they be overcome, and if so, how?
2. Depictions of graphic violence have become commonplace in contemporary popular culture. How might an anthropologist explain this phenomenon?

KEY TERMS:

diaspora   (p. 245)
ethnocide   (p. 243)
genocide   (p. 243)
refugees   (p. 245)

GLOSSARY

achieved status An identity that is believed to be in flux and that is dependent upon the actions and achievements of an individual. (p. 168)

agroecological approaches Agricultural methods that incorporate indigenous practices of food production along with contemporary agricultural research yet preserve the environment. (p. 72)

armchair anthropologist Refers to an approach to the study of various societies that dominated anthropology in the late 1800s. It involved the collection, study, and analysis of the writings of missionaries, explorers, and colonists who had sustained contact with non-Western peoples. Armchair anthropologists used these documents to make comparisons and generalizations about the ways of life of various groups. (p. 9)

ascribed status An identity that is perceived as fixed and unchanging because a person is believed to be born with it. In Canadian society, race is often assumed to be ascribed at birth. (p. 168)

balanced reciprocity A form of exchange in which items of equal or near-equal value are exchanged on the spot. (p. 186)

bands A term used by anthropologists to refer to egalitarian units of social organization, found mostly among foragers, that usually consist of fewer than 100 people. (p. 43)

bilateral kinship A system in which individuals trace their descent through both parents. (p. 111)

biomedical model A term, also known as Western medicine, scientific medicine, or modern medicine, that combines biology with the diagnosis and treatment of illness and that views the body as a machine, independent of social context, that must be repaired periodically. (p. 65)

brideservice The requirement that when a couple marries, the groom must work for the bride's parents for some specified period of time. (p. 113)

bridewealth The valuables that a groom or his family are expected or obligated to present to the bride's family. (p. 122)

caste A form of social stratification and identity in India where individuals are assigned at birth to the ranked social and occupational groups of their parents. (p. 168)

clan A unilineal descent group whose members claim descent from a common ancestor. (p. 43)

class A form of identity informed by perceptions of an individual's economic worth or status. It is also a form of social hierarchy. (p. 167)

commodity Traditionally, commodities are items that involve a transfer of value and a counter-transfer: A sells something to B, and the transaction is finished. A longstanding personal relationship between buyer and seller is not established. This is typical of capitalist market-exchange systems. (p. 154)

creole A term used commonly to refer to the formation of slave societies in the Caribbean in which elements of African and European cultures were merged, blended, or combined into something uniquely Caribbean. (p. 102)

cultural relativism The attempt to understand the beliefs and behaviours of other cultures in terms of the culture in which they are found. (p. 19)

cultural text A way of thinking about culture as a text of significant symbols—words, gestures, drawings, natural objects—that carries meaning. (p. 25)

culture The system of meanings about the nature of experience that are shared by a people and passed on from one generation to another, including the meanings that people give to things, events, activities, and people. (p. 6)

culture change The changes in meanings that a people ascribe to experience and changes in their way of life. (p. 43)

culture of poverty A term coined by anthropologist Oscar Lewis to describe the lifestyle and world view of people who inhabit urban and rural slums. (p. 185)

diaspora A population whose members are dispersed and living outside of their homeland. (p. 245)

domain of experience An area of human experience (e.g., business, war, science, family life) from which people borrow meaning to apply to other areas. (p. 79)

dowry The goods and valuables a bride's family supplies to the groom's family or to the couple. (p. 125)

economic development The term used to identify an increase in level of technology, and by some, standard of living of a population. Others view it as an ideology based on three key assumptions: (1) that economic growth and development is the solution to national as well as global problems; (2) that global economic integration will contribute to solving global ecological and social problems; and (3) that foreign assistance to undeveloped countries will make things better. (p. 59)

economic systems   The rules, mechanisms, institutions, and systems of relations through which goods and services are distributed and people get what they want. (p. 202)

egocentric   A view of the self that defines each person as a replica of all humanity, as the location of motivations and drives, and as capable of acting independently from others. (p. 146)

enculturation   The process through which individuals learn an identity. This can encompass parental socialization, the influence of peers, the mass media, government, or other forces. (p. 141)

endogamy   A rule that requires a person to marry someone inside one's own group (the group could be a lineage, an ethnic group, a religious group, etc.). (p. 122)

essentialism   The act of creating generalizations or stereotypes about the behaviour or culture of a group of people. (p. 14)

ethnocentric fallacy   The mistaken notion that the beliefs and behaviours of other cultures can be judged from the perspective of one's own culture. (p. 19)

ethnocentrism   The tendency to judge the beliefs and behaviours of other cultures from the perspective of one's own culture. (p. 19)

ethnocide   The attempt to destroy the culture of a people. (p. 243)

ethnographic method   The immersion of researchers in the lives and cultures of the peoples they are trying to understand in order to comprehend the meanings these people ascribe to their existence. (p. 10)

ethnographic present   Use of the present tense to describe a culture, although the description may refer to situations that existed in the past. (p. 110)

ethnography   A written description and analysis of a particular group of people, usually based upon anthropological fieldwork. (p. 11)

exogamy   A rule that requires a person to marry someone outside one's own group. (p. 122)

extended family   A family group based on blood relations of three or more generations. (p. 116)

factory model   An energy-intensive, ecologically damaging form of agriculture intended to grow or raise as many crops or livestock as possible in the shortest amount of time. (p. 71)

factory system   A system of production characterized by the concentration of labour and machines in specific places. It is associated with the Industrial Revolution. (p. 53)

fieldwork   Anthropologists engage in long-term interactions (usually a year or more) with various groups of people. This often involves living with people, observing and contributing to daily chores and tasks (participant observation), and conducting interviews. Most fieldwork in anthropology has historically been qualitative in nature. (p. 10)

free trade   The removal of barriers to the free flow of goods and capital between nations by eliminating import and export taxes as well as subsidies paid to farmers and business people. It may also mean reducing environmental or social laws when they restrict the flow of goods and capital. (p. 203)

gender   Culturally constructed ideals of behaviour, dress, occupations, roles, and comportment for particular sexes. (p. 178)

generalized reciprocity   A form of exchange in which people share what they have with others but expect them to reciprocate later. (p. 186)

genocide   The attempt to exterminate a people. (p. 243)

globalization   Defined by Anthony Giddens as the intensification of worldwide social relations that link distant localities in such a way that local happenings are shaped by events occurring many miles away, and vice versa. (p. 200)

hegemonic masculinity   Refers to ideals and norms of masculinity in a society, which are often privileged over others. (p. 181)

holistic   When an individual's sense of self cannot be conceived as existing separately from society or apart from his or her status or role. (p. 145)

identity   Learned personal and social types of affiliation, including gender, sexuality, race, class, nationalism, and ethnicity, for example. (p. 140)

imagined community   A term coined by Benedict Anderson in 1983. It refers to the fact that even in the absence of face-to-face interactions, a sense of community (e.g., nationalism) is culturally constructed by forces such as the mass media. (p. 142)

impartible inheritance A form of inheritance in which family property is passed undivided to one heir. (p. 130)

incest taboo A rule that prohibits sexual relations among certain categories of kin, such as brothers or sisters, parents and children, or, in some cases, cousins. (p. 119)

indigenous peoples Groups of people whose ancestors pre-date the arrival of European or other forms of colonialism, who share a culture and/or way of life that they often identify as distinct from "mainstream" society, and who often feel that they have a right to self-government. (p. 158)

individualistic A view of the self in which the individual is primarily responsible for his or her own actions. (p. 145)

Industrial Revolution A period of European history, generally identified as occurring in the late 18th century, marked by a shift in production from agriculture to industrial goods, urbanization, and the factory system. (p. 52)

International Monetary Fund Formed in 1944 at the Bretton Woods Conference to regulate currency transactions among countries. The IMF now makes loans and regulates the economies of lending countries. (p. 60)

interpersonal theory of disease A view of disease in which it is assumed that illness is caused by tensions or conflicts in social relations. (p. 68)

irrigation agriculture A form of cultivation in which water is used to deliver nutrients to growing plants. (p. 43)

key metaphors A term to identify metaphors that dominate the meanings that people in a specific culture attribute to their experience. (p. 82)

key scenarios Dominant stories or myths that portray the values and beliefs of a specific society. (p. 88)

kula ring A system of inter-island gift exchange documented by anthropologist Bronislaw Malinowski in the Trobriand Islands. It involves the exchange of shell necklaces and armbands. According to Malinowski, the *kula* ring serves, among other things, to create alliances and social ties among individuals living on different islands. (p. 152)

market externalities Costs that are not included in the prices people pay, such as health risks and environmental degradation. (p. 204)

matrilineage A lineage that is formed by tracing descent in the female line. (p. 113)

matrilineal kinship A system of descent in which persons are related to their kin through the mother only. (p. 112)

metaphor A figure of speech in which linguistic expressions are taken from one area of experience and applied to another. (p. 79)

multiculturalism A term that Eva Mackey defines as a Canadian policy in which all hyphenated cultures, such as African-Canadians and French-Canadians, are described and celebrated as part of a "cultural mosaic." Contrast with the "cultural melting pot" image that is used in the United States. (p. 214)

multi-sited fieldwork This term, coined by George Marcus in 1995, refers to the process of connecting localized experiences of fieldwork with broader, global processes. It necessitates understanding various issues from multiple "sites" or perspectives. (p. 13)

myth A story or narrative that portrays the meanings people give to their experience. (p. 82)

nation A collection of people who share a common language, world view, and ancestry. (p. 205)

nation-state A political community that has clearly defined territorial borders and centralized authority. (p. 205)

nature versus nurture This phrase, coined by Francis Galton in 1874, references a longstanding scholarly debate concerning whether or not human behaviours and identities are the result of nature (biological and genetic factors) or nurture (learned and cultural factors). (p. 142)

negative reciprocity A form of exchange in which the object is to get something for nothing or to make a profit. (p. 186)

neoliberalism An economic philosophy that argues for minimal government involvement in the economy and greatly accelerated economic growth. Well-being, neoliberals argue, is best served by liberating individual entrepreneurs to operate in a framework of strong property rights, free markets, and free trade. (p. 203)

nuclear family The family group consisting of father, mother, and their biological or adopted children. (p. 112)

partible inheritance A form of inheritance in which the goods or property of a family is divided among the heirs. (p. 130)

participant observation An element of fieldwork that can involve participating in daily tasks, and observing daily interactions among a particular group. (p. 10)

pathogen An infectious agent such as a bacteria or a virus that can cause disease. (p. 66)

patrilineage A lineage that is formed by tracing descent in the male line. (p. 116)

patrilineal kinship A system of descent in which persons are related to their kin through the father only. (p. 112)

polyandry A form of marriage in which a woman is permitted to have more than one husband. (p. 128)

polygamy A form of marriage in which a person is permitted to have more than one spouse. (p. 127)

polygyny A form of marriage in which a man is permitted to have more than one wife. (p. 127)

population density The number of people in a given geographic area. (p. 48)

potlach A celebration, usually involving elaborate feasting and the redistribution of gifts, found among many indigenous Northwest Coast groups, such as the Tsimshian. The potlatch is a means of creating a new identity or of reinforcing social status within a group. (p. 153)

principle of reciprocity According to Marcel Mauss, gift giving involves reciprocity. The idea is that the exchange of gifts creates a feeling of obligation, in that the gift must be repaid. (p. 152)

progress The idea that human history is the story of a steady advance from a life dependent on the whims of nature to a life of control and domination over natural forces. (p. 42)

"putting out" system A means of production, common in the 16th and 17th centuries and surviving today, in which a manufacturer or merchant supplies the materials and sometimes the tools to workers, who produce the goods in their own homes. (p. 53)

race A culturally constructed form of identity and social hierarchy, *race* refers to the presumed hereditary, phenotypic characteristics of a group of people. These physical or phenotypic differences are often erroneously correlated with behavioural attributes. (p. 166)

racism Refers to the discrimination and mistreatment of particular "racial" groups. (p. 170)

refugees Groups of people who have been forced from their homeland due to warfare, forced expulsion, acts of terrorism, or other factors. (p. 245)

relativistic fallacy The idea that it is impossible to make moral judgments about the beliefs and behaviours of members of other cultures. (p. 20)

representation The way in which a group of people is depicted in writing or through images. Anthropologists are increasingly conscious of the fact that when they write about a group of people, they are constructing particular representations that may have positive or negative long-term effects for a group of people. (p. 13)

revitalization movements The term suggested by Anthony F.C. Wallace for attempts by a people to construct a more satisfying culture. (p. 99)

rites of passage This term, coined in 1908 by Arnold Van Gennep, refers to rituals that accompany changes in status, such as the transition from boyhood to manhood, living to dead, or student to graduate. (p. 150)

ritual A dramatic rendering or social portrayal of meanings shared by a specific body of people in a way that makes them seem correct and proper (*see also* symbolic actions). (p. 78)

salvage anthropology An approach to anthropology that arose in the late 1800s when anthropologists witnessed the extinction and/or assimilation of indigenous groups throughout the world. In response, some anthropologists, such as Franz Boas, suggested that anthropologists rapidly document the oral stories, songs, histories, and other traditions of indigenous groups before they disappeared. (p. 12)

sedentary A mode of livelihood characterized by permanent or semi-permanent settlements. (p. 42)

sex Hormonal, chronosomal, or physical differences between men and women. (p. 178)

slash-and-burn (or swidden) agriculture A mode of livelihood in which forests are cleared by burning trees and brush, and crops are planted among the ashes of the cleared ground. (p. 43)

social stratification/hierarchy The ordering and ranking of individuals within society. Those at the top of the hierarchy are generally afforded more power, wealth, prestige, or privileges in a society. Hierarchies can be based on race, gender, class, caste, ethnicity, national affiliation, or other factors. (p. 165)

sociocentric A context-dependent view of self. The self exists as an entity only within the concrete situations or roles occupied by the person. (p. 146)

sociocultural anthropology An anthropological approach that retains the British focus on social anthropology at the same time as it adds the American focus on culture to produce something slightly different from either one. (p. 3)

state A form of society characterized by a hierarchical ranking of people and centralized political control. (p. 43)

structural violence Actions of remote government or international agencies that result in denial to the poor of basic rights of food, shelter, or livelihood. (p. 194)

symbolic actions The activities including ritual, myth, art, dance, and music—that dramatically depict the meanings shared by a specific body of people. (p. 79)

syncretization The term given to the combination of old beliefs or religions and new ones that are often introduced during colonization. (p. 100)

third gender A gender role given to someone who does not fit within strictly masculine or feminine gender roles in a given society. (p. 178)

totemism The use of a symbol, generally an animal or a plant, as a physical representation for a group, generally a clan (p. 78)

transnational Involving more than one nation-state; reaching beyond or transcending national boundaries. (p. 208)

vector An organism, such as a mosquito, tick, flea, or snail, that can transmit disease to another animal. (p. 66)

white privilege Refers to the fact that in many societies, "white" people have access to greater power, authority, and privileges than non white people. (p. 171)

World Bank One of the institutions created at the Bretton Woods, New Hampshire, meeting in 1944 of Allied nations. The World Bank (or the Bank for Reconstruction and Development) functions as a lending institution to nations largely for projects related to economic development. (p. 60)

world view An encompassing picture of reality based on shared cultural assumptions about how the world works. (p. 79)

BIBLIOGRAPHY

Abu-Lughod, Lila. 1995. "A Tale of Two Pregnancies." In *Women Writing Culture*. Edited by Ruth Behar and Deborah A. Gordon. Berkeley: University of California Press.

Adelson, Naomi. 2000. *"Being alive well": Health and the Politics of Cree Well-Being*. Toronto: University of Toronto Press.

Aditjondro, George. 2000. "Ninjas, Nanggalas, Monuments, and Mossad Manuals." In *Death Squad: The Anthropology of State Terror*. Edited by Jeffery A. Sluka. Philadelphia: University of Pennsylvania Press.

Alford, Richard D. 1988. *Naming and Identity: A Cross-Cultural Study of Personal Naming Practices*. New Haven: HRAF Press.

American Anthropological Association 1998 Statement on Race. http://www.aaanet.org/stmts/racepp.htm

American Anthropological Association. 2005. *Anthropology News* 46:1.

Anderson, Benedict R. O'G. 1991. *Imagined Communities: Reflections on the Origin and Spread of Nationalism*. New York: Verso.

Anderson, Margaret (Seguin). 1984. *Interpretive Contexts for Traditional and Current Coast Tsimshian Feasts*. Ottawa: Canadian Ethnology Service Paper, National Museum of Canada, 98.

———. 2004. "Understanding Tsimshian Potlatch." In *Native Peoples: The Canadian Experience*. Edited by R. Bruce Morrison and C. Roderick Wilson. Toronto: Oxford University Press.

———, ed. 1984. *The Tsimshian: Images of the Past, Views for the Present*. Vancouver: UBC Press.

Anderson, Margaret (Seguin), and Marjorie Halpin, eds. 2000. *Potlatch at Getsegukla*. Vancouver: UBC Press.

Anderson-Levy, Lisa. 2000. "Colliding/Colluding Identities: Race, Class, and Gender in Jamaican Family Systems." In *New Directions in Anthropological Kinship*. Edited by Linda Stone. Lanham: Rowman and Littlefield.

Anelauskas, Valdas. 1999. *Discovering America As It Is*. Atlanta: Clarity.

Angeloni, Elvio. 1990. *Anthropology 90/91*. Guilford: Dushkin.

Arat-Koc, Sedef. 1999a. "'Good Enough to Work but Not Good Enough to Stay': Foreign Domestic Workers and the Law." In *Locating Law: Race/Class/Gender Connections*. Edited by Elizabeth Comack. Halifax: Fernwood.

———. 1999b. "Neoliberalism, State Restructuring, and Immigration: Changes in Canadian Policies in the 1990s." *Journal of Canadian Studies* 34(2): 31–57.

Asch, Michael, ed. 2002. *Aboriginal and Treaty Rights in Canada: Essays on Law, Equality, and Respect for Difference*. Vancouver: UBC Press.

Austin-Broos, Diane. 1997. *Jamaica Genesis: Religion and the Politics of Moral Orders*. Chicago: University of Chicago Press.

Bannerji, Himani. 2000. *The Dark Side of the Nation: Essays on Multiculturalism, Nationalism, and Gender*. Toronto: Canadian Scholars' Press.

Barker, John, ed. 1990. *Christianity in Oceania: Ethnographic Perspectives*. Lanham: University Press of America.

Barrett, Stanley R. 1987. *Is God a Racist? The Right Wing in Canada*. Toronto: University of Toronto Press.

———. 1996. *Anthropology: A Student's Guide to Theory and Method*. Toronto: University of Toronto Press.

———. 2002. *Culture Meets Power*. Westport: Praeger.

Barsh, Russel Lawrence. 2002. "Netukulimk Past and Present: Mikmaw Ethics and the Atlantic Fisheries." *Journal of Canadian Studies* 37(1): 15–44.

Basok, Tanya. 2004. *Tortillas and Tomatoes: Transmigrant Mexican Harvesters in Canada*. Montreal and Kingston: McGill–Queen's University Press.

Beaud, Michel. 1983. *A History of Capitalism, 1500–1980*. New York: Monthly Review Press.

Becker, Gay. 1997. *Disrupted Lives: How People Create Meaning in a Chaotic World*. Berkeley: University of California Press.

Behar, Ruth, and Deborah Gordon, eds. 1995. *Women Writing Culture*. Berkeley: University of California Press.

Bellah, Robert, Richard Madsen, William M. Sullivan, Ann Swidler, and Steven M. Tipton. 1984. *Habits of the Heart*. Berkeley: University of California Press.

Belmonte, Thomas. 1989. *The Broken Fountain*. New York: Columbia University Press.

Benedict, Ruth. 1934. *Patterns of Culture*. New York: Houghton Mifflin.

Bielawski, Ellen. 2004. *Rogue Diamonds: Northern Riches on Dene Land*. Seattle: University of Washington Press.

Blackwood, Evelyn. 2005. "Wedding Bell Blues: Marriage, Missing Men, and Matrifocal Follies." *American Ethnologist* 32(1): 3–19.

Blaikie, Piers, and Harold Brookfield. 1987. *Land Degradation and Society*. London: Methuen.

Blaser, Mario, Harvey Feit, and Glenn McRae, eds. 2004. *In the Way of Development: Indigenous Peoples Life Projects and Globalization*. London and New York: Zed.

Blundell, Valda. 1989. "The Tourist and the Native." In *A Different Drummer: Readings in Anthropology with a Canadian Perspective*. Edited by Bruce Alden Cox, Jacques Chevallier, and Valda Blundell. Ottawa: Carleton University Press.

Boas, Franz. 1940. *Race, Language and Culture*. New York: Macmillan.

Boas, Franz, and George Hunt. 1905. *Kwakiutl Texts*. Memoir of the American Museum of Natural History, vol. 5.

Bodley, John. 1985. *Anthropology and Contemporary Problems*, 2nd ed. Palo Alto: Mayfield.

——. 1994. *Cultural Anthropology: Tribes, States, and the Global System*. Mountain View: Mayfield.

——. 1999. *The Victims of Progress*. Mountain View: Mayfield.

Boellstorff, Tom. 2008. *Coming of Age in Second Life: An Anthropologist Explores the Virtually Human*. Princeton: Princeton University Press.

Bohannan, Laura. 1966. "Shakespeare in the Bush." *Natural History Magazine*, August/September.

Bonanno, Alessandro, Lawrence Busch, William Friedland, Lourdes Gouveia, and Enzo Mingione, eds. 1994. *From Columbus to ConAgra: The Globalization of Agriculture and Food*. Lawrence: University Press of Kansas.

Bossen, Laurel. 2002. *Chinese Women and Rural Development: Sixty Years of Change in Lu Village, Yunnan*. Lanham: Rowman and Littlefield.

Bourgois, Philippe. 1995. *In Search of Respect: Selling Crack in El Barrio*. Cambridge: Cambridge University Press.

Branford, Sue, and Jan Rocha. 2002. *Cutting the Wire: The Story of the Landless Movement in Brazil*. London: Latin American Bureau.

Braudel, Fernand. 1982. *Civilization and Capitalism 15th–18th Century: Volume II, The Wheels of Commerce*. New York: Harper and Row.

Brettell, Caroline, and Carolyn Sargent, eds. 2005. *Gender in Cross-Cultural Perspective*. Upper Saddle River: Prentice Hall.

Briggs, Jean. 1970. *Never in Anger*. Cambridge, MA: Harvard University Press.

Brody, Hugh. 2000. *The Other Side of Eden: Hunters, Farmers, and the Shaping of the World*. Vancouver: Douglas and McIntyre.

Brown, Karen McCarthy. 1991. *Mama Lola: A Vodou Priestess in Brooklyn*. Berkeley: University of California Press.

Burt, Ben. 1994. *Tradition and Christianity: The Colonial Transformation of a Solomon Islands Society*. Philadelphia: Harwood.

Burt, Martha. 1992. *Over the Edge: The Growth of Homelessness in the 1980s*. New York: Russell Sage Foundation.

Cagan, Leslie. 1983. "Feminism and Militarism." In *Beyond Survival: New Directions for the Disarmament Movement*. Edited by M. Albert and D. Dellinger. Boston: South End.

Canadian Council on Learning. 2009. *The State of Aboriginal Learning in Canada: A Holistic Approach to Measuring Success*. Ottawa.

Carneiro, Robert. 1978. "Political Expansion as an Expression of the Principle of Competitive Exclusion." In *Origins of the State: The Anthropology of Political Evolution*. Edited by Ronald Cohn and Elman Service. Philadelphia: Institute for the Study of Human Issues.

——. 1979. "Slash-and-Burn Cultivation Among the Kuikuru and Its Implication for Cultural Development in the Amazon Basin." In *The Evolution of Horticultural Systems in Native South America: Causes and Consequences. Anthropologica Supplement 2*. Edited by J. Wilbert. Caracas.

——. 1990. "Chiefdom-Level Warfare as Exemplified in Fiji and Cauca Valley." In *The Anthropology of War*. Edited by Jonathan Hass. New York: Cambridge University Press.

Carrier, James G. 1993. "The Rituals of Christmas Giving." In *Unwrapping Christmas*. Edited by Daniel Miller. Oxford: Clarendon.

——. 1995. *Gifts and Commodities: Exchange and Western Capitalism Since 1700*. London: Routledge.

Carter, Sarah. 1999. *Aboriginal People and Colonizers of Western Canada to 1900*. Toronto: University of Toronto Press.

Cesara, Manda. 1982. *Reflections of a Woman Anthropologist: No Hiding Place*. Toronto: Academic Press.

Chagnon, Napoleon. 1968. *Yanomamö, The Fierce People*. Toronto: Holt.

——. 1990. "Reproductive and Somatic Conflicts of Interest in the Genesis of Violence and Warfare Among Tribesmen." In *The Anthropology of War*. Edited by Jonathan Hass. New York: Cambridge University Press.

Chambers, Erve. 2000. *Native Tours: The Anthropology of Travel and Tourism*. Prospect Heights: Waveland.

Chen, Zhongping. 2004. "Chinese Minority and Everyday Racism in Canadian Towns and Small Cities: An Ethnic Study of the Case of Peterborough, Ontario, 1892–1951." *Canadian Ethnic Studies* 36(1): 71–91.

Chimbinda, Jorge. 2006. "The Umbundu Naming System." M.A. thesis, Department of Anthropology, University of Western Ontario, London.

Chodkiewicz, Jean-Luc, and Raymond E. Wiest, eds. 2004. *Globalization and Community*. Winnipeg: University of Manitoba Press.

Chomsky, Noam. 1984. *Turning the Tide: U.S. Intervention in Central America and the Struggle for Peace*. Boston: South End.

Churchill, Ward. 1994. *Indians Are Us? Culture and Genocide in Native North America*. Monroe: Common Courage.

Clammer, John, Sylvie Poirier, and Eric Schwimmer, eds. 2004. *Figured Worlds: Ontological Obstacles in Intercultural Relations*. Toronto: University of Toronto Press.

Clark, Kim. 2005. "Ecuadorian Indians, the Nation, and Class in Historic Perspective: Rethinking a 'New Social Movement.'" *Anthropologica* 47(1): 53–65.

Cohen, Mark. 1977. *The Food Crisis in Prehistory*. New Haven: Yale University Press.

——. 1989. *Health and the Rise of Civilization*. New Haven: Yale University Press.

Cohn, Carol. 1987. "Sex and Death in the Rational World of Defense Intellectuals." *Signs* 12: 687–718.

——. 1991. "Decoding Military Newspeak." *Ms.* 5.

Cole, Sally. 2000. "Reflections on Anthropology in Canada: Introduction." *Anthropologica* 42(2): 123–26.

Collier, Jane E., and Michelle Rosaldo. 1981. "Politics and Gender in Simple Societies." In *Sexual Meanings: The Cultural Construction of Gender and Sexuality*. Edited by Sherry B. Ortner and Harriet Whitehead. New York: Cambridge University Press.

Collings, Peter, and Richard G. Condon. 1996. "Blood on Ice: Status, Self-Esteem, and Ritual Injury Among Inuit Hockey Players." *Human Organization* 55(3): 253–62.

Comaroff, Jean, and John Comoraff. 2009. "Alien-Nation: Zombies, Immigrants, and Millenial Capitalism." In *Enchantments of Modernity: Empire, Nation, Globalization*. Edited by S. Dube. New Delhi: Routledge India. 451–81.

Conklin, Beth. 2001. *Consuming Grief: Compassionate Cannibalism in an Amazonian Society*. Austin: University of Texas Press.

Corten, Andre, and Ruth Marshall-Fratani. 2001. *Between Babel and Pentecost: Transnational Pentecostalism in Africa and Latin America*. Bloomington: Indiana University Press.

Counts, David, and Dorothy Counts. 1998. "Fictive Families in the Field." In *Fieldwork and Families: Constructing New Models for Ethnographic Research*. Edited by Juliana Flinn, Leslie Marshall, and Jocelyn Armstrong. Honolulu: University of Hawai'i Press.

Cowan, Jane K., Marie-Benedicte Dembour, and Richard A. Wilson, eds. 2001. *Culture and Rights: Anthropological Perspectives*. Cambridge: Cambridge University Press.

Cowell, Daniel David. 1985/86. "Funerals, Family, and Forefathers: A View of Italian-American Funeral Practices." *Omega* 16: 69–85.

Cox, Bruce Alden, Jacques Chevalier, and Valda Blundell, eds. 1989. *A Different Drummer: Readings in Anthropology with a Canadian Perspective*. Ottawa: Carleton University Press.

Crick, Malcolm R. 1982. "Anthropology of Knowledge." *Annual Review of Anthropology* 11: 287–313. Palo Alto: Annual Reviews.

Crowley, Aleister. 1985. *The Book of Thoth*. Stamford: U.S. Games Systems.

Cruikshank, Julie. 1998. *The Social Life of Stories: Narrative and Knowledge in the Yukon Territory*. Lincoln: University of Nebraska Press.

——. 1990. *Life Lived Like a Story: Life Stories of Three Yukon Native Elders*. Lincoln: University of Nebraska Press.

——. 2005. *Do Glaciers Listen? Local Knowledge, Colonial Encounters, and Social Imagination*. Vancouver: UBC Press.

Culhane, Dara. 1998. *The Pleasures of the Crown: Anthropology, Law, and First Nations*. Burnaby: Talonbooks.

Culhane Speck, Dara. 1987. *An Error in Judgement: The Politics of Medical Care in an Indian/White Community*. Vancouver: Talonbooks.

Cummins, Bryan D. 2004. *"Only God Can Own the Land": The Attawapiskat Cree*. Toronto: Pearson Education.

Cummings, Maggie. 2008. "The Trouble with Trousers: Gossip, *Kastom*, and Sexual Culture in Vanuatu." In *Making Sense of AIDS: Culture, Sexuality, and Power in Melanesia*. Edited by Leslie Butt and Richard Eves Honolulu: University of Hawai'i Press. 133–49.

Daniel, Valentine. 1996. *Charred Lullabies: Chapters in an Anthropology of Violence*. Princeton: Princeton University Press.

Darnell, Regna. 1990. *Edward Sapir: Linguist, Anthropologist, Humanist*. Berkeley: University of California Press.

——. 1998. *And Along Came Boas: Continuity and Revolution in Americanist Anthropology*. Amsterdam and Philadelphia: John Benjamins.

——. 1998. "Toward a History of Canadian Departments of Anthropology: Retrospect, Prospect, and Common Cause." *Anthropologica* 40(2): 153–68.

——. 2000. "Canadian Anthropologists, the First Nations, and Canada's Self-Image at the Millennium." *Anthropologica* 42(2): 165–74.

Davis, D.L., and R.G. Whitten. 1987. "The Cross-Cultural Study of Human Sexuality." In *Annual Review of Anthropology* 16: 69–98. Palo Alto: Annual Reviews.

D'Andrade, Roy. 1995. "Moral Models in Anthropology." *Current Anthropology* 36: 399–408.

Day, Richard J.F. 2000. *Multiculturalism and the History of Canadian Diversity*. Toronto: University of Toronto Press.

Delaney, Carol. 1991. *The Seed and the Soil: Gender and Cosmology in a Turkish Village Society*. Berkeley: University of California Press.

Desai, Ashok V. 1972. "Population and Standards of Living in Akbar's Time." In *Indian Economic and Social History Review* 9: 42–62.

Devita, Philip, ed. 1990. *The Humbled Anthropologist: Tales from the Pacific*. Belmont: Wadsworth.

——. 1991. *The Naked Anthropologist: Tales from Around the World*. Belmont: Wadsworth.

Dickason, Olive Patricia. 2002. *Canada's First Nations: A History of Founding Peoples from Earliest Times*. 3rd ed. Toronto: Oxford University Press.

Divale, William Tulio, and Marvin Harris. 1976. "Population, Warfare, and the Male Supremacist Complex." *American Anthropologist* 78: 521–38.

Douglas, Mary. 1966. *Purity and Danger*. New York: Praeger.

Douglas, Mary, and Aaron Wildavsky. 1982. *Risk and Culture: An Essay on the Selection of Technical and Environmental Changes*. Berkeley: University of California Press.

Douglas, Ngaire. 1996. *They Came for Savages: 100 Years of Tourism in Melanesia*. Lismore: Southern Cross University Press.

Dréze, Jean, and Amartya Sen. 1991. *Hunger and Public Action*. New York: Cambridge University Press.

Dumont, Louis. 1970. *Homo Hierarchicus: An Essay on the Caste System*. Chicago: University of Chicago Press.

Durham, William H. 1990. "Advances in Evolutionary Culture Theory." *Annual Review of Anthropology* 19: 187–210. Palo Alto: Annual Reviews.

Durkheim, Emile. 1961. *The Elementary Forms of the Religious Life*. New York: Collier.

Dyck, Noel. 2000. "Games, Bodies, Celebrations, and Boundaries: Anthropological Perspectives on Sports." In *Sports, Games and Cultures*. Edited by Noel Dyke. Oxford: Berg.

Dyck, Noel, and James B. Waldram, eds. 1993. *Anthropology, Public Policy, and Native Peoples in Canada*. Montreal and Kingston: McGill–Queen's University Press.

Eckert, Penelope, and Sally McConnell-Ginet. 2003. *Language and Gender*. Cambridge: Cambridge University Press.

Edmonds, Alexander. 2010. *Pretty Modern: Beauty, Sex, and Plastic Surgery in Brazil*. Durham: Duke University Press.

Eisler, Riane. 1987. *The Chalice and the Blade*. New York: Harper and Row.

Eller, Jack. 1999. "Quebec: Masters in Our Own House." In *From Culture to Ethnicity to Conflict: An Anthropological Perspective on International Ethnic Conflict*. Ann Arbor: University of Michigan Press.

Epp, Marlene, Francis Iacovetta, and Francis Swyripa, eds. 2004. *Sisters or Strangers? Immigrant, Ethnic, and Racialized Women in Canadian History*. Toronto: University of Toronto Press.

Erasmus, Charles. 1977. *In Search of the Common Good*. Glencoe: The Free Press.

Ervin, Alexander M. 2001. *Canadian Perspectives in Cultural Anthropology*. Toronto: Nelson Education.

——. 2005. *Applied Anthropology: Tools and Perspectives for Contemporary Practice*. Boston: Allyn and Bacon.

Escobar, Arturo. 1995. *Encountering Development: The Making and Unmaking of the Third World*. Princeton: Princeton University Press.

Evans-Pritchard, E.E. 1940. *The Nuer: A Description of the Modes of Livelihood and Political Institutions of a Nilotic People*. Oxford: Clarendon.

——. 1985. *Theories of Primitive Religion*. San Francisco: Greenwood.

Farah, Randa. 2003. "The Marginalization of Palestinian Refugees." In *Problems of Protection: The UNHCR, Refugees, and Human Rights*. Edited by Niklaus Steiner, Mark Gibney, and Gil Loescher. New York and London: Routledge.

——. 2004. "But Where Shall I Return? Where To? 1948 Palestinian Refugees: Land and Return." *Mediterranean Journal of Human Rights* 8(2): 157–84.

——. 2005. "Out of the Shadows: Listening to Place-Based Narratives of Palestinian Women." In *Women and the Politics of Place*. Edited by Wendy Harcourt and Arturo Escobar. Bloomfield: Kumarian.

Farmer, Paul. 1992. *AIDS and Accusation: Haiti and the Geography of Blame*. Berkeley: University of California Press.

——. 2003. *Pathologies of Power: Health, Human Rights, and the New War on the Poor*. Berkeley: University of California Press.

Fausto-Sterling, Anne. 1993. "The Five Sexes: Why Male and Female Are Not Enough." *The Sciences* 33: 20–24.

Fei, Hsiao-Tung. 1939. *Peasant Life in China: A Field Study of Country Life in the Yangtze Valley*. London: Routledge and Kegan Paul.

Feinberg, Richard. 2001. "Introduction: Schneider's Cultural Analysis of Kinship and Its Implications for Anthropological Relativism." In *The Cultural Analysis of Kinship: The Legacy of David M. Schneider*. Edited by Feinberg and M. Ottenheimer Urbana: University of Illinois Press.

Feit, Harvey A. 1973. "The Ethno-Ecology of the Waswanipi Cree; or How Hunters Manage Their Resources." In *Cultural Ecology*. Edited by B. Cox. Toronto: McClelland & Stewart.

——. 1982. "The Income Security Program for Cree Hunters in Quebec: An Experiment in Increasing the Autonomy of Hunters in a Developed Nation State." *Canadian Journal of Anthropology* 3(1): 57–70.

——. 2001. "Hunting, Nature, and Metaphor: Political and Discursive Strategies in James Bay Cree Resistance and Autonomy." In *Indigenous Traditions and Ecology: The Interbeing of Cosmology and Community*. Edited by John A. Grim. Cambridge, MA: Harvard Divinity School.

——. 2004a. "Hunting and the Quest for Power: The James Bay Cree and Whiteman Development." In *Native Peoples: The Canadian Experience*. Edited by R. Bruce Morrison and C. Roderick Wilson. Don Mills, ON: Oxford University Press.

——. 2004b. "James Bay Crees' Life Projects and Politics: Histories of Place, Animal Partners and Enduring Relationships." In *In The Way of Development: Indigenous Peoples, Life Projects, and Globalization*. Edited by Mario Blaser, Harvey A. Feit, and Glenn McRae. London and New York: Zed Books in association with the International Development Research Centre, Ottawa.

Fenton, Cameron. 2010. "The Ethnography of an Airstrike: Canada's Military Academics in the Afghan War and at Home." http://www.dominionpaper.ca/articles/3295

Ferguson, R. Brian. 1992. "A Savage Encounter: Western Contact and the Yanomami War Complex." In *War in the Tribal Zone: Expanding States and Indigenous Warfare*. Edited by R. Brian Ferguson and Neil L. Whitehead. Santa Fe: School of American Research Press.

Ferguson, R. Brian. 1995. *Yanomami Warfare: A Political History*. Santa Fe: School of the American Research Press.

Fernandez, James W. 1978. "African Religious Movements." In *Annual Review of Anthropology* 7: 195–234. Palo Alto: Annual Reviews.

Fienup-Riordan, Ann. 1990. *Eskimo Essays: Yup'ik Lives and How We See Them*. New Brunswick: Rutgers University Press.

Fisher, William. 1997. "Doing Good? The Politics and Antipolitics of NGO Practices." *Annual Review of Anthropology* 26: 439–64.

Fleras, Augie, and Jean Leonard Elliot. 2002. *Engaging Diversity: Multiculturalism in Canada*. Toronto: Nelson Education.

Foucault, Michel. 1979. *Discipline and Punish: The Birth of the Prison*. New York: Vintage.

Francis, Daniel. 1992. *The Imaginary Indian: The Image of the Indian in Canadian Culture*. Vancouver: Arsenal Pulp.

Franklin, Sarah, and Susan McKinnin, eds. 2001. *Relative Values: Reconfiguring Kinship Studies*. Durham: Duke University Press.

French, Hilary. 2000. *Vanishing Borders: Protecting the Planet in the Age of Globalization*. New York: Norton.

Frideres, James. 2003. *Native Peoples in Canada: Contemporary Conflicts*. Toronto: Prentice Hall.

Frideres, James S., and Rene Gadacz. 2001. *Aboriginal Peoples in Canada: Contemporary Conflicts*. Toronto: Prentice Hall.

Fried, Morton, Marvin Harris, and Robert Murphy. 1967. *War: The Anthropology of Armed Conflict and Aggression*. Garden City: Natural History Press.

Furniss, Elizabeth. 1992. *Victims of Benevolence: Discipline and Death at the Williams Lake Indian Residential School, 1891–1920*. Williams Lake: Cariboo Tribal Council.

Gagne, Marie-Anik. 1994. *A Nation Within a Nation: Dependency and the Cree*. Montreal: Black Rose.

Galton, Francis. 1879. *Hereditary Genius: An Inquiry into Its Laws and Consequences*. New York: Appleton.

Gardner, Katy, and David Lewis. 1996. *Anthropology, Development, and the Post-Modern Challenge*. London: Pluto.

Geertz, Clifford. 1972. "Deep Play: Notes on the Balinese Cockfight." *Daedalus* 101: 1–37.

—— . 1973. "The Impact of Culture on the Concept of Man." In *The Interpretation of Cultures*. New York: Basic.

Gellner, Ernest. 1983. *Nations and Nationalism*. Ithaca: Cornell University Press.

George, Susan, and Fabrizio Sabelli. 1994. *Faith and Credit: The World Bank's Secular Empire*. Boulder: Westview.

Gerber, Linda. 1990. "Multiple Jeopardy: A Socio-Economic Comparison of Men and Women Among the Indian, Metis, and Inuit Peoples of Canada." *Canadian Ethnic Studies* 22(3): 69–84.

Geschiere, Peter. 1997. *The Modernity of Witchcraft: Politics and the Occult in Postcolonial Africa*. Charlottesville: University Press of Virginia.

Gibson, Thomas. 1990. "Raiding, Trading, and Tribal Autonomy in Insular Southeast Asia." In *The Anthropology of War*. Edited by Jonathan Hass. New York: Cambridge University Press.

Giddens, Anthony. 1990. *The Consequences of Modernity*. Cambridge: Polity.

Gilmore, David D. 1990. *Manhood in the Making: Cultural Concepts of Masculinity*. New Haven: Yale University Press.

Ginsburg, Faye, and Rayna Rapp. 1991. "The Politics of Reproduction." In *Annual Review of Anthropology* 20: 311–43. Palo Alto: Annual Reviews.

Gledhill, John. 1994. *Power and Its Disguises: Anthropological Perspectives on Politics*. London: Pluto.

Goffman, Erving. 1999. *The Presentation of Self in Everyday Life*. New York: Peter Smith.

Gonzales, Roberto. 2009. *American Counterinsurgency: Human Science and the Human Terrain*. New York: Prickly Paradigm.

Gould, Stephen Jay. 1981. *The Mismeasure of Man*. New York: Norton.

Goulet, Jean-Guy A. 1998. *Ways of Knowing: Experience, Knowledge, and Power Among the Dene Tha*. Vancouver: UBC Press.

—— . 2004 "The Dene Tha of Chateh: Continuities and Transformations." In *Native Peoples: The Canadian Experience*. Edited by R. Bruce Morrison and C. Roderick Wilson. Toronto: Oxford University Press.

Green, Linda. 1995. "Living in a State of Fear." In *Fieldwork Under Fire: Contemporary Studies of Violence and Survival*. Edited by Carolyn Nordstrom and Antonius C.G. Robben. Berkeley: University of California Press.

Greenhouse, Carol. 1987. "Cultural Perspectives on War." In *The Quest for Peace: Transcending Collective Violence and War Among Societies, Cultures, and States*. Edited by R. Varynen. Beverly Hills: Sage.

Gremillon, Helen. 2003. *Feeding Anorexia: Gender and Power at a Treatment Center*. Durham: Duke University Press.

Gregor, Thomas. 1990. "Uneasy Peace: Intertribal Relations in Brazil's Upper Xingu." In *The Anthropology of War*. Edited by Jonathan Hass. New York: Cambridge University Press.

Grim, John A., ed. 2001. *Indigenous Traditions and Ecology: The Interbeing of Cosmology and Community*. Cambridge, MA: Harvard University Press.

Gruneau, Richard, and David Whitson, eds. 1993. *Artificial Ice: Hockey, Commerce, and Culture*. Peterborough: Broadview.

Gusterson, Hugh. 1995. *Nuclear Rites: A Weapons Laboratory at the End of the Cold War*. Berkeley: University of California Press.

Gwynne, Margaret A. 2003. *Applied Anthropology: A Career-Oriented Approach*. Boston: Allyn and Bacon.

Hall, Edgar T. 1966. *The Hidden Dimension*. Garden City: Doubleday.

Handler, Richard. 1988. *Nationalism and the Politics of Culture in Quebec*. Madison: University of Wisconsin Press.

Hanson, Allan. 1993. *Testing Testing*. Berkeley: University of California Press.

Hartman, Anne. 2009. "'Here for a Little Pickup?' Notes on Women's Shinny Hockey in Toronto Public Parks." In *Now is the Winter: Thinking about Hockey*. Edited by Jamie Dobb and Richard Harrison. Toronto: Wolsak and Wynn.

Hass, Jonathan, ed. 1990. *The Anthropology of War*. Cambridge: Cambridge University Press.

Harris, Marvin. 1977. *Cannibals and Kings: The Origins of Culture*. New York: Vintage.

Harris, Marvin, and Eric Ross. 1987. *Food and Evolution: Toward a Theory of Human Food Habits*. Philadelphia: Temple University Press.

Hedican, Edward J. 1986. *The Ogoki River Guides: Emergent Leadership Among the Northern Ojibwa*. Waterloo: Wilfrid Laurier University Press.

——. 1995. *Applied Anthropology in Canada: Understanding Aboriginal Issues*. Toronto: University of Toronto Press.

——. 2001. *Up in Nipigon Country: Anthropology as a Personal Experience*. Halifax: Fernwood.

Hedley, Max. 1998. "Shadow of Domination: Colonialism, Household, and Community Relations." In *Transgressing Borders: Critical Perspectives on Gender, Household, and Culture*. Edited by Suzan Ilcan and Lynne Phillips. Westport: Bergin and Garvey.

Helly, Denise. 2004. "Are Muslims Discriminated Against Since September 2001?" *Canadian Ethnic Studies* 36(1): 24–47.

Helm, June. 1965. "Bilaterality in the Social Organization of the Arctic Drainage Dene." *Ethnology* 4: 361–85.

Henare, Manuka. 2001. "Tapu, Mana, Mauri, Hau, Wairua: A Maori Philosophy of Vitalism and Cosmos." In *Indigenous Traditions and Ecology: The Interbeing of Cosmology and Community*. Edited by John A. Grim. Cambridge, MA: Harvard University Press.

Henderson, Paul. 1976. "Class Structure and the Concept of Intelligence." In *Schooling and Capitalism: A Sociological Reader*. Edited by Roger Dale, Geoff Esland, and Madeleine MacDonald. London: Routledge and Kegan Paul in association with Open University Press.

Henry, Paget. 1997. "Rastafarianism and the Reality of Dread." In *Existence in Black: An Anthology of Black Existential Philosophy*. Edited by L.R. Gordon. New York: Routledge.

Herrnstein, Richard J., and Charles Murray. 1994. *The Bell Curve: Intelligence and Class Structure in American Life*. New York: The Free Press.

Hertz, Robert. 1960. *Death and the Right Hand*. Glencoe: The Free Press.

Herzfeld, Michael. 2001. *Anthropology: Theoretical Practice in Culture and Society*. Malden: Blackwell.

Hobbes, Thomas. 1881[1651]. *Leviathan*. London: Oxford University Press.

Hoben, Allan. 1982. "Anthropologists and Development." In *Annual Review of Anthropology* 11: 349–75. Palo Alto: Annual Reviews.

Hobsbaum, Eric. 1959. *Primitive Rebels: Studies in Archaic Forms of Social Movement in the 19th and 20th Centuries*. New York: Praeger.

Hoerder, Dirk. 2002. *Cultures in Contact: World Migrations in the Second Millennium*. Durham: Duke University Press.

Holmes, Teresa. 1997. "Contested Kinship and the Dispute of Customary Law in Colonial Kenya." *Anthropologica* 39: 79–90.

Honigmann, John J. 1963. *Understanding Culture*. New York: Harper and Row.

——. 1976. *The Development of Anthropological Ideas*. Homewood: Dorsey.

Hoodfar, Homa. 2003. "More Than Clothing: Veiling as an Adaptive Strategy." In *The Muslim Veil in North America*. Edited by Sajida Sultana Alvi, Homa Hoodfar, and Sheila McDonough. Toronto: Women's Press.

Hostetler, John. 1974. *Hutterite Society*. Baltimore: Johns Hopkins University Press.

House, James S., Karl R. Landis, and Debra Umberson. 1988. "Social Relationships and Health." *Science* 241: 540–45.

Howell, Signe, and Roy Willis, eds. *Societies at Peace: Anthropological Perspectives.* London and New York: Routledge.

Hsu, Francis L.K. 1967. *Under the Ancestor's Shadow.* New York: Anchor.

Hutchinson, John, and Anthony D. Smith, eds. 1994. *Nationalism.* Oxford: Oxford University Press.

Inhorn, Marcia C., and Peter J. Brown. 1990. "The Anthropology of Infectious Disease." In *Annual Review of Anthropology* 19: 89–117. Palo Alto: Annual Reviews.

Irwin, Anne. 2002. "The Social Organization of Soldiering: A Canadian Infantry Company in the Field." Ph.D. diss., Manchester University.

——. 2012. "'There Will Be a Lot of Old Young Men Coming Home': Combat and Becoming a Man in Afghanistan." In *Young Men in Uncertain Times.* Edited by V. Amit and N. Dyck. New York: Berghahn.

Isbister, John. 2003. *Promises Not Kept: Poverty and Betrayal of Third World Development.* Bloomfield: Kumarian.

Jensen, Arthur. 1972. *Genetics and Education.* New York: Harper and Row.

Johnson, Norris Brock. 1985. *Westhaven: Classroom Culture and Society in a Rural Elementary School.* Chapel Hill: University of North Carolina Press.

Jorgensen, Dan. 1990. "Placing the Past and Moving the Present: Myth and Contemporary History in Telefolmin." *Culture* 10(2): 47–56.

——. 1996. "Regional History and Ethnic Identity in the Hub of New Guinea: The Emergence of the Min." *Oceania* 66(3): 189–210.

——. 1997. "Who and What Is a Landowner? Mythology and Marking the Ground in a Papua New Guinea Mining Project." *Anthropological Forum* 7(4): 599–627.

Judd, Ellen R. 1994. *Gender and Power in Rural North China.* Stanford: Stanford University Press.

Juergensmeyer, Mark. 2004. *Terror in the Mind of God: The Global Rise of Religious Violence.* Berkeley: University of California Press.

Kafka, Peter. 2005. "Top Earning Dead Celebrities." *Forbes.* http://www.forbes.com/2005/10/25/highest-earning-dead-celebrities_deadceleb05_land.html.

Karier, Clarence J. 1976. "Testing for Order and Control in the Corporate Liberal State." In *Schooling and Capitalism: A Sociological Reader.* Edited by Roger Dale, Geoff Esland, and Madeleine MacDonald. London: Routledge and Kegan Paul in association with the Open University Press.

Kazemipur, Abdolmohammad, and Shiva S. Halli. 2001. "The Changing Colour of Poverty in Canada." *Canadian Review of Sociology and Anthropology* 38(2): 217–38.

Kearney, Michael. 1991. "A Very Bad Disease of the Arms." In *The Naked Anthropologist: Tales from Around the World.* Edited by Philip Devita. Belmont: Wadsworth.

Keesing, Roger. 1991. "Not a Real Fish: The Ethnographer as Inside Outsider." In *The Naked Anthropologist: Tales from Around the World.* Edited by Philip Devita. Belmont: Wadsworth.

Kehoe, Alice. 1989. *The Ghost Dance: Ethnohistory and Revitalization.* New York: Holt, Rinehart, and Winston.

Keiser, Lincoln. 1969. *The Vice Lords: Warriors of the Streets.* New York: Holt, Rinehart, and Winston.

Kelly, John D., and Martha Kaplan. 1990. "History, Structure, and Ritual." In *Annual Review of Anthropology* 19: 119–50. Palo Alto: Annual Reviews.

Kennedy, Paul. 1993. *Preparing for the Twenty-First Century.* New York: Random House.

Keohane, Kieran. 1997. *Symptoms of Canada: An Essay on the Canadian Identity.* Toronto: University of Toronto Press.

Kets de Vries, Manfred, and Danny Miller. 1987. "Interpreting Organizational Texts." *Journal of Management Studies* 24: 233–47.

Kidder, Tracy. 2003. *Mountains Beyond Mountains.* New York. Random House.

Kiefer, Christie. 1976. "The Danchi Zoku and the Evolution of the Metropolitan Mind." In *Japan: The Paradox of Progress.* Edited by Lewis Austin, with the assistance of Adrienne Suddard and Nancy Remington. New Haven: Yale University Press.

Kinkade, Kathleen. 1973. *A Walden Two Experiment: The First Five Years of Twin Oaks Community.* New York: William Morrow.

Klaits, Frederick. 2005. "The Widow in Blue: Blood and the Morality of Remembering in Botswana's Time of AIDS." *Africa* 75(1): 46–62.

Korten, David C. 1995. *When Corporations Rule the World.* Hartford: Kumarian.

Kotlowitz, Alex. 1991. *There Are No Children Here.* New York: Anchor.

Kramer, Jennifer. 2007. *Switchbacks: Art, Ownership and Nuxalk National Identity.* Vancouver: UBC Press.

Kroeber, Alfred L. 1948. *Anthropology.* New York: Harcourt, Brace.

Kuper, Leo. 1981. *Genocide: Its Political Use in the Twentieth Century.* New Haven: Yale University Press.

Lakoff, George, and Mark Johnson. 1980. *Metaphors We Live By.* Chicago: University of Chicago Press.

Lakoff, Robin. 1975. *Language and Women's Place.* New York: Harper and Row.

Lambek, Michael. 2002. "General Introduction." In *A Reader in the Anthropology of Religion.* Edited by Michael Lambek. Malden: Blackwell.

Lang, Sabine. 1998. *Men as Women, Women as Men: Changing Gender in Native American Cultures.* Austin: University of Texas Press.

Langlois, Kellie, and Didier Garriguet. 2011. *Sugar Consumption Among Canadians of All Ages.* http://www.statcan.gc.ca.myaccess.library.utoronto.ca/pub/82-003-x/2011003/article/11540-cng.htm

Lappé, Frances Moore, and Joseph Collins. 1977. *Food First: Beyond the Myth of Scarcity.* New York: Random House.

Lee, Richard. 1969. "Eating Christmas in the Kalihari." *Natural History Magazine.* December.

——. 1984. *The Dobe !Kung.* New York: Holt, Rinehart, and Winston.

Lee, Richard, and Irven DeVore, eds. 1968. *Man the Hunter.* Chicago: Aldine.

Lee, Richard, and Ida Susser. 2002. "Facing the Challenge of HIV/AIDS." *Cultural Survival Quarterly* 26(1). http://www.culturalsurvival.org/publications/cultural-survival-quarterly/botswana/facing-challenge-hivaids

Leslie, Heather Young. 1998. "The Anthropologist, the Mother, and the Cross-cultured Child." In *Fieldwork and Families: Constructing Models for Ethnographic Research.* Edited by Juliana Flinn, Leslie Marshall, and Jocelyn Armstrong. Honolulu: University of Hawai'i Press.

Levi-Strauss, Claude. 1966. *The Savage Mind.* Chicago: University of Chicago Press.

——. 1974. *Tristé Tropiques.* New York: Atheneum.

Lewellen, Ted. 2002. *The Anthropology of Globalization: Cultural Anthropology Enters the 21st Century.* Westport: Bergin and Garvey.

Lewin, Ellen, and William L. Leap, eds. 2002. *Out in Theory: The Emergence of Lesbian and Gay Anthropology.* Chicago: University of Chicago Press.

Lewis, Oscar. 1959. *Five Families: Mexican Case Studies in the Culture of Poverty.* New York: Basic.

Li, Tania. 1999a, ed. *Transforming the Indonesian Uplands: Marginality, Power, and Production.* Amsterdam: Harwood.

——. 1999b. "Compromising Power: Development, Culture, and Rule in Indonesia." *Cultural Anthropology* 14(3): 295–322.

Li, Tania. 2002. "Local Histories, Global Markets: Cocoa and Class in Upland Sulawesi." *Development and Change* 33(3): 415–37.

Lightner, Sara, and Anna Naupa. 2005. *Histri Blong Yumi Long Vanuatu.* Port Vila: Vanuatu Cultural Centre.

Lithman, Yngve G. 2004. "Anthropologists on Home Turf: How Green Is the Grass?" *Anthropologica* 46(1): 17–27.

Lofgren, Orvar. 1999. *On Holiday: A History of Vacationing.* Berkeley: University of California Press.

Long, David, and Olive Patricia Dickason, eds. 2000. *Visions of the Heart: Canadian Aboriginal Issues.* Toronto: Harcourt Canada.

Longres, John F. 1990. *Human Behavior in the Social Environment.* Itasca: F.E. Peacock.

Lorber, Judith. 1994. *Paradoxes of Gender.* New Haven: Yale University Press.

Lorway, Robert. 2006. "Dispelling 'Heterosexual African AIDS' in Namibia: Same-Sex Sexuality in the Township of Katutura." *Culture, Health, and Sexuality* 8(5): 435–49.

——. 2007. "Breaking a Public Health Silence: HIV Risk and Male–Male Sexual Practices in the Windhoek Urban Area." In *Unravelling Taboos: Gender and Sexuality in Namibia.* Edited by S. Lafont and D. Hubbard. Windhoek: Gender Research and Advocacy Project, Legal Assistance Centre.

Luhrmann, T.M. 1989. *Persuasions of the Witch's Craft: Ritual Magic in Contemporary England.* Cambridge, MA: Harvard University Press.

Luxton, Meg, ed. 1997. *Feminism and Families: Critical Policies and Changing Practices*. Halifax: Fernwood.

Lyons, Andrew P., and Harriet D. Lyons. 2004. *Irregular Connections: A History of Anthropology and Sexuality*. Lincoln: University of Nebraska Press.

Mackey, Eva. 1999. *The House of Difference: Cultural Politics and National Identity in Canada*. London and New York: Routledge.

Macnair, Peter. 2004. "From Kwakiutl to Kwakwaka'wakw." In *Native Peoples: The Canadian Experience*. Edited by R. Bruce Morrison and C. Roderick Wilson. Toronto: Oxford University Press.

Malinowski, Bronislaw. 1929. *The Sexual Life of Savages in North-Western Melanesia*. New York: Halcyon House.

——. 1944. *A Scientific Theory of Culture, and Other Essays*. Chapel Hill: University of North Carolina Press.

——. 1948. *Magic, Science, and Religion, and Other Essays*. Boston: Beacon.

——. 1961[1922]. *Argonauts of the Western Pacific*. New York: Dutton.

Marchak, Patricia M. 2003. *Reins of Terror*. Montreal and Kingston: McGill–Queen's University Press.

Marcus, George E. 1995. Ethnography in/of the World System: The Emergence of Multi-Sited Ethnography. *Annual Review of Anthropology* 24(1): 95-117.

Marshall, Lorna. 1976. *The !Kung of Nyae Nyae*. Cambridge, MA: Harvard University Press.

Martin, Emily. 1987. *The Woman in the Body: A Cultural Analysis of Reproduction*. Boston: Beacon.

Martin-Hill, Dawn . 2004. "Resistance, Determination, and Perseverance of the Lubicon Cree Women." In *In the Way of Development: Indigenous peoples, Life Projects, and Globalization*. Edited by H.A. Feit, M. Blaser, and G. McRae. New York: Palgrave Macmillan.

——. 2008. *The Lubicon Lake Nation: Indigenous Knowledge and Power*. Toronto: University of Toronto Press.

Marwick, Max. 1965. *Sorcery in Its Social Setting*. Manchester: University of Manchester Press.

Matsubara, Hisako. 1985. *Cranes at Dusk*. New York: Dial.

Mattingly, Cheryl, Mary Lawlor, and Lanita Jacobs-Huey. 2002. "Narrating September 11: Race, Gender, and the Play of Cultural Identities." *American Anthropologist* 104(743): 743–53.

Mauss, Marcel. 1967[1925]. *The Gift: Forms and Functions of Exchange in Archaic Societies*. Translated by Ian Cunnison. New York: Norton.

Maybury-Lewis, David. 1997. *Indigenous Peoples, Ethnic Groups, and the State*. Boston: Allyn and Bacon.

McCauley, Clark. 1990. "Conference Overview." In *The Anthropology of War*. Edited by Jonathan Hass. New York: Cambridge University Press.

McElroy, Ann, and Patricia Townsend. 1979. *Medical Anthropology*. North Scituate: Duxbury.

McFate, Montgomery. 2005. "Anthropology and Counterinsurgency: The Strange Story of their Curious Relationship." *Military Review*, March–April.

McFate, Montgomery and Andrea Jackson. "An Organizational Solution for DOD's Cultural Knowledge Needs." *Military Review*, May–June.

McGarry, Karen. 2011. "Mass Media and Gender Identity in High Performance Canadian Figure Skating." In *The Gendered Society Reader*. Edited by M. Kimmel, A. Aronson, and A. Kaler. 2nd Can. Ed. Cambridge: Oxford University Press.

McGee, R. Jon, and Richard Warms. 2000. *Anthropological Theory: An Introductory History*. Mountain View: Mayfield.

McIntosh, Peggy. 1988. "White Privilege and Male Privilege: A Personal Account of Coming to See Correspondences Through Work in Women's Studies." Working Paper no. 189. Wellesley College Center for Research on Women, Wellesley, MA.

McNally, David. 2002. *Another World Is Possible: Globalization and Anti-Capitalism*. Winnipeg: Arbeiter Ring.

Mead, Margaret. 1928. *Coming of Age in Samoa: A Psychological Study of Primitive Youth for Western Civilization*. New York: Morrow.

Miller, Bruce Granville. 2003. *Invisible Indigenes: The Politics of Nonrecognition*. Lincoln: University of Nebraska Press.

Mills, Antonia. 1988. "A Preliminary Investigation of Cases of Reincarnation Among the Beaver and Gitksan Indians." *Anthropologica* 30: 23–59.

Mills, Antonia, and Richard Slobodin, eds. 1994. *Amerindian Rebirth: Reincarnation Belief Among North American Indians and Inuit*. Toronto: University of Toronto Press.

Mintz, Sidney W. 1985. *Sweetness and Power: The Place of Sugar in World History*. New York: Viking.

Mishkin, Bernard. 1940. *Rank and Warfare Among the Plains Indians*. Monograph No. 3, American Ethnological Society. Seattle: University of Washington Press.

Moffat, Tina, and Elizabeth Finnis. 2005. "Considering Social and Material Resources: The Political Ecology of a Peri-Urban Squatter Community in Nepal." *Habitat International* 29: 453–468.

Monture-Angus, Patricia A. 2000. "Lessons in Decolonization: Aboriginal Over-Representation in Canadian Criminal Justice." In *Visions of the Heart: Canadian Aboriginal Issues*. Edited by David Long and Olive Patricia Dickason. Toronto: Harcourt Canada.

Mooney, James. 2011[1897]. *The Ghost Dance Religion and the Sioux Outbreak of 1890*. Chicago: University of Chicago Press.

Moore, Henrietta. 1988. *Feminism and Anthropology*. Cambridge: Polity.

Moore, Henrietta, and Todd Sanders, eds. 2005. *Anthropology in Theory: Issues in Epistemology*. Malden: Blackwell.

Moore, Patrick, Angela Wheelock, and Dene Wodih Society. 1990. *Wolverine Myths and Visions: Dene Traditions from Northern Alberta*. Lincoln: University of Nebraska Press.

Moore, Robert B. 1976. *Racism in the English Language*. New York: Council on Interracial Books for Children.

Moore, Sally Falk. 2005. *Law and Anthropology: A Reader*. Oxford: Blackwell.

Moos, Robert, and Robert Brownstein. 1977. *Environment and Utopia*. New York: Plenum.

Morgan, Lewis Henry. 1964[1877]. *Ancient Society*. Cambridge, MA: Belknap.

Morrison, David. 2000. "Canadian Aid: A Mixed Record and an Uncertain Future." In *Transforming Development, Foreign Aid for a Changing World*. Edited by J. Freedman. Toronto: University of Toronto Press.

Morrison, R. Bruce, and C. Roderick Wilson, eds. 2004. *Native Peoples: The Canadian Experience*. Toronto: Oxford University Press.

Morton, Samuel G. 1844. *An Inquiry into the Distinctive Characteristics of the Aboriginal Race of America*. Philadelphia: Penington.

Mukhopadhyay, Carol C., and Patricia J. Higgins. 1988. "Anthropological Studies of Women's Status Revisited: 1977–1987." In *Annual Review of Anthropology* 17: 461–495. Palo Alto: Annual Reviews.

Murray, David A.B. 2002 *Opacity: Gender, Sexuality, Race, and the "Problem" of Identity in Martinique*. New York: Peter Lang.

Myer, Fred R. 1988. "Critical Trends in the Study of Hunters-Gatherers." In *Annual Review of Anthropology* 17: 261–82. Palo Alto: Annual Reviews.

Nader, Laura, ed. 1996. *Naked Science: Anthropological Inquiry into Boundaries, Power, and Knowledge*. New York: Routledge.

Nagengast Carole. 1994. "Violence, Terror, and the Crisis of the State." In *Annual Review of Anthropology* 23: 109–36. Palo Alto: Annual Reviews.

Nagengast, Carole, and Carlos G. Velez-Ibanez, eds. 2004. *Human Rights: The Scholar as Activist*. Oklahoma City: Society for Applied Anthropology.

Narayan, Kirin. 1993. "How Native Is a 'Native' Anthropologist?" *American Anthropologist* 95(3): 671-86.

Nations, James D. 1994. "The Ecology of the Zapatista Revolt." *Cultural Survival Quarterly* 18: 31–33.

Neider, Charles. 1966. *The Complete Travel Books of Mark Twain*. New York: Doubleday.

Neizen, Ronald. 1993. "Power and Dignity: The Social Consequences of Hydro-Electric Development for the James Bay Cree." *Canadian Review of Sociology and Anthropology* 30(4): 510.

———. 2003. *The Origins of Indigenism: Human Rights and the Politics of Identity*. Berkeley: University of California Press.

———. 2004. "Indigenous Peoples in a Global Era." In *Globalization and Community: Canadian Perspectives*. Edited by Jean-Luc Chodkiewicz and Raymond E. Wiest. Winnipeg: University of Manitoba Press.

Ng, Roxana. 2002. "Freedom for Whom? Globalization and Trade from the Standpoint of Garment Workers." *Canadian Woman Studies* 21/22(4/1): 74–81.

———. 2007. "Garment Production in Canada: Social and Political Implications. *Studies in Political Economy* 79 (Spring): 3-11.

Nichter, Mimi. 2000. *Fat Talk: What Girls and Their Parents Say About Dieting*. Cambridge, MA: Harvard University Press.

Nigh, Ronald. 1995. "Animal Agriculture for the Reforestation of Degraded Tropical Rainforests." *Culture and Agriculture* 51–52: 2–5.

Nordstrom, Carolyn. 2004. *Shadows of War: Violence, Power, and International Profiteering in the Twenty-First Century.* Berkeley: University of California Press.

Omohundro, John T. 2001. *Careers in Anthropology.* Mountain View: Mayfield.

Ontario Ministry of Aboriginal Affairs. Aboriginal Labour Force. http://www.aboriginalaffairs.gov.on.ca/english/services/datasheets/labour.asp.

Ortner, Sherry B., and Harriet Whitehead, eds. 1981. *Sexual Meanings: The Cultural Construction of Gender and Sexuality.* Cambridge: Cambridge University Press.

Otterbein, Keith F. 2004. *How War Began.* College Station: Texas A&M University Press.

Pagels, Elaine H. 1995. *The Origin of Satan.* New York: Random House.

Paine, Robert, ed. 1985. *Advocacy and Anthropology: First Encounters.* St. John's: Institute of Social and Economic Research.

Palgi, Phyllis, and Henry Abramovitch. 1984. "Death: A Cross-Cultural Perspective." In *Annual Review of Anthropology* 13: 385–417. Palo Alto: Annual Reviews.

Parkin, Robert, and Linda Stone, eds. 2004. *Kinship and Family: An Anthropological Reader.* Malden: Blackwell.

Patrick, Donna. 2003. *Language, Politics, and Social Interaction in an Inuit Community.* Berlin: Mouton de Gruyter.

Paulson, Susan, Lisa L. Gezon, and Michael Watts. 2003. "Locating the Political in Political Ecology: An Introduction." *Human Organization* 62(3): 205–17.

Pearson, Karl. 1901. "On the Inheritance of Mental Characteristics in Man." In *Proceedings of the Royal Society of London* 69: 153–55.

Pengelly, Ryan. D., and Irwin, Anne. 2011. "Twenty-first Century Narratives from Afghanistan: Storytelling, Morality, and War. In *The Routledge Handbook of War and Society: Iraq and Afghanistan.* Edited by M.G. Ender and S. Carlton-Ford. New York: Routledge.

Philips, Susan U. 1980. "Sex Differences and Language." In *Annual Review of Anthropology* 9: 523–44. Palo Alto: Annual Reviews.

Polanyi, Karl. 1957[1944]. *The Great Transformation.* Boston: Beacon.

Pratt, Cranford. 2000. "Alleviating Global Poverty or Enhancing Security: Competing Rationales for Canadian Development Assistance." In *Transforming Development: Foreign Aid for a Changing World.* Edited by J. Freedman. Toronto: University of Toronto Press.

Preston, Richard J. 1975. *Cree Narrative: Expressing the Personal Meaning of Events.* Ottawa: Natioanl Museum of Canada.

——. 2004. "Cumulative Cultural Change in the Moose and Rupert River Basins: Local Cultural Sites Affected by Global Influences." In *Globalization and Community.* Edited by J.L. Chodkiewicz and Raymond E. Wiest. Winnipeg: University of Manitoba Press.

Pryce, Paula. 1999. *"Keeping the Lakes' Way": Reburial and the Re-Creation of a Moral World Among an Invisible People.* Toronto: University of Toronto Press.

Psacharopoulos, George, and Harry A. Patrinos. 1994. "Indigenous People and Poverty in Latin America." *Finance and Development* 31.

Read, Kenneth E. 1965. *The High Valley.* New York: Columbia University Press.

Reardon, Betty. 1985. *Sexism and the War System.* New York: Columbia University Teachers College Press.

Reed, Richard. 1997. *Forest Dwellers, Forest Protectors: Indigenous Models for International Development.* Boston: Allyn and Bacon.

Rich, Bruce. 1994. *Mortgaging the Earth: The World Bank, Environmental Impoverishment, and the Crisis of Development.* Boston: Beacon.

Ridington, Robin. 1990. *Little Bit Know Something: Stories in a Language of Anthropology.* Iowa City: University of Iowa Press.

Rindos, David. 1984. *The Origins of Agriculture.* New York: Academic Press.

Rivoli, Pietra. 2005. *The Travels of a T-Shirt in the Global Economy: An Economist Examines the Markets, Power, and the Politics of World Trade.* Hoboken: John Wiley.

Robarchek, Clayton. 1990. "Motivations and Material Causes: On the Explanation of Conflict and War." In *The Anthropology of War.* Edited by Jonathan Hass. New York: Cambridge University Press.

Robbins, Richard H. 2005. *Global Problems and the Culture of Capitalism.* 3rd ed. Boston: Allyn and Bacon.

Rosaldo, Renato. 1989. *Culture and Truth: The Remaking of Social Analysis.* Boston: Beacon.

Rosaldo, Michele, and Jane Monnig Atkinson. 1975. "Man the Hunter and Woman: Metaphors for the

Sexes in Ilongot Magical Spells." In *The Interpretation of Symbolism*. Edited by Roy Willis. New York: John Wiley.

Ross, Rupert. 1992. *Dancing with a Ghost: Exploring Indian Reality*. Markham: Octopus.

Rothstein, Frances Abrahamer, and Michael L. Blim, eds. 1992. *Anthropology and the Global Factory: Studies of the New Industrialism in the Late Twentieth Century*. New York: Bergin and Garvey.

Rowe, Allen. 2004. "'The Mysterious Oriental Mind': Ethnic Surveillance and the Chinese in Canada During the Great War." *Canadian Ethnic Studies* 36(1): 48–70.

Roy, Ramashray. 1985. *Self and Society: A Study in Gandhian Thought*. Beverly Hills: Sage.

Rubel, Arthur. 1964. "The Epidemiology of a Folk Illness: Susto in Hispanic America." *Ethnology* 3: 268–83.

Ruoff, Jeffrey. 1996. "'Can a Documentary Be Made of Real Life?': The Reception of *An American Family*. In *The Construction of the Viewer: Media Ethnography and the Anthropology of Audiences*. Edited by P.I. Crawford and S.B. Hafsteinnsson. Denmark: Intervention.

Russell, Wendy. 2004. "The People Had Discovered Their Own Approach to Life: Politicizing Development Discourse." In *In the Way of Development: Indigenous Peoples, Life Projects, and Globalization*. Edited by Mario Blaser, Harvey A. Feit, and Glenn McRae. London and New York: Zed Books in association with International Development Research Centre, Ottawa.

Rutherford, Blair. 1999. "To Find a Witch: Anthropology, Witch-Finding in North-West Zimbabwe." *Critique of Anthropology* 19: 89–109.

Sahlins, Marshall. 1968. *Tribesmen*. New York: Prentice Hall.

Sanday, Peggy Reeves. 1981. "The Socio-Cultural Context of Rape: A Cross-Cultural Study." *Journal of Social Issues* 37: 5–27.

——. 2007[1990]. *Gang Rape: Sex, Brotherhood and Privilege on Campus*. 2nd ed. New York: NYU Press.

Satzewich, Vic. 1991. *Racism and the Incorporation of Foreign Labour: Farm Labour Migration to Canada Since 1945*. London: Routledge.

——, ed. 1992. *Deconstructing a Nation: Immigration, Multiculturalism, and Racism in '90s Canada*. Halifax: Fernwood.

Scaglion, Richard. 1990. "Ethnocentrism and the Abelam." In *The Humbled Anthropologist: Tales from the Pacific*. Edited by Philip Devita. Belmont: Wadsworth.

Schieffelin, Bambi B., and Elinor Ochs. 1986. "Language Socialization." In *Annual Review of Anthropology* 15: 163–91. Palo Alto: Annual Reviews.

Scheper-Hughes, Nancy. 1992. *Death Without Weeping: The Violence of Everyday Life in Brazil*. Berkeley: University of California Press.

——. 1995. "The Primacy of the Ethical: Propositions for a Militant Anthropology." *Current Anthropology* 36: 409–420.

Scheper-Hughes, Nancy, and Philippe Bourgois, eds. 2004. *Violence in War and Peace*. Malden: Blackwell.

Schmidt, Bettina E., and Ingo W. Schroder, eds. 2001. *Anthropology of Violence and Conflict*. London and New York: Routledge.

Schneider, David M. 1984. *A Critique of the Study of Kinship*. Ann Arbor: University of Michigan Press.

Schrire, Carmel. 1984. "Wild Surmises on Savage Thoughts." In *Past and Present in Hunter Gatherer Studies*. Edited by Carmel Schrire. Orlando: Academic Press.

Sharma, Parnesh. 1998. *Aboriginal Fishing Rights: Laws, Courts, Politics*. Halifax: Fernwood.

——. 2001. "On Not Being Canadian: The Social Organization of 'Migrant Workers' in Canada." *Canadian Review of Sociology and Anthropology* 38(4): 415–39.

Shewell, Hugh. 2004. *"Enough to Keep Them Alive": Indian Welfare in Canada, 1873–1965*. Toronto: University of Toronto Press.

Shipton, Parker. 1990. "African Famines and Food Security." In *Annual Review of Anthropology* 19: 353–94. Palo Alto: Annual Reviews.

Shore, Chris, and Susan Wright. 1997. *Anthropology of Policy: Critical Perspectives on Governance and Power*. London: Routledge.

Shostak, Marjorie. 1983. *Nisa: The Life and Words of a !Kung Woman*. New York: Vintage.

Shweder, Richard A., and Edmund J. Bourne. 1984. "Does the Concept of the Person Vary Cross-Culturally?" In *Cultural Conceptions of Mental Health and Therapy*. Edited by A.J. Marsella and G.M. White. Boston: Reidel.

Sidel, Ruth. 1986. *Women and Children Last: Social Stratification in America*. New York: Penguin.

Silverman, Martin G. 1979. "'Kinship': An Informal, Critical Guide to Some Problems." In *Challenging Anthropology*. Edited by David H. Turner and Gavin A. Smith. Toronto: McGraw-Hill Ryerson.

Sipes, Richard G. 1973. "War, Sports, and Aggression: An Empirical Test of Two Rival Theories." *American Anthropologist* 74: 64–86.

Skinner, B.F. 1962. *Walden Two*. New York: Macmillan.

Slobodin, Richard. 1994. "Kutchin Concepts of Reincarnation." In *Amerindian Rebirth: Reincarnation Belief Among North American Indians and Inuit*. Edited by Antonia Mills and Richard Slobodin. Toronto: University of Toronto Press.

Smith, Adam. 1994[1776]. *The Wealth of Nations*. Edited by Edwin Cannan. New York: Modern Library.

Smith, Gavin. 1999. *Confronting the Present: Towards a Politically Engaged Anthropology*. Oxford and New York: Berg.

Smith, Raymond T. 1984. "Anthropology and the Concept of Social Class." In *Annual Review of Anthropology* 13: 467–94. Palo Alto: Annual Reviews.

Smith, Robert J. 1983. *Japanese Society: Tradition, Self, and the Social Order*. New York: Cambridge University Press.

Solway, Jacqueline, ed. 2003. "Politics and Practice in Critical Anthropology: The Work of Richard B. Lee." Special Edition of *Anthropologica* 45(1): 1–128.

Solway, Jacqueline S., and Richard B. Lee. 1990. "Foragers, Genuine or Spurious? Situating the Kalahari San in History." *Current Anthropology* 31(2): 109–46.

Spearman, Charles. 1904. "General Intelligence." *American Journal of Psychology* 115: 201–92.

Stack, Carol. 1974. *All Our Kin: Strategies for Survival in a Black Community*. New York: Harper and Row.

Stafford, James. 1992. "The Impact of the New Immigration Policy on Racism in Canada." In *Deconstructing a Nation: Immigration, Multiculturalism, and Racism in '90s Canada*. Edited by Vic Satzewich. Halifax: Fernwood.

Stephenson, Peter H. 1991. *The Hutterian People: Ritual and Rebirth in the Evolution of Communal Life*. Lanham: University Press of America.

Stern, Jessica. 2003. *Terror in the Name of God: Why Religious Militants Kill*. New York: HarperCollins.

Stevens, Jacqueline. 1999. *Reproducing the State*. Princeton: Princeton University Press.

Stewart, Pamela J., and Andrew Strathern. 2002. *Violence: Theory and Ethnography*. London and New York: Continuum.

Stone, Linda, ed. 2001. *New Directions in Anthropological Kinship*. Lanham: Rowman and Littlefield.

Strong, William. 1929. "Cross-Cousin Marriage and the Culture of the Northeast Algonkian." *American Anthropologist* 31: 277–88.

Susser, Ida. 2006. The Other Side of Development: HIV/AIDS Among Men and Women in Ju/'hoansi Villages." In *The Politics of Egalitarianism: Theory and Practice*. Edited by J.S. Solway. New York: Berghahn.

—— . 2009. "Ju/'hoansi Women in the Age of HIV: An Exceptional Case." In *AIDS, Sex, and Culture: Global Politics and Survival in Southern Africa*. Edited by Ida Susser. Malden: Blackwell.

Taft, Michael. 1997. "Men in Women's Clothes: Theatrical Transvestites on the Canadian Prairie." In *Undisciplined Women: Tradition and Culture in Canada*. Edited by Pauline Greenhill and Diane Tye. Kingston and Montreal: McGill–Queen's University Press.

Tator, Carol, and Francis Henry. 2000. "The Role and Practice of Racialized Discourse in Culture and Cultural Production." *Journal of Canadian Studies* 35(3): 120–41.

Thomas, Elizabeth. 1959. *The Harmless People*. New York: Knopf.

Thompson, E.P. "Time, Work-Discipline, and Industrial Capitalism." *Past and Present* 38: 56–97.

Thrasher, Frederic. 1963[1927]. *The Gang*. Chicago: University of Chicago Press.

Todaro, Michael. 2000. *Economic Development*. Reading: Addison Wesley.

Toynbee, Jason. 2007. *Bob Marley: Herald of Postcolonial World?* Cambridge: Polity.

Trigger, Bruce. 1986. "Evolutionism, Relativism, and Putting Native People into Historical Context." *Culture* 6(2): 65–79.

Turner, Terence. 2005. "Ethical Issues Arising from Patrick Tierney's *Darkness in El Dorado* and the Ensuing Controversy." In *The Fierce Controversy and What We Can Learn from It*. Edited by R. Borofsky.

Turner, Victor. 1967. *The Forest of Symbols: Aspects of Ndembu Ritual*. Ithaca: Cornell University Press.

—— . 1995[1969]. *The Ritual Process*. Hawthorne: Aldine de Gruyter.

Tylor, Edward. 1871. *Primitive Culture*. London: Murray.

Valentine, Charles A. 1968. *Culture and Poverty: Critique and Counter-Proposals*. Chicago: University of Chicago Press.

van den Berghe, Pierre L. 1965. *South Africa: A Study in Conflict*. Middletown: Wesleyan University Press.

——. 1970. *Race and Ethnicity*. New York: Basic.

——. 1992. "The Modern State: Nation-Builder or Nation-Killer?" *International Journal of Group Tensions* 22: 191–208.

van den Berghe, Pierre L., and George P. Primov. 1977. *Inequality in the Peruvian Andes: Class and Ethnicity in Cuzco*. Columbia: University of Missouri Press.

van Gennep, Arnold. 1960[1906]. *The Rites of Passage*. Translated by Monica B. Vizedom and Gabrielle L. Chaffe. Chicago: University of Chicago Press.

VanWynsberghe, Robert M. 2002. *AlterNatives: Community, Identity, and Environmental Justice on Walpole Island*. Toronto: Allyn and Bacon.

Vincent, Joan, ed. 2002. *The Anthropology of Politics*. Oxford: Blackwell.

Von Gernet, Alexander. 1994. "Saving the Souls: Reincarnation Beliefs of the Seventeenth-Century Huron." In *American Rebirth: Reincarnation Belief Among North American Indians and Inuit*. Edited by Antonia Mills and Richard Slobodin. Toronto: University of Toronto Press.

Wagner, Roy. 1984. "Ritual as Communication: Order, Meaning, and Secrecy in Melanesian Initiation Rites." In *Annual Review of Anthropology* 13: 143–55. Palo Alto: Annual Reviews.

Waldram, James B. 1997. *The Way of the Pipe: Aboriginal Spirituality and Symbolic Healing in Canadian Prisons*. Peterborough: Broadview.

Waldram, James B., and J. O'Neil. 1989. "Native Health Research in Canada." Special Issue of *Native Studies Review* 5(1): 1–213.

Walens, Stanley. 1981. *Feasting With Cannibals: An Essay on Kwakiutl Cosmology*. Princeton: Princeton University Press.

Wall, Denis. 2000. "Aboriginal Self-Government in Canada: The Cases of Nunavut and the Alberta Metis Settlements." In *Visions of the Heart: Canadian Aboriginal Issues*. Edited by David Long and Olive Patricia Dickason. Toronto: Harcourt Canada.

Wall, Ellen. 1992. "Personal Labour Relations and Ethnicity in Ontario Agriculture." In *Deconstructing a Nation: Immigration, Multiculturalism and Racism in '90s Canada*. Edited by Vic Satzewich. Halifax: Fernwood.

Wallace, Anthony F.C. 1966. *Religion: An Anthropological View*. New York: Random House.

Wallerstein, Immanuel. 1989. *The Modern World-System III. The Second Era of Great Expansion of the Capitalist World-Economy, 1730–1840s*. New York: Academic.

Walsh, Andrew. 2002a. "Responsibility, Taboos, and 'The Freedom to Do Otherwise' in Ankarana, Northern Madagascar." *Journal of the Royal Anthropological Institute* 8(3): 451–68.

——. 2002b. "Saving Souls, Preserving Bodies: Religious Incongruity in a Northern Malagasy Mining Town." *Journal of Religion in Africa* 32(3): 366–92.

——. 2003. "'Hot Money' and Daring Consumption in a Northern Malagasy Town." *American Ethnologist* 30(2): 290–305.

——. 2004. "In the Wake of Things: Speculating in and about Sapphires in Northern Madagascar." *American Anthropologist* 106(2): 225–37.

——. 2010. "The Commodification of Fetishes: Telling the Difference Between Natural and Synthetic Sapphires." *American Ethnologist* 37(1): 98–114.

Washburn, Sherwood L., and C.S. Lancaster. 1968. "The Evolution of Hunting." In *Man the Hunter*. Edited by R.B. Lee and Irvene Devore. New York: Aldine.

Watson-Ellam, Linda. 2001. "Living Against the Wind. Pathways Chosen by Chinese Immigrants." *Canadian Ethnic Studies* 33(1): 71–101.

Weiner, Annette B. 1976. *Women of Value, Men of Renown*. Austin: University of Texas Press.

——. 1988. *The Trobrianders of Papua New Guinea*. New York: Holt, Rinehart, and Winston.

Weston, Kath. 1991. *Families We Choose: Lesbians, Gays, Kinship*. New York: Columbia University Press.

White, Leslie. 1949. *The Science of Culture*. New York: Farrar, Straus and Giroux.

——. 1959. *The Evolution of Culture*. New York: McGraw-Hill.

Whitehead, Harriet. 1981. "The Bow and the Burden Strap: A New Look at Institutionalized Homosexuality in Native North America." In *Sexual Meanings: The*

Cultural Construction of Gender and Sexuality. Edited by Sherry B. Ortner and Harriet Whitehead. New York: Cambridge University Press.

Whitehead, Neil Lancelot. 1990. "The Snake Warriors—Sons of the Tiger's Teeth: A Descriptive Analysis of Carib Warfare, ca. 1500–1820." In *The Anthropology of War*. Edited by Jonathan Hass. New York: Cambridge University Press.

Williams, Walter L. 1986. *The Spirit and the Flesh: Sexual Diversity in American Indian Culture*. Boston: Beacon.

Wilmsen, Edwin N., and James R. Denbow. 1990. "Paradigmatic History of San-Speaking Peoples and Current Attempts at Revision." *Current Anthropology* 31: 489–512.

Wilson, Richard A. 1997. *Human Rights, Culture, and Context: Anthropological Perspectives*. London: Pluto.

Wise, Amanda. 2006. *Exile and Return Among the East Timorese*. Philadelphia: University of Pennsylvania Press.

Wolf, Eric. 1964. *Anthropology*. Englewood Cliffs: Prentice-Hall.

——. 1966. *Peasants*. Englewood Cliffs: Prentice Hall.

——. 1969. *Peasant Wars of the Twentieth Century*. New York: Harper and Row.

——. 1982. *Europe and the People Without History*. Berkeley: University of California Press.

Wolf, Margery. 1968. *The House of Lim*. Englewood Cliffs: Prentice Hall.

Woodburn, James. 1968. "An Introduction to Hadza Ecology." In *Man the Hunter*. Edited by Richard Lee and Irven DeVore, with the assistance of Jill Nash. Chicago: Aldine.

Worsley, Peter. 1982. "Non-Western Medical Systems." In *Annual Review of Anthropology* 11: 315–48. Palo Alto: Annual Reviews.

Yan, Yunxiang. 2002. "Practicing Kinship in Rural North China." In *Practicing Kinship: Lineage and Descent in Late Imperial China*. Edited by Michael Szonyi. Stanford: Stanford University Press.

Yanagisako, Sylvia Junko. 1979. "Family and Household: The Analysis of Domestic Groups." In *Annual Review of Anthropology* 8: 161–205. Palo Alto: Annual Reviews.

Yanagisako, Sylvia, and Carol Delaney, eds. 1995. *Naturalizing Power: Essays on Feminist Cultural Analysis*. New York: Routledge.

Young, Allan. 1982. "The Anthropologies of Illness and Sickness." In *Annual Review of Anthropology* 11: 257–85. Palo Alto: Annual Reviews.

Young, K. 1988. *Health Care and Culture Change: The Indian Experience in the Central Subarctic*. Toronto: University of Toronto Press.

Zechenter, Elizabeth. 1997. "In the Name of Culture: Cultural Relativism and the Abuse of the Individual." *Journal of Anthropological Research—Universal Human Rights Versus Cultural Relativity* 53: 319–48.

Ziegler-Otero, Lawrence. 2004. *Resistance in an Amazonian Community: Huaorani Organizing Against the Global Economy*. New York and Oxford: Berghahn.

INDEX

Book of Revelation, 233–234
Bossen, Laurel, 131
Botswana, AIDS epidemic in, 134
Bourgois, Philippe, 23
Bourne, Edmund, 146
Brahmins, 168
Brazil, 60–61
    class in, 177–178
    debts, 60–61
    economic development, 61
    mortality rate for children, 69
    race in, 177–178
    social hierarchies in, 177–178
Bretton Woods Agreement, 60
Brideservice, 113, 240, 257
Bridewealth, 122, 257
Brière, Elaine, 246
British East India Company, 55
British North America Act of
    1867, 149
British Petroleum, 208
Brody, Hugh, 140, 141
Brown, Karen McCarthy, 102
Browning, Kurt, 221
Burt, Ben, 97

C
Cagan, Leslie, 241
Calder, Frank, 216
Cambodia, 242
Cameroon, modern witchcraft in,
    94–95
Canada
    garment industry, 210–211
    globalization and Canadian
        identity, 220–224
    hockey, 28–31, 142
    identity, 142
    immigration, 213
    multicultural policy, 214
    potato industry in, 51
    poverty rates among
        immigrants, 166
    races in, 213
    soldiers in Kandahar, 253–254
Canadian Forces, 253–254

Canadian identity, 141–142
Canadian International
    Developmental Agency
    (CIDA), 70
Canadian Nazi Party, 171
Canadian Pacific Railway, 205, 213
Cannibal Dance, 85–86
Cannibal Society, 85–86
Cannibalism, 21
Carib, 229–230
Carnegie Mellon University, 252
Carneiro, Robert L., 51, 241
Carpet bombing, 248
Carrier, James, 154–155, 157
Caste, 168–169, 257
Cecil, Ashley, 40f
Central America, 209
Chagnon, Napoleon, 15, 232, 239
Cherokee, 57–58
Cherokee Removal, 57f
Chewa, 67–68
Cheyenne, 178
Chiapas, Mexico, 62
Chimbinda, Jorge, 144–145
China, 7
    death in, 7
    family composition of rural
        Chinese, 116–119
    family cycle of rural Chinese,
        124–125
    food, 7
    marriage, 124–125
    opium trade, 55–56
Chinese, rural
    family composition of rural
        Chinese, 116–119
    family cycle of, 124–125
    marriage in, 124–125
    sex, love and wealth among,
        126–127
    threats to family, 129–130
Christianity, 187
    Dene Tha and, 96
    in Solomon Islands, 96–97
Christmas, 156–158
Christmas Carol, A (Dickens),
    156, 189

Christmas tree farms, 248
Church Missionary Society, 154
Churchill, Ward, 185
Clans, 43, 122, 257
Clark, Kim, 158
Class, 167, 173–176
    in Brazil, 177
    definition of, 257
    as form of social hierarchy, 168
    intelligence and, 173–176
Classroom chairs, 3–4
Clean bombs, 248
Clocks, 25
Clothing, as identity marker,
    151–152
Cockfight, Balinese, 26–28
Code of Conduct for Trademark
    Licensees, 211
Cohen, Mark, 48–49
Cohn, Carol, 248–249
Cola drink, 32
Collateral damage, 248
Collective identity, 158–162
Collings, Peter, 30–31
Columbus, Christopher, 9, 63
Comaroff, Jean, 88
Comaroff, John, 88
Coming of Age in Samoa (Mead), 14
Coming of Age in Second Life
    (Boelstorff), 12–13
Commodities, 154–155, 257
Common sense, 176
CONAIE (Confederation of
    Indigenous Nations of
    Ecuador), 158–159, 218
Condon, Richard, 30–31
Confederation of Indigenous
    Nations of Ecuador
    (CONAIE), 158–159, 218
Conklin, Beth, 21
Consuming Grief (Conklin), 21
Contraception, 244
Convention on the Prevention and
    Punishment of the Crime of
    Genocide, 190
Corps of Engineer, 194
Cotton gin, 56